GRAPHIS DESIGN 92

The International Annual on Design and Illustration

Das internationale Jahrbuch über Design und Illustration

Le Répertoire Internationale de Design et d'Illustration

Edited by/Herausgegeben von/Réalisé par

B. Martin Pedersen

Publisher and Creative Director: B. Martin Pedersen

Assistant Editors: Heinke Jenssen, Annette Crandall

Photographer: Walter Zuber

Graphis Press Corp., Zurich (Switzerland)

GRAPHIS PUBLICATIONS

GRAPHIS, THE INTERNATIONAL BI-MONTHLY JOURNAL OF VISUAL COMMUNICATION
GRAPHIS DESIGN, THE INTERNATIONAL ANNUAL OF DESIGN AND ILLUSTRATION
GRAPHIS PHOTO, THE INTERNATIONAL ANNUAL OF PHOTOGRAPHY
GRAPHIS POSTER, THE INTERNATIONAL ANNUAL OF POSTER ART
GRAPHIS PACKAGING, AN INTERNATIONAL SURVEY OF PACKACKING DESIGN
GRAPHIS LETTERHEAD 1, AN INTERNATIONAL SURVEY OF LETTERHEAD DESIGN
GRAPHIS DIAGRAM, THE GRAPHIC VISUALIZATION OF ABSTRACT, TECHNICAL AND
    STATISTICAL FACTS AND FUNCTIONS
GRAPHIS LOGO, AN INTERNATIONAL SURVEY OF LOGOS
GRAPHIS PUBLICATION DESIGN, AN INTERNATIONAL SURVEY OF THE BEST
    IN MAGAZINE DESIGN
GRAPHIS ANNUAL REPORTS, AN INTERNATIONAL COMPILATION OF THE BEST DESIGNED
    ANNUAL REPORTS
GRAPHIS CORPORATE IDENTITY, AN INTERNATIONAL COMPILATION OF THE BEST IN
    CORPORATE IDENTITY DESIGN
42 YEARS OF GRAPHIS COVERS, AN ANTHOLOGY OF ALL GRAPHIS COVERS FROM 1944-86 WITH ARTISTS'
    SHORT BIOGRAPHIES AND INDEXES OF ALL GRAPHIS ISSUES
POSTERS MADE POSSIBLE BY A GRANT FROM MOBIL, A COLLECTION OF 250 INTERNATIONAL POSTERS
    COMMISSIONED BY MOBIL AND SELECTED BY THE POSTER SOCIETY

GRAPHIS PUBLIKATIONEN

GRAPHIS, DIE INTERNATIONALE ZWEIMONATSZEITSCHRIFT DER VISUELLEN KOMMUNIKATION
GRAPHIS DESIGN, DAS INTERNATIONALE JAHRBUCH ÜBER DESIGN UND ILLUSTRATION
GRAPHIS PHOTO, DAS INTERNATIONALE JAHRBUCH DER PHOTOGRAPHIE
GRAPHIS POSTER, DAS INTERNATIONALE JAHRBUCH DER PLAKATKUNST
GRAPHIS PACKAGING, EIN INTERNATIONALER ÜBERBLICK ÜBER DIE PACKUNGSGESTALTUNG
GRAPHIS LETTERHEAD 1, EIN INTERNATIONALER ÜBERBLICK ÜBER BRIEFPAPIERGESTALTUNG
GRAPHIS DIAGRAM, DIE GRAPHISCHE DARSTELLUNG ABSTRAKTER TECHNISCHER UND
    STATISTISCHER DATEN UND FAKTEN
GRAPHIS LOGO, EINE INTERNATIONALE AUSWAHL VON FIRMEN-LOGOS
GRAPHIS PUBLICATION DESIGN, EINE INTERNATIONALE ZUSAMMENSTELLUNG DES BESTEN
    ZEITSCHRIFTEN-DESIGNS
GRAPHIS ANNUAL REPORT, EIN INTERNATIONALER ÜBERBLICK ÜBER DIE GESTALTUNG
    VON JAHRESBERICHTEN
GRAPHIS CORPORATE IDENTITY, EINE INTERNATIONALE AUSWAHL DES BESTEN
    CORPORATE IDENTITY DESIGNS
42 YEARS OF GRAPHIS COVERS, EINE SAMMLUNG ALLER GRAPHIS-UMSCHLÄGE VON 1944-86 MIT
    INFORMATIONEN ÜBER DIE KÜNSTLER UND INHALTSÜBERSICHTEN ALLER AUSGABEN DER
    ZEITSCHRIFT GRAPHIS
POSTERS MADE POSSIBLE BY A GRANT FROM MOBIL, EINE SAMMLUNG VON 250 INTERNATIONALEN
    PLAKATEN, VON MOBIL IN AUFTRAG GEGEBEN UND VON DER POSTER SOCIETY AUSGEWÄHLT

PUBLICATIONS GRAPHIS

GRAPHIS, LA REVUE BIMESTRIELLE INTERNATIONALE DE LA COMMUNICATION VISUELLE
GRAPHIS DESIGN, LE RÉPERTOIRE INTERNATIONAL DE LA COMMUNICATION VISUELLE
GRAPHIS PHOTO, LE RÉPERTOIRE INTERNATIONAL DE LA PHOTOGRAPHIE
GRAPHIS POSTER, LE RÉPERTOIRE INTERNATIONAL DE L'AFFICHE
GRAPHIS PACKAGING, LE RÉPERTOIRE INTERNATIONAL DE LA CRÉATION D'EMBALLAGES
GRAPHIS LETTERHEAD, LE RÉPERTOIRE INTERNATIONAL DU DESIGN DE PAPIER À LETTRES
GRAPHIS DIAGRAM, LE RÉPERTOIRE GRAPHIQUE DE FAITS ET DONNÉES ABSTRAITS,
    TECHNIQUES ET STATISTIQUES
GRAPHIS LOGO, LE RÉPERTOIRE INTERNATIONAL DU LOGO
GRAPHIS PUBLICATION DESIGN, LE RÉPERTOIRE INTERNATIONAL DU DESIGN DE PÉRIODIQUES
GRAPHIS ANNUAL REPORTS, PANORAMA INTERNATIONAL DU MEILLEUR DESIGN DE RAPPORTS
    ANNUELS D'ENTREPRISES
GRAPHIS CORPORATE IDENTITY, PANORAMA INTERNATIONAL DU MEILLEUR DESIGN D'IDENTITÉ CORPORATE
42 YEARS OF GRAPHIS COVERS, RECUEIL DE TOUTES LES COUVERTURES DE GRAPHIS 1944 À 1986
    AVEC DES NOTICES BIOGRAPHIQUES DES ARTISTES ET LE SOMMAIRE DE TOUS LES NUMÉROS DU
    MAGAZINE GRAPHIS
POSTERS MADE POSSIBLE BY A GRANT FROM MOBIL, UNE COLLECTION DE 250 AFFICHES
    INTERNATIONALES COMMANDÉES PAR MOBIL ET SÉLECTIONNÉES PAR LA POSTER SOCIETY

PUBLICATION No. 204 (ISBN 3-85709-192-4)
© COPYRIGHT UNDER UNIVERSAL COPYRIGHT CONVENTION
COPYRIGHT © 1991 BY GRAPHIS PRESS CORP., DUFOURSTRASSE 107, 8008 ZURICH, SWITZERLAND
JACKET AND BOOK DESIGN COPYRIGHT © 1991 BY PEDERSEN DESIGN
    141 LEXINGTON AVENUE, NEW YORK, N.Y. 10016 USA
FRENCH CAPTIONS BY NICOLE VIAUD

PRINTED IN JAPAN BY TOPPAN PRINTING CO., LTD.

CONTENTS · INHALT · SOMMAIRE

ABBREVIATIONS 7

COMMENTARY BY MICHAEL VANDERBYL 8

COMMENTARY BY TAKENOBU IGARASHI 14

COMMENTARY BY BEN BOS 20

INDEX TO ART DIRECTORS 250

DESIGNERS 252

ARTISTS 255

AGENCIES 258

COPYWRITERS AND STYLISTS 260

CLIENTS AND PUBLISHERS 261

CALL FOR ENTRIES 264

ABKÜRZUNGEN 7

KOMMENTAR VON MICHAEL VANDERBYL ... 10

KOMMENTAR VON TAKENOBU IGARASHI 16

KOMMENTAR VON BEN BOS 22

KÜNSTLERISCHE LEITER 250

GESTALTER 252

KÜNSTLER 255

AGENTUREN 258

TEXTER UND STYLISTEN 260

AUFTRAGGEBER UND VERLAGE 261

EINLADUNG 264

ABRÉVIATIONS 7

COMMENTAIRE PAR MICHAEL VANDERBYL .12

COMMENTAIRE PAR TAKENOBU IGARASHI .18

COMMENTAIRE PAR BEN BOS 24

DIRECTEURS ARTISTIQUES 250

DESIGNERS 252

ARTISTES 255

AGENCES 258

REDACTEURS ET STYLISTES 260

CLIENTS ET EDITEURS 261

APPEL D'ENVOIS 264

ADVERTISING 27

BROCHURES 77

EDITORIAL DESIGN 137

ILLUSTRATION 181

CORPORATE IDENTITY 203

PACKAGING 217

BOOKS AND CALENDARS 231

WERBUNG 27

BROSCHÜREN 77

REDAKTIONELLES DESIGN 137

ILLUSTRATIONEN 181

CORPORATE IDENTITY 203

PACKUNGEN 217

BÜCHER UND KALENDER 231

PUBLICITÉ 27

BROCHURES 77

DESIGN DE PÉRIODIQUES 137

ILLUSTRATION 181

CORPORATE IDENTITY 203

PACKAGING 217

LIVRES ET CALENDRIERS 231

AUSTRIA	AUT	AUSTRALIEN	AUS	AFRIQUE DU SUD	SAF
AUSTRALIA	AUS	BRASILIEN	BRA	ALLEMAGNE	GER
BRAZIL	BRA	DEUTSCHLAND	GER	AUSTRALIE	AUS
CANADA	CAN	FRANKREICH	FRA	AUTRICHE	AUT
CZECHOSLOVAKIA	CFR	GROSSBRITANNIEN	GBR	BRÉSIL	BRA
FRANCE	FRA	IRAN	IRN	CANADA	CAN
GERMANY	GER	ITALIEN	ITA	ESPAGNE	SPA
GREAT BRITAIN	GBR	JAPAN	JPN	ÉTATS-UNIS	USA
IRAN	IRN	KANADA	CAN	FRANCE	FRA
ITALY	ITA	NIEDERLANDE	NLD	GRANDE-BRETAGNE	GBR
JAPAN	JPN	NORWEGEN	NOR	IRAN	IRN
NETHERLANDS	NLD	ÖSTERREICH	AUT	ITALIE	ITA
NORWAY	NOR	POLEN	POL	JAPON	JPN
POLAND	POL	PORTUGAL	POR	NORVÈGE	NOR
PORTUGAL	POR	SCHWEDEN	SWE	PAYS-BAS	NLD
SOUTH AFRICA	SAF	SCHWEIZ	SWI	POLOGNE	POL
SPAIN	SPA	SPANIEN	SPA	PORTUGAL	POR
SWEDEN	SWE	SÜDAFRIKA	SAF	SUÈDE	SWE
SWITZERLAND	SWI	TSCHECHOSLOWAKEI	CFR	SUISSE	SWI
TURKEY	TUR	TÜRKEI	TUR	TCHÉCOSLOVAQUIE	CFR
USA	USA	USA	USA	TURQUIE	TUR

REMARKS
WE EXTEND OUR HEARTFELT THANKS TO CONTRIBUTORS THROUGHOUT THE WORLD WHO HAVE MADE IT POSSIBLE FOR US TO PUBLISH A WIDE AND INTERNATIONAL SPECTRUM OF THE BEST WORK IN THIS FIELD.

ENTRY INSTRUCTIONS MAY BE REQUESTED AT: GRAPHIS PRESS CORP., DUFOURSTRASSE 107, 8008 ZURICH, SWITZERLAND

ANMERKUNGEN
UNSER HERZLICHER DANK GILT DEN EINSENDERN AUS ALLER WELT, DIE ES UNS DURCH IHRE BEITRÄGE MÖGLICH GEMACHT HABEN, EIN BREITES, INTERNATIONALES SPEKTRUM DER BESTEN ARBEITEN ZU VERÖFFENTLICHEN.

TEILNAHMEBEDINGUNGEN:
GRAPHIS VERLAG AG, DUFOURSTRASSE 107, 8008 ZÜRICH, SCHWEIZ

ANNOTATIONS
TOUTE NOTRE RECONNAISSANCE VA AUX DESIGNERS DU MONDE ENTIER DONT LES ENVOIS NOUS ONT PERMIS DE CONSTITUER UN VASTE PANORAMA INTERNATIONAL DES MEILLEURS TRAVAUX.

MODALITÉS D'ENVOI DE TRAVAUX:
EDITIONS GRAPHIS SA, DUFOURSTRASSE 107, 8008 ZURICH, SUISSE

MICHAEL VANDERBYL

PORTRAIT OF MICHAEL VANDERBYL BY MONICA LEE

ONE OF THE THINGS THAT SETS AN ARTIST—A GRAPHIC ARTIST—APART IS CONVICTION. MAKING ART OR DESIGNING AS IF IT MATTERED, AS IF THE WORLD MATTERED. □ GRAPHIC DESIGN IS GENERALLY HELD TO BE A MINOR ART. RATHER THAN TRANSFORMING REALITY, A FEAT CLAIMED BY PAINTERS AND SCULPTORS, GRAPHIC DESIGN IS SEEN AS AN AUXILIARY TO SALES. A DECADE AGO, PAUL RAND WROTE: "IT IS NO SECRET THAT THE REAL WORLD IN WHICH THE DESIGNER FUNCTIONS IS...THE WORLD OF BUYING AND SELLING, ...BUT WITHOUT GOOD DESIGN THE MARKETPLACE WOULD BE A SHOWCASE OF VISUAL VULGARITY." I AGREE. ESPECIALLY WITH THE "BUT" AND I WOULD ONLY ADD THAT THE GRAPHIC DESIGNER CAN BE A POSITIVE FORCE IN TRANSFORMING THE MARKETPLACE AND SHAPING A RICHER COLLECTIVE LIFE. DESIGNERS SERVE CLIENTS JUST AS RENAISSANCE ARTISTS BOWED TO THE POPE OR NOBLEMEN WHO COMMISSIONED A CHAPEL FRESCOE OR TAPESTRY. BUT LIKE THOSE ARTISTS, WE CANNOT LIMIT OURSELVES TO THE SPECIFIC ENDS OF SOLVING THE IMMEDIATE PROBLEM. WE MUST NOT FALL PREY TO THE CYNICAL SPIRIT OF A DECADE THAT WOULD HAVE US BELIEVE THAT OUR WORK IS JUST ANOTHER DISPOSABLE PART OF A TRASH CULTURE. GOOD DESIGN REQUIRES THE UNFASHIONABLE QUALITIES OF FEELING AND COMMITMENT IF IT IS TO OUTLAST THE CURRENT TREND OF SPLICING STYLES AND SURFACES. BOTH DESIGNERS AND CLIENTS SHOULD KNOW THAT GOOD DESIGN CAN BE MORE THAN A VISUAL FIX OR A SALES PITCH JUST AS CATHEDRALS, STATUARY AND PORTRAITURE DELIVERED MORE THAN THEIR SPECIFIC MESSAGES OF WEALTH AND POWER. □ IT IS PERHAPS ONLY IN THE LAST CENTURY THAT ART HAS BEEN KICKED UPSTAIRS INTO AN IVORY TOWER (WHERE THERE'S A VERY EXCLUSIVE HIGH-STAKES GAME GOING ON BETWEEN COLLECTORS, CURATORS, AND ARTISTS), CLOISTERED IN MUSEUMS AND COLLECTIONS, ADORED BY CRITICS AND CONNOISSEURS AND CEOS LIKE A GOLDEN CALF. THE POSTURE OF THE ARTIST AS CREATIVE GENIUS AND THE CONSUMING INTEREST IN DEALS AND IMAGE HAS

(LEFT) A POSTER CREATED FOR THE '91 STANFORD CONFERENCE ON DESIGN (RIGHT) A POSTER FOR THE EXHIBITOR SHOW '91

both elevated and reduced art to a glamorous commodity. If the style of post-modern art is a garage sale of perspectives, materials, genres, etc. the prices are certainly not. And if post-modern art has moved away from the "silence" of modern minimalism, it still fails to speak to the public. It is neither seen or heard in the real life of the community which goes on in the workplace, the shops, and cafes. That's where you find graphic art—hanging out on street corners, in the corporate offices, public and private institutions, the retail environment, and in peoples' homes, informing, transforming, enlightening, and clarifying everyday life. □ Let's acknowledge the importance of the visual history and visual world created by graphic design in the artifacts and images with which we continually interact in our daily life. Why, after all, do we study the baskets, clay jars, religious

objects, and public architecture of a people? The artist leaves the imprint of this individual sensitivity to proportion, space and materials and his personal passions, strengths and flaws; but we also find there the traces of the myths, traditions, and social history of a culture; their sense of relatedness to each other and to nature. Just as our comic strips, neon signs, toasters, shoe boxes, lipsticks, magazines, posters, etc. tell us about our science, our fantasies, our mating rituals, and so forth. □ The value of graphic design is tied not only to form and function, but to the feeling one has for life and our work as designers is not limited to specific functional or educative ends. We can contribute directly to the pleasure, ease, color of life—the way life feels. Designers not only open the channels of desire with seductive images or streamline tasks with models of efficiency. Designers can no

ONE OF MICHAEL VANDERBYL'S MANY RENOWNED INTERIOR DISPLAY DESIGNS. HERE, THE ESPRIT SHOE SHOWROOM IN NEW YORK

longer think of themselves as simply engineers of information, tools of the corporate world and marketing strategies. We must find sources of self-expression and meaning as well as solving problems. The trend has been to look outside and into the past for inspiration, borrowing from other times and tribes, but we can also turn inside by exploring personal feeling and memory—our own passions, our own ironic sense of humanity and of tragedy, our own hungers, anxieties and pleasures. In this way, our design will be not only accessible and appropriate, but truly new, interesting and meaningful. Design can inspire us as individuals, move us as members of a world community, help us to achieve understanding, *enhance our work, make us laugh, give us pleasure, startle, surprise, and prevent us from being swamped in a "showcase of ... vulgarity." We must also convey to our clients their responsibility as contemporary patrons of the applied arts, with the sincere desire to contribute something of long-lasting worth alongside the daily life in the fast track. □ Graphis represents the work of designers who have achieved not only solutions to problems, but who have made contributions to our collective culture. Not content to passively render mere fragments of style, their personal commitment to design can serve to inspire us all (as designers, producers of culture, members of a community) that it does matter.* ∎

MICHAEL VANDERBYL DIRECTS VANDERBYL DESIGN, A MULTI-DISCIPLINARY DESIGN FIRM KNOWN FOR CONSISTENTLY PRODUCING AWARD-WINNING DESIGNS IN FURNITURE, GRAPHICS, TEXTILES, AND INTERIORS FOR SUCH CLIENTS AS ESPRIT, IBM, POLAROID, THE AMERICAN INSTITUTE OF ARCHITECTS, AND HICKORY BUSINESS FURNITURE. HE WILL CHAIR THE PRESIDENTIAL JURY FOR THE 1992 NATIONAL ENDOWMENT FOR THE ARTS PRESIDENTIAL DESIGN AWARDS. ∎

Was einen Künstler – einen Graphik-Designer – zu etwas Besonderem macht, ist seine Gesinnung, ist die Tatsache, dass er Kunst macht oder etwas gestaltet, als ob es darauf ankäme, als ob die Welt wichtig wäre. □ Im allgemeinen gilt Graphik-Design als eine geringe Kunst. Statt die Realität neu zu gestalten, wie dies Maler und Bildhauer für sich in Anspruch nehmen, wird Graphik-Design als Verkaufsinstrument betrachtet. Vor zehn Jahren schrieb Paul Rand: «Es ist kein Geheimnis, dass die reale Welt, in welcher der Designer arbeitet, die Welt des Kaufens und Verkaufens ist, ...aber ohne gutes Design wäre der Markt ein Schaufenster visueller Geschmacklosigkeiten.» □ Ich teile seine Meinung, besonders was das «aber» angeht, und möchte nur hinzufügen, dass der Graphik-Designer eine positive Kraft bei der Neugestaltung des Marktes und der Bereicherung des täglichen Lebens sein kann. Designer dienen ihren Auftraggebern so wie die Künstler der Renaissance dem Papst oder dem Adel gedient haben, ihren Auftraggebern für Fresken, Bildteppiche und Ähnliches. Aber wie jene Künstler können auch wir uns nicht darauf beschränken, nur eine Aufgabe zu lösen. Wir dürfen nicht Opfer des Zynismus einer Dekade werden, die uns glauben machen will, dass unsere Arbeit nichts weiter als ein Teil der Wegwerfkultur ist. Gutes Design, das über den gegenwärtigen Trend der Zersplitterung von Stilen und Oberflächen hinaus Gültigkeit behalten soll, verlangt ganz unmodische Qualitäten von Gefühl und Einsatz. Designer und Auftraggeber sollten wissen, dass gutes Design mehr als ein visueller Anziehungspunkt oder Verkaufsförderung sein muss. □ Eigentlich wurde die Kunst erst im letzten Jahrhundert hinauf in ihren Elfenbeinturm befördert (wo ein exklusives Spiel mit hohem Einsatz zwischen Sammlern, Kuratoren und Künstlern stattfindet). Die Stellung des Künstlers als kreatives Genie und das brennende Interesse an Geschäften und Image hat die Kunst zu einer Luxusware gemacht. □ Wir sollten die Bedeutung der durch Graphik-Design geschaffenen visuellen Geschichte und visuellen Welt – sei es durch Gegenstände oder Bilder – erkennen. Warum befassen wir uns denn mit den Körben, den Tongefässen, den religiösen Gegenständen und der Architektur der Völker? Der Künstler hinterlässt Zeichen seines persönlichen Gespürs für Proportionen, Raum und Material sowie seiner persönlichen Leidenschaften, Stärken und Schwächen; gleichzeitig aber finden wir in diesen Werken Spuren der Mythen, der Traditionen und der Geschichte einer Kultur; die Beziehung zwischen den Dingen und ihre Beziehung zur Natur wird sichtbar. Genauso verhält es sich mit unseren Comic Strips, der Neon-Werbung, Toastern, Schuhschachteln, Lippenstiften, Zeitschriften, Plakaten etc. Sie erzählen etwas über unsere Wissenschaft, unsere Phantasien, die Rituale zwischen den Geschlechtern usw. □ Der Wert des Graphik-Designs ist nicht nur an Form und Funktion gebunden, sondern er betrifft auch die Einstellung zum Leben. Unsere Arbeit als Designer beschränkt sich nicht auf spezifische funktionelle oder erzieherische Aufgaben. Wir können direkt dazu beitragen, das Leben angenehmer, leichter und farbiger zu machen. Designer erwecken nicht nur Wünsche mit verführerischen Bildern oder erleichtern Aufgaben mit Anleitungen für organisiertes Vorgehen. Designer können sich nicht länger einfach als Aufbereiter von Informationen, als Werkzeuge der Geschäftswelt und ihrer Marketing-Strategien verstehen. Wir müssen Möglichkeiten finden, uns selbst auszudrücken, müssen neben der Lösung von Problemen der Arbeit eine Bedeutung geben. Es war bisher üblich, sich draussen umzusehen und die Inspiration in der Vergangenheit zu suchen, bei anderen Völkern und Zeiten Anleihen zu machen, aber wir sollten auch unsere eigenen Gefühle und Erinnerungen einbeziehen. Unsere Arbeit wird nicht nur zugänglich und angemessen sein, sondern wirklich neu, interessant und bedeutsam. Design kann uns als Individuen inspirieren, uns als Angehörige der Weltgemeinschaft bewegen, zur Verständigung beitragen, unsere Arbeit bereichern, uns zum Lachen bringen, Freude bereiten, erstaunen, überraschen und uns davor behüten, in «Geschmacklosigkeiten» unterzugehen. Wir müssen unsere Auftraggeber dazu bringen, zu zeitgenössischen Mäzenen der angewandten Künste zu werden, mit der Verpflichtung, trotz der Schnellebigkeit etwas von Wert zurückzulassen. □ Graphis steht für die Arbeit von Designern, die nicht nur Aufgaben gelöst, sondern gleichzeitig einen Beitrag zu unserer gemeinsamen Kultur geleistet haben. Die blosse Herstellung von stilistischen Fragmenten genügt diesen Designern nicht; ihre persönliche Einstellung zum Design sollte uns alle (als Designer, Kulturschaffende und Mitglieder einer Gemeinschaft) überzeugen, dass gutes Design nicht gleichgültig ist. ■

VANDERBYL DESIGN ERHÄLT UNTER DER LEITUNG VON MICHAEL VANDERBYL STÄNDIG AUSZEICHNUNGEN FÜR IHRE ARBEITEN (MÖBEL, GRAPHIK, TEXTILIEN UND INNENAUSSTATTUNGEN) FÜR KUNDEN WIE ESPRIT, IBM, POLAROID, THE AMERICAN INSTITUTE OF ARCHITECTS UND HICKORY BUSINESS FURNITURE. VANDERBYL WIRD DER JURY DER 1992 NATIONAL ENDOWMENT FOR THE ARTS PRESIDENTIAL DESIGN AWARDS VORSTEHEN. ■

L'une des choses qui distingue l'artiste – c'est la conviction qui l'habite. Faire de l'art ou du design comme si cela avait de l'importance, comme si le monde importait. □ Le design graphique est généralement tenu pour un art mineur, il est considéré comme un auxiliaire de la vente. Il y a dix ans, Paul Rand écrivait ceci: «Ce n'est un secret pour personne que le monde dans lequel le designer évolue est... celui de l'achat et de la vente, ...mais sans un bon design, le marché ne serait qu'une vitrine de vulgarité visuelle.» Je suis d'accord. J'ajouterais seulement que le designer graphique peut agir de manière positive en transformant le marché et en suscitant une vie collective plus riche. Les designers sont au service de leurs clients tout comme les artistes de la Renaissance qui s'inclinaient devant le Pape ou les nobles qui leur avaient commandé une fresque pour une chapelle ou une tapisserie. Mais, comme eux, nous ne pouvons nous limiter à résoudre un problème immédiat. Nous ne devons pas succomber à cet esprit cynique qui caractérise la décennie et qui voudrait nous faire croire que notre travail n'est rien d'autre que ce qu'on jette dans cette société de consommation. Un bon design doit avoir deux qualités indémodables, à savoir la sensibilité et l'engagement. Les designers et les clients devraient savoir qu'un bon design peut être plus qu'un impact visuel ou un aiguillon pour la vente. □ C'est peut-être seulement au cours du siècle dernier que l'art est sorti de sa tour d'ivoire. La position de l'artiste, considéré comme un génie, et l'intérêt que suscite l'image ont contribué à élever l'art, mais aussi à le réduire à un produit séduisant. Si l'art postmoderne est un libre-service de perspectives, d'articles, de genres, etc., les prix ne le sont certes pas. Et s'il s'est dégagé du «silence» du minimalisme, il ne réussit toujours pas à parler au public. On ne le rencontre guère dans la vie réelle de la communauté, sur les lieux de travail, dans les magasins et les cafés. C'est là par contre que vous trouvez l'art graphique – accroché au coin de la rue, dans les bureaux, les institutions publiques ou privées, dans les magasins et chez les gens, informant, transformant et clarifiant la vie quotidienne. □ Il est temps de reconnaître l'importance de l'histoire visuelle et du monde visuel créé par le design graphique dans les produits manufacturés et les images auxquelles nous sommes confrontés dans notre vie quotidienne. Pourquoi, après tout, étudions-nous donc les jarres en terre cuite, les objets religieux et l'architecture publique d'un peuple? L'artiste laisse l'empreinte de sa sensibilité individuelle dans les proportions, l'espace, la matière; ceux-ci témoignent de ses passions personnelles, de sa force et de ses faiblesses. Mais nous y découvrons aussi la trace des mythes, des traditions et de l'histoire sociale d'une culture; comment ils sont reliés entre eux et à la nature. Tout comme nos bandes dessinées, nos enseignes au néon, nos grille-pain, magazines, affiches, etc. traduisent notre savoir, notre imagination, nos rituels amoureux. □ La valeur du design graphique ne dépend pas seulement de sa forme et de sa fonction, mais du sentiment que quelqu'un peut avoir de la vie et du travail du designer, à condition que celui-ci ne soit pas limité à une fonction spécifique ou à des fins purement éducatives. Nous pouvons directement contribuer au bien-être, transformer la vie – la façon dont la vie est vécue. Les designers n'ouvrent pas seulement les portes du désir avec des images alléchantes de produits d'avant-garde. Ils ne doivent plus se considérer comme de simples techniciens de l'information, les outils du monde commercial et des stratégies de marché. Nous devons trouver des sources d'expression et de signification tout en résolvant des problèmes. Une certaine mode nous a conduit à chercher dans le passé notre inspiration, à emprunter des choses à d'autres époques et à d'autres peuples, mais nous pouvons aussi explorer le sentiment et la mémoire personnels – nos passions propres, notre sens de l'humour ou du tragique, nos désirs, nos angoisses et nos plaisirs. Notre design sera ainsi véritablement nouveau, intéressant et chargé de signification. Le design peut nous inspirer en tant qu'individus, nous émouvoir en tant que membre de la société, nous aider à comprendre, mettre en valeur notre travail, nous faire rire, nous donner du plaisir, nous surprendre, et nous empêcher d'être submergés par cette «vitrine de vulgarité». Nous devons par ailleurs inciter nos clients à participer: mécènes contemporains de l'art appliqué, qu'ils s'attachent à laisser quelque chose de valable derrière eux. □ Graphis présente le travail de designers qui, non seulement sont arrivés à trouver des solutions à des problèmes, mais qui ont contribué à notre culture collective, qui ne se sont pas contentés de reproduire passivement des fragments de style. Leur engagement personnel devrait nous convaincre (comme designers, producteurs d'une culture et membres d'une communauté) que celui-ci a de l'importance. ■

MICHAEL VANDERBYL EST À LA TÊTE DE VANDERBYL DESIGN, UNE FIRME DE DESIGN PLURIDISCIPLINAIRE CÉLÈBRE POUR SES CRÉATIONS DE MEUBLES, PRODUITS GRAPHIQUES, TEXTILES ET INTÉRIEURS POUR DES CLIENTS TELS QUE ESPRIT, IBM, POLAROÏD, THE AMERICAN INSTITUTE OF ARCHITECTS ET HICKORY BUSINESS FURNITURE. IL PRÉSIDERA LE JURY DU CONCOURS 1992 DE LA FONDATION NATIONALE POUR LES ARTS DU DESIGN AUX USA.■

TAKENOBU IGARASHI

PORTRAIT OF TAKENOUBU IGARASHI BY STEVEN A. HELLER

INDIVIDUALITY IS DIFFICULT TO FIND IN DESIGN THESE DAYS. AS DESIGNERS PURSUE THE NEEDS OF THE INTERNATIONAL MARKET, THE NEEDS OF THE CLIENT AND RESPOND TO CURRENT TRENDS, ORIGINALITY BECOMES SECONDARY. DESIGN IS FURTHERMORE ALL TOO FREQUENTLY PRODUCED UNDER SUCH CONSTRAINTS THAT DESIGNERS ARE NOT ALLOWED AMPLE TIME TO THINK DEEPLY ABOUT WHAT THEY ARE PRODUCING. □ DESIGNERS' IDENTITIES FURTHER LOST IN A MASS OF INFORMATION: GLOBALLY, DESIGN LOOKS THE SAME. AS SUCH, WE FIND OURSELVES AT A CRITICAL MOMENT IN THE HISTORY OF OUR INDUSTRY. THIS TRANSITIONAL PERIOD IS FURTHER ACCENTUATED BY A GENERATION OF DESIGNERS—MANY WHO COMPRISE THE FOUNDATION OF TODAY'S PROFESSION— WHO WILL SOON RETIRE. HOW TO REGAIN A SENSE OF IDENTITY WITHIN OUR WORK? THE SEARCH FOR ORIGINALITY BEGINS WITH THE BASICS OF DESIGN. AND THE PASSION TO BE FOUND IN THE ALL-ENCOMPASSING BOND BETWEEN THE ARTIST AND HIS OR HER WORK. □ ISN'T IT TIME FOR DESIGNERS TO RECONSIDER THE CONCEPT OF DESIGN IN ORDER TO ESTABLISH THEIR OWN IDENTITY? DECIDING WHAT TO SUBSTITUTE IN PLACE OF MEAT, FOR EXAMPLE, IS THE IDEA BEHIND THE CONCEPT OF VEGETARIANISM. THERE ARE MORE THAN ENOUGH IDEAS BUT VERY FEW CONCEPTS. THE INDIVIDUALITY OF A DESIGNER AND THE DESIGNS HE OR SHE PRODUCES WILL BE INDISTINGUISHABLE IF DESIGN IS PRACTICED ONLY AS A BUSINESS. OUR RESPONSIBILITY AS DESIGNERS AND OUR OBLIGATION TO SOCIETY IS TO PURSUE AND ESTABLISH CONCEPTS WITHIN OUR CREATIVE WORK.■

TAKENOBU IGARASHI IS AN INTERNATIONALLY-RENOWNED DESIGNER AND SCULPTOR WHOSE WORK INCLUDES PRINT MEDIA DESIGN, CORPORATE IDENTITY, ENVIRONMENTAL DESIGN AND INDUSTRIAL DESIGN. HE IS KNOWN FOR A SERIES OF AXONOMETRIC POSTERS USING ALPHABETS AND LETTERFORMS AS WELL AS SHOPPING BAGS AND CALENDARS FOR THE MUSEUM OF MODERN ART, NEW YORK (MOMA); CORPORATE IDENTITY PROJECTS FOR THE MITSUI BANK, MEIJI MILK PRODUCTS AND SUNTORY HALL IN TOKYO; LIMITED EDITION SCULPTURES DESIGNED FOR THE NISSAN "INFINITY" SHOWROOMS IN THE UNITED STATES AND PRODUCT DESIGN SUCH AS THE LEGAME CORDLESS TELEPHONE. □ A GRADUATE OF TAMA UNIVERSITY OF FINE ARTS IN TOKYO, IGARASHI OBTAINED A MASTER OF ARTS DEGREE IN ART FROM THE UNIVERSITY OF CALIFORNIA IN LOS ANGELES. IN 1970 IGARASHI STUDIO WAS ESTABLISHED. WHILE CURRENTLY RUNNING OFFICES IN TOKYO AND LOS ANGELES, HE IS AN ACTIVE MEMBER OF AGI (ALLIANCE GRAPHIQUE INTERNATIONALE), TEACHES AT UCLA AND SERVES AS THE DEAN OF DESIGN AT THE DESIGN DEPARTMENT OF TAMA ART UNIVERSITY IN TOKYO.■

MEIJI

HEUTE FÄLLT ES SCHWER, INDIVIDUALITÄT IM DESIGN ZU ENTDECKEN. DIE GRAPHIK-DESIGNER ERFÜLLEN IN ERSTER LINIE DIE ANFORDERUNGEN DES INTERNATIONALEN MARKTES UND BERÜCKSICHTIGEN DIE BEDÜRFNISSE DES AUFTRAGGEBERS SOWIE DIE GÄNGIGEN TRENDS—ORIGINALITÄT KOMMT ERST AN ZWEITER STELLE. SIE MÜSSEN IHRE ARBEIT SO SCHNELL ERLEDIGEN, DASS IHNEN KEINE ZEIT BLEIBT, WIRKLICH DARÜBER NACHZUDENKEN, WAS SIE PRODUZIEREN. ☐ DIE IDENTITÄT DER DESIGNER GEHT IN DER MASSEN-INFORMATION VERLOREN: IN ALLER WELT SIEHT GRAPHIK-DESIGN GLEICH AUS. IN DIESEM SINNE KÖNN-TE MAN SAGEN, DASS WIR HEUTE SCHWERE ZEITEN HABEN, WAS DAS DESIGN ANGEHT. ES KOMMT NOCH ERSCHWEREND HINZU, DASS DIE LEUTE, DIE DEN GRUNDSTOCK FÜR DAS HEUTIGE DESIGN SCHUFEN, SICH ALLMÄHLICH ZURÜCKZIEHEN. WIE KÖNNEN WIR EIN GEFÜHL VON IDENTITÄT IN UNSERER ARBEIT ZURÜCKGEWINNEN? DIE SUCHE NACH ORIGINALITÄT BEGINNT MIT DER BESINNUNG AUF DAS WESENTLICHE DES DESIGNS. DIE LEIDENSCHAFT, DIE DEN KÜNSTLER MIT SEINER ARBEIT VERBINDET, DARF NICHT VERLORENGEHEN. ☐ WIRD ES NICHT HÖCHSTE ZEIT, DASS DIE GRAPHIKER SICH ERNEUT MIT DEM WESEN DES DESIGNS AUSEINANDERSETZEN, UM IHRE EIGENE IDENTITÄT ZU DEFINIEREN? SICH DARÜBER GEDANKEN ZU MACHEN, WOMIT MAN FLEISCH ERSETZEN KANN, IST ZUM BEISPIEL DIE IDEE HINTER DEM KONZEPT DES VEGETARISMUS. IDEEN FINDET MAN IN ZAHLREICHEN ARBEITEN, KONZEPTE GANZ SELTEN. WENN DER DESIGNER SEINE ARBEIT NUR ALS GESCHÄFT BETRACHTET, WERDEN WIR WEDER SEINE PERSÖNLICHKEIT NOCH ORIGINALITÄT IN SEINER ARBEIT ENTDECKEN KÖNNEN. UNSERE AUFGABE ALS DESIGNER BESTEHT DARIN, EIN KONZEPT ZU FINDEN, AN DAS WIR UNS HALTEN KÖN-NEN, UM UNSERER VERANTWORTUNG GEGENUBER DER GESELLSCHAFT GERECHT ZU WERDEN.■

TAKENOBU IGARASHI, 1944 IN HOKKAIDO GEBOREN, IST EIN INTERNATIONAL ANERKANNTER DESIGNER UND BILDHAUER. ZU SEINEM BREITEN ARBEITSBEREICH GEHÖREN GRAPHIK-DESIGN FÜR DIE DRUCKMEDIEN, CORPORATE IDENTITY, UMWELTGRAPHIK UND INDUSTRIE-DESIGN. SEINE ARBEITEN BEFINDEN SICH IN DEN SAMMLUNGEN DES MUSEUM OF MODERN ART IN NEW YORK UND, FÜR DAS ER AUCH TRAGTASCHEN UND KALENDAR GESTALTETE, ANDERER MUSEEN UND UNIVERSITÄTEN IN ALLER WELT. ☐ TAKENOBU IGARASHI SCHLOSS SEIN STUDIUM AN DER TAMA-KUNSTAKADEMIE IN TOKIO AB UND BEKAM DEN «MASTER OF ARTS»-TITEL FÜR KUNST VON DER UNIVERSITY OF CALIFORNIA IN LOS ANGELES. 1970 GRÜNDETE ER DAS IGARASHI-STUDIO. HEUTE HAT ER BÜROS IN TOKIO UND LOS ANGELES UND IST AKTIVES MITGLIED DER AGI (ALLIANCE GRAPHIQUE INTERNATIONALE). ZUDEM IST ER GASTPROFESSOR AN DER UCLA UND DEKAN FÜR DESIGN AN DER TAMA-KUNSTAKADEMIE IN TOKIO.■

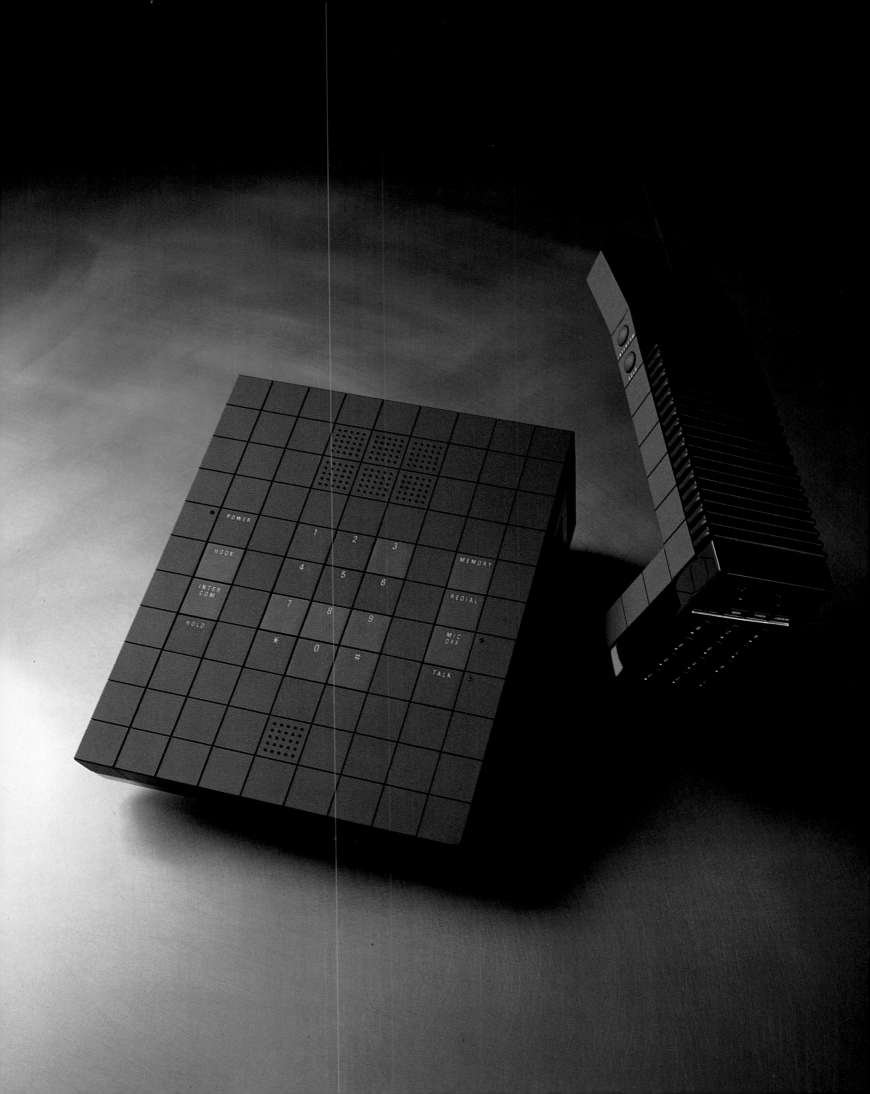

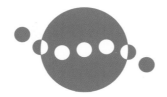

(OPPOSITE) LEGAME, CORDLESS TELEPHONE (ABOVE) A CORPORATE SYMBOL CREATED FOR THE CALPIS FOOD INDUSTRY CO. LTD.

DE NOS JOURS, DANS LE DESIGN, IL EST DIFFICILE DE DISCERNER L'INDIVIUALITÉ DES CRÉATEURS. LES DESIGNERS CHERCHENT À RÉPONDRE AUX BESOINS DU MARCHÉ INTERNATIONAL, AUX EXIGENCES DE LEURS CLIENTS ET ILS SUIVENT LES MODES, AU POINT QUE L'ORIGINALITÉ EST DEVENUE CHOSE SECONDAIRE. D'AILLEURS, TROP SOUVENT, LES DÉLAIS DE PRODUCTION SONT SI CONTRAIGNANTS QUE LES DESIGNERS N'ONT MÊME PAS LE LOISIER DE RÉFLÉCHIR EN PROFONDEUR À CE QU'ILS ÉLA-BORENT. □ L' IDENTITÉ DU DESIGNER SE PERD DANS LA MASSE D'INFORMATIONS; DANS L'ENSEMBLE, LES DESIGNS FINISSENT PAR TOUS SE RESSEMBLER. NOUS NOUS TROUVONS EN L'OCCURRENCE À UN MOMENT CRITIQUE DE L'HISTOIRE DU DESIGN, UNE PÉRIODE DE TRANSITION. CELA RESSORT ENCORE DAVANTAGE DU FAIT QUE LA GÉNÉRATION DE CEUX QUI ONT JETÉ LES BASES DU DESIGN D'AUJOURD 'HUI VA BIENTôT PRENDRE SA RETRAITE. COMMENT RETROUVER UN SENS DE L'IDENTITÉ DANS NOTRE TRAVAIL? LA RECHERCHE DE L'ORIGINALITÉ EST L'UN DES FONDEMENTS MÊME DU DESIGN. IL NOUS FAUT RETROUVER LA PASSION DU MÉTIER DANS CETTE RELATION ABSOLUE QUI UNIT L'ARTISTE À SON ŒUVRE. □ LE MOMENT N'EST-IL PAS VENU POUR LES DESIGNERS DE RECONSIDÉRER LE CONCEPT DU DESIGN AFIN D'ÉTABLIR LEUR IDENTITÉ PROPRE? DÉCIDER PAR EXEMPLE DE CE QU'ON VA MANGER EN PLACE DE VIANDE EST L'IDÉE QUI SOUS-TEND LE CONCEPT DE VÉGÉTARISME. IL Y A DES TONNES ET DES TONNES D'IDÉES, MAIS FORT PEU DE CONCEPTS. L'INDIVIDUALITÉ D'UN DESIGNER ET L'ORIGI-NALITÉ DE SON DESIGN NE SERONT PERCEPTIBLES QUE S'IL PRATIQUE LE DESIGN AUTREMENT QUE COMME UN BUSINESS. EN TANT QUE DESIGNERS, IL EST DE NOTRE DEVOIR ENVERS LA SOCIÉTÉ ET DE NOTRE RESPONSABILITÉ DE SUIVRE ET DE DÉFINIR UN CONCEPT À L'INTÉRIEUR DE NOTRE DESIGN. ∎

NÉ À HOKKAIDO EN 1944, **TAKENOBU IGARASHI** EST UN DESIGNER ET UN SCULPTEUR DE RENOMMÉE INTERNATIONALE. SON ŒUVRE COUVRE DES DOMAINES D'ACTIVITÉS AUSSI VARIÉS QUE LE DESIGN GRAPHIQUE, L'IDENTITÉ CORPORATE, LE DESIGN ENVIRON-NEMENTAL ET LE DESIGN INDUSTRIEL. SON ŒUVRE EST CONSERVÉE DANS LES COLLECTIONS PERMANENTES DU MUSEUM OF MODERN ART DE NEW YORK (MOMA), AINSI QUE DANS D'AUTRES MUSÉES ET UNIVERSITÉS DU MONDE ENTIER. □ DIPLOMÉ DE L'ECOLE SUPÉRIEURE DES BEAUX-ARTS TAMA DE TOKYO, TAKENOBU IGARASHI A OBTENU UNE LICENCE ÉS ART DE L'UNIVERSITÉ DE CALIFORNIE À LOS ANGELES (UCLA). LE STUDIO IGARASHI. A OUVERT SES PORTES EN 1970. ACTUELLEMENT, TOUT EN DIRIGEANT SES BUREAUX DE TOKYO ET DE LOS ANGELES, IL EST MEMBRE ACTIF DE L'ALLIANCE GRAPHIQUE INTERNATIONALE (AGI), PRO-FESSEUR À L'UCLA ET DOYEN EN DESIGN DE LA SECTION DESIGN DE L'ECOLE SUPÉRIEURE DES BEAUX-ARTS TAMA DE TOKYO.∎

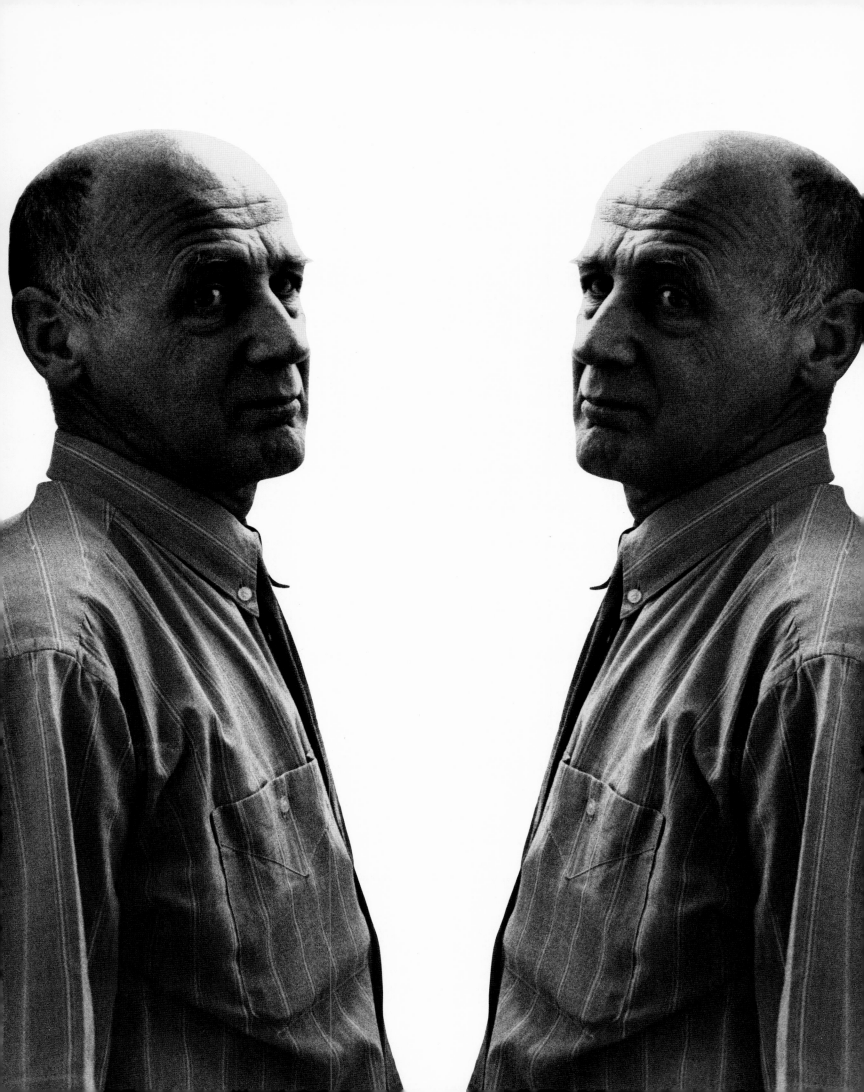

BEN BOS

IN THIS YOUNG PROFESSION OF OURS, MANY DESIGNERS ARE STILL FULL OF IDEALISM ABOUT THE ROLE OF DESIGN IN SOCIETY. AS A CONSEQUENCE NUMEROUS PROFESSIONALS DEVOTE A LOT OF ENERGY TO THE EDUCATION OF THE NEXT GENERATION OF GRAPHIC DESIGNERS. AT UNIVERSITITES, COLLEGES, AND ACADEMIES WE RAISE OUR FUTURE COLLEAGUES AND COMPETITORS: EVERY YEAR "SHIPLOADS" OF YOUNG DESIGNERS, WHO WILL BE TRYING TO JOIN OUR RANKS, AFTER THEIR GRADUATION. THE PROFES-SION, BE IT IN GRAPHIC DESIGN OR IN ADVERTISING, STILL ATTRACTS TALENTED YOUNG PEOPLE, BECAUSE THE ACTIVITY TAKES PLACE ON THE FRONTIERS OF ART AND INDUSTRY, AND SEEMS TO OFFER A KIND OF LIFE THAT BRINGS ABOUT PERSONAL SATISFACTION, FULFILLMENT AND RESPECTABILITY. IT IS NOT JUST ANOTHER WAY TO EARN ONE'S LIVING. GRAPHIC DESIGN IS IN MOST CASES HUMANISTIC ENOUGH TO COMPLY WITH A CERTAIN FEELING OF ETHICAL RESPONSIBILITY, RATHER THAN JUST HARD BUSINESS (WHICH, WE ALL KNOW, IT CAN BE AS WELL...). □ WE HAVE SEEN IMPORTANT CHANGES TAK-ING PLACE DURING THE LAST TWO DECADES. THE RAPIDLY GROWING ROLE FOR THE TECHNICAL ILLUS-TRATION, THE INTEREST FOR AIRBRUSH TECHNIQUE, THE OUTBURST OF MOVING IMAGES. I FEEL THAT PART OF THIS "EXPLOSION OF VISUAL IMAGES" HAS BEEN MADE POSSIBLE BY THE FACT THAT QUITE A FEW PEOPLE WHO COULD HAVE CHOSEN A CAREER IN FINE ART, CHANGED OVER TO DESIGN AND ILLUS-TRATION, BECAUSE THEY WERE AWARE OF THE FACT THAT APPLIED ARTS SEEM TO OFFER BETTER CHANCES FOR A SATISFACTORY INCOME. N WE HAVE SEEN THE NEW WAVE IN GRAPHIC DESIGN, IN BASLE AND IN CALIFORNIA, IN GREAT BRITAIN AND HOLLAND. THE INFLUENCES OF TECHNOLOGIES, OF DTP, SOPHISTICATED COMPUTERS, PAINT BOXES AND OTHER NEW TOOLS. I ATTENDED THE PIRA CONFERENCE IN LONDON, 1990, ON DESIGN AND TECHNOLOGY, FINDING OUT THAT AT LEAST THERE, MOST PEOPLE WERE ONLY SPEAKING ABOUT THE SUBJECT, RATHER THAN BEING INVOLVED IN IT THEMSELVES. AND IF

(LEFT) A POSTER CELEBRATING 20 YEARS OF RANDSTAD INTERIM, AN EMPLOYMENT AGENCY, IN BELGIUM (RIGHT) A 1991 INTERNATIONAL AWARD WINNING POSTER FOR KEILER WOCHE OR KIEL WEEK, A SAILING AND CULTURAL EVENT THAT BEGAN IN 1885.

they were involved, it was sometimes leading to better performances, but certainly not always. Their handwriting, if they had had one, seemed to have been taken over by a robot; the tricks were often too obvious and too predictable. These tools also cannot do without the talents, fortunately. □ This annual is a showcase to the profession. It's readers and "spectators" will largely consist of contributors, designers, and design students, and the proud clients who find their projects honored by publication in this famous book. It is a souce for pride and envy, for inspiration and imitation. n The annual is also one of the barometers that register the "highs" of the previous year. Its pages show the subjective choice of the editor and his team. At the same time a number of famous Design Biennales or Art Directors' and Type

Directors' Shows register the judges' visions on real quality in present day design. n Graphis Design has always, certainly under the direction of Walter Herdeg, laid great emphasis on ideas and on illustrative work, rather than for instance on functionalists' typography. The poster events in Lahti, Warsaw and Colorado all seem to have their own set of rules for selecting winners, national flavors being added by the "locals" in the jury. □ One cannot deny the different approach in design, nearer to fine art, in the former East block countries. It comes from both a different philosophy and different educational approach. Even now, after all their revolutions, one still sees more work from (former) communist countries at the Biennale of Brno. On the whole, that Biennale received entries from over 40 countries,

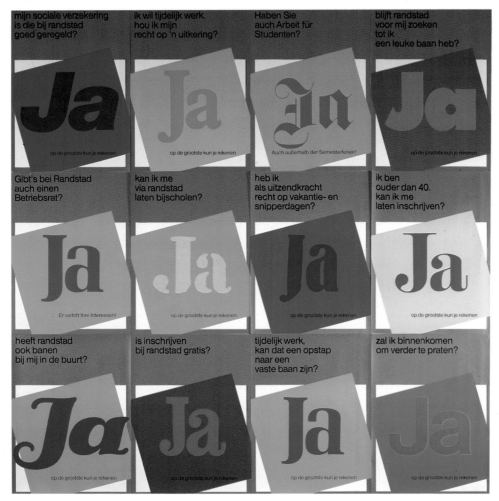

mijn sociale verzekering
is die bij randstad
goed geregeld?

ik wil tijdelijk werk.
hou ik mijn
recht op 'n uitkering?

Haben Sie
auch Arbeit für
Studenten?

blijft randstad
voor mij zoeken
tot ik
een leuke baan heb?

Ja
op de grootste kun je rekenen

Ja
op de grootste kun je rekenen

Ja
Auch außerhalb der Semesterferien?

Ja
op de grootste kun je rekenen

Gibt's bei Randstad
auch einen
Betriebsrat?

kan ik me
via randstad
laten bijscholen?

heb ik
als uitzendkracht
recht op vakantie- en
snipperdagen?

ik ben
ouder dan 40.
kan ik me
laten inschrijven?

Ja
Er vertritt Ihre Interessen!

Ja
op de grootste kun je rekenen

Ja
op de grootste kun je rekenen

Ja
op de grootste kun je rekenen

heeft randstad
ook banen
bij mij in de buurt?

is inschrijven
bij randstad gratis?

tijdelijk werk,
kan dat een opstap
naar een
vaste baan zijn?

zal ik binnenkomen
om verder te praten?

Ja
op de grootste kun je rekenen

Ja
op de grootste kun je rekenen

Ja
op de grootste kun je rekenen

Ja
op de grootste kun je rekenen

(THIS PAGE, ABOVE) A SERIES OF POSTERS FOR RANDSTAD MITZENDBUREAU (NETHER-LANDS) AND RANDSTAD ZEIT-ARBEIT (GERMAN DEMOCRATIC REPUBLIC) IN 1988.

amongst which I noticed surprisingly mature entries from places where you would never expect any graphic design to take place at all. Design is going global. □ Serving as a judge in 1991 at the New York Type Directors' Show, I was confronted with the fact that we were constantly reminded of our responsibility to select work that found its true level of superiority in typography, rather than in astonishing visuals. So in all there seem to be various platforms to honor quite different talents. □ The worldwide distribution of information about these top performances in our profession, will no doubt play its part in spreading the message of design throughout the world. There is no reason to sit back in complacent satisfaction. Certainly, we can admire many great pieces of design, but we must also always be aware of the fact that there is still an enormous, universal demand for decent, functional or attractive visual information, sometimes with emotional "added value". The fate of far too many people is still determined by the fact that they cannot read any of the messages, and therefore also miss most of our "written words". There is still an overwhelming need for design that can serve to create a more livable environment and generate greater understanding in a better world. ■

BEN BOS (BORN IN 1930) JOINED TOTAL DESIGN, AMSTERDAM, WHEN IT WAS FOUNDED BACK IN 1963. HE BECAME A CREATIVE DIRECTOR OF THIS FIRST DUTCH DESIGN GROUP A FEW YEARS LATER AND REMAINS IN THAT POSITION UP TO THE PRESENT DAY. SPECIALIZED IN CORPORATE IDENTITY PROGRAMS, HE WRITES ABOUT DESIGN, IS A PHOTOGRAPHER AND A LECTURER. HE HAS BEEN AN ACTIVE MEMBER OF THE PROFESSIONAL ORGANISATIONS OF HOLLAND AND BECAME A MEMBER OF AGI IN 1978. HE IS AGI'S NATIONAL PRESIDENT AND THE EDITOR OF THE AGI BULLETIN. HE HAS WON NUMEROUS DESIGN AWARDS AND HAD AN EXHIBITION OF HIS WORK IN BREDA IN 1988. ■

In unserer sehr jungen Branche sind viele Designer noch voller Idealismus, was die Rolle des Designs in unserer Gesellschaft betrifft. Viele von ihnen verwenden deshalb eine Menge Energie auf die Ausbildung der nächsten Generation von Graphik-Designern. An Hochschulen und Fachschulen ziehen wir unsere zukünftigen Kollegen und Konkurrenten heran: jedes Jahr Scharen von jungen Designern, die versuchen werden, es uns gleich zu tun, sobald sie die Abschlussprüfungen hinter sich haben. Sei es im Bereich des Graphik-Designs oder der Werbung, die Branche zieht talentierte junge Leute an, weil sie sich zwischen Kunst und Wirtschaft bewegt und offenbar ein Leben zu bieten scheint, das persönliche Befriedigung, Erfüllung und Anerkennung mit sich bringt. Für die meisten ist Graphik-Design nicht nur ein hartes Geschäft (was es, wie wir alle wissen, oft genug ist), sondern auch humanistisch genug, um ein gewisses Gefühl ethischer Verantwortung zuzulassen. □ In den vergangenen zwei Jahrzehnten haben wir wichtige Veränderungen miterlebt. Die wachsende Bedeutung technischer Illustration, das Interesse für die Airbrush-Technik, die Flut der bewegten Bilder. □ Wir haben die New Wave im Graphik-Design erlebt, den Einfluss neuer Technologien, des DTP, hochentwickelter Computer, Paint Boxes und anderer neuer Arbeitsgeräte. Ich nahm 1990 an der PIRA-Konferenz in London teil und stellte fest, dass zumindest dort die meisten Leute nur über das Thema sprachen, aber kaum selbst in der Praxis damit zu tun hatten. Bei denen, die tatsächlich damit arbeiteten, führte die Technik in einigen wenigen Fällen zu einem besseren Ergebnis, es war durchaus nicht bei allen der Fall. Ihre persönliche Handschrift, falls sie eine besessen hatten, schien von einem Roboter übernommen zu sein; die Tricks waren in vielen Fällen zu offensichtlich, zu kalkulierbar. Ohne Begabung nützen diese Geräte – zum Glück – nichts. □ Das Jahrbuch Graphis Design ist ein Schaufenster der Branche. Seine Leser und «Betrachter» werden zum grössten Teil aus Betroffenen bestehen, aus Designern und Studenten und natürlich aus den stolzen Auftraggebern, die ihre Projekte durch dieses berühmte Buch geehrt sehen. Es ruft Stolz und Neid hervor, verursacht Inspiration und Imitation. □ Das Jahrbuch ist zudem eines der Barometer, das die «Hochs» des vergangenen Jahres registriert. Seine Seiten zeigen die sub-jektive Auswahl des Herausgebers und seines Teams. Daneben gibt es noch eine Reihe berühmter Design-Biennalen oder Art Directors' und Type Directors' Shows, die die Meinung ihrer Juroren hinsichtlich wirklicher Qualität des heutigen Designs reflektieren. □ Graphis Design hat immer grossen Wert auf Ideen und illustrative Arbeiten gelegt. Auch die Plakat-Biennalen in Lahti, Warschau und Colorado scheinen alle von eigenen Kriterien für die Auswahl der Gewinner auszugehen, wobei die ortsansässigen Mitglieder der Juries dem Gesamtbild zuweilen einen nationalen Anstrich geben. □ Man kann nicht übersehen, dass Graphik-Design in den ehemaligen Ostblockstaaten näher bei der Kunst liegt. Das ist auf eine andere Einstellung und eine andere Ausbildung zurückzuführen. Sogar jetzt, nach den Umwälzungen, sah man an der letzten Biennale in Brno immer noch mehr Arbeiten aus den (ehemaligen) kommunistischen Ländern. Es kamen zwar Einsendungen aus über 40 Ländern, und darunter waren überraschend reife Arbeiten aus Gebieten, von denen man kaum vermutet hätte, dass Graphik-Design dort überhaupt existiert. Design ist überall. □ Bei der New York Type Directors Show 1991 gehörte ich zur Jury und musste feststellen, dass wir unentwegt ermahnt wurden, Arbeiten auszuwählen, die sich durch hohes Niveau in der Typographie auszeichnen, dass es nicht um eindrucksvolle visuelle Einfälle geht. Das heisst, dass es tatsächlich verschiedene Gesichtspunkte gibt, nach denen die verschiedenen Talente gewürdigt werden. □ Die weltweite Verbreitung von Informationen über die Topleistungen in unserer Branche dient zweifellos auch der Verbreitung guten Designs. Man kann sich nicht einfach zufrieden im Sessel zurücklehnen und nichts tun. Natürlich wurde bereits Bewundernswertes im Design-Bereich vollbracht, aber man kann es nicht einfach dabei belassen. Wir müssen uns klar darüber sein, dass es überall noch immer einen enormen Bedarf an guter, verständlicher und ansprechender visueller Information gibt, wobei manchmal auch Emotionen zusätzlich ins Spiel kommen müssen. Das Schicksal zu vieler Leute wird noch immer durch die Tatsache bestimmt, dass sie keine Botschaft lesen können. Zudem gibt es noch immer einen enormen Bedarf an Design für die Schaffung einer lebenswerten Umwelt und einer Welt, die durch grösseres gegenseitiges Verständnis geprägt ist. ■

BEN BOS (1930) GEHÖRT SEIT 1963 ZU TOTAL DESIGN, AMSTERDAM, D.H. SEIT DER GRÜNDUNG DIESER ERSTEN HOLLÄNDISCHEN DESIGN-GRUPPE. NACH EIN PAAR JAHREN WURDE ER CREATIVE DIRECTOR, WAS ER HEUTE NOCH IST. ER HAT SICH AUF CORPORATE IDENTITY-PROGRAMME SPEZIALISIERT, SCHREIBT ÜBER DESIGN, PHOTOGRAPHIERT UND HÄLT VORTRÄGE. ER IST BEI VERSCHIEDENEN BERUFSVERBÄNDEN DER GRAPHISCHEN BRANCHE IN HOLLAND ALS AKTIVES MITGLIED TÄTIG UND SEIT 1978 MITGLIED DER AGI. ER IST HEUTE PRÄSIDENT DER HOLLÄNDISCHEN SEKTION DER AGI UND HERAUSGEBER DES AGI-BULLETINS. FÜR SEINE ARBEITEN HAT ER ZAHLREICHE AUSZEICHNUNGEN ERHALTEN. 1988 WURDEN SIE IN EINER AUSSTELLUNG IN BREDA GEZEIGT.■

Dans notre jeune profession, on trouve toujours autant d'idéalistes en ce qui concerne le rôle du design dans la société. La conséquence est que de nombreux professionnels consacrent une grande part de leur énergie à l'éducation de la prochaine génération de designers graphiques. Ce sont eux qui forment nos futurs collègues et concurrents dans les universités, les collèges et les académies; chaque année, des cargaisons de jeunes designers essaieront de rejoindre nos rangs après leur diplôme. Les métiers du design et de la publicité continuent d'attirer les jeunes talents, car ces activités se situent aux frontières de l'art et de l'industrie et semblent offrir un style de vie qui apporte satisfaction et respectabilité, tout en permettant l'accomplissement personnel. Ce n'est pas seulement une autre manière de gagner sa vie. Le design graphique est dans la plupart des cas assez humaniste pour se soumettre à une certaine éthique, au lieu d'être uniquement du business pur et dur (ce qu'il peut aussi être, nous le savons tous). □ Nous avons pu constater que d'importants changements s'étaient produits au cours des deux dernières décades: le rôle croissant de l'illustration technique, l'intérêt pour la technique de l'aérographe, l'explosion du secteur de l'animation. □ Nous avons pu voir l'éclosion de la New Wave dans le design graphique, l'influence des nouvelles technologies, du desktop publishing, des ordinateurs sophistiqués, des palettes graphiques et bien d'autres nouveaux outils. En 1990, j'ai assisté à la conférence PIRA de Londres sur les rapports du design et de la technologie et j'ai réalisé que la plupart des participants abordaient cette question sans être vraiment directement concernés. Et lorsqu'ils l'étaient, cela pouvait améliorer les résultats, mais pas toujours... Leur écriture propre, s'ils en avaient une, semblait être devenue celle d'un robot; les trucs étaient souvent trop évidents et prévisibles. Les outils, heureusement, n'apportent donc rien sans le talent. □ Ce répertoire annuel est une vitrine pour la profession. Ses lecteurs et «spectateurs» sont pour la plupart des protagonistes, des designers et des étudiants en arts graphiques, ainsi que des clients fiers de voir leurs projets honorés d'une publication dans ce livre fameux. Il suscite l'orgueil et la jalousie, c'est une source d'inspiration, un modèle. □ Ce répertoire annuel est aussi l'un de ces baromètres qui enregistrent les «hauts» de l'année précédente. Dans ses pages, on découvre le choix subjectif de l'éditeur et de l'équipe qui l'entoure. En même temps, une quantité de Biennales du design ou d'expositions des Arts Directors et Type Directors Clubs tiennent compte de l'opinion du jury sur la qualité véritable du design d'aujourd'hui. □ Graphis Design a, dès ses débuts, attaché une importance plus grande aux idées et aux images qu'aux travaux typographiques fonctionnels par exemple. Les expositions d'affiches de Lahti, Varsovie ou du Colorado semblent avoir leurs propres critères de sélection des candidats, les caractères nationaux venant s'ajouter aux «particularités locales» du jury. □ Nul ne saurait nier l'approche différente du design, plus proche du domaine de l'Art proprement dit, dans l'ancien bloc des pays de l'Est. Cela vient à la fois d'une philosophie et d'une éducation différentes. Aujourd'hui encore, même après toutes leurs révolutions, à la Biennale de Brno, la majorité des travaux exposés vient des (anciens) pays communistes. Cette Biennale a reçu des envois de plus de 40 pays, parmi lesquels j'ai remarqué, avec quelque surprise, des projets très élaborés provenant de contrées où vous ne vous attendriez jamais à trouver du design graphique. □ Membre du jury de l'exposition du New York Type Directors Club de 1991, je me suis aperçu d'une chose: nous devions toujours nous rappeler qu'il est de notre devoir de sélectionner des travaux dont la supériorité réside dans la qualité de la typographie plutôt que dans des visuels époustouflants. Il existe en réalité toute une échelle de critères qui permette d'honorer les talents les plus divers. □ Les informations concernant ces manifestations de haut niveau dans notre profession sont diffusées à une échelle internationale et cela contribue sans aucun doute à répandre le message du design dans le monde entier. Il n'y a cependant pas lieu de se reposer sur ses lauriers. Certes, nous pouvons admirer de grandes réalisations, mais nous devons être conscients du fait que la demande est énorme: partout l'on a besoin d'une information visuelle honnête, fonctionnelle et attrayante, avec l'émotion en plus quelquefois. Le destin de beaucoup trop de gens est déjà décidé du fait qu'ils ne peuvent lire aucun message et donc qu'ils ne comprennent pas la plupart de nos «messages écrits». Il est urgent de créer un design qui contribue à créer un environnement vivable et plus de compréhension dans un monde meilleur. ■

BEN BOS (NÉ EN 1930) A REJOINT L'AGENCE TOTAL DESIGN D'AMSTERDAM DÈS SA FONDATION EN 1963. IL DEVINT DIRECTEUR DE LA CRÉATION DE CE PREMIER STUDIO DE DESIGN HOLLANDAIS QUELQUES ANNÉES PLUS TARD ET IL EST RESTÉ À CE POSTE JUSQU'À CE JOUR. SPÉCIALISÉ DANS LES PROGRAMMES D'IDENTITÉ CORPORATE, IL ÉCRIT SUR LE DESIGN, FAIT DE LA PHOTO ET DES CONFÉRENCES. LONGTEMPS ACTIF AU SEIN DES ORGANISMES PROFESSIONNELS HOLLANDAIS, IL EST MEMBRE DE L'AGI DEPUIS 1978. IL A ÉTÉ NOMMÉ PRÉSIDENT NATIONAL DE L'AGI ET IL ÉDITE LE BULLETIN DE L'ASSOCIATION. IL A REMPORTÉ DE NOMBREUX PRIX ET SON ŒUVRE A ÉTÉ EXPOSÉE À BREDA EN 1988. ■

ADVERTISING

WERBUNG

PUBLICITÉ

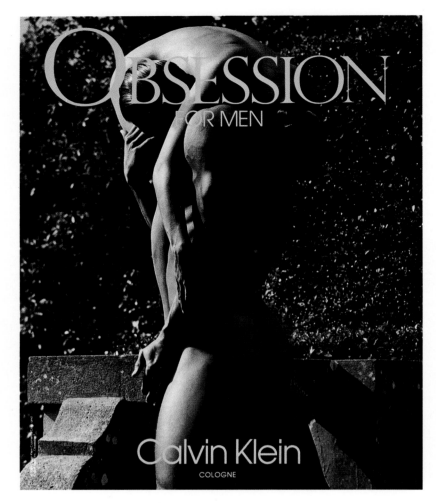

(PRECEDING PAGE)

ART DIRECTORS:

DOUGLAS JOSEPH

RIK BESSER

DESIGNER:

DOUGLAS JOSEPH

ARTIST:

STEVE JOHNSON

AGENCY:

BESSER JOSEPH

PARTNERS

CLIENT:

◄ LINCOLN BANCORP

ART DIRECTOR:

MAURO MORTAROLI

DESIGNER:

MAURO MORTAROLI

PHOTOGRAPHER:

NINO MASCARDI

COPYWRITER:

MAURIZIO SALA

AGENCY:

ARMANDO TESTA

S.P.A.

CLIENT:

SCHIAPPARELLI

BENESSERE

PIKENZ S.P.A.

■ 1

ART DIRECTOR:

SAM SHAHID

PHOTOGRAPHER:

BRUCE WEBER

STYLIST:

TONNE GOODMAN

AGENCY:

CRK ADVERTISING

CLIENT:

CALVIN KLEIN

COSMETICS COMPANY

■ 2, 3

■ 1 "MAKE A WISH" SAYS THIS AD FOR ARROGAN-TISSIMA, A FRAGRANCE CREATED FOR THE SELF-CONFIDENT, ELEGANT, CLASSIC WOMAN. THE MESSAGE SUGGESTS THAT ARROGANTISSIMA IS A PERFUME, THAT ONCE CHOSEN, WILL NOT BE CHANGED, THAT JUST LIKE A WISH IT CAN FULFILL EVERY DESIRE AND EXPECTATION. (ITA)

■ 2, 3 A FULL-PAGE AND A DOUBLE-SPREAD MAGAZINE ADVERTISEMENT FOR CALVIN KLEIN'S OBSESSION LINE. (USA)

● (VORHERGEHENDE SEITE) ILLUSTRATION VON STEVE JOHNSON, ÖL AUF AQUARELLPAPIER. (USA)

● 1 «WÜNSCH DIR WAS» SAGT DIESE ANZEIGE FÜR ARROGANTISSIMA, EIN PARFUM FÜR DIE SELBST-BEWUSSTE, ELEGANTE FRAU. DIE BOTSCHAFT IST, DASS DIE ENTSCHEIDUNG, HAT MAN EINMAL ARRO-GANTISSIMA GEWÄHLT, UNWIDERRUFLICH IST. WIE BEI EINEM WUNSCH, DEN MAN FREI HAT, WIRD ES ALLE ERWARTUNGEN ERFÜLLEN. (ITA)

● 2, 3 EINE GANZSEITIGE UND EINE DOPPELSEITIGE ANZEIGE FÜR DIE OBSESSION-LINIE VON CALVIN KLEIN. (USA)

▲ (PAGE PRÉCÉDENTE) ILLUSTRATION DE STEVE JOHNSON, HUILE SUR PAPIER AQUARELLE. (USA)

▲ 1 «EXPRIME UN DÉSIR»: PUBLICITÉ POUR ARRO-GANTISSIMA, UN PARFUM CRÉÉ POUR LA FEMME SÛRE D'ELLE, ÉLÉGANTE ET CLASSIQUE. SI L'ON EN CROIT CE SLOGAN, CHOISIR ARROGANTISSIMA RE-VIENT À FAIRE UN VŒU ET TOUS LES SOUHAITS LES PLUS CHERS DE LA FEMME QUI UTILISERA CE PARFUM SERONT EXAUCÉS. (ITA)

▲ 2, 3 ANNONCE PLEINE PAGE ET ANNONCE DOUBLE PAGE POUR LA LIGNE DE PRODUITS POUR LE CORPS OBSESSION DE CALVIN KLEIN. (USA)

ART DIRECTOR:
STAN LÉVY
DESIGNER:
STAN LÉVY
PHOTOGRAPHER:
ALDO FALLAI
AGENCY:
SUCCESS SLAD
CLIENT:
GIORGIO ARMANI
PARFUMS
■ 4, 5

ART DIRECTOR:
BRUCE BLOCH
PHOTOGRAPHER:
PIERO GEMELLI
COPYWRITER:
PATTY ROCKMORE
AGENCY:
WELLS, RICH, GREENE
CLIENT:
RICHARDSON-VICKS
■ 6

■ 4, 5 EXAMPLES OF THE CONTINUOUS CLASSICAL STYLE OF ADVERTISING FOR PRODUCTS BY GIORGIO ARMANI THAT CORRESPONDS WITH THE CLASSICAL STYLE OF HIS FASHIONS. (ITA)

■ 6 DOUBLE-SPREAD ADVERTISEMENT FOR OIL OF OLAY WITH A CLOSE-UP VIEW OF THE BOTTLE. COLOR AND SHAPE OF THIS DETAIL SUGGEST THE HUMAN BODY AND SKIN, EMPHASIZING THE CLAIM THAT THIS FLUID CAN MAKE UP FOR THE LOSS OF THE SKIN'S NATURAL FLUID. (USA)

● 4, 5 BEISPIELE DES KONSEQUENT VERFOLGTEN KLASSISCHEN WERBESTILS FÜR PRODUKTE VON GIORGIO ARMANI, IM EINKLANG MIT DEM KLASSISCHEN STIL SEINER MODEKREATIONEN. (ITA)

● 6 DOPPELSEITIGES INSERAT FÜR DAS HAUTPFLEGEMITTEL OIL OF OLAZ MIT DETAIL DER FLASCHE. FORM UND FARBE DIESES AUSSCHNITTS ERINNERN AN DEN MENSCHLICHEN KÖRPER UND DIE HAUT, DER GEMÄSS TEXT DURCH DIESES MITTEL FEUCHTIGKEIT ZURÜCKGEGEBEN WIRD. (USA)

▲ 4, 5 EXEMPLES D'ANNONCES D'UN STYLE TRÈS CLASSIQUE POUR LES PRODUITS DE GIORGIO ARMANI, QUI CORRESPONDENT AU CLASSICISME DE SES CRÉATIONS DE MODE. (ITA)

▲ 6 ANNONCE DOUBLE PAGE MONTRANT LE DÉTAIL D'UN FLACON D'HUILE D'OLAZ, UN PRODUIT HYDRATANT POUR LA PEAU DONT ON VANTE ICI LES QUALITÉS D'ABSORPTION. LA FORME ET LA COULEUR DE CE DÉTAIL ÉVOQUENT LE CORPS HUMAIN ET LES PROPRIÉTÉS DU PRODUIT. (USA)

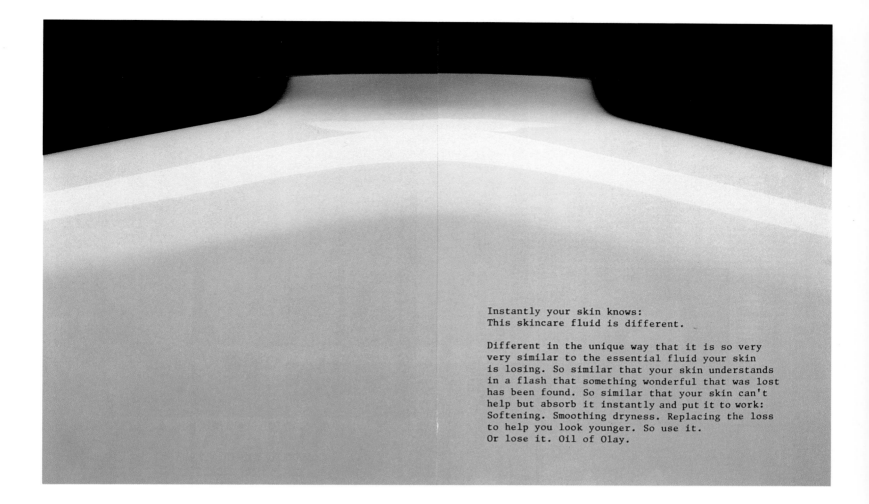

Instantly your skin knows:
This skincare fluid is different.

Different in the unique way that it is so very
very similar to the essential fluid your skin
is losing. So similar that your skin understands
in a flash that something wonderful that was lost
has been found. So similar that your skin can't
help but absorb it instantly and put it to work:
Softening. Smoothing dryness. Replacing the loss
to help you look younger. So use it.
Or lose it. Oil of Olay.

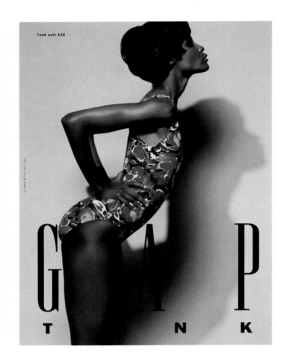

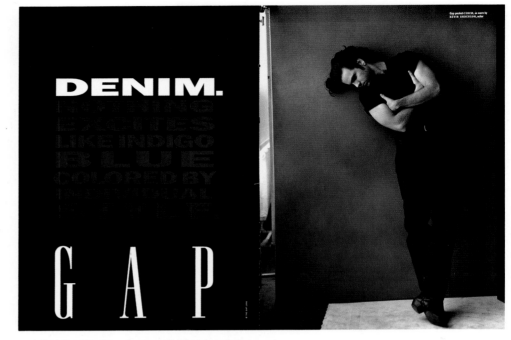

CREATIVE DIRECTOR:
MAGGIE GROSS
DESIGNERS:
ROZ ROMNEY
RUTH SAKHEIM   ART DIRECTOR:
PHOTOGRAPHERS: ARTY TAN
GUZMAN   DESIGNER:
ANNIE LEIBOVITZ   ARTY TAN
HERB RITTS   PHOTOGRAPHER:
COPYWRITER: SHAWN MICHIENZI
TIM COHRS   COPYWRITER:
AGENCY: MIKE GIBBS
GAP/IN-HOUSE   AGENCY:
CLIENT: FALLON MCELLIGOTT
THE GAP   CLIENT:
■ 7-9   THE LEE COMPANY
                              ▶▶■ 10-12

Lee Lites. Lightweight denim.

Light, cool, comfortable jeans with a remarkably soft hand. Perfect for all seasons. Available in two different finishes: Aged Stone and Aged Blue. Call your Lee sales representative today. Because Lee Lites are just what the market ordered. And everyone will be reaching for them.

Lee Lites. A new line of lightweight denim.

Light, cool, comfortable jeans with a remarkably soft hand. Perfect for all seasons. Available in two different finishes: Aged Stone and Aged Blue. Call your Lee sales representative today. Because Lee Lites are just what the market ordered. And they just might take off without you.

Lee Lites. Lightweight denim.

Light, cool, comfortable jeans with a remarkably soft hand. Perfect for all seasons. Available in two different finishes: Aged Stone and Aged Blue. Call your Lee sales representative today. Because Lee Lites are just what the market ordered. And they're raising eyebrows everywhere.

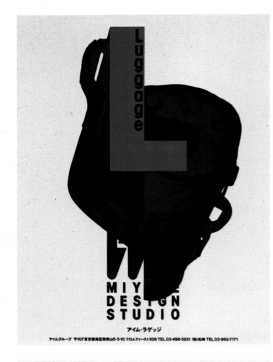

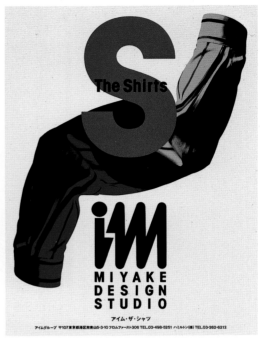

■ 13-18 THE INITIAL LETTERS OF THE ENGLISH WORDS FOR THE TEXTILES PRESENTED ARE THE MAJOR ELEMENT IN THIS SERIES OF MAGAZINE ADVERTISEMENTS FOR AN ISSEY MIYAKE LICENSE GROUP. (JPN)

■ 19-21 DOUBLE-SPREAD ADVERTISEMENTS FOR KIKIT FASHIONS BY MAURICE SASSON, AVAILABLE IN THE MOST PRESTIGIOUS STORES. (USA)

● 13-18 DIE ANFANGSBUCHSTABEN DER ENGLISCHEN BEZEICHNUNGEN FÜR DIE DARGESTELLTEN TEXTILIEN SIND DAS ZENTRALE ELEMENT DIESER ANZEIGENREIHE FÜR EINEN LIZENZNEHMER DES MODESCHÖPFERS ISSEY MIYAKE. (JPN)

● 19-21 DOPPELSEITIGE ANZEIGEN FÜR KIKIT-MODE VON MAURICE SASSON, DIE IN ERSTKLASSIGEN KAUFHÄUSERN ERHÄLTLICH IST. (USA)

▲ 13-18 LES INITIALES DU NOM ANGLAIS DE CHAQUE PRODUIT REPRÉSENTÉ CONSTITUENT L'ÉLÉMENT CENTRAL DE CETTE CAMPAGNE D'ANNONCES POUR UN REVENDEUR SOUS LICENCE DES VÊTEMENTS ET ACCESSOIRES ISSEY MIYAKE. (JPN)

▲ 19-21 ANNONCES DOUBLE PAGE POUR LA COLLECTION KIKIT DE MAURICE SASSON, VENDUE DANS LES MAGASINS LES PLUS PRESTIGIEUX. (USA)

ART DIRECTOR:
MASAAKI HIROMURA
DESIGNERS:
MASAAKI HIROMURA
TAKAFUMI KUSAGAYA
PHOTOGRAPHER:
YUTAKA SAKANO
AGENCY:
IKKS, INC.
CLIENT:
MIYAKE DESIGN
STUDIO
◀■ 13-18

ART DIRECTOR:
FABIEN BARON
DESIGNER:
MAURICE SASSON
PHOTOGRAPHER:
WAYNE MASER
AGENCY:
IN-HOUSE
CLIENT:
MAURICE SASSON
■ 19-21

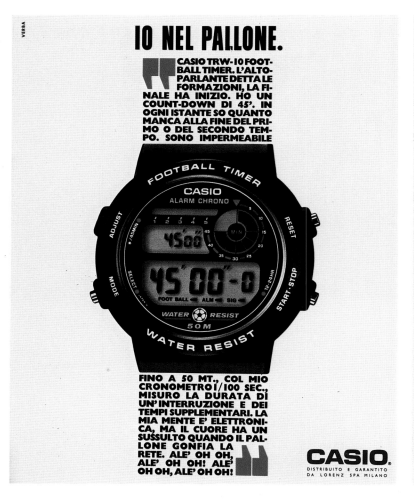

ART DIRECTOR:

DANIELE CIMA

DESIGNER:

DANIELE CIMA

PHOTOGRAPHER:

YOSHI KAZUMOTO

COPYWRITERS:

DANIELE RAVENNA

ENRICO BONOMINI

AGENCY:

VERBA

CLIENT:

CASIO

■ 22, 23

ART DIRECTOR:

ALBERTO BACCARI

ILLUSTRATOR:

ROBERTO RODRIGUEZ

COPYWRITER:

ROBERT SCHULMAN

AGENCY:

ARMANDO TESTA

ADVERTISING INC.

CLIENT:

TIME EXCHANGE

■ 24, 25

■ 22, 23 "I THE FOOTBALL PLAYER" AND "I THE RALLY DRIVER." THE WATCHES IN THIS CAMPAIGN INTRODUCE THEMSELVES. THEY ARE SPECIALLY DESIGNED FOR CERTAIN SPORTS. (ITA)

■ 24, 25 A COMBINATION OF TWO ADVERTISEMENTS PLACED ON CONSECUTIVE PAGES. THEY ARE DONE IN THE STYLE OF POST-REVOLUTIONARY ART OF THE SOVIET UNION, FOR A WATCH MADE IN THE USSR AND SOLD ON THE US MARKET. (USA)

● 22, 23 «ICH, DER FUSSBALLSPIELER» UND «ICH, DER RALLYEFAHRER» – DIE UHREN STELLEN SICH IN DIESER KAMPAGNE SELBST VOR. SIE SIND SPEZIELL FÜR BESTIMMTE SPORTARTEN KONZIPIERT. (ITA)

● 24, 25 EINE KOMBINATION VON ZWEI ANZEIGEN, IM STIL DER SOWJETISCHEN KUNST NACH DER OKTOBERREVOLUTION, FÜR EINE IN DER UDSSR HERGESTELLTE UHR. DIE ANZEIGEN ERSCHIENEN AUF AUFEINANDERFOLGENDEN SEITEN. (USA)

▲ 22, 23 «MOI, LE FOOTBALLEUR» ET «MOI, LE COUREUR DE RALLYES»: LES MONTRES SE PRÉSENTENT ICI DIRECTEMENT, CHAQUE MODÈLE ÉTANT CONÇU POUR UN SPORT DIFFÉRENT. (ITA)

▲ 24, 25 CES ANNONCES POUR UNE MONTRE FABRIQUÉE EN URSS, PRÉSENTÉES SUR DEUX PAGES CONSÉCUTIVES, ONT ÉTÉ RÉALISÉES DANS LE STYLE DES AFFICHES DE LA RÉVOLUTION D'OCTOBRE. (USA)

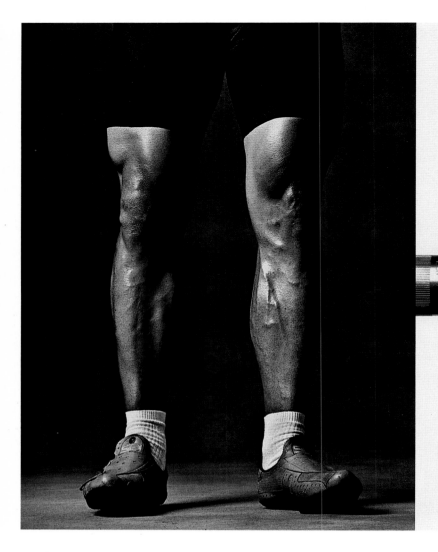

A Timex you wind with your feet.

If you think the Timex Velo-Trak is another Timex watch you're only half right.

Actually, it's the first sports watch that's

Using the Velo-Trak is as easy as riding a bike. Buttons are large, and the readouts clear.

also a bicycle computer. The first bike computer cyclists can wear

With its ingenious mounting bracket the Velo-Trak shifts from a cycle computer to wristwatch in about the time it takes to shift.

on their wrist when they're not wearing it on their bike.

Yet despite all its versatility, the Velo-Trak is no compromise.

Like other sophisticated cycle computers it features current and maximum speed, trip and total season distance, current and maximum

cadence, 24-hour countdown timer, and a 24-hour chronograph with lap and split.

But unlike any other cycle computer it's also a wristwatch with

features like time and calendar, hourly chime, and alarm. It's even water-resistant to 25 meters. Which makes it perfect for the growing triathlete market.

Of course, with its three-year lithium battery your customers don't really have to wind it.

But once they get one on their bike they may want to crank it. **TIMEX** *VELO-TRAK*

Suggested retail price $75.00. Available only to bicycle and sporting goods retailers. For the Timex sporting goods representative nearest you call 1-800-FOR-WATCH. © 1989 Timex Corp.

ART DIRECTOR:
HOUMAN PIRDAVARI
DESIGNER:
HOUMAN PIRDAVARI
PHOTOGRAPHER:
JIM ARNDT
COPYWRITER:
BRUCE BILDSTEN
AGENCY:
FALLON MCELLIGOTT
CLIENT:
TIMEX CORP.
■ 26

ART DIRECTOR:
HOUMAN PIRDAVARI
DESIGNER:
HOUMAN PIRDAVARI
PHOTOGRAPHER:
HIRO
COPYWRITER:
BRUCE BILDSTEN
AGENCY:
FALLON MCELLIGOTT
CLIENT:
TIMEX CORP.
▶■ 27-35

■ 26 DOUBLE-SPREAD AD FOR TIMEX VELO-TRAK, A SPORTS WATCH THAT IS ALSO A BICYCLE COMPUTER. IT CAN BE FIXED TO THE BIKE OR WORN BY THE CYCLISTS ON THEIR WRISTS. (USA)

■ 27-35 THE LEADING THEME OF THIS SERIES IS THAT "THE MOST REMARKABLE PEOPLE IN THIS WORLD ARE JUST ORDINARY (THOUGH RATHER ACTIVE) PEOPLE WHO HAPPENED TO HAVE EXPERIENCED SOMETHING EXTRAORDINARY, AND SURVIVED." THESE PEOPLE ARE WEARING A SPECIAL WATCH FROM THE TIMEX COLLECTION. (USA)

● 26 ANZEIGE FÜR TIMEX VELO- TRAK, EINE SPORT-UHR, DIE AUCH ALS RENNRAD-COMPUTER DIENT. SIE KANN AM FAHRRAD ANGEBRACHT ODER AM HANDGELENK GETRAGEN WERDEN. (USA)

● 27-35 DAS LEITTHEMA DIESER KAMPAGNE IST, DASS »DIE BEMERKENSWERTESTEN LEUTE GANZ GEWÖHNLICHE (WENN AUCH SEHR AKTIVE) MENSCHEN SIND, DENEN ETWAS ZUGESTOSSEN IST, UND DIE ÜBERLEBT HABEN«. SIE SIND ETWAS BESONDERES UND TRAGEN EINE BESONDERE UHR AUS DER TIMEX-KOLLEKTION. (USA)

▲ 26 ANNONCE DOUBLE PAGE POUR VELO-TRAK, UNE MONTRE DE SPORT ÉLECTRONIQUE AVEC CHRONOMÈTRE, QUI PEUT ÊTRE FIXÉE AU GUIDON DE VÉLO OU AU POIGNET DU CYCLISTE. (USA)

▲ 27-35 LE LEITMOTIV DE CETTE CAMPAGNE EST QUE «LES GENS LES PLUS REMARQUABLES SONT DES GENS ORDINAIRES (QUOIQUE PLUTÔT ACTIFS), QUI ONT FAIT L'EXPÉRIENCE DE QUELQUE CHOSE D'EXTRAORDINAIRE ET ONT SURVÉCU.» CHACUN D'EUX PORTE UN MODÈLE DE MONTRE BIEN PARTICULIER DE LA COLLECTION TIMEX. (USA)

The most remarkable people in this world don't appear on movie screens or in sports arenas or on television tubes. They drive cabs and work in offices and operate machinery. They're just ordinary people like us who happened to have experienced something extraordinary. And survived.

IT WILL RETURN TO MEMORY, LONG AFTER IT HAS RETURNED TO PORT.

Experienced travellers know that a great vacation is not merely fascinating destinations. It is, rather, a series of moments – strung together like a necklace that you will carry with you long after you return home.

Who knows what detail handled just so, will one day be the key to a lasting memory? It may be something as simple as a gentle knock at the door that brings a bottle of Dom Perignon from a cellar of 17,000 selections; an exquisite dinner created by 33 chefs. At the latch, perhaps, will be your first sample of the gracious service that inspired *Travel-Holiday* magazine to vote us Most Courteous Cruise Line for three years running; or perhaps the loafers you left outside your door last night now returned and, miraculously, shined.

When a vacation is such an important transaction, is there any room for compromise?

Your own necklace of moments awaits you aboard the five-star-plus ships of Royal Viking Line. A call to your travel agent, or to us at (800) 426-0821 will bring details on our whereabouts throughout the year. As always, we look forward to seeing you on board.

ROYAL VIKING LINE
THE WORLD'S FINEST

En route to an adventure on the East African coast: the gleaming white Royal Viking Sun, rated the world's best ship by Berlitz.

Outside the windowed walls of your forward observation lounge, the scenery changes pleasantly day after day, and so do you.

Bahamian Registry.

© Royal Viking Line 1990

ART DIRECTORS:
STEVE STONE
JEREMY POSTAER
RICH SILVERSTEIN
TRACY WONG
BETSY ZIMMERMANN
DESIGNERS:
STEVE STONE
JEREMY POSTAER
RICH SILVERSTEIN
TRACY WONG
BETSY ZIMMERMANN
PHOTOGRAPHERS:
DUNCAN SIM
JAY MAISEL
HARVEY LLOYD
FERNANDO BATISTA
RANDY MILLER
GWENNE WILCOX
HANK BENSON
COPYWRITERS:
ED CRAYTON
DAVID FOWLER
ROB BAGOT
AGENCY:
GOODBY, BERLIN &
SILVERSTEIN
CLIENT:
ROYAL VIKING LINE

■ 36-40

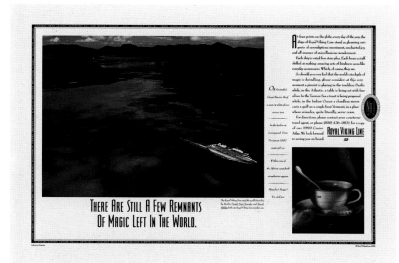

THERE ARE STILL A FEW REMNANTS
OF MAGIC LEFT IN THE WORLD.

HALFWAY BETWEEN MANHATTAN AND BERMUDA,
AN ENCHANTED ISLAND THAT BOASTS THE BEST OF BOTH.

ARRIVING AT THE PROPER STATE OF MIND REQUIRES JUST THE RIGHT VEHICLE.

■ 36-40 EXAMPLES FROM A CAMPAIGN FOR THE 1990 CRUISES OF THE ROYAL VIKING LINE EMPHASIZING THE COMFORT A CRUISE OFFERS TO ITS PASSENGERS EVEN IN THE REMOTEST PLACES. THE COPY CLAIMING THAT THE LINE IS THE WORLD'S BEST IS BASED ON A JUDGEMENT OF THE READERS OF THE MAGAZINES *CONDÉ NAST TRAVELER* AND *TRAVEL HOLIDAY*. (USA)

● 36-40 BEISPIELE AUS EINER KAMPAGNE FÜR DIE KREUZFAHRTEN DER ROYAL VIKING LINE IM JAHR 1990, IN DER DER KOMFORT BETONT WIRD, DER DEN REISENDEN AUCH AN DEN ENTLEGENDSTEN ORTEN GEBOTEN WIRD. DIE ANZEIGE, IN DER DIE LINIE ALS DIE «BESTE DER WELT» BEZEICHNET WIRD, STÜTZT SICH AUF DAS URTEIL DER LESER VON *CONDÉ NAST TRAVELER* UND *TRAVEL HOLIDAY*. (USA)

▲ 36-40 EXEMPLES D'UNE CAMPAGNE D'ANNONCES POUR LE PROGRAMME DE CROISIÈRES 90 DE LA COMPAGNIE ROYAL VIKING LINE: L'ACCENT EST MIS SUR LE CONFORT PROPOSÉ AUX VOYAGEURS. DANS CES ANNONCES, ROYAL VIKING LINE EST APPELÉE «LA MEILLEURE LIGNE DU MONDE», UN JUGEMENT BASÉ SUR L'OPINION DES LECTEURS DE *CONDÉ NAST TRAVELER* ET *TRAVEL HOLIDAY*. (USA)

ART DIRECTOR:
JACQUI COATES
ANDREW LEES
PHOTOGRAPHER:
PETER JEFFS
ILLUSTRATOR:
JACQUI COATES
COPYWRITER:
ANDREW LEES
AGENCY:
CHIAT/DAY/MOJO
CLIENT:
CLUB
MÉDITERRANÉE
■ 41-43

■ 41-43 EXAMPLES FROM AN ADVERTISING CAM-
PAIGN FOR THE CLUB MÉDITERRANÉE IN AUSTRALIA.
COLLAGES WITH ALL KINDS OF THINGS THAT SPEAK
OF THE COUNTRY CONCERNED IN THE PARTICULAR
ADVERTISEMENT ARE USED, HERE MALAYSIA, TAHITI
AND THAILAND. THE IDEA WAS TO CONVEY THE
NATURAL, RELAXING YET LUXURIOUS LIFE OFFERED
BY THIS CLUB. (AUS)

● 41-43 BEISPIELE AUS EINER WERBEKAMPAGNE
FÜR DEN CLUB MÉDITERRANÉE IN AUSTRALIEN:
«NACH NUR 7 TAGEN LESEN SIE DIESE ZEILE 50%
LANGSAMER»; «IN TAHITI HAT DAS ALPHABET NUR 13
BUCHSTABEN. WIE IM CLUB IST HIER ALLES EIN-
FACHER»; «FRANZÖSISCHE RESTAURANTS MIT THAI-
LÄNDISCHEN MEERESFRÜCHTEN, AN DER SCHÖN-
STEN KÜSTE ASIENS.» (AUS)

▲ 41-43 EXEMPLES D'ANNONCES POUR UNE
CAMPAGNE PUBLICITAIRE DU CLUB MÉDITERRANÉE.
«AU BOUT DE 6 JOURS, VOUS LIREZ CETTE ANNONCE
50% PLUS LENTEMENT»; «L'ALPHABET TAHITIEN N'A
QUE 13 LETTRES. COMME AU CLUB, TOUT Y EST
PLUS SIMPLE»; «DES RESTAURANTS FRANÇAIS AVEC
DES FRUITS DE MER THAÏLANDAIS, SUR LA PLUS
BELLE PLAGE D'ASIE». (AUS)

The legendary Alfa Romeo 6C 1750 Gran Sport. Winner of the 1929, 1930 and 1931 Mille Miglia.

Coming soon: A legend for the new age. The incredible front-wheel-drive Alfa Romeo 164 high-performance luxury sedan. With an Alfa Romeo Assurance Program so comprehensive, it even pays for things like brake pads. See your dealer for details. For more information, call 1-800-245-ALFA.

©1990 Alfa Romeo Distributors of North America.

Alfa Romeo. The legendary marque of high performance.

ART DIRECTORS:
TOM LICHTENHELD
ARTY TAN
DESIGNERS:
TOM LICHTENHELD
ARTY TAN
PHOTOGRAPHER:
MARK LAFAVOR
COPYWRITERS:
PHIL HANFT
JAMIE BARRETT
AGENCY:
FALLON MCELLIGOTT
CLIENT:
AMOCO OIL CO.
◄■ 45, 46

ART DIRECTOR:
GARY WISE
PHOTOGRAPHER:
ROB GAGE
COPYWRITER:
LANCE ALDRICH
AGENCY:
ROSS ROY
ADVERTISING
CLIENT:
ALFA ROMEO
DISTRIBUTORS OF
AMERICA
■ 44, 47

■ 44, 47 ADVERTISEMENTS FROM A CAMPAIGN FOR ALFA ROMEO IN THE UNITED STATES. THE PHOTOS ON THE LEFT SHOW A DETAIL OF THE LEGENDARY FORERUNNERS OF THE MODERN COUNTERPARTS PRESENTED ON THE RIGHT. 44: THE ALFA BIMOTORE MONOPOSTO OF 1935 AND THE LATEST PININFARINA DESIGNED 164 HIGH PERFORMANCE LUXURY SEDAN. 47: DETAIL OF THE TIRE OF THE 6C 1750 GRAN SPORT AND ITS COUNTERPART BELONGING TO THE 164 SEDAN. (USA)

■ 45, 46 WITH THESE ADVERTISEMENTS RETAILERS ARE TOLD THAT AMOCO LDO MOTOR OIL CAN BE USED BY ANY OF THEIR CUSTOMERS. (USA)

● 44, 47 ANZEIGEN AUS EINER US-KAMPAGNE FÜR ALFA ROMEO. AUF DER LINKEN SEITE DER INSERATE WERDEN DETAILS DER LEGENDÄREN VORLÄUFER DES NEUSTEN MODELLS GEZEIGT, DAS RECHTS VORGE-STELLT WIRD. 44: DER ALFA BIMOTORE MONOPOSTO VON 1935 UND DAS NEUSTE, VON PININFARINA ENTWORFENE MODELL, EINE 164 LUXUSLIMOUSINE. 47: DETAIL DES REIFENS EINES 6C 1750 GRAN SPORT UND DAS MODERNE GEGENSTÜCK EINER 164-LIMOUSINE. (USA)

● 45, 46 MIT DIESEN ANZEIGEN WIRD DEN HÄNDLERN MITGETEILT, DASS SICH AMOCO LDO MOTORENÖL FÜR ALLE AUTOS EIGNET. (USA)

▲ 44, 47 ANNONCES D'UNE CAMPAGNE POUR ALFA ROMEO AUX ÉTATS-UNIS. CHAQUE IMAGE OPPOSE DEUX PHOTOS DE DÉTAILS DE VOITURES, CELLE D'UN MODÈLE HISTORIQUE ET CELLE DU MODÈLE LE PLUS RÉCENT. 44: LA LÉGENDAIRE ALFA ROMEO BIMOTORE MONOPOSTO DE 1935 ET LA LIMOUSINE DE LUXE 164, DESSINÉE PAR PININFARINA. 47: UN DÉTAIL DU PNEU DE LA 6C 1750 GRAN SPORT, GAGNANTE DES MILLE MIGLIA EN 1929, 1930, 1931 ET LA ROUE DE L'ALFA ROMEO 164. (USA)

▲ 45, 46 SUR CES ANNONCES, ON SIGNALE AUX DÉTAILLANTS QUE L'HUILE POUR MOTEURS AMOCO LDO CONVIENT À TOUTES LES VOITURES. (USA)

THINK OF IT AS A PORTFOLIO OF THE BEST ENGINEERING MINDS IN EUROPE.

Every new BMW, it appears, serves as a magnet to attract the greatest automotive thinkers. Which may be the only credible theory to explain the existence of the BMW 750iL. After all, it takes a rare blend of genius and focus to create a 296-horsepower 12-cylinder engine so uncannily smooth. Or a sedan so renowned for its luxury, yet perfectly at home on the critics' lists of the world's most exhilarating performance cars. We invite you to visit your nearest BMW dealer (for locations, call 800-334-4BMW) and test drive the 750iL sedan: the collective inspiration of Europe's engineering elite. You'll discover a car that not only outclasses its rivals, but completely outthinks them. THE ULTIMATE DRIVING MACHINE.

A CAR DESIGNED TO CONTROL FATE, NOT TEMPT IT.

The term "high performance" means many things to many people. But to the designers of the BMW 5-Series, it has but one meaning: a car that can prevent split-second decisions from turning into catastrophic events. Which explains why the 5-Series was endowed with sophisticated third-generation anti-lock brakes. And a suspension system that's both internationally patented and universally coveted. And an engine that can effortlessly power you past everything from bad roads to bad drivers. If you enjoy the idea of reducing your reaction time to the barest minimum, see how quickly you can react to this invitation. Visit your nearby BMW dealer for a thorough test drive. THE ULTIMATE DRIVING MACHINE.

THE WORLD'S MOST SOPHISTICATED HARDWARE ALSO COMES WITH THE WORLD'S MOST ELEGANT SOFTWARE.

Recently, the 12-cylinder BMW 750iL earned its place on Motor Trend Magazine's list of the world's best performance cars—alongside Ferrari, Lamborghini and Porsche. Not surprising, for a BMW. But very surprising, considering the 750iL is also a four-door luxury sedan. Few interiors, even those without wheels, can compete with the BMW 750iL for quietness and tasteful elegance. Its leather seating is a tribute to craftsmanship. Its next-century electronics exist not to dazzle, but instead to supplement the natural driving instincts. Test drive the 750iL at your BMW dealer. It's truly one of the world's greatest performance cars. Even when it's standing still. THE ULTIMATE DRIVING MACHINE.

AT LAST, BUMPERS THAT ACTUALLY TAKE BUMPS.

In one fell swoop, the engineers at BMW have shattered the theory that a safe car can never be exciting as well. Witness the BMW 5-Series: a performance sedan designed so thoughtfully, it has safety systems to protect its safety systems. Rather than offer only symbolic protection, its regenerating bumpers absorb impacts up to 5 mph with virtually no damage to the car. Also standard are antilock brakes and a driver's airbag. To experience the 5-Series' unparalleled defense system for yourself, just visit your nearest BMW dealer (call 800-334-4BMW for locations or more information). In the right car, you'll find that safety can be a thrilling feature indeed. **THE ULTIMATE DRIVING MACHINE:**

ART DIRECTOR:
JAMES DALTHORP
PHOTOGRAPHERS:
ERNST HERMANN
RUTH
TERRY HEFFERNAN
COPYWRITERS:
KEN SEGALL
GALEN GREENWOOD
RAV FRIEDEL
AGENCY:
AMMIRATI & PURIS
CLIENT:
BMW OF NORTH
AMERICA INC.
■ 48-51

After years of buying everything from the "Porsche of toasters" to the "Porsche of stereos," perhaps you're ready for the Porsche of cars.

There is a small group of individuals in the world for whom perfection is almost an obsession. Somewhere in the evolution of this group's vernacular, the name Porsche came to represent far more than sheetmetal. It became a benchmark.

For their part, these purists have used Porsche as an analogy for anything inimitable. For our part, we have continued to craft unique, exciting automobiles which make the analogy viable. The new 944 S2 Cabriolet is a powerful basis for such comparison.

The 944 convertible continues a tradition of racebred, open-top cars. Professor Porsche's first car, an open roadster hand-built in 1948, won the first race it entered. Thus began the story.

The 944 chapter opened in 1981, when the car was created for the famous 24 hour race at LeMans. The new Cabriolet possesses the engineering that has since made the 944 victorious on racetracks around the globe.

A transaxle design provides near-perfect 50-50 weight balance. Cornering is uncannily stable. Pressure-cast alloy wheels are mated to huge, 4-piston internally vented disc brakes with ABS. Suspension, steering, braking and drive systems are all carefully matched to work as one. Even tire tread is meticulously calculated. (Obsessive enough for you?)

The painting process alone requires 26 steps. Body parts are hot-dip zinc galvanized before a single weld is done, sealing zinc even in the seams to prevent corrosion. (To weld through these panels, we had to develop our own tools.)

So after nearly a decade of setting standards against which other sports cars are measured, about the only way left to make the 944 more fun was to take the top off. Naturally, in typical Porsche fashion.

The thick, 4-layer top is hand-stitched, then hand-assembled. For a precise fit on each individual car. The Porsche philosophy is that a convertible must truly be 4-season. A specially reinforced windshield sweeps air around the vehicle, creating an effect that has been described as "like being in the eye of a hurricane." An eerie calm, with a tempest swirling about you.

For those who measure value strictly in terms of exclusivity, we offer this thought; just over 1,600 of these 1990 Cabriolets will be made available in the U.S. Or, to put it another way, fewer than 140 per month for the entire country.

If you have spent a lifetime acquiring a collection of preeminent products, and are now ready for the automobile which inspired many of them, we invite you to visit your authorized Porsche dealership for a test-drive.

As a final side-benefit, you can also experience our new 4x25 watt Reno II sound system. It is, in fact, the Porsche of stereos.

The new Porsche 944 S2 Cabriolet.

Maybe we'll build another like it next month. Maybe not.

Incomprehensible as it may seem, in any given month, we rarely build two Porsche cars that are identical.

The simple fact is, it was never Professor Porsche's intention to build a lot of cars. Just a limited number of very special sports cars, for perfectionists like himself who could appreciate them.

It is this fierce individuality and self-expression which has always made a Porsche a Porsche. First, we do things our own way technologically. Seeking the most perfect solution. Then, we virtually sculpt each vehicle into a distinctive statement for the individual who will occupy it.

The new generation 911 Carrera 4 Cabriolet is the latest evolution in this rather unconventional philosophy.

Simply by virtue of this Porsche heritage and construction, it stands uniquely apart. Welding alone takes over 4 working days for each body. Engines are bench-built by hand. Convertible tops are individually hand-stitched, then hand-assembled.

Incorporating an electronic all-wheel drive system that makes it literally a landmark car, the Carrera 4 elevates sports cars to a new level of useable power and performance.

It is after all this, however, that each Porsche truly becomes singular, allowing for individualization almost unheard of in this day and age. We offer over 350 different seat variations. Our current exterior color palette numbers 13, but we have available over 200 selections, including every production color we have ever used. You could even have the same silver that Professor Porsche used on his first roadster in 1947.

Or, send us a sample to match. One gentleman provided us with his girlfriend's lipstick. A woman sent a swatch of her favorite dress. After a tour, one customer wrote, "In many ways, your plant has more in common with an artist's workshop than with a 'normal' automobile factory."

Of course, all this takes time. Which is why we can only promise 776 Carrera 4 Cabriolets to the U.S. this year. Ample reason to make time now for a test-drive at your authorized Porsche dealership.

But be forewarned: If you acquire one, and can't wait to exchange a knowing wave with someone on the road in a car just like yours, don't hold your breath. You may never see one.

The new Porsche 911 Carrera 4 Cabriolet.

Eight guys hand-built the engine on a bench. Crazy, isn't it?

Every now and then in Germany, a Porsche driver will have a stranger walk up, scrutinize his or her car, and ask to examine it. Checking the code number, the stranger will proudly announce, "This is one of mine. I helped create this one."

Since Professor Porsche and his followers lovingly gave life to their first handcrafted roadster in 1947, the passion and process they spawned have continued unbroken.

A Porsche is not so much built as it is born. Brought into this world by what has been described as an extended family. The 1990 Porsche 928 GT is part of the current generation in what is truly a living heritage.

Everyone who touches the cars must first apprentice for nearly four years. Newcomers are carefully paired with "the old ones," so that not just methods, but the Porsche spirit is passed on. The 326 hp aluminum engine of the 928 GT is constructed by sophisticated technicians, each capable of building an entire engine themselves.

Regularly trading jobs, a team of eight meticulously paired handbuilds an engine. Once complete, it is hooked up and run on a stand for 30 minutes, being taken all the way to redline and carefully checked for output and performance.

Upon approval, the engine is entirely re-torqued before finally being delicately settled into the car. So, true to our racing heritage, each power plant will perform to its full potential right off the showroom floor without typical engine break-in.

The body is built from approximately 500 different sheet metal parts, all either two-sided zinc galvanized steel or aluminum. Leather seats are carefully stitched by hand. Leather consoles and door panels are painstakingly stretched and fitted one at a time.

If you were to take a 928 apart piece by piece, in many places you would find the signatures of the individuals who worked on the car. If this sounds extraordinary, then only a test-drive in a 928 at your authorized Porsche dealer will help you to put their pride into perspective. We must caution you, however, that you may well find yourself swept up in the irresistible desire to put your own name on one.

In which case we say, welcome to the family.

The new Porsche 928 GT.

As you can see, we've changed more than our slogan.

The new Scoupe.

Tell the truth. You were surprised to see our name on this car, right? Well, it's true—this sleek, sporty 2+2 is the new Hyundai Scoupe.

But don't think its beauty is only sheetmetal deep. Because the Scoupe is just as much fun to drive as it is to be seen in. With its performance-engineered suspension and fuel-injected overhead-cam engine, you may never want to take a shortcut again.

In fact, you may never want to get out of your new Scoupe LS once you get in. And start enjoying its contoured sport bucket seats. Power windows and mirrors. Power steering. Four-speaker AM/FM stereo cassette system. Even its available CD player.

And to make sure the fun goes on and on, your new Scoupe comes equipped with a 3-year/36,000-mile bumper-to-bumper no-deductible limited warranty.*

So go see for yourself. Scoupe will change what you think about, well, you know who. **HYUNDAI**

Hyundai. Yes, Hyundai.

*See dealer for details.
DO BUCKLE UP. DON'T DRINK AND DRIVE. © 1990 HYUNDAI

ART DIRECTOR:
MARK JOHNSON
DESIGNER:
MARK JOHNSON
PHOTOGRAPHER:
JEFF ZWART
COPYWRITER:
JOHN STINGLEY
AGENCY:
FALLON MCELLIGOTT
CLIENT:
PORSCHE CARS
NORTH AMERICA
◀■ 52-54

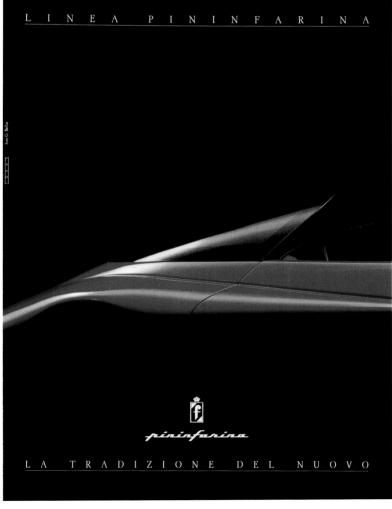

ART DIRECTOR:
JERRY PFIFFNER
DESIGNER:
JOHN BERNARDIN
PHOTOGRAPHER:
MIKE RAUSCH
COPYWRITER:
STEVE STEIN
AGENCY:
BACKER SPIELVOGEL
BATES
CLIENT:
HYUNDAI MOTOR
AMERICA
■ 55

ART DIRECTORS:
AUGUSTO CONCATO
ROLANDO COLOMBO
PHOTOGRAPHER:
GIORGIO BELLIA
AGENCY:
STUDIO FORMA
CLIENT:
PININFARINA
■ 56

Contrary to popular belief, this is not the ideal physique for a bank.

These days, most banks are groping for just about any kind of business opportunity they can get their hands on. Whether it's little Billy's passbook savings account, or the cash management responsibilities at William Sr.'s corporation.

Not Continental Bank, however. Rather than grasp indiscriminately at eight different opportunities at once, we've chosen to focus our energies exclusively on one: business banking. The result is a bank undivided in its interests, and wholly committed to serving you, the business banking customer.

If this concept sounds familiar, that's because it is. Everywhere you look, in virtually every American industry (with the sole exception of banking), forward-thinking companies are pulling in their tentacles. At Continental, we hopped on this specialization bandwagon well ahead of most other banks. Which means now, with fewer items on our plate, we're able to concentrate on developing a more sophisticated set of financial services and products. Like corporate investment strategies, for instance. Restructuring advice. Capitalization ideas. And a whole host of innovative financial risk management tools ranging from caps to captions to collars to corridors—as well as a few that don't happen to begin with the letter "c."

So how has all this paring down, this channeling of resources, and this tightening of focus affected Continental Bank? We're infinitely stronger and more competitive. And so, more importantly, are our clients. If you'd like to learn more about our unique singlemindedness, and how it can help your company grow, we encourage you to call us at (312)828-5799. Or, if you'd prefer, we'd be happy to visit you in person. We can promise you one thing about our bankers— they all have a maximum of two legs.

⊕ Continental Bank
A new approach to business.

ART DIRECTOR:
BOB BARRIE
DESIGNER:
BOB BARRIE
PHOTOGRAPHERS:
RICK DUBLIN
KERRY PETERSON
COPYWRITER:
JAMIE BARRETT
AGENCY:
FALLON MCELLIGOTT
CLIENT:
CONTINENTAL BANK
▶■ 57-61

SINK OR SWIM.

Whether it's a small interior project or one that'll be the envy of the neighborhood, our home improvement loans fill the bill.

✿ FIRST OF AMERICA.

An Equal Opportunity Lender.   Member FDIC.

ART DIRECTOR:
JEFF MARTIN
PHOTOGRAPHER:
RANDY MAYOR
COPYWRITER:
LEE SLOAN
AGENCY:
LAWLER BALLARD
CLIENT:
FIRST OF AMERICA
BANK
■ 62

ART DIRECTOR:

TOM MACMANUS

PHOTOGRAPHER:

STEVE BRONSTEIN

COPYWRITER:

DAVID WARREN

AGENCY:

TBWA ADVERTISING

CLIENT:

CARILLON

IMPORTERS, LTD.

■ 63, 64

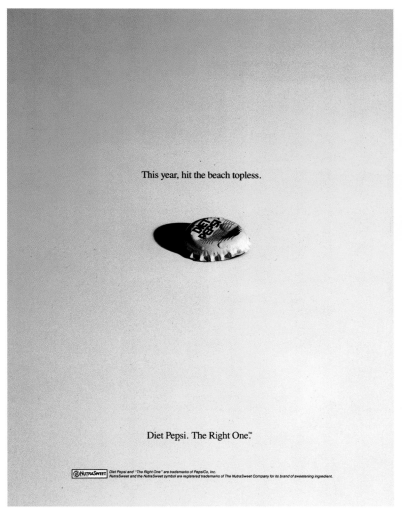

This year, hit the beach topless.

Diet Pepsi. The Right One.™

1886   1882

THE ONLY VODKA TO RECEIVE
A FOUR-CZAR RATING.

1877   1896

THE IMPERIAL RUSSIAN COURT

PURVEYORS TO   1885 · 1917

FOR OVER A CENTURY
THE REIGNING VODKA.

05-1005-01

ART DIRECTOR:

PAUL KIRNER

PHOTOGRAPHER:

CHRIS COLLINS

COPYWRITER:

BILL BRUCE

AGENCY:

BBDO

CLIENT:

PEPSI CO, INC.

■ 65

ART DIRECTOR:

BOB COLE

PHOTOGRAPHER:

JODY DOLE

COPYWRITER:

SUE TROTT

AGENCY:

MCCANN ERICKSON

CLIENT:

HEUBLEIN, INC.

■ 66

■ 63, 64 EXAMPLES FROM A CAMPAIGN FOR ABSO-
LUT VODKA, A SWEDISH PRODUCT ON THE US MAR-
KET. THIS "BOTTLE" CAMPAIGN HAS BEEN PURSUED
OVER THE YEARS. JUST SIX YEARS AFTER ITS
INTRODUCTION ABSOLUT BECAME THE BEST SELLING
IMPORTED VODKA ON THE US MARKET. (USA)

■ 65 "THIS YEAR, HIT THE BEACH TOPLESS"—WITH A
MINIMUM OF COPY AND ILLUSTRATION, A MAXIMUM
EFFECT IS OBTAINED IN THIS DIET PEPSI ADVER-
TISEMENT. (USA)

■ 66 "THE ONLY VODKA TO RECEIVE A FOUR-CZAR
RATING"—TRADITION, QUALITY AND ORIGIN OF
SMIRNOFF VODKA ARE EMPHASIZED BY THIS CLOSE
UP VIEW OF A GLASS AND THE BOTTLE LABEL. (USA)

● 63, 64 AUS EINER KAMPAGNE FÜR ABSOLUT-
WODKA, EIN SCHWEDISCHES PRODUKT AUF DEM US-
MARKT. DIESES «FLASCHEN»-INSERAT WIRD SEIT
JAHREN KONSEQUENT DURCHGEZOGEN. NUR SECHS
JAHRE NACH DER EINFÜHRUNG WURDE ABSOLUT ZUM
BESTVERKAUFTEN IMPORTIERTEN WODKA. (USA)

● 65 «ZEIGEN SIE SICH DIESES JAHR AM STRAND
OBEN OHNE.» EINE MAXIMALE WIRKUNG MIT EINEM
MINIMUM AN TEXT UND ILLUSTRATION FÜR EINE
DIÄT-PEPSI-ANZEIGE. (USA)

● 66 «DER EINZIGE WODKA, DER EINE VIER-ZAREN-
AUSZEICHNUNG BEKAM.» DIE BETONUNG DIESER
SMIRNOFF-WERBUNG LIEGT AUF TRADITION, QUALI-
TÄT UND DEM HERKUNFTSLAND. (USA)

▲ 63, 64 D'UNE CAMPAGNE POUR ABSOLUT VODKA,
UN PRODUIT SUÉDOIS VENDU AUX ÉTATS-UNIS.
L'ANNONCE SUR LE THÈME DES BOUTEILLES SE
POURSUIT DEPUIS DES ANNÉES. SIX ANS APRÈS SON
INTRODUCTION, ABSOLUT EST LA MARQUE DE VODKA
IMPORTÉE LA PLUS VENDUE SUR CE MARCHÉ. (USA)

▲ 65 «CETTE ANNÉE, ENLEVEZ LE HAUT SUR LA
PLAGE.» UN EFFET MAXIMUM OBTENU AVEC UN
MINIMUM DE TEXTE ET D'IMAGE DANS CETTE
ANNONCE POUR UN NOUVEAU PEPSI ALLÉGÉ. (USA)

▲ 66 «LA SEULE VODKA QUI AIT REÇU QUATRE
TSARS.» CETTE PUBLICITÉ POUR LA VODKA
SMIRNOFF MET L'ACCENT SUR LA TRADITION, LA
QUALITÉ ET L'ORIGINE DE CE PRODUIT. (USA)

ART DIRECTOR:

ARTY TAN

DESIGNER:

ARTY TAN

PHOTOGRAPHER:

JIM ARNDT

COPYWRITER:

MIKE GIBBS

AGENCY:

FALLON MCELLIGOTT

CLIENT:

ICEBOX

■ 67-69

ART DIRECTOR:

RICH SILVERSTEIN

PHOTOGRAPHERS:

TERRY HEFFERNAN

JOHN BLAUSTEIN

GORDON EDWARDES

ROGER RESSMEYER

COPYWRITER:

DAVE O'HARE

AGENCY:

GOODBY, BERLIN &

SILVERSTEIN

CLIENT:

SPECIALIZED

BICYCLES

■ 70-72

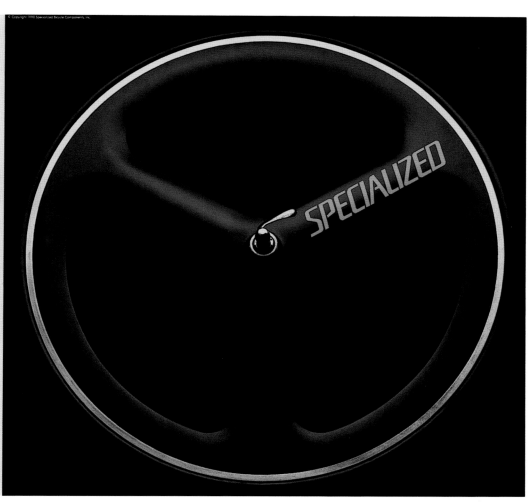

THE 1990 CARBON AND ALUMINIUM
ALLEZ® EPIC™

YOU JUST CREATED MORE DRAG TURNING THE PAGE THAN THIS WHEEL WILL CREATE AT 30 MPH.

IT WAS DESIGNED WITH THE AID OF A CRAY® SUPER COMPUTER, BY ENGINEERS WHO MAINLY DREAM UP THINGS FOR OUTER SPACE. IT'S COMPOSED OF CARBON FIBER, KEVLAR® ARAMID AND GLASS FIBERS, WITH A 6061 T6 ALUMINUM RIM. COOL, HUH? AT LEAST THAT'S WHAT THE GUYS OVER AT DUPONT® SAID WHEN THEY SAT DOWN TO HELP US MAKE THIS PROJECT A REALITY. AND IT'S WHAT USCF NATIONAL TEAM MEMBERS AND FORMER OLYMPIANS BOB MIONSKE AND JIM COPELAND SAID AFTER THEY TESTED IT. AND WE'RE PRETTY CONFIDENT YOU'LL SAY THE SAME THING WHEN YOU REALIZE A PAIR OF SPECIALIZED COMPOSITE WHEELS CAN SAVE OVER TEN MINUTES IN A 100-MILE TIME TRIAL OR TRIATHLON. VERY COOL INDEED.

SPECIALIZED®

THE ULTRA-COMFORTABLE
AIR FORCE 3® HELMET.

USED BY MORE HARDCORE ENTHUSIASTS.

SPECIALIZED®

WHAT GOOD IS A TRIATHLON BIKE IF IT CAN'T HANDLE A LITTLE HEAD WIND?

SPECIALIZED®

■ 67-69 THE PURPOSE OF THIS CAMPAIGN WAS TO COMMUNICATE TO MEMBERS OF THE ART COMMUNITY THAT ICEBOX IS A CUSTOM FRAMING STUDIO AND ART GALLERY BY SHOWING THEM AN INTERESTING PERSPECTIVE OF WHAT FRAMES CAN DO TO IMAGES. (USA)

■ 70-72 FROM A CAMPAIGN FOR SPECIALIZED BICYCLES, A COMPANY THAT PRODUCES NOT ONLY SPECIALIZED BIKES BUT ALSO SPECIALIZED ACCESSORIES. THE IMAGE OF MR. GORBACHEV IS AN ALLUSION TO THE FACT THAT THE RUSSIAN NATIONAL TEAM USES THEIR HELMETS. (USA)

● 67-69 MIT DIESER KAMPAGNE SOLLTE DEN KUNST-INTERESSIERTEN MITGETEILT WERDEN, DASS ICEBOX RAHMEN ANFERTIGT UND GLEICHZEITIG EINE GALERIE IST. DIE AUSSCHNITTE DER PHOTOGRA-PHISCHEN ILLUSTRATIONEN DEMONSTRIEREN, WAS RAHMEN BEWIRKEN KÖNNEN. (USA)

● 70-72 BEISPIELE AUS EINER KAMPAGNE FÜR SPECIALIZED BICYCLES, EINE FIRMA, DIE NICHT NUR SPEZIELLE SPORTRÄDER, SONDERN AUCH SPEZIEL-LES ZUBEHÖR HERSTELLT. GORBATSCHOV SYMBOLI-SIERT DIE TATSACHE, DASS DAS NATIONAL-TEAM DER UDSSR DIE HELME DIESER FIRMA TRÄGT. (USA)

▲ 67-69 CETTE CAMPAGNE DEVAIT ATTIRER L'ATTENTION DES AMATEURS D'ART SUR LE FAIT QU'EN DEHORS D'ÊTRE UNE GALERIE, ICEBOX RÉALISE DES ENCADREMENTS. LES DÉTAILS DU PAYSAGE ENCADRÉS METTENT LE RÉSULTAT FINAL EN ÉVIDENCE. (USA)

▲ 70-72 D'UNE CAMPAGNE POUR SPECIALIZED BICYCLES. CE FABRICANT NE PRODUIT PAS SEULE-MENT DES VÉLOS DE COURSE, MAIS AUSSI DES ACCESSOIRES. LE PERSONNAGE DE GORBATSCHOV RAPPELLE QUE L'ÉQUIPE RUSSE PORTE DES CASQUES DE CETTE MARQUE. (USA)

During rush hour,
this is the sane lane.

While everyone else is hopping into car pools at 5 o'clock, you could be jumping into an eight-lane swimming pool instead.

It's just one of the ways you can clear your mind and tone your body at the new Downtown YMCA.

We also offer the latest strength equipment, step aerobics, and racquetball and squash courts.

Individual memberships cost just $29 per month and also include the use of all other Minneapolis metro Ys.

Just call 371-8740 to join. Located on Ninth Street between Hennepin and LaSalle Avenues. **THE NEW DOWNTOWN YMCA.**

PROTEZIONE
DISEGNATA DAL TEMPO

L'evoluzione della forma è il completamento di un processo progettuale destinato a lasciare un segno nel tempo. La tecnologia K.one si evolve all'interno di un progetto che oltre alla ricerca estetica punta a realizzare il massimo livello di protezione.

k.one

K.one è un marchio registrato da MODASOLARIS S.p.A.

ART DIRECTOR:
JAC COVERDALE
PHOTOGRAPHERS:
JOE MICHL
JIM ARNDT
COPYWRITER:
LEE SCHMIDT
AGENCY:
CLARITY
COVERDALE RUEFF
CLIENT:
YMCA OF
MINNEAPOLIS
■ 73

ART DIRECTOR:
CIRIANO ZANON
DESIGNER:
ELENA STRATOTI
PHOTOGRAPHER:
GIANNI BACCEGA
COPYWRITER:
CIRIANO ZANON
AGENCY:
ZAN ON DESIGN
COMMUNICATION
CLIENT:
K.ONE-MODASOLARIS
■ 74

ART DIRECTOR:
MICHAEL PRIEVE
DESIGNER:
MICHAEL PRIEVE
PHOTOGRAPHER:
PEGGY SIROTA
COPYWRITER:
JIM RISWOLD
AGENCY:
WIEDEN & KENNEDY
CLIENT:
NIKE
▲ ■ 75

ART DIRECTOR:
KEVIN MCCARTHY
DESIGNER:
KEVIN MCCARTHY
ARTISTS:
STEVEN SCOTT
JONATHAN WRIGHT
PHOTOGRAPHERS:
MARK GERVASE
PAUL GERSTEN
COPYWRITER:
BRIAN BELEFANT
AGENCY:
STEIN ROBAIRE
HELM
CLIENT:
GIRO SPORT DESIGN
▶ ■ 76

■ 73 THE YMCA OF MINNEAPOLIS ADVERTISES THEIR NEW DOWNTOWN FACILITIES, INCLUDING AN 8-LANE SWIMMING POOL. (USA)

■ 74 "PROTECTION DESIGNED BY SPEED", AN ADVERTISEMENT FOR PROTECTIVE GOGGLES BY K.ONE. (ITA)

■ 75 "THERE IS AIR IN YOUR CROSS TRAINING SHOES SO THAT THERE IS ENOUGH FOR THE SQUASH COURTS, THE STREETS, THE TENNIS COURTS, THE BASKET BALL FIELDS AND IN THE GYMS". BO JACKSON, AMERICAN BASEBALL AND FOOTBALL PLAYER, IS THE STAR OF THIS NIKE AD. (FRA)

■ 76 THE COPY OF THIS ADVERTISEMENT TELLS THE STORY OF THE DEVELOPMENT OF THIS LIGHT-WEIGHT GIRO HELMET. (USA)

● 73 «WÄHREND DER RUSH HOUR IST DIES DIE VERNÜNFTIGSTE BAHN.» DAS YMCA VON MINNEAPOLIS WIRBT FÜR SEINE NEUEN SPORTANLAGEN. (USA)

● 74 «SCHUTZ, VOM TEMPO BESTIMMT». ANZEIGE FÜR EINE K.ONE-SCHUTZBRILLE, DIE DURCH GUTES DESIGN MAXIMALEN SCHUTZ BIETET. (ITA)

● 75 «IN IHREN TRAININGSSCHUHEN IST LUFT, DAMIT SIE GENUG LUFT FÜR DIE SQUASH-HALLEN, DIE STRASSE, DIE TENNISPLÄTZE, DIE BASKETBALL-PLÄTZE UND DIE SPORTHALLEN HABEN.» STAR DIESER NIKE-WERBUNG IST BO JACKSON, AMERIKANISCHER BASEBALL- UND FOOTBALL-PROFI. (FRA)

● 76 IN DIESER ANZEIGE WIRD DIE GESCHICHTE DER ENTWICKLUNG EINES LEICHTGEWICHTIGEN SCHUTZHELMS FÜR RADFAHRER ERZÄHLT. (USA)

▲ 73 PUBLICITÉ POUR LES NOUVELLES INSTALLATIONS SPORTIVES DE L'YMCA DE MINNEAPOLIS, AVEC PISCINE À HUIT COULOIRS. (USA)

▲ 74 «UNE PROTECTION DESSINÉE PAR LE TEMPS»: ANNONCE POUR LES LUNETTES K.ONE DONT LE DESIGN PERMET UNE PROTECTION MAXIMUM. (ITA)

▲ 75 ANNONCE DOUBLE PAGE POUR LES CHAUSSURES DE SPORT NIKE AIR DONT LA SEMELLE RENFERME UNE COUCHE D'AIR. ON Y ÉNUMÈRE LES TERRAINS APPROPRIÉS À LEUR USAGE. LE SPORTIF DE CETTE PUBLICITÉ EST LE JOUEUR DE BASEBALL ET DE FOOTBALL AMÉRICAIN BO JACKSON. (FRA)

▲ 76 «UNE COURSE D'OBSTACLES AVEC LES CASQUES GIRO.» L'ANNONCE RETRACE L'HISTOIRE DE CES CASQUES DE PROTECTION POUR CYCLISTES. (USA)

THERE'S AIR IN OUR CROSS TRAINING SHOES

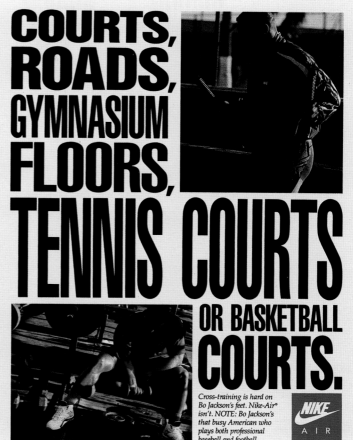

Air Trainer SC High

BECAUSE THERE'S NONE IN SQUASH

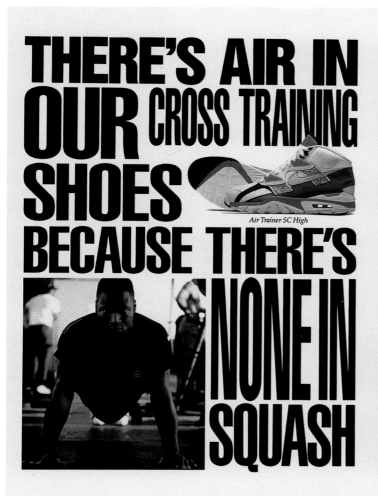

COURTS, ROADS, GYMNASIUM FLOORS, TENNIS COURTS OR BASKETBALL COURTS.

Cross-training is hard on Bo Jackson's feet. Nike-Air® isn't. NOTE: Bo Jackson's that busy American who plays both professional baseball and football.

A CRASH COURSE IN GIRO HELMETS.

Four years ago, while tooling around Santa Cruz on his bicycle, an industrial designer named Jim Gentes was struck with a revolutionary thought. Why, Jim wondered to himself, did bicycle helmets need to weigh so much?

Jim may not have been the first to want a lighter helmet, but he was certainly the first to do something about it.

He got ahold of a NASA Supercomputer and designed himself an entirely new type of helmet. One that was safe enough to meet ANSI Z904 safety standards and be certified by the Snell Memorial Foundation, yet was so light that it weighed barely half what his old helmet did. The Prolight.

THIS IS THE HELMET EVERYONE ELSE IS TRYING TO CATCH UP WITH.

What's more impressive than the Prolight's light weight is the way its ventilation keeps a rider's head cool. And even more impressive than its ventilation is its aerodynamic design, which actually allows a rider to expend less energy in order to go fast.

In fact, so many cyclists were so impressed with the Prolight that Jim hocked his grandfather's pocket watch and started a company named Giro® to manufacture it.

It's been such a remarkable success that today, other companies are scrambling to create helmets as light, as aerodynamic, and as

What our Roll Cage Technology does is offer unparalleled protection against your helmet breaking apart in an accident.

We believe that the better a helmet fits, the better it'll work. So we make helmets in more sizes than anybody else.

Giro does hundreds of hours of research just to create the lightest-weight expanded polystyrene foam with the greatest impact absorbency possible.

Another thing you want in a helmet—comfortable straps. Because studies show that even the best helmet doesn't do you any good if you don't wear it.

safe as the Prolight. What they fail to realize is that one of the things that makes Giro helmets so remarkable is the way we go about making them.

Instead of being built on an assembly line, for instance, each helmet is started and finished by the same person. No, it's probably not the most efficient way to work, but it certainly makes for a better helmet.

Another thing is the way we're constantly working to improve our helmets. The company's policy has always been that if you crash within a year of buying a Giro helmet, we'll replace it for only the cost of shipping and handling. That way, we can examine wrecked helmets to determine how they could be made safer.

The Hammerhead, as you can pretty much tell just by looking at it, is a Prolight with Hardbody™ Construction—a lightweight copolymer shell bonded to it. As a result, it's not only a very durable helmet, but it's also incredibly ventilated and more aerodynamic.

And what's particularly amazing is that a Hammerhead only weighs an ounce more than a Prolight—making it not only lighter than any other hard shell helmet (except one, but we'll get to that in a minute), but actually lighter than many soft shell helmets.

Now that may sound pretty good to you and me, but there are cyclists out there who want even more. Greg LeMond, for instance.

You know who Greg LeMond is, the guy who won the Tour de France? If you watched the race, you saw him

One direct result of that research is Roll Cage™ Technology, a structural reinforcement you'll find on every helmet you see in this ad simply because it could save your life, regardless of the fact that Snell and ANSI standards don't require it.

Another direct result of that research is the second-generation of Giro helmets: The Hammerhead.

NOW WE'RE MAKING IT EVEN HARDER.

wearing two different Giro helmets. For most of the race, Greg wore the Air Attack, a helmet he helped Jim Gentes design.

ARE WE GOING TOO FAST FOR YOU?

The Air Attack incorporates both our Roll Cage Technology and Hardbody Construction. And because its nine oversized vents are aerodynamically tuned, it's not only more aerodynamic, but actually weighs thirteen percent less than the Hammerhead. Yet it still exceeds all Snell safety standards.

In the time trials, Greg wore the Aerohead. (Actually, he wore about 90% of an Aerohead, because of UCI regulations.) As the name would imply, the Aerohead is the most aerodynamic of all the Giro helmets.

You'd probably like to see the Aerohead. Sorry. We don't have room to show it, and besides, it's a pure racing helmet. So if you're in the market for one, you probably already know what it looks like.

In fact, we don't even have room to tell you what kinds of things you can expect to see from Giro in the future. All we can say is that Jim Gentes hasn't stopped riding his bike.

Giro is located at 2880 Research Park Drive, Soquel, California 95073. Our phone number is (800) 969-GIRO. U.S. and foreign patents pending. One more thing. The three-panel design and the Air Attack side wave are trademarks of Giro Sport Design.

The

Brian Kane

Collection.

For Bernhardt.

An Introduction.

Westweek

1990

PDCLA.

BERNHARDT

circle 28

ART DIRECTOR:

MICHAEL VANDERBYL

DESIGNER:

MICHAEL VANDERBYL

AGENCY:

VANDERBYL DESIGN

CLIENT:

BERNHARDT

FURNITURE CO.

■ 77

Solo.
A table for one...
or two.

A new line
with a fresh slant
from Johnson

Duo.
A task table
for your type.

A new line
with a fresh slant
from Johnson

ART DIRECTOR:
JEFF BARNES
DESIGNER:
JEFF BARNES
PHOTOGRAPHER:
GINA UHLMANN
COPYWRITER:
PAM RUBIN
STYLIST:
DONNA FORST
AGENCY:
BARNES DESIGN
OFFICE
CLIENT:
JOHNSON
INDUSTRIES
■ 78, 79

■ 77 A DOUBLE-SPREAD MAGAZINE AD INTRODUCING THE BRIAN KANE COLLECTION FOR BERNHARDT FURNITURE COMPANY. (USA)

■ 78, 79 TWO ADVERTISEMENTS INTRODUCING A NEW LINE OF TABLES, EMPHASIZING THE SLANT OF THE LEGS. (USA)

● 77 EINE DOPPELSEITIGE ZEITSCHRIFTENANZEIGE FÜR DIE EINFÜHRUNG DER BRIAN KANE KOLLEKTION DER MÖBELFIRMA BERNHARDT. (USA)

● 78, 79 DIESE ANZEIGEN STELLEN EINE NEUE TISCHREIHE VOR, BEI DER ES UM DIE BESONDERE STELLUNG DER BEINE GEHT. (USA)

▲ 77 ANNONCE DE MAGAZINE SUR DOUBLE PAGE POUR LE LANCEMENT DE LA COLLECTION BRIAN KANE POUR LES MEUBLES BERNHARDT. (USA)

▲ 78, 79 CES ANNONCES PRÉSENTENT UNE NOUVELLE LIGNE DE TABLES DONT LES PIEDS ONT UNE POSITION ORIGINALE. (USA)

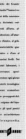

ART DIRECTOR:

GAVINO SANNA

PHOTOGRAPHER:

FRANCESCO CORNELLI

COPYWRITER:

GASPARE GIUA

AGENCY:

YOUNG & RUBICAM

CLIENT:

CASTELLARANO

FIANDRE CERAMICHE

■ 80-83

ART DIRECTOR:

MICHAEL VANDERBYL

DESIGNER:

MICHAEL VANDERBYL

PHOTOGRAPHERS:

OMEGA STUDIOS

STONE & STECCATI

AGENCY:

VANDERBYL DESIGN

CLIENT:

HICKORY BUSINESS

FURNITURE

►■ 84-86

■ 80-83 FOUR ADS FOR FIANDRE GRANITE: "IN DALLAS WE DON'T SUFFER FROM VERTIGO" (SHOWN IS THE OAKLAWN BUILDING); "THIS ICECREAM SHOP IS FAMOUS FOR ITS GRANITE"; "WE CAME TO COLORADO TO REFLECT" (THE ITT BUILDING IN AURORA); "WE STAYED TOUGH WHEN THE GERMANS CAME" (THE BMW SHOWROOM IN MILAN FEATURES FIANDRE GRANITE). (ITA)

■ 84 MAGAZINE ADVERTISEMENT SHOWING THE DESIGNER ROBERT A.M. STERN IN ONE OF HIS SOFAS FOR HICKORY BUSINESS FURNITURE. (USA)

■ 85, 86 THE CHAIR IN THE ADVERTISEMENT ON THE LEFT WAS DESIGNED BY ROBERT A.M. STERN, THE "MEETING HOUSE SERIES" IN THE ONE AT RIGHT IS BY DAVIS ALLEN. FROM A CAMPAIGN FOR HBF FURNITURE. (USA)

● 80-83 VIER ANZEIGEN FÜR FIANDRE-GRANIT: «IN DALLAS WIRD UNS NICHT SCHWINDLIG» (GEZEIGT IST DAS OAKLAWN BUILDING); «DIESES EIS-CAFÉ IST WEGEN SEINES GRANITBODENS BERÜHMT»; «WIR KAMEN NACH COLORADO, UM ZU REFLEKTIEREN» (ITT-GEBÄUDE IN AURORA); «WIR BLIEBEN HART ALS DIE DEUTSCHEN KAMEN» (DER BMW-SHOWROOM IN MAILAND HAT EINEN FIANDRE-GRANITBODEN). (ITA)

● 84 DER DESIGNER ROBERT A.M. STERN AUF EINEM DER VON IHM FÜR HICKORY BUSINESS FURNITURE ENTWORFENEN SOFAS. MAGAZINANZEIGE. (USA)

● 85, 86 DER STUHL IN DER ANZEIGE (GEGENÜBER UNTEN LINKS) IST EIN DESIGN VON ROBERT A.M. STERN, DIE «MEETING HOUSE-SERIE» RECHTS DANEBEN WURDE VON DAVIS ALLEN FÜR HBF-MÖBEL ENTWORFEN. (USA)

▲ 80-83 QUATRE ANNONCES POUR LE GRANIT FIANDRE: «À DALLAS, NOUS NE SOUFFRONS PAS DU VERTIGE» (PHOTO DU OAKLAWN BUILDING); «CE GLACIER EST CÉLÈBRE POUR SES GRANITS»; «NOUS SOMMES ALLÉS AU COLORADO POUR REFLÉTER» (LE BÂTIMENT ITT À AURORA); «NOUS AVONS ÉTÉ TRÈS DURS AVEC LES ALLEMANDS» (LE SOL DU MAGASIN D'EXPOSITION BMW À MILAN). (ITA)

▲ 84 LE DESIGNER ROBERT A.M. STERN ASSIS SUR UN SOFA QU'IL A CRÉÉ POUR HICKORY BUSINESS FURNITURE. ANNONCE DE MAGAZINES. (USA)

▲ 85, 86 LA CHAISE DE L'ANNONCE DE LA PAGE CI-CONTRE, EN BAS À GAUCHE, EST UNE CRÉATION DE ROBERT A.M. STERN. LA SÉRIE «MEETING HOUSE» DE DROITE A ÉTÉ DESSINÉE PAR DAVIS ALLEN POUR LES MEUBLES HBF. (USA)

HBF

Hickory
Business
Furniture

Robert
A.M.
Stern

Designs
For
HBF

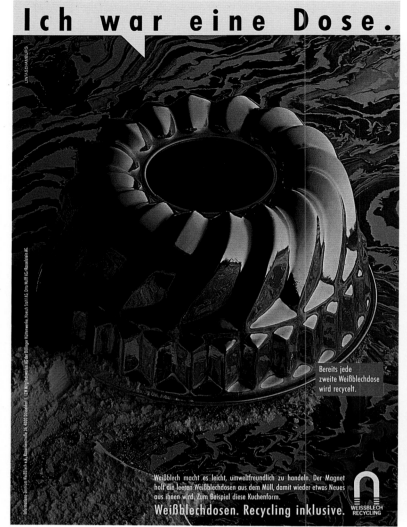

ART DIRECTOR:

GERD WOLF

PHOTOGRAPHER:

HANS HANSEN

COPYWRITER:

JENS SCHARFF

AGENCY:

LINTAS:HAMBURG

CLIENT:

INFORMATIONS-

ZENTRUM

WEISSBLECH

■ 87, 88

ARTIST:

KLAUS DOBRUNZ

COPYWRITER:

KLAUS DOBRUNZ

CLIENT:

ROBIN WOOD

▶■ 89

■ 87, 88 ADVERTISEMENTS DEMONSTRATING HOW TIN CANS CAN BE RECYCLED: "I ONCE WAS A CAN". THIS CAMPAIGN FOR THE INFORMATION CENTER ON TINPLATE WAS TO PRESENT THIS MATERIAL AS A MODERN, VALUABLE AND ENVIRONMENTALLY FRIENDLY MATERIAL AND THUS HELP REDUCE IGNORANCE AND PREJUDICE AGAINST TIN CANS. (GER)

■ 89 FROM A CAMPAIGN AGAINST THE DESTRUCTION OF THE TROPICAL RAIN FORESTS. EIGHT PIECES THAT CAN ALSO STAND ALONE BUILD UP TO A LARGE-FORMAT POSTER. EACH PART CONTAINS INFORMATION ON WHAT IS HAPPENING AND WHAT WILL BE THE CONSEQUENCES FOR THE WORLD IF THE EXPLOITATION IS NOT STOPPED. (GER)

● 87, 88 NEUE PRODUKTE, DIE AUS DOSEN GEMACHT WURDEN. DIESE KAMPAGNE FÜR DAS INFORMATIONS-ZENTRUM WEISSBLECH SOLL UNWISSEN UND VORBEHALTE ABBAUEN UND DAZU BEITRAGEN, DASS ALLE ZIELGRUPPEN WEISSBLECH ALS MODERNES, HOCHWERTIGES UND UMWELTFREUNDLICHES MATERIAL VERSTEHEN LERNEN. (GER)

● 89 AUS EINER KAMPAGNE GEGEN DIE ZERSTÖRUNG DER TROPISCHEN REGENWÄLDER. ACHT EINZELNE TEILE, DIE AUCH ALLEIN STEHEN KÖNNEN, ERGEBEN ZUSAMMEN EIN GROSSPLAKAT. JEDES EINZELPLAKAT INFORMIERT ÜBER DEN RAUBBAU UND DIE MÖGLICHEN KONSEQUENZEN FÜR DIE WELT, WENN DIE ZERSTÖRUNG NICHT AUFHÖRT. (GER)

▲ 87, 88 PRODUITS FAITS À PARTIR DE BOÎTES EN FER BLANC RECYCLÉES. LA CAMPAGNE POUR LE CENTRE D'INFORMATION DU FER BLANC DOIT PERMETTRE DE LUTTER CONTRE LES IDÉES FAUSSES ET LES PRÉJUGÉS CONCERNANT LE FER BLANC. IL S'AGIT DE LE CONSIDÉRER COMME UN MATÉRIAU RESPECTUEUX DE L'ENVIRONNEMENT. (GER)

▲ 89 D'UNE CAMPAGNE CONTRE LA DESTRUCTION DE LA FORÊT ÉQUATORIALE. LES HUIT IMAGES, QUI PEUVENT ÊTRE VUES SÉPARÉMENT, CONSTITUENT ENSEMBLE UNE GRANDE AFFICHE. CHACUNE INFORME DES ÉTAPES DE CETTE DÉVASTATION ET DES CONSÉQUENCES QUE CETTE DESTRUCTION PEUT ENTRAÎNER POUR L'HUMANITÉ. (GER)

ART DIRECTOR:
SEYMON O'STILLY
DESIGNER:
SEYMON O'STILLY
PHOTOGRAPHER:
DENNIS MANARCHY
COPYWRITER:
LYNN STILES
AGENCY:
LORD, DENTSU &
PARTNERS
CLIENT:
THE NEW YORKER
■ 90

ART DIRECTOR:
TOM LICHTENHELD
DESIGNER:
TOM LICHTENHELD
PHOTOGRAPHER:
TOM CONNERS
COPYWRITER:
JOHN STINGLEY
AGENCY:
FALLON MCELLIGOTT
CLIENT:
WORLD MONITOR
■ 91

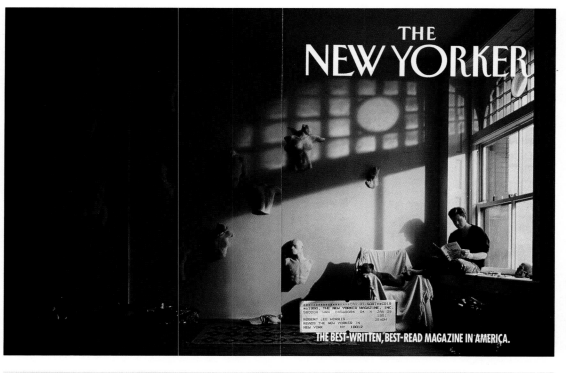

THE BEST-WRITTEN, BEST-READ MAGAZINE IN AMERICA.

One of our writers on China knows so much, we can't begin to tell you about him.

In June 1989, he was a student protesting in Tiananmen Square. He avoided the tanks. He avoided arrest. Now, incredibly, he's a Chinese ministry official, pushing democracy from the inside.

When we wanted an article on China one year after the student uprising, he was perfect to write it. Who is he? We can't tell you. That was part of the deal.

At World Monitor magazine, we believe highly involved stories call for highly involved writers. Experts who have been there. Who possess unique knowledge, and understand its significance.

We go wherever we have to in the world to find them. From Communist officials, to American schoolteachers, to former presidents. Then, we let them explain things in their own words. For an insider's perspective no journalist could uncover in a traditional interview.

It's the kind of insight needed to understand complex global issues. That's why the people you find reading World Monitor, like the people who write for it, are leaders. Individuals looking for informed assessments and speculation on what may come next, so they can prosper in the global village we all now share.

World Monitor. Conceived, created and followed by those who understand that in today's world there is, more than ever, no substitute for experience.

WORLD MONITOR
THE CHRISTIAN SCIENCE MONITOR, MONTHLY
Where the people in the news report the news.

■ 90 JEWELRY DESIGNER ROBERT LEE MORRIS READING *THE NEW YORKER*. EXAMPLE FROM A CAMPAIGN EMPHASIZING THAT IMPORTANT PEOPLE ALL OVER THE COUNTRY ARE READING THIS MAGAZINE. (USA)

■ 91 THIS ADVERTISEMENT INTRODUCES *WORLD MONITOR* MAGAZINE TO THE TRADE AS A PUBLICATION IN WHICH INSIDERS AND EXPERTS RATHER THAN TRADITIONAL JOURNALISTS, WRITE ABOUT ECONOMIC, POLITICAL AND CULTURAL TOPICS OF INTERNATIONAL SIGNIFICANCE. (USA)

■ 92 "FREQUENT OUR NEW 3000 SQUARE FOOT SHOP AT PROGRESS SQUARE—OF COURSE YOU CAN ALWAYS GET HER THE PORSCHE" CLAIMS THIS ADVERTISEMENT FOR A FLOWER SHOP. (USA)

■ 93 "MADAME GAUGUIN AND HER DAUGHTERS CLEANING THE FLOOR". ADVERTISEMENT FOR A HOUSEHOLD CLEANSER. (FRA)

● 90 DER NEW YORKER SCHMUCKDESIGNER ROBERT LEE MORRIS BEIM LESEN DER ZEITSCHRIFT *THE NEW YORKER*, «DIE ZEITSCHRIFT MIT DEN BESTEN AUTOREN UND DEN BESTEN LESERN» (IM GANZEN LAND). (USA)

● 91 IN DIESER ANZEIGE STELLT SICH DAS MAGAZIN *WORLD MONITOR* VOR: «EINER UNSERER AUTOREN IN CHINA WEISS SO VIEL, DASS WIR IHNEN NICHTS ÜBER IHN SAGEN DÜRFEN.» DAMIT WIRD UNTERSTRICHEN, DASS INSIDER FÜR DIESES INTERNATIONALE MAGAZIN SCHREIBEN. (USA)

● 92 BESUCHEN SIE UNSEREN 1000 QUADRATMETER GROSSEN LADEN AM PROGRESS SQUARE. DEN PORSCHE KÖNNEN SIE IHR IMMER NOCH KAUFEN.» ANZEIGE FÜR EINEN BLUMENLADEN. (USA)

● 93 «MADAME GAUGUIN UND IHRE TÖCHTER REINIGEN DEN FUSSBODEN.» ANZEIGE FÜR EIN HAUSHALTREINIGUNGSMITTEL. (FRA)

▲ 90 LE CRÉATEUR DE BIJOUX ROBERT LEE MORRIS LISANT *THE NEW YORKER*, LE MAGAZINE LE MIEUX ÉCRIT ET LE PLUS LU D'AMÉRIQUE». EXEMPLE TIRÉ D'UNE CAMPAGNE MONTRANT DES CÉLÉBRITÉS DE TOUT LE PAYS QUI LISENT CETTE REVUE. (USA)

▲ 91 *WORLD MONITOR* SE PRÉSENTE AINSI: «L'UN DE NOS AUTEURS EN CHINE SAIT TELLEMENT DE CHOSES QUE NOUS NE POUVONS VOUS PARLER DE LUI.» CETTE ANNONCE SOULIGNE LE FAIT QUE DES PROTAGONISTES DIRECTS, ET NON DES JOURNALISTES, ÉCRIVENT POUR CE MAGAZINE INTERNATIONAL. (USA)

▲ 92 «VENEZ VISITER NOTRE MAGASIN DE 1000 MÈTRES CARRÉS À PROGRESS SQUARE. BIEN ENTENDU, VOUS POURREZ TOUJOURS LUI ACHETER LA PORSCHE.» POUR UN MAGASIN DE FLEURS. (USA)

▲ 93 ANNONCE POUR L'EAU DE JAVEL LACROIX TIRÉE D'UNE SÉRIE BASÉE SUR UNE PARODIE DE TABLEAUX IMPRESSIONNISTES. (FRA)

CREATIVE DIRECTOR:
AUSTIN HOWE
ART DIRECTOR:
AARON SMITH
PHOTOGRAPHERS:
HENRY NGAN
BOB RANDALL
COPYWRITER:
AUSTIN HOWE
AGENCY:
A.K.A. ADVERTISING
& SASS
CLIENT:
RAINYDAY FLOWERS
■ 92

ART DIRECTOR:
PHILIPPE
VANSEGHBROECK
ARTIST:
DARIGO
COPYWRITER:
HERVÉ DE VAUBLANC
AGENCY:
CATO JOHNSON
CLIENT:
COLGATE-PALMOLIVE
■ 93

MADAME GAUGUIN ET SES FILLES ASSAINISSENT LE SOL

ART DIRECTOR:

PIETER VAN VELSEN

PHOTOGRAPHER:

HANS KROESKAMP

COPYWRITER:

AAD KUYPER

AGENCY:

PPGH/J. WALTER

THOMPSON

CLIENT:

DE VOLKSKRANT

■ 94-96

ART DIRECTOR:

BILL ZABOWSKI

PHOTOGRAPHERS:

PETER WONG

DENNIS MANARCHY

COPYWRITER:

JOHN JARVIS

AGENCY:

MARTIN/WILLIAMS

ADVERTISING, INC.

CLIENT:

YELLOW PAGES

PUBLISHERS ASSOC.

►■ 97-99

No Other Medium Offers This Kind Of Reach.

Let's face it. A lot of media can talk about how many people they reach, but how many can talk about how many people reach for them? We, on the other hand, can tell you that 82.7 percent of purchasers using the Yellow Pages make a contact with a business they found in the directory. We can tell you that over 45% of them make a purchase. And from there we can get specific about dozens of product-specific categories, including yours. For example, we can tell you how many people looked in the Yellow Pages before buying tires. Or how many people made a purchase from a florist based on an ad in the directory. The fact is, we have a surprising amount of data showing consumer usage of the Yellow Pages, and it's all organized by category in easy-to-read reports. If you want to be in the right place when the buying decisions are made, call 1-800-325-8455 to learn more about Yellow Pages usage in your category. Or write to the Yellow Pages Publishers Association at the address below. And start getting the kind of reach that really matters. **The Yellow Pages. Be There When The Decision Is Made.**

If Only It Were This Easy To Tell When A Prospect Turns Into A Buyer.

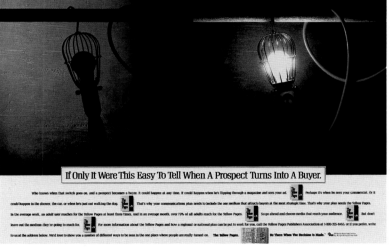

If Only It Were This Easy To Tell When A Prospect Turns Into A Buyer.

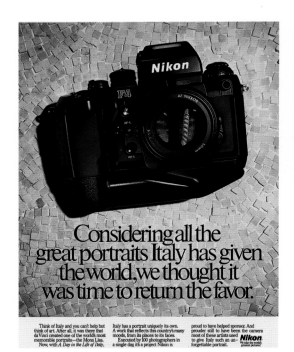

Shot by Art Wolfe on Fujichrome Velvia 35mm.

FUJI. A new way of seeing things.

ART DIRECTOR:
ANGELO JULIANO
DESIGNER:
ANGELO JULIANO
PHOTOGRAPHER:
FRANK SPINELLI
COPYWRITER:
JUDITH ATWOOD
AGENCY:
SCALI, MCCABE,
SLOVES
CLIENT:
NIKON
■ 100

ART DIRECTOR:
JEFF GRIFFITH
PHOTOGRAPHER:
ART WOLFE
COPYWRITER:
BOB SHIFFRAR
AGENCY:
HAL RINEY &
PARTNERS
CLIENT:
FUJI PHOTO FILM USA
■ 101

ART DIRECTOR:
KAI MUI
PHOTOGRAPHERS:
BARRY LATEGAN
TYEN
MITCHELL FEINBERG
COPYWRITER:
ANN HAYDEN
AGENCY:
RUMRILL-HOYT
CLIENT:
PROFESSIONAL
PHOTOGRAPHY
DIVISION,
EASTMAN KODAK CO.
▶■ 102-104

■ 100 IN THIS AD NIKON, WHO CLAIMS TO "TAKE THE WORLD'S GREATEST PICTURES", REFERS TO THE BOOK ENTITLED *A DAY IN THE LIFE OF ITALY*, A PROJECT NIKON HAS HELPED TO SPONSOR. (USA)

■ 101 MONO LAKE IN CALIFORNIA PHOTOGRAPHED BY ART WOLFE WHO USED A FUJICHROME VELVIA FILM. THE CITATIONS OF PROFESSIONALS ALL DESCRIBE THE ADVANTAGES OF THIS FILM. (USA)

■ 102-104 DOUBLE-SPREAD ADVERTISEMENTS FOR EASTMAN KODAK. FROM TOP TO BOTTOM: BARRY LATEGAN'S BOLD CONTRASTS IN COLORS AND SHAPES; THE REFINED BLACK AND WHITE OF TYEN (GARMENTS BY ISSEY MIYAKE); THE IMPACT OF BLACK WITH BRIGHT COLORS, BY MITCHELL FEINBERG. (USA).

● 100 «ITALIEN HAT UNS SO VIELE MEISTERWERKE GESCHENKT, ES WAR AN DER ZEIT, UNS ZU REVANCHIEREN.» INSERAT FÜR NIKON-KAMERAS, DIE «DIE BESTEN BILDER DER WELT MACHEN». (USA)

● 101 MONO LAKE IN KALIFORNIEN, VON ART WOLFE MIT EINEM FUJICHORME VELVIA-FILM PHOTOGRA-PHIERT. IN ALLEN ZITATEN BESCHREIBEN PROFIS DIE VORTEILE DES FILMMATERIALS. (USA)

● 102-104 DOPPELSEITIGE ANZEIGEN FÜR EASTMAN KODAK. VON OBEN NACH UNTEN: BARRY LATEGANS GEWAGTE KONTRASTE IN FORM UND FARBE; ISSEY MIYAKES MODE IN RAFFINIERTEM SCHWARZWEISS, VON TYEN PHOTOGRAPHIERT; DIE WIRKUNG VON FARBEN IM ZUSAMMENSPIEL MIT SCHWARZ, VON MITCHELL FEINBERG. (USA)

▲ 100 «L'ITALIE NOUS A DONNÉ TELLEMENT DE CHEFS-D'ŒUVRE QU'IL ÉTAIT BIEN TEMPS DE LUI RENDRE HOMMAGE À NOTRE TOUR.» ANNONCE POUR LES APPAREILS PHOTO NIKON. (USA)

▲ 101 LE MONO LAKE EN CALIFORNIE PHOTOGRA-PHIÉ PAR ART WOLFE QUI A UTILISÉ UN FILM FUJI-CHROME VELVIA. DES EXTRAITS DE CITATIONS ÉNU-MÉRENT LES QUALITÉS DE CETTE PELLICULE. (USA)

▲ 102-104 ANNONCES DOUBLE PAGE POUR EASTMAN KODAK. EN HAUT, LES CONTRASTES AUDACIEUX DE FORMES ET DE COULEURS DE BARRY LATEGAN; AU CENTRE, LES RAFFINEMENTS DU NOIR ET BLANC DE TYEN, IMPERMÉABLE D'ISSEY MIYAKE; EN BAS, LES SUBTILITÉS DU NOIR ET DE LA COULEUR PAR MITCHELL FEINBERG. (USA)

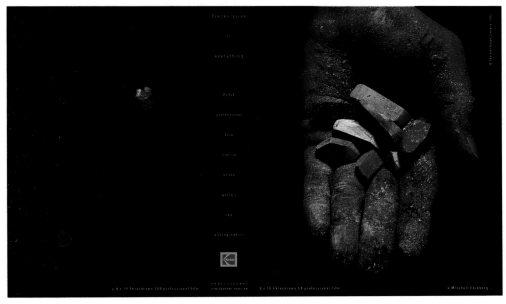

"Sex was like a drug. I'd do anything to get it. Yet when I did, all I felt was shame."

"For me, sex was the only thing that mattered.

It took control of everything in my life; where I went, how I dressed. It wasn't just my top priority, it was my only priority.

Male, female it didn't matter. What mattered was the fantasy. The excitement of seduction. Yet the sex didn't bring me pleasure. It made me feel guilty and ashamed.

I knew what I was doing with sex and pornography was destructive, but I couldn't control myself. And when I did try to stop acting out sexually, I had to use alcohol or drugs to medicate myself.

I was slipping away,

yet I didn't know who I could go to for help, or even if I could trust anyone with my secrets. When I actually started to plan my suicide, I knew I had to get help.

Fortunately, a friend knew a therapist who had heard of this program. I probably would've been in the obituaries rather than working on my recovery, if it weren't for him."

For patients like Gregg, admitting that they have a sexual addiction and deciding to get some help is one of the hardest decisions of their lives.

That's why it's important for you to know that the treatment environment at Golden Valley Health Center is one where you can feel totally safe and unthreatened.

Since 1985, we've treated over 1500 men and women for sexual dependency.

All of these people trusted us with their innermost fears and secrets. In return, we treated them with respect, complete confidentiality, and in a caring, nurturing way, helped them work towards their recovery.

For a free booklet on sexual addiction or for information on a free confidential consultation, call the SDU Response Center at 1-800-321-2273.

Golden Valley Health Center
4101 Golden Valley Road, Golden Valley, MN 55422

"What my parents taught me about incest I'm still trying to forget."

"It all started when I was about six. My parents would take me into the bath with them and do things I'm still ashamed to talk about. Sometimes they even took pictures.

I used to cry and beg them not to hurt me. But then they told me they loved me. And they said if I loved

them, I would let them do it.

The abuse stopped when I was in junior high because my parents got divorced. My mother switched her interest to alcohol and never touched me sexually again.

Unfortunately, the abuse didn't really end. The memories haunted me for years. Finally, I started using alcohol to medicate the pain I felt from being abused and

abandoned by my parents.

My self-esteem was so low, the only time I felt like I was worth anything was when someone would have sex with me. Yet when it was over, all I felt was guilt and shame. My life wasn't worth living.

I'd still be trapped by my sexual dependency, instead of working on my recovery, if a friend hadn't told me about this program."

For patients like Glenn, admitting that they have a sexual addiction and deciding to get some help is one of the hardest decisions of their lives.

That's why it's important for you to know that the treatment environment at Golden Valley Health Center is one where you can feel totally safe and unthreatened.

Since 1985, we've treated over 1500 men and women for sexual dependency.

All of these people trusted us with their innermost fears and secrets. In return, we treated them with respect, complete confidentiality, and in a caring, nurturing way, helped them work towards their recovery.

If you would like a free booklet on sexual addiction or would like information on a free confidential consultation, call 1-800-321-2273 and ask for the SDU Response Center.

Golden Valley Health Center
4101 Golden Valley Road, Golden Valley, MN 55422

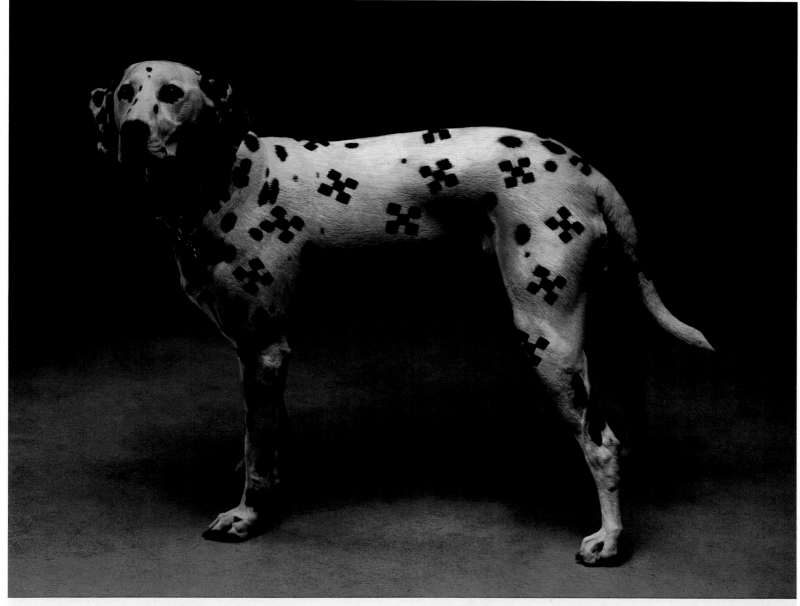

Hire Fallon McElligott and a lot of dogs will be switching brands.
With Fallon McElligott and Ralston working together, dog owners all across the country will begin to see Purina dogfood as the only choice.

ART DIRECTOR:
JAC COVERDALE
PHOTOGRAPHER:
JIM ARNDT
COPYWRITER:
JERRY FURY
AGENCY:
CLARITY
COVERDALE RUEFF
CLIENT:
GOLDEN VALLEY
HEALTH CENTER
◀■ 105, 106

ART DIRECTOR:
ARTY TAN
DESIGNER:
ARTY TAN
PHOTOGRAPHER:
KERRY PETERSEN
COPYWRITER:
MIKE GIBBS
AGENCY:
FALLON MCELLIGOTT
CLIENT:
FALLON MCELLIGOTT
■ 107

■ 105, 106 TWO NEWSPAPER ADS FOR A THERA-
PEUTIC CENTER WHERE PEOPLE ARE TREATED FOR
SEXUAL DEPENDENCY. AT LEFT, A VICTIM OF
INCEST, AT RIGHT A YOUNG MAN FOR WHOM "SEX
WAS THE ONLY THING THAT MATTERED." (USA)

■ 107 SELF-PROMOTION BY FALLON MCELLIGOTT
COMMUNICATING TO PURINA THAT THEY COULD HELP
THEIR BUSINESS IMPROVE, AS THEY ARE ABLE TO
COMMUNICATE IN A UNIQUE WAY. (USA)

● 105, 106 ZEITUNGSANZEIGEN FÜR EIN THERA-
PEUTISCHES ZENTRUM FÜR MENSCHEN MIT SCHWE-
REN SEXUELLEN PROBLEMEN. LINKS EIN OPFER VON
INZEST, RECHTS EIN JUNGER MANN, FÜR DEN »SEX
DAS EINZIGE WAR, WAS ZÄHLTE«. (USA)

● 107 EIGENWERBUNG FÜR FALLON MCELLIGOTT,
DIE SICH AN DEN HUNDEFUTTERHERSTELLER PURINA
RICHTET: DIE AGENTUR MÖCHTE DAS BUDGET; SIE
BIETET EINZIGARTIGE WERBEIDEEN AN. (USA)

▲ 105, 106 ANNONCES POUR UN CENTRE THÉRAPEU-
TIQUE POUR LES PERSONNES SOUFFRANT DE DÉ-
SÉQUILIBRES SEXUELS: À G., UNE VICTIME DE L'IN-
CESTE, À DR., UN JEUNE HOMME POUR LEQUEL «LE
SEXE ÉTAIT COMME UNE DROGUE». (USA)

▲ 107 ANNONCE DE FALLON MCELLIGOTT QUI VEUT
DÉMONTRER COMMENT L'AGENCE POURRAIT FAIRE
PROGRESSER LE CHIFFRE D'AFFAIRES DE PURINA,
UN FABRICANT D'ALIMENTS POUR CHIENS. (USA)

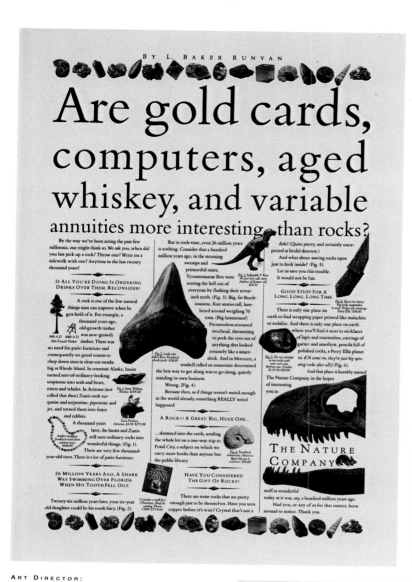

BY L. BAKER RUNYAN

Are gold cards, computers, aged whiskey, and variable
annuities more interesting than rocks?

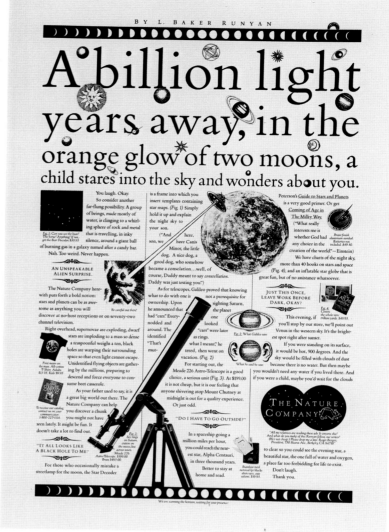

BY L. BAKER RUNYAN

A billion light years away, in the
orange glow of two moons, a
child stares into the sky and wonders about you.

ART DIRECTOR:
TRACY WONG
DESIGNER:
TRACY WONG
PHOTOGRAPHERS:
GERRY BYBEE
DENNIS MORELLA
BARRY ROBINSON
COPYWRITER:
DAVID FOWLER
AGENCY:
GOODBY, BERLIN &
SILVERSTEIN
CLIENT:
THE NATURE COMPANY
■ 108, 109

Macht Ihren Ohren Beine.

maxell
Audio- und Videokassetten

Wer Testberichten glaubt, sieht, dass Audio-Kassetten von Maxell die besten sind.
Wer Testberichten nicht glaubt, hört, dass man Testberichten ruhig glauben darf.

ART DIRECTOR:
DANY BIERI
DESIGNER:
ANITA LUSSMANN
PHOTOGRAPHER:
WOLF NEIDHART
COPYWRITER:
PATRICK SENN
AGENCY:
WIRZ WERBE-
BERATUNG AG
CLIENT:
MUSICA AG
◄■ 110

The voice of Philips.

▶▶ Nuovi Maxi Philips C2, ideali per esaltare la purezza del suono CD ▶ Telecomando multifunzionale ▶ Controllo Volume Motorizzato ▶ Tre soluzioni di potenza hi-fi: 80, 120 e 180 watt con Surround Sound e Dynamic Bass Booster ▶ Tuner Digitale con sintesi di frequenza e 30 memorie ▶ Lettore Compact Disc a 16 bit ▶ Equalizzatore grafico a 20 bande stereo ▶ Casse acustiche Bass Reflex a 3 vie. ◀◀

NUOVI SISTEMI MAXI
Modelli C2 - C6 - C8.

ART DIRECTOR:
GIOVANNI BEDESCHI
CREATIVE DIRECTORS:
MAURIZIO D'ADDA
GIANPIETRO
VIGORELLI
PHOTOGRAPHERS:
OLIVIERO TOSCANI
F. & M. PAPETTI
COPYWRITER:
MICHELE TOSI
AGENCY:
SAATCHI & SAATCHI
ADVERTISING, MILAN
CLIENT:
PHILIPS
■ 111

■ 108, 109 TWO ADVERTISEMENTS FOR THE NATURE COMPANY WHICH PUBLISHES BOOKS ON NATURE AND SPACE, MINERALS AND NATURAL HISTORY, AS WELL AS SELLS ALL KINDS OF OBJECTS RELATED TO NATURE. (USA)

■ 110 ADVERTISEMENT FROM AN IMAGE CAMPAIGN FOR MAXELL AUDIO AND VIDEO-CASSETTES THAT "GO RIGHT INTO YOUR LEGS". (SWI)

■ 111 AN ITALIAN ADVERTISEMENT WITH AN ENGLISH HEADLINE, PRESENTING THE NEW MAXI PHILIPS HI-FI EQUIPMENT. (ITA)

● 108, 109 ZWEI ANZEIGEN FÜR DIE NATURE COMPANY, DIE BÜCHER ÜBER THEMEN WIE NATUR, WELTRAUM, MINERALIEN, NATURGESCHICHTE HERAUSGIBT UND AUCH DINGE VERKAUFT, DIE MIT DIESEN GEBIETEN ZUSAMMENHÄNGEN. (USA)

● 110 AUS EINER IMAGE-KAMPAGNE FÜR MAXELL AUDIO- UND VIDEO-KASSETTEN. DIE BOTSCHAFT: MAXELL BRINGT SIE AUF TRAB. (SWI)

● 111 «DIE STIMME VON PHILIPS» – EIN GANZSEITIGES INSERAT, MIT DEM DIE NEUE HIFI-ANLAGE MAXI PHILIPS C2 VORGESTELLT WIRD. (ITA)

▲ 108, 109 DEUX ANNONCES POUR THE NATURE COMPANY, UNE MAISON D'ÉDITIONS PUBLIANT DES LIVRES SUR LA NATURE ET L'ESPACE, LES MINÉRAUX ET L'HISTOIRE NATURELLE, ET DES OBJETS SE RAPPORTANT À CES DOMAINES. (USA)

▲ 110 ANNONCE D'UNE CAMPAGNE POUR LES CASSETTES AUDIO ET VIDÉO MAXELL, AU RYTHME DESQUELLES VOUS NE POURREZ RÉSISTER. (SWI)

▲ 111 «LA VOIX DE PHILIPS.» ANNONCE PLEINE PAGE PRÉSENTANT LA NOUVELLE CHAÎNE HIFI MAXI PHILIPS C2. (ITA)

ART DIRECTOR:

MARISA ACOCELLA

PHOTOGRAPHER:

WILLIAM WEGMAN

COPYWRITER:

DAN GREGORY

AGENCY:

HAL RINEY &

PARTNERS

CLIENT:

FUJI

■ 112

Could it be that the fastest way to a corner office is no office at all?

286/386sx notebook computers   [800] 248-4880

Librex.
THE FREEDOM OF ONE.

ART DIRECTOR:
ERICH JOINER
DESIGNER:
ERICH JOINER
PHOTOGRAPHER:
NADAV KANDER
COPYWRITER:
CLAY WILLIAMS
AGENCY:
GOODBY, BERLIN &
SILVERSTEIN
CLIENT:
LIBREX COMPUTERS
■ 113

■ 112 IN CASE YOU WANT TO TAPE THE SOUND OF THESE TWO, A FUJI AUDIO CASSETTE IS THE PRODUCT TO CHOOSE! (USA)

■ 113 ADVERTISEMENT FOR PORTABLE NOTEBOOK COMPUTERS BY LIBREX. THIS CAMPAIGN IS BASED ON THE IDEA OF PERSONAL FREEDOM AND MOBILITY OFFERED BY THESE COMPUTERS, SO THAT EVEN THE OFFICE BECOMES SUPERFLUOUS. (USA)

● 112 «AUF EINER FUJI-AUDIO-KASSETTE KLINGT ALLES BESSER» – SOLLTE MAN DEN WUNSCH HABEN, DIESE BEIDEN ÖFTER ZU HÖREN! (USA)

● 113 ANZEIGE FÜR TRAGBARE COMPUTER VON LIBREX. DIESE KAMPAGNE BAUT AUF DER VORSTEL-LUNG VON PERSÖNLICHER FREIHEIT UND MOBILITÄT AUF, DIE DIESE COMPUTER BIETEN, SO DASS SELBST EIN BÜRO ÜBERFLÜSSIG WIRD. (USA)

▲ 112 PUBLICITÉ POUR LES CASSETTES AUDIO FUJI QUI RESTITUENT À LA PERFECTION LA QUALITÉ DU SON DE CHAQUE CHOSE. (USA)

▲ 113 ANNONCE POUR LES ORDINATEURS PORTA-TIFS DE LIBREX. CETTE CAMPAGNE EST BASÉE SUR LA NOTION DE LIBERTÉ INDIVIDUELLE; LE SLOGAN FAIT ALLUSION À LA MOBILITÉ QU'OFFRENT CES OR-DINATEURS, RENDANT LE BUREAU SUPERFLU. (USA)

Nothing Hits It Like A MerCruiser.

When you say "Hit it" behind a MerCruiser® 5.7L Competition Ski Inboard, be ready to hold on tight. There's 260 HP that wants to get up and go even more than you do.

Designed to meet the specific demands of competition

skiing, the 5.7L delivers powerful, smooth and steady acceleration across the entire speed range. It's specially calibrated four-barrel carb maintains speed precisely, without surging. Exclusive PlusPower™ exhaust maximizes horse-

power for more top end speed and better fuel economy.

And, because it's a MerCruiser, you know it was made to perform flawlessly. That's why the 5.7L has been certified in 10 AWSA tournament tow boats for 1990, more than any other manufacturer.

Factor in the industry's largest network of servicing dealers and you realize that the 5.7L Ski Inboard, like every other MerCruiser, is the only logical choice.

MerCruiser. The Only Logical Choice.

© 1990 Brunswick Corporation. Mercury Marine, Fond du Lac, WI. A Brunswick Company.

OUR ABILITY TO REPRODUCE DOTS IS PERFECT FOR THAT PET PROJECT.

It takes a special breed to provide the kind of printing that stands out from the pack. That's why HM Graphics is the hot spot for sharper dot reproduction up to 300 line screens. ✦ After all, dogged

attention to detail, state-of-the-art presses and faithful service have always been our strong points. ✦ If you want some doggone good reproduction, call HM. ✦ We'll get back to you on the dot.

Photograph courtesy of The Chamber of Coal Traders, London.

ART DIRECTOR:
MARK HAUMERSEN

PHOTOGRAPHER:
MARVY!

COPYWRITER:
PETE SMITH

AGENCY:
MARTIN/WILLIAMS
ADVERTISING, INC.

CLIENT:
MERCURY MARINE

■ 114

ART DIRECTOR:
KRIS JENSON

PHOTOGRAPHER:
CHAMBER OF COAL
TRADERS

AGENCY:
FRANKENBERRY,
LAUGHLIN +
CONSTABLE

CLIENT:
HM GRAPHICS

■ 115

■ 114 FROM A CAMPAIGN FOR MERCRUISER BOAT MOTORS AND THEIR POWER OF ACCELERATION WHICH IS DEMONSTRATED IN THIS PICTURE. (USA)

■ 115 THE QUALITY OF REPRODUCTION BY THESE LITHOGRAPHERS IS APTLY DEMONSTRATED BY THIS IMAGE, A SCENE EVOKING WALT DISNEY'S "101 DALMATIANS." (USA)

● 114 AUS EINER KAMPAGNE FÜR MERCRUISER-BOOTSMOTOREN, DEREN BESCHLEUNIGSKRAFT MIT DIESEM BILD DEMONSTRIERT WIRD. (USA)

● 115 «UNSER KÖNNEN IN DER REPRODUKTION VON PUNKTEN IST FÜR DIESES PROJEKT BESTENS GEEIGNET». WERBUNG EINES LITHOGRAPHEN, MIT EINER ANLEIHE BEI DISNEYS «101 DALMATINER». (USA)

▲ 114 PUBLICITÉ POUR LES MOTEURS DE BATEAUX MERCRUISER, DONT LA PUISSANCE D'ACCÉLÉRATION FAIT BONDIR LES AMATEURS DE SKI NAUTIQUE. (USA)

▲ 115 LA QUALITÉ DE LA REPRODUCTION DE CE LITHOGRAPHE PERMET DE RÉALISER DES PROJETS EXCEPTIONNELS COMME CETTE RECONSTITUTION D'UNE SCÈNE DES «101 DALMATIENS» DE DISNEY. (USA)

BROCHURES

BROSCHÜREN

BROCHURES

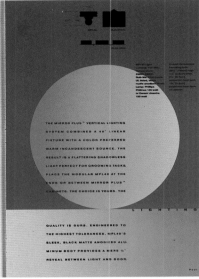

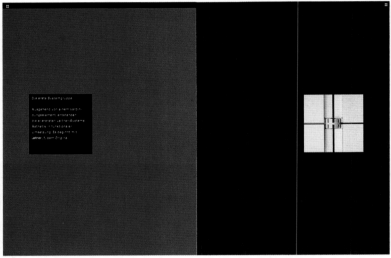

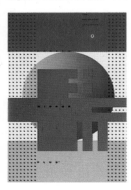

DESIGNERS:
MICHAEL
GUNSELMAN
KERRY POLITE
PHOTOGRAPHER:
TOM CRANE
COPYWRITER:
HOWARD KATZ
AGENCY:
GUNSELMAN +
POLITE
CLIENT:
ROBERN, INC.
■ 116-119, 124

■ 116-119, 124 (THIS DOUBLE SPREAD AND BOTTOM OF LEFT PAGE) DOUBLE SPREADS AND COVER OF A BROCHURE PRESENTING A RANGE OF BATHROOM APPLIANCES MARKETED BY ROBERN INC. UNDER THE "MIRROR PLUS" BRAND. THEY OFFER MORE THAN A MIRROR AND MORE THAN A CABINET. THE COLORS RED, BLUE AND YELLOW DOMINATE THIS BROCHURE. ON THE COVER, A SILVER TONE IS ADDED. (USA)

■ 120-123, 125 EXAMPLES OF THE DOUBLE SPREADS AND COVER (THIS PAGE SECOND ROW AND RIGHT PAGE BOTTOM) OF A CATALOG FOR LEITNER, A COMPANY SPECIALIZING IN EXHIBITION SYSTEMS. THE PHOTOGRAPHS ON THE DOUBLE SPREADS FOCUS ON THE ESTHETIC DESIGN AND FUNCTION OF EACH PRODUCT RANGE. THE PURITY OF THE DESIGN AND THE EASY CONSTRUCTION IS THE MAIN THEME. THE SQUARE IS THE DOMINANT ELEMENT OF THE PAGE DESIGN. (GER)

● 116-119, 124 DOPPELSEITEN UND UMSCHLAG EINER BROSCHÜRE (DIESE DOPPELSEITE GANZ OBEN UND LINKE SEITE UNTEN), IN DER BADEZIMMER-EINRICHTUNGEN VORGESTELLT WERDEN: «MIRROR PLUS» VON ROBERN IST «MEHR ALS EIN SPIEGEL UND MEHR ALS EIN SCHRANK». DIE FARBEN ROT, BLAU UND GELB DOMINIEREN; AUF DEM UMSCHLAG WURDE EIN SILBERTON HINZUGEFÜGT. (USA)

● 120-123, 125 (DIESE DOPPELSEITE, UNTERE REIHE, UND RECHTE SEITE UNTEN) BEISPIELE DER DOPPELSEITEN UND UMSCHLAG EINES KATALOGS FÜR AUSSTELLUNGSSYSTEME DER FIRMA LEITER. DIE PHOTOS AUF DEN DOPPELSEITEN HEBEN DIE FUNKTIONALE AESTHETIK JEDER PRODUKTGRUPPE HERVOR. DIE REINHEIT DER FORM UND DIE UNPROBLEMATISCHE KONSTRUKTION SIND DAS ZENTRALE THEMA. DAS QUADRAT DOMINIERT DIE GESTALTUNG DER SEITEN. (GER)

▲ 116-119, 124 (SUR CETTE DOUBLE PAGE, EN HAUT ET CI-CONTRE, EN BAS) DOUBLES PAGES ET COUVERTURE DE LA BROCHURE PRÉSENTANT LA GAMME D'ARMOIRES À GLACE POUR SALLES DE BAINS «MIRROR PLUS» DE ROBERN. «PLUS QU'UN MIROIR ET PLUS QU'UNE ARMOIRE», IL S'AGIT D'ÉLÉMENTS MODULABLES; LES REFLETS DU MIROIR SONT ATTÉNUÉS GRÂCE À UN ÉCLAIRAGE ADÉQUAT. (USA)

▲ 120-123, 125 (SUR CETTE DOUBLE PAGE, DEUXIÈME RANGÉE ET PAGE DE DROITE, EN BAS) EXEMPLES DE DOUBLES PAGES ET COUVERTURE DU CATALOGUE DE LEITNER, UNE FIRME SPÉCIALISÉE DANS LES SYSTÈMES D'EXPOSITION. LES PHOTOS SUR DOUBLE PAGE METTENT EN ÉVIDENCE L'ESTHÉTIQUE ET LA FONCTION DE CHAQUE GAMME DE PRODUITS. L'ACCENT EST MIS SUR LA PURETÉ DE LA FORME DE CES ÉLÉMENTS ET LA SIMPLICITÉ DE LA CONSTRUCTION. (GER)

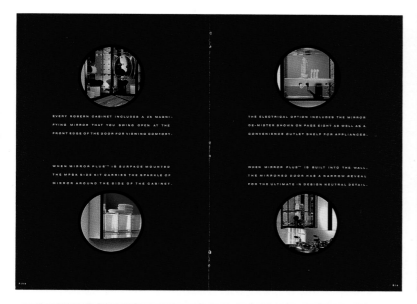

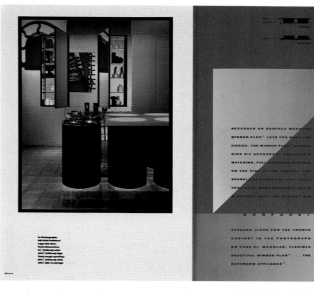

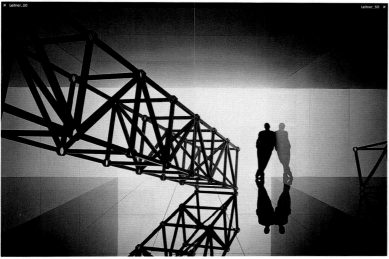

ART DIRECTOR:

SABINE MESCHER

DESIGNER:

SABINE MESCHER

PHOTOGRAPHER:

DIETMAR HENNEKA

COPYWRITER:

MAX RAUSCHER

CLIENT:

LEITNER GMBH

■ 120-123, 125

ERCO Lichtfabrik

Vom schönen Schein
der Lampe
zum besseren Schein
des Lichtes

Ernst & Sohn

■ 126 JACKET OF A BOOK PUBLISHED BY ERCO LEUCHTEN, A PRODUCER OF LIGHTING SYSTEMS, FOR WHOM DESIGN PLAYS AN OUTSTANDING ROLE. THE BOOK DEALS WITH THE PHILOSOPHY, BACKGROUND AND AIMS OF THE COMPANY AND ITS CORPORATE CULTURE. (GER)

● 126 SCHUTZUMSCHLAG EINES BUCHES, DAS VON DER ERCO LICHTFABRIK HERAUSGEGEBEN WURDE. DESIGN SPIELT EINE HERAUSRAGENDE ROLLE. DAS BUCH BEFASST SICH MIT GRUNDSÄTZEN, HINTERGRÜNDEN, UMSTÄNDEN UND ZIELSETZUNGEN, MIT DER FIRMENKULTUR. (GER)

▲ 126 JAQUETTE D'UN LIVRE SUR ERCO, UN FABRICANT DE LAMPES ET PROJECTEURS QUI ACCORDE UNE GRANDE IMPORTANCE AU DESIGN, AUSSI BIEN AU NIVEAU DES LOCAUX DE PRODUCTION QUE DANS L'ÉLABORATION DES PRODUITS ET LA DÉCORATION DES POINTS DE VENTE. (GER)

■ 127-131 FROM A BROCHURE FOR BERNHARDT FURNITURE. THE NEW LINE OF TEXTILES INTRODUCED WAS INSPIRED BY THE MOSAICS FOUND IN THE NEW YORK CITY SUBWAY SYSTEM, CREATED BY ARTISANS OF THE TURN OF THE CENTURY. (USA)

● 127-131 DOPPELSEITEN UND UMSCHLAG EINER KLEINEN, SPIRALGEBUNDENEN BROSCHÜRE FÜR BERNHARDT-MÖBEL. DIE DARIN VORGESTELLTEN NEUEN MÖBELSTOFFE WURDEN VON DEN MOSAIKEN DER NEW YORKER U-BAHN INSPIRIERT. (USA)

▲ 127-131 D'UNE PETITE BROCHURE DES MEUBLES BERNHARDT PRÉSENTANT UNE NOUVELLE COLLECTION DE TISSUS D'AMEUBLEMENT EN LIN. LES MOTIFS DES ÉTOFFES SONT INSPIRÉS DES MOSAÏQUES DU MÉTRO DE NEW YORK. (USA)

ART DIRECTOR:
OTL AICHER
PHOTOGRAPHER:
HANS HANSEN
CLIENT:
ERCO LEUCHTEN

◀■ 126

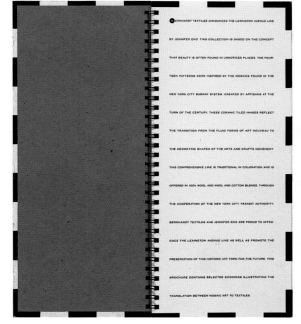

ART DIRECTOR:
MICHAEL VANDERBYL
DESIGNER:
MICHAEL VANDERBYL
PHOTOGRAPHERS:
ROSE HODGES
DAVID LUBARSKY
COPYWRITER:
VANDERBYL DESIGN
AGENCY:
VANDERBYL DESIGN/
IN COOPERATION
WITH THE NEW YORK
CITY TRANSIT
AUTHORITY
CLIENT:
BERNHARDT
FURNITURE CO.

■ 127-131

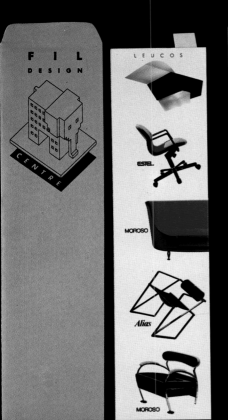

F I L
D E S I G N
C E N T R E

LEUCOS

ESTEL

MOROSO

Alias

MOROSO

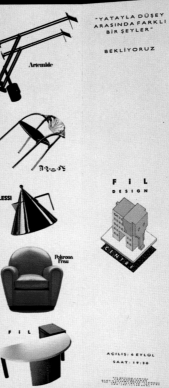

Artemide

ALESSI

Poltrona Frau

FIL

F i L
D E S I G N
C E N T R E

"YATAYLA DÜŞEY
ARASINDA FARKLI
BİR ŞEYLER"

BEKLİYORUZ

AÇILIŞ: 6 EYLÜL
SAAT: 19:30

LEUCOS

ESTEL

MOROSO

Alias

MOROSO

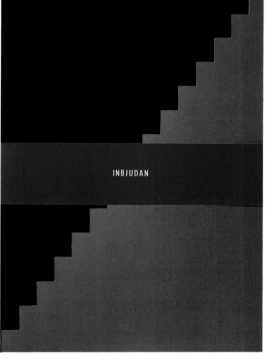

ART DIRECTOR:
MESUT KAYALAR
DESIGNER:
MESUT KAYALAR
AGENCY:
EMA ADVERTISING
CLIENT:
FIL DESIGN CENTRE
◀■ 132, 133

ART DIRECTOR:
KLAS BJÖRKMAN
DESIGNER:
KLAS BJÖRKMAN
COPYWRITER:
MARGARETA
REGEBRO
AGENCY:
ERVACO/BJÖRKMAN
& MITCHELL AB
CLIENT:
SVENSK MÖBEL-
CENTER
■ 134-136

■ 132, 133 INVITATION CARD OF THE FIL DESIGN CENTRE IN ISTANBUL: AT LEFT, THE ENVELOPE, IN A VERY NARROW HIGH FORMAT AND THE CLOSED CARD; AT RIGHT, THE OPENED CARD. (TUR)

■ 134-136 INVITATION TO AN "OPEN HOUSE" OF A FURNITURE CENTER IN STOCKHOLM. ON TOP, THE CARD IN THE OPEN FOLDER; AT BOTTOM, THE OUT-SIDE OF THE CLOSED ENVELOPE WITH THE WORD "INVITATION" PRINTED ON THE WRAPPER. (SWE)

● 132, 133 EINLADUNG DES FIL DESIGN CENTRE IN ISTANBUL. LINKS, DER SEHR SCHMALE, HOHE UM-SCHLAG UND DIE GESCHLOSSENE KARTE, RECHTS DIE GEÖFFNETE KARTE. (TUR)

● 134-136 EINLADUNG ZU EINEM «TAG DER OFFENEN TÜR» EINES MÖBELZENTRUMS IN STOCKHOLM. OBEN DIE KARTE, GANZ AUFGESCHLAGEN; UNTEN DER GE-SCHLOSSENE UMSCHLAG MIT DEM WORT «EINLA-DUNG» AUF DEM STREIFBAND. (SWE)

▲ 132, 133 INVITATION D'UN CENTRE DE DESIGN D'ISTANBUL: À GAUCHE, L'ENVELOPPE DU DÉPLIANT, DE FORMAT TRÈS ALLONGÉ ET LA CARTE FERMÉE; À DROITE, LA CARTE OUVERTE. (TUR)

▲ 134-136 INVITATION À UNE OPÉRATION «PORTE OUVERTE» D'UN CENTRE DE MEUBLES. EN HAUT, LA CARTE OUVERTE; EN BAS, LA CARTE FERMÉE EST GLISSÉE DANS UNE BANDE DE PAPIER COLORÉ QUI PORTE L'INSCRIPTION «INVITATION». (SWE)

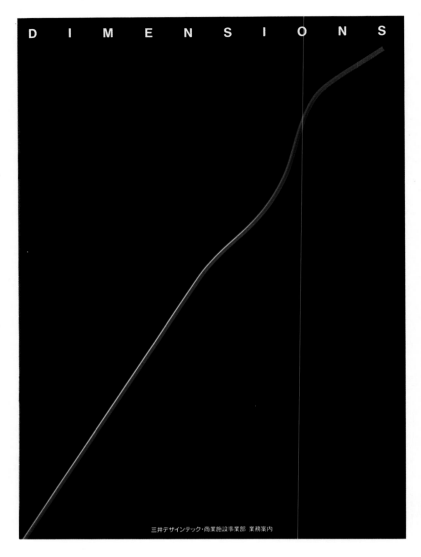

ART DIRECTOR:
HIROYUKI HAYASHI
DESIGNER:
KEN SHINOHARA
PHOTOGRAPHER:
HARUO KOISHIZAWA
STYLISTS:
HIROYUKI HAYASHI
KEN SHINOHARA

COPYWRITER:
OSAMU TOKUNARI
AGENCY:
KANSAI SUPER
STUDIO
CLIENT:
MITSUI DESIGNTEC
■ 137

ART DIRECTOR:
ANTHONY RUSSELL
DESIGNER:
BARBARA NIEMINEN
ARTIST:
ROY WIEMANN
AGENCY:
ANTHONY RUSSEL
& ASSOCIATES
CLIENT:
KIDDER, PEABODY
■ 138

■ 137 COVER OF A BROCHURE FOR MITSUI DESINTEC. (JPN)

■ 138 THE WORLDWIDE OPERATIONS OF KIDDER, PEABODY & CO., AN INVESTMENT FIRM, ARE THE THEME OF THE COVER OF THIS RECRUITMENT BROCHURE. (USA)

■ 139-144 JACKET AND SPREADS FROM A HARD-BOUND BROCHURE FOR BROWN AND ROOT ENGINEERING. THE COVER PHOTOGRAPH WAS TAKEN IN THE SAHARA DESERT OF LIBYA. THE COMPANY DESIGNED A WATER PIPELINE SYSTEM TO BRING THE WATER HIDDEN BENEATH THIS DESERT TO THE POPULOUS COAST OF THE COUNTRY. THE ILLUSTRATIONS DESCRIBE VARIOUS PROJECTS: MOHOLE, A SCIENTIFIC PROJECT OF THE SIXTIES WHICH USED EXTREMELY DEEP DRILLINGS THROUGH THE CRUST TO THE MANTLE OF THE EARTH; THE OPERATION SOMBRERO CONCERNING THE BLOWOUT OF OIL WELLS; A DEEP SEA PLATFORM WHICH IS HIGHER THAN THE EMPIRE STATE BUILDING. (USA)

● 137 UMSCHLAG EINER BROSCHÜRE FÜR MITSUI DESINTEC. (JPN)

● 138 DIE WELTWEITEN OPERATIONEN VON KIDDER, PEABODY & CO., EINER INVESTMENT-FIRMA, SIND DAS THEMA DES UMSCHLAGS DIESER BROSCHÜRE, MIT DER PERSONAL ANGEWORBEN WIRD. (USA)

● 139-144 SCHUTZUMSCHLAG UND DOPPELSEITEN AUS EINER LEINENGEBUNDENEN BROSCHÜRE FÜR EINE INTERNATIONALE BAU- UND INGENIEURSFIRMA. DAS UMSCHLAGPHOTO WURDE IN LIBYEN AUFGENOMMEN. DIE FIRMA BAUT DORT EIN PIPELINE-SYSTEM, UM DAS UNTER DER WÜSTE VORHANDENE WASSER IN DIE STÄDTE ZU LEITEN. ANHAND DER ILLUSTRATIONEN WERDEN VERSCHIEDENE PROJEKTE ERLÄUTERT: MOHOLE, EIN WISSENSCHAFTLICHES PROJEKT AUS DEN 60ER JAHREN, BEI DEM ES UM EXTREM TIEFE BOHRUNGEN GING; DIE OPERATION «SOMBRERO» 1979, EIN PLAN ZUR LÖSCHUNG BRENNENDER ÖL-QUELLEN; DER UNTERBAU EINER ÖLINSEL, HÖHER ALS DAS EMPIRE STATE BUILDUNG. (USA)

▲ 137 COUVERTURE D'UNE BROCHURE POUR MITSUI DESINTEC. (JPN)

▲ 138 COUVERTURE D'UNE BROCHURE DE RECRUTEMENT POUR KIDDER, PEABODY & CO., UNE SOCIÉTÉ D'INVESTISSEMENTS BANCAIRES TRAVAILLANT À L'ÉCHELLE MONDIALE. (USA)

▲ 139-143 JAQUETTE ET DOUBLES PAGES D'UN LIVRE DOCUMENTANT LES RÉALISATIONS ET LES PROJETS D'UNE SOCIÉTÉ DE CONSTRUCTION ET D'INGÉNIERIE INTERNATIONALE. LA PHOTO DE LA JAQUETTE A ÉTÉ PRISE DANS LE DÉSERT DE LIBYE OÙ L'ENTREPRISE DOIT CONSTRUIRE UN PIPE-LINE POUR ACHEMINER L'EAU DE CETTE RÉGION VERS LA CÔTE; «MOHOLE», UN PROJET DES ANNÉES 60 VISANT À EFFECTUER DES FORAGES POUR ÉTUDIER LES MOUVEMENTS DE L'ÉCORCE TERRESTRE; L'OPÉRATION «SOMBRERO» EN 1979, PLAN DE SAUVETAGE D'UNE PLATE-FORME PÉTROLIÈRE EN FEU; LA SUBSTRUCTURE D'UNE PLATE-FORME EST PLUS ÉLEVÉE QUE L'EMPIRE STATE BUILDING. (USA)

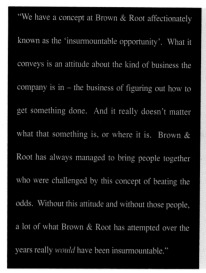

"We have a concept at Brown & Root affectionately known as the 'insurmountable opportunity'. What it conveys is an attitude about the kind of business the company is in – the business of figuring out how to get something done. And it really doesn't matter what that something is, or where it is. Brown & Root has always managed to bring people together who were challenged by this concept of beating the odds. Without this attitude and without those people, a lot of what Brown & Root has attempted over the years really *would* have been insurmountable."

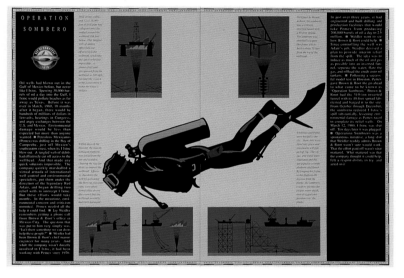

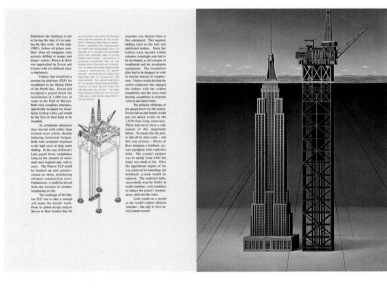

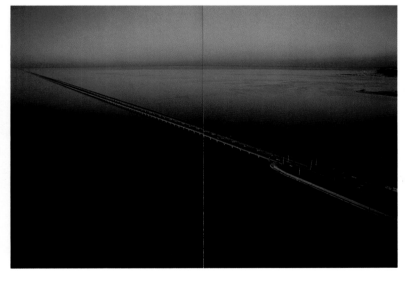

ART DIRECTOR:
LOWELL WILLIAMS
DESIGNERS:
BILL CARSON
ANDY DEARWATER
LOWELL WILLIAMS
PHOTOGRAPHER:
JEFF CORWIN
ARTISTS:
ANDY DEARWATER
TROY FORD

COPYWRITER:
JOANN STONE
AGENCY:
LOWELL WILLIAMS
DESIGN
CLIENT:
BROWN & ROOT USA,
INC.
■ 139-144

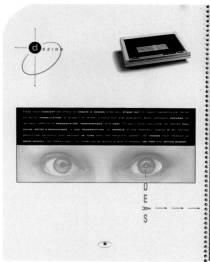

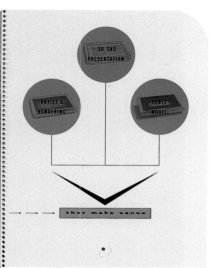

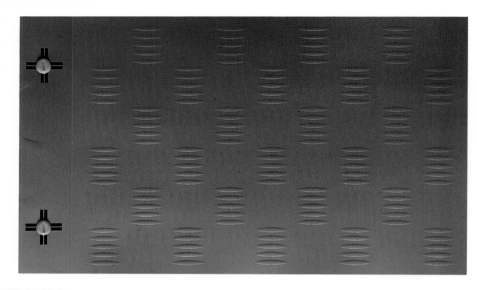

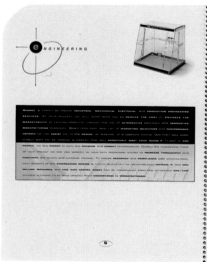

■ 145-147 FROM A SPIRAL-BOUND PROMOTIONAL BROCHURE FOR APOGEE DESIGNS, A PLASTICS FABRICATION SPECIALIST. THIS PIECE FEATURES A FORMED TRANSPARENT COVER CONCEIVED AND MANUFACTURED BY THE CLIENT. (USA)

■ 148-151 FROM A BROCHURE FOR THE TRANSPORT DESIGN CONSORTIUM, AN ASSOCIATION OF FOUR COMPANIES WHO WORK IN THE AREAS OF INTERIOR, INDUSTRIAL, ENGINEERING, CORPORATE GRAPHIC, AND ARCHITECTURAL DESIGN FOR TRANSPORT RELATED INDUSTRIES. (USA)

● 145-147 AUS EINER SPIRALGEBUNDENEN PROMO-TIONSBROSCHÜRE FÜR APOGEE DESIGNS, HERSTEL-LER VON PLASTIKMATERIAL. DER SCHUTZUMSCHLAG AUS GEFORMTEN, TRANSPARENTEM PLASTIK WURDE VOM AUFTRAGGEBER HERGESTELLT. (USA)

● 148-151 UMSCHLAG UND SEITEN AUS EINER BRO-SCHÜRE FÜR DAS TRANSPORT DESIGN CONSORTIUM, DAS AUS VIER FIRMEN BESTEHT, DIE IM BEREICH DER INNENAUSSTATTUNG UND DES INDUSTRIE-DESIGN AUF DEM GEBIET DES TRANSPORTWESENS TÄTIG SIND. (USA)

▲ 145-147 DOUBLES PAGES ET COUVERTURE EN RELIEF DE PLASTIQUE MOULÉ TRANSPARENT POUR UNE BROCHURE DE PROMOTION À RELIURE SPIRALE D'APOGEE DESIGNS, UN SPÉCIALISTE DU PLAS-TIQUE. (USA)

▲ 148-151 D'UNE BROCHURE POUR UNE FIRME QUI REGROUPE QUATRE SOCIÉTÉS TRAVAILLANT DANS LE SECTEUR DU DESIGN INDUSTRIEL ET D'INTÉ-RIEUR DES MOYENS DE TRANSPORT. LA COUVER-TURE ARGENT AVEC GAUFRAGE RAPPELLE LA STRUCTURE DES MARCHEPIEDS DE CAMIONS. (USA)

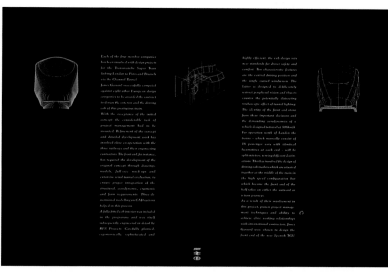

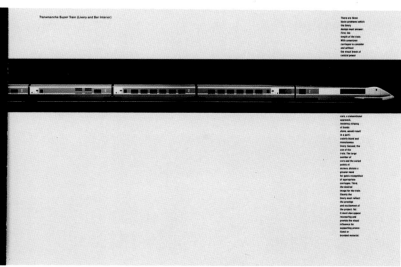

Transmanche Super Train (Livery and Bar Interior)

Transport design consortium

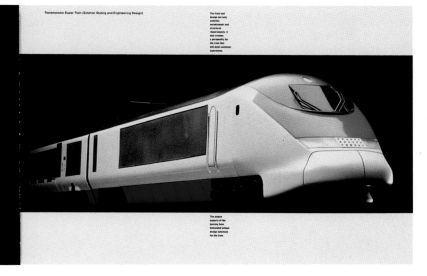

Transmanche Super Train (Exterior Styling and Engineering Design)

ART DIRECTOR:
TIM THOMPSON

DESIGNER:
JOE PARISI

PHOTOGRAPHER:
ED WHITMAN/LIGHT-
STRUCK STUDIO

COPYWRITER:
BOB FLESHER

AGENCY:
GRAFFITO

CLIENT:
APOGEE DESIGNS

◀■ 145-147

ART DIRECTOR:
MICHAEL DENNY

DESIGNERS:
JOHN BATESON
CHRIS BRADLEY
RACHAEL DINNIS

COPYWRITER:
HEATHER SMITH

AGENCY:
ROUNDEL DESIGN
GROUP

CLIENT:
TRANSPORT DESIGN
CONSORTIUM

■ 148-151

ART DIRECTORS:
EDDIE LEE
JEAN CRAIG-
TEERLINK
DESIGNERS:
JEAN CRAIG-
TEERLINK
JOAN HOWARD
PHOTOGRAPHER:
JOHN GREENLEIGH
ARTIST:
JAY CAPELA
AGENCY:
NEXT COMPUTER
◀■ 152, 153

ART DIRECTOR:
LOWELL WILLIAMS
DESIGNER:
BILL CARSON
PHOTOGRAPHER:
JOE BARABAN
AGENCY:
LOWELL WILLIAMS
DESIGN
CLIENT:
USPCI
■ 154

CREATIVE DIRECTOR:
MONICA LITTLE
ART DIRECTOR:
BETH MADSEN
ARTIST:
KRISTIN STAUBITZ
AGENCY:
LITTLE & COMPANY
CLIENT:
INTERNATIONAL
DAIRY QUEEN
■ 155

■ 152, 153 COVERS OF CATALOGS OF CURRENT SOFTWARE AND PERIPHERAL HARDWARE AVAILABLE FOR NEXT COMPUTERS. THESE CATALOGS ARE PUBLISHED EACH SEASON. (USA)

■ 154 COVER FOR A BROCHURE OUTLINING CAPABILITIES OFFERED BY AN ENVIRONMENTAL SERVICE FIRM, A SUBSIDIARY OF THE UNION PACIFIC CORPORATION. THE COVER PHOTOGRAPH, REPEATED ON THE BACK, REFERS TO THE COMPANY'S EXTENSIVE TRUCK TRANSPORT FLEETS. (USA)

■ 155 A BOOK ON CORPORATE HISTORY DOCUMENTING THE FIRST FIFTY YEARS OF INTERNATIONAL DAIRY QUEEN, WITH ONE OF ITS MOST FAMOUS PRODUCTS ILLUSTRATING THE COVER. (USA)

● 152, 153 UMSCHLÄGE FÜR KATALOGE ÜBER SOFTWARE UND HARDWARE-TEILE, DIE FÜR NEXT COMPUTER ERHÄLTLICH SIND. DIE KATALOGE ERSCHEINEN EINMAL IN JEDER JAHRESZEIT. (USA)

● 154 UMSCHLAG DER BROSCHÜRE EINER FIRMA, DIE SICH UM UMWELTGERECHTEN TRANSPORT UND ENTSORGUNG VON INDUSTRIE-ABFÄLLEN KÜMMERT. DAS PHOTO, DAS SICH AUF DEN UMFANGREICHEN LASTWAGENPARK DER FIRMA BEZIEHT, WIRD AUF DER RÜCKSEITE WIEDERHOLT. (USA)

● 155 EIN BUCH ÜBER DIE FIRMENGESCHICHTE ANLÄSSLICH DES 50JÄHRIGEN BESTEHENS DER FIRMA INTERNATIONAL DAIRY QUEEN. SOFT-EIS IST EINES DER BEKANNTESTEN PODUKTE DER FIRMA. (USA)

▲ 152, 153 COUVERTURES DE DEUX CATALOGUES PRÉSENTANT LES NOUVEAUX LOGICIELS ET LE MATÉRIEL INFORMATIQUE DE NEXT COMPUTER INC., PUBLIÉS CHAQUE SAISON. (USA)

▲ 154 COUVERTURE D'UNE BROCHURE INFORMANT SUR LES SERVICES OFFERTS PAR UNE FILIALE DE LA UNION PACIFIC CORPORATION. CETTE SOCIÉTÉ EST SPÉCIALISÉE DANS LES PROBLÈMES D'ENVIRONNEMENT, NOTAMMENT DANS LE TRANSPORT ET LE TRAITEMENT DES DÉCHETS INDUSTRIELS. (USA)

▲ 155 «LE CÔNE AVEC LA PETITE BOUCLE»: COUVERTURE DE LA BROCHURE PUBLIÉE À L'OCCASION DU 50E ANNIVERSAIRE D'INTERNATIONAL DAIRY QUEEN, LA FIRME QUI LANÇA LES SOFT ICE. (USA)

■ 156 ONE OF THE CATALOGS PUBLISHED EACH SEA-SON BY THE AVIA GROUP, PRESENTING ITS FOOT-WEAR COLLECTION FOR ATHLETES. (USA)

■ 157 COVER OF A PROMOTIONAL BROCHURE PUB-LISHED BY NIKE ON BASEBALL AND FOOTBALL STAR BO JACKSON. (USA)

■ 158-161 COVER AND SPREADS FROM A BROCHURE FOR INSERTION INTO TRADE PUBLICATIONS. THE BRIEF WAS TO ESTABLISH A NEW IMAGE FOR A SHOE MANUFACTURER, WHO IS OFFERING SHOES UNDER THE BRAND OF "REVELATIONS" THAT COMBINE COM-FORT WITH STYLE. (USA)

● 156 «NUR FÜR ATHLETEN» – EINER DER JEDE SAISON ERSCHEINENDEN KATALOGE EINES SPORT-SCHUHHERSTELLERS. (USA)

● 157. UMSCHLAG EINER VON NIKE VERÖFFENT-LICHTEN BROSCHÜRE ÜBER DEN BASEBALL- UND FOOTBALL-STAR BO JACKSON. (USA)

● 158-161 UMSCHLAG UND DOPPELSEITEN AUS EINER BROSCHÜRE, DIE IN FACHZEITSCHRIFTEN EINGEHEFTET WIRD. ES GEHT UM EIN NEUES IMAGE FÜR EINEN SCHUHFABRIKANTEN, DER SCHUHE AN-BIETET, DIE BEQUEM UND ELEGANT SIND. DER MAR-KENNAME: «OFFENBARUNGEN». (USA)

▲ 156 L'UN DES CATALOGUES SAISONNIERS DES CHAUSSURES DE SPORT AVIA, «DESTINÉES UNIQUE-MENT AUX ATHLÈTES». (USA)

▲ 157 COUVERTURE D'UN DÉPLIANT PROMOTIONNEL POUR BO JACKSON, UN CHAMPION DE BASEBALL AUX MULTIPLES TALENTS SPORTIFS. (USA)

▲ 158-161 COUVERTURE ET PAGES INTÉRIEURES DE LA BROCHURE D'UN FABRICANT DE CHAUSSURES PRÉSENTANT LES MODÈLES CONFORTABLES ET ÉLÉGANTS DE LA LIGNE «RÉVÉLATIONS». IL S'AGISSAIT DE DONNER À CETTE MARQUE UNE NOUVELLE IMAGE. (USA)

ART DIRECTOR:
STEVEN SANDSTROM
DESIGNERS:
JENNIFER LYON
STEVEN SANDSTROM
PHOTOGRAPHER:
C.B. HARDING
AGENCY:
SANDSTROM
DESIGN, INC.
CLIENT:
AVIA GROUP
INTERNATIONAL
■ 156

ART DIRECTOR:
JOSEPH PARSLEY
DESIGNER:
JOSEPH PARSLEY
PHOTOGRAPHER:
DAN LAMB
AGENCY:
NIKE DESIGN
CLIENT:
NIKE INC.
■ 157

ART DIRECTOR:
JOHN DOYLE
DESIGNER:
DALE EDMONDSON
PHOTOGRAPHER:
GEORGE PETRAKES
COPYWRITER:
GEOFF COURRIER
AGENCY:
DOYLE ADVERTIS-
ING/DESIGN
CLIENT:
LOWELL SHOE INC.
▶■ 158-161

SPIRIT

Spring · 1991

ART DIRECTOR:
WALTER
HERRINGTON
DESIGNER:
WALTER
HERRINGTON
PHOTOGRAPHER:
CARLO DALLA
CHIESA
COPYWRITER:
EDWARD PARONE
STUDIO:
DESIGN MATTERS
CLIENT:
SPIRIT ACTIVWEAR

■ 162-165

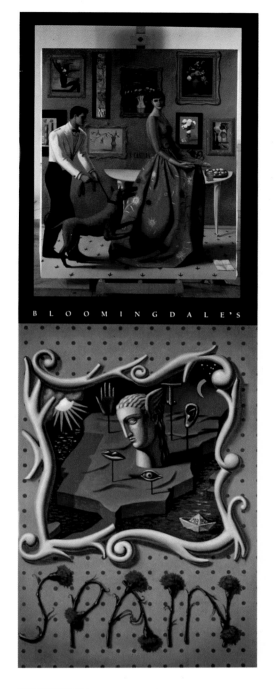

ART DIRECTOR:

SUSANNA MORALDI

AGENCY:

ARNELL/BICKFORD

CLIENT:

DKNY COVERINGS

◄■ 166

CREATIVE DIRECTOR:

JOHN JAY

ART DIRECTOR:

ROBERT VALENTINE

PHOTOGRAPHER:

KURT MARKUS

ARTIST:

SIGREDO MARTIN

BEGUÉ

AGENCY:

BLOOMINGDALE'S

CLIENT:

BLOOMINGDALE'S

■ 167, 168

■ 162-165 TRADE SHOW BROCHURE FOR SPIRIT ACTIVEWEAR, A LINE OF CLOTHES WITH A SIMPLE, CLASSIC STYLE. (USA)

■ 166 PRESS KIT AND BUYERS' FOLDER FOR THE LAUNCH OF A DKNY HOSIERY LINE. THE PAPER CORRESPONDS WITH THE ACTUAL PACKAGING. THE LOGO USED ON THE COVER IS WELL-KNOWN. (USA)

■ 167 COVER OF A PROMOTIONAL BOOKLET FOR SPANISH WEEKS AT BLOOMINGDALE'S, AN HOMAGE TO THE CULTURE OF THIS COUNTRY (USA)

■ 168 COVER OF A BROCHURE FOR BLOOMINGDALE'S PRESENTING THE FALL/WINTER MEN'S FASHION. THE RIBBON HOLDS A SMALLER BROCHURE ENTITLED: "INFINITE STYLE." (USA)

● 162-165 MESSEKATALOG FÜR SPIRIT, IN DEM KLEIDUNG GEZEIGT WIRD, DIE SCHLICHT, KLASSISCH UND NATÜRLICH IST. (USA)

● 166 PRESSE/VERKAUFSMAPPE FÜR DIE LANCIERUNG EINER STRUMPFLINIE VON DKNY, EIN BEKANNTES LOGO. DAS PAPIER DER MAPPE WIRD AUCH FÜR DIE STRUMPFVERPACKUNG VERWENDET. (USA)

● 167 DIE KULTUR SPANIENS ALS THEMA EINER BROSCHÜRE FÜR «SPANISCHE WOCHEN» DES KAUFHAUSES BLOOMINGDALE'S. (USA)

● 168 UMSCHLAG EINER BROSCHÜRE FÜR BLOOMINGDALE'S MIT DER HERBST/WINTER-HERRENMODE. AN DEM AUSSEN SICHTBAREN BAND IST EINE KLEINERE, ZWEITE BROSCHÜRE BEFESTIGT. (USA)

▲ 162-165 PETITE BROCHURE POUR SPIRIT PRÉSENTANT UNE LIGNE DE VÊTEMENTS SIMPLES, CLASSIQUES ET FACILES D'ENTRETIEN. (USA)

▲ 166 COUVERTURE D'UNE POCHETTE RENFERMANT DU MATÉRIEL PUBLICITAIRE POUR LE LANCEMENT D'UNE LIGNE DE COLLANTS. LE PAPIER UTILISÉ A ÉTÉ CHOISI EN FONCTION DES EMBALLAGES. (USA)

▲ 167 COUVERTURE D'UN PROSPECTUS DES MAGASINS BLOOMINGDALE'S POUR DES SEMAINES DE PROMOTION CONSACRÉES À L'ESPAGNE. (USA)

▲ 168 COUVERTURE D'UNE BROCHURE POUR LA MODE MASCULINE AUTOMNE/HIVER DE BLOOMINGDALE'S. UNE AUTRE PETITE BROCHURE EST FIXÉE À LA PREMIÈRE À L'AIDE D'UN LIEN. (USA)

BLACK IS BLACK IS BLACK

k.one

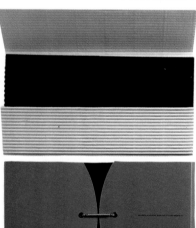

ART DIRECTOR:
CIRIANO ZANON
DESIGNER:
FRANCO CARDIN
PHOTOGRAPHER:
GIANNI BACCEGA
AGENCY:
ZAN ON DESIGN
COMMUNICATION
CLIENT:
K. ONE MODA-
SOLARIS
◀■ 169-174

ART DIRECTOR:
DEL TERRELONGE
DESIGNER:
DEL TERRELONGE
PHOTOGRAPHER:
RON BAXTER SMITH
COPYWRITER:
JOHN MACKAY
AGENCY:
TERRELONGE
DESIGN INC.
CLIENT:
MARC LAURENT
■ 175-181

■ 169-174 CATALOG FOR K.ONE SUNGLASSES. THE MAT CARTON COVER IS CONTAINED IN A LAMINATED JACKET BEARING A SLOGAN THAT TAKES UP THE FAMOUS "A ROSE IS A ROSE IS A ROSE" BY GERTRUDE STEIN. DIFFERENT STRUCTURES AND VARIOUS SHADES OF BLACK WITH ACCENTS OF COLOR, MOSTLY RED, DOMINATE ALL SPREADS. (ITA)

■ 175-181 A PROMOTIONAL BROCHURE FOR FASHION BY MARK LAURENT AND OTHER DESIGNERS. IT IS SPIRAL-BOUND. THE DIFFERENT BRANDS ARE PRINTED ON TRANSPARENT PAPER. CARDBOARD PAGES IN A SPECIAL REDUCED FORMAT INTRODUCE THE ILLUSTRATIONS. THE SPIRAL-BOUND CATALOG IS PROTECTED BY CORRUGATED CARDBOARD (SHOWN HALF OPENED) AND A CARDBOARD COVER WITH A SPECIAL RUBBERBAND/SPRING SEAL. (CAN)

● 169-174 KATALOG FÜR K.ONE.-SONNENBRILLEN. DER MATTE KARTONEINBAND STECKT IN EINEM LAMINIERTEN SCHUTZUMSCHLAG MIT EINEM SLOGAN, DER AUF DEN BERÜHMTEN AUSSPRUCH VON GERTRUDE STEIN «A ROSE IS A ROSE IS A ROSE» ZURÜCKGREIFT. STRUKTUREN UND VERSCHIEDENE ABSTUFUNGEN VON SCHWARZ DOMINIEREN. (ITA)

● 175-181 EIN KATALOG FÜR MARC LAURENT UND ANDERE DESIGNER-MODE. ER IST SPIRALGEBUNDEN, DIE VERSCHIEDENEN MARKEN SIND AUF EIN TRANS- PARENTPAPIER GEDRUCKT, WÄHREND KARTONSEI- TEN IN SPEZIELLEM FORMAT ALS EINFÜHRUNGEN ZU DEN ABBILDUNGEN DIENEN. DER SPIRALGEBUNDENE KATALOG IST DURCH WELLKARTON UND EINEN KARTONUMSCHLAG MIT GUMMIBAND/SPIRALFEDER- VERSCHLUSS GESCHÜTZT. (CAN)

▲ 169-174 CATALOGUE DES LUNETTES DE SOLEIL K.ONE. LA COUVERTURE DE CARTON MAT EST RE- COUVERTE D'UNE JAQUETTE DE PAPIER GLACÉ; LE SLOGAN REPREND LA FORMULE DE GERTRUDE STEIN, «A ROSE IS A ROSE IS A ROSE». LA COMPO- SITION GRAPHIQUE EST DOMINÉE PAR DES JEUX DE STRUCTURE ET DES DÉGRADÉS DE NOIR. (ITA)

▲ 175-181 UN CATALOGUE À RELIURE SPIRALE DE MARC LAURENT ET D'AUTRES GRANDS COUTURIERS. LES DIVERSES MARQUES SONT IMPRIMÉES SUR PAPIER TRANSPARENT; DES PAGES CARTONNÉES DE FORMAT PARTICULIER INTRODUISENT LA PRÉSEN- TATION PHOTOGRAPHIQUE. CE CATALOGUE À RE- LIURE SPIRALE EST PROTÉGÉ D'UNE ENVELOPPE DE CARTON ONDULÉ ET GLISSÉ DANS UNE BANDE DE CARTON RIGIDE FERMÉE PAR UN RESSORT. (CAN)

P H O T O G R A P H E R :
JUAN DE LA FUENTE
A G E N C Y :
STUDIO GATTI
C L I E N T :
SYBILLA
■ 182-191

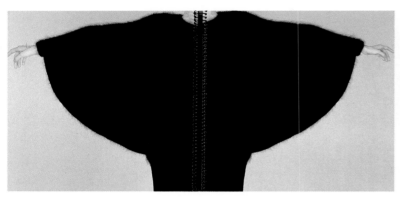

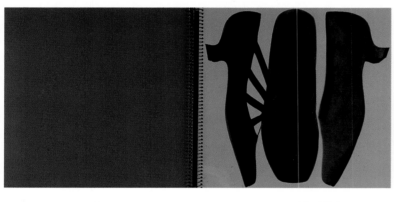

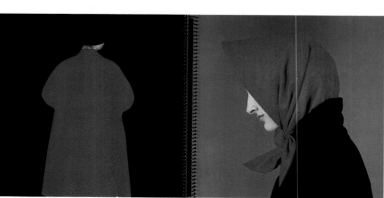

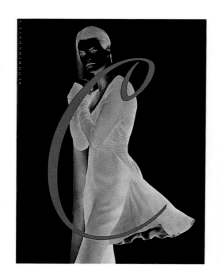

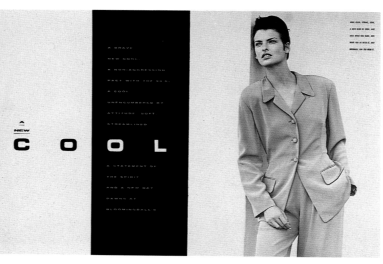

COOL

ART DIRECTOR:
JOHN JAY
DESIGNER:
JOHN JAY
PHOTOGRAPHER:
STEVEN MEISEL
AGENCY:
BLOOMINGDALE'S
CLIENT:
BLOOMINGDALE'S
■ 192-196

■ 182-191 SPIRAL-BOUND CATALOG PRESENTING THE CREATIONS OF A SPANISH FASHION DESIGNER. ALL MODELS ARE SHOWN SILHOUETTED ON MONOCHROME PAGES. SOME MOTIFS ARE PRINTED ON TRANSPARENT PLASTIC PAGES, LIKE THE ONE WITH THE SHOES, PRODUCING A SPECIAL EFFECT WHEN SUPERIMPOSED OVER ANOTHER MOTIF. (SPA)

■ 192-196 "A NEW COOL" IS THE TITLE OF THIS CATALOG FOR BLOOMINGDALE'S. PLAYING ON THE SUBJECT OF POSITIVE AND NEGATIVE, THE CATALOG IS PRINTED IN BLACK-AND-WHITE IN HARMONY WITH A SOFT, STREAMLINED FASHION, DESCRIBED AS A STATEMENT OF THE SPIRIT OF THE TIMES. (USA)

● 182-191 SPIRALGEBUNDENER KATALOG MIT DEM «SYBILLA»-SCHRIFTZUG. DIE NEUSTEN KREATIONEN DIESER SPANISCHEN MODESCHÖPFERIN SIND AUF EINFARBIGEN SEITEN FREIGESTELLT GEZEIGT. EINIGE SEITEN SIND AUS DURCHSICHTIGEM, TRANSPARENTEM PLASTIK. DURCH DIE ÜBERLAGERUNG ENTSTEHT EIN SPEZIELLER EFFEKT. (SPA)

● 192-196 DIESER KATALOG FÜR BLOOMINGDALE'S IST GANZ IN SCHWARZWEISS GEDRUCKT. ER SPIELT MIT DEM THEMA POSITIV/NEGATIV UND PRÄSENTIERT EINE SANFTE, UNKOMPLIZIERTE MODE, DIE ALS ZEICHEN DES ZEITGEISTES, DES AUSDRUCKS DER PERSÖNLICHKEIT BEZEICHNET WIRD. (USA)

▲ 182-191 COUVERTURE D'UN CATALOGUE À RELIURE SPIRALE PORTANT LA SIGNATURE DE SYBILLA. LES MODÈLES DE LA COLLECTION AUTOMNE/HIVER 90/91 SONT PRÉSENTÉS SUR DES FONDS UNIS. DES JEUX DE SUPERPOSITIONS DE FORMES (186) SONT OBTENUS GRÂCE À DES MOTIFS IMPRIMÉS SUR RHODOID TRANSPARENT. (SPA)

▲ 192-196 CATALOGUE POUR BLOOMINGDALE'S AVEC PHOTOGRAPHIES EN NOIR ET BLANC JOUANT SUR LES EFFETS DE NÉGATIF ET DE POSITIF. LE RAFFINEMENT DES NUANCES DE GRIS MET EN VALEUR CETTE MODE DÉCONTRACTÉE QUI DOIT SOULIGNER L'ORIGINALITÉ DE LA PERSONNALITÉ. (USA)

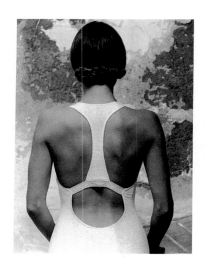

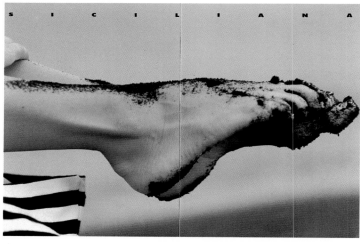

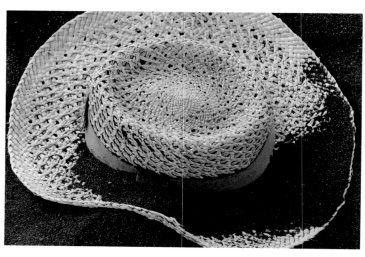

ART DIRECTORS:
FRANCA GORI
GIANNI SINNI
PHOTOGRAPHER:
ALDO FALLAI
AGENCY:
LCD GRAPHICS
PUBLISHER:
EMPORIO ARMANI
◀■ 197-209

ART DIRECTOR:
WOLFGANG
HASLINGER
AGENCY:
WERKSTUDIO
CLIENT:
CILAG GMBH
■ 210, 211

Hier verbergen sich...

■ 197-209 FRONT AND BACK COVER AND SPREADS FROM A SEMESTRIAL MAGAZINE PUBLISHED BY THE FASHION HOUSE EMPORIO ARMANI. ITALIAN HIGH-SPIRITED LIFESTYLE IS THE KEY TO HIS FASHION AND IN CONTEXT WITH THIS PHILOSOPHY, THE MAGAZINE WAS CREATED TO INFORM NOT ONLY ON THE LATEST FASHIONS BUT ALSO ON ITALIAN CULTURE. THIS ISSUE FOCUSES ON SICILY. (ITA)

● 197-209 AUS EINEM MAGAZIN DES MODEHAUSES EMPORIO ARMANI. ITALIENISCHE LEBENSART PRÄGT DIESE RAFFINIERTEN, SINNLICHEN KREATIONEN ARMANIS. IM EINKLANG MIT DIESER PHILOSOPHIE IST DIESE ZEITSCHRIFT ENTSTANDEN, DIE NICHT NUR ÜBER DIE NEUSTEN MODELLE, SONDERN AUCH ÜBER DIE ITALIENISCHE KULTUR INFORMIERT. DIESE AUSGABE IST SIZILIEN GEWIDMET. (ITA)

▲ 197-209 RECTO ET VERSO DE LA COUVERTURE ET DOUBLES PAGES DU CATALOGUE SEMESTRIEL PRÉSENTANT LA COLLECTION PRINTEMPS/ÉTÉ 90 EMPORIO ARMANI. CETTE MODE RAFFINÉE ET SENSUELLE REFLÈTE LE STYLE DE VIE ITALIEN. CONSACRÉ À LA SICILE, LE CATALOGUE EST ILLUSTRÉ D'IMAGES DE LA VIE QUOTIDIENNE; IL ÉVOQUE ÉGALEMENT DES PERSONNALITÉS, LITTÉRAIRES OU AUTRES. (ITA)

■ 210, 211 A DIRECT MAIL PIECE WITH REAL ZIPPER SHOWN CLOSED AND OPENED FOR A PHARMACEUTICAL PRODUCT FOR THE TREATMENT OF MYCOSE INFECTIONS, MANUFACTURED BY CILAG. (AUT)

● 210, 211 WERBESENDUNG FÜR EIN MEDIKAMENT GEGEN MYKOSE-INFEKTIONEN. HIER DER MIT EINEM REISSVERSCHLUSS VERSCHLOSSENE UMSCHLAG UND DIE GEÖFFNETE BROSCHÜRE. (AUT)

▲ 210, 211 PETITE BROCHURE PUBLICITAIRE POUR UN MÉDICAMENT CONTRE LES INFECTIONS MYCOSIQUES. À G., LA COUVERTURE AVEC FERMETURE ÉCLAIR; À DR., LA BROCHURE OUVERTE. (AUT)

ART DIRECTOR:
JOHN SAYLES
DESIGNERS:
JOHN SAYLES
JOE BUSTAD
PHOTOGRAPHER:
BILL NELLANS
ARTIST:
JOHN SAYLES
COPYWRITER:
JULIE SOMMERLOT
AGENCY:
SAYLES GRAPHIC
DESIGN
CLIENT:
GILBERT PAPER
■ 212-216

ART DIRECTORS:
CHARLES S.
ANDERSON
DAN OLSON
DESIGNERS:
CHARLES S.
ANDERSON
DAN OLSON
ARTIST:
RANDALL DAHLK
AGENCY:
CHARLES S.
ANDERSON DESIGN
CLIENT:
FRENCH PAPER CO.
▶■ 217

■ 212-216 SPREADS AND COVER OF A BROCHURE DESIGNED TO SHOW THE UNUSUAL USE OF COLORED STOCK MADE BY GILBERT PAPER. THE POWER OF PRINT AND PAPER IS THE LEADING THEME. (USA)

● 212-216 DOPPELSEITEN UND UMSCHLAG EINER BROSCHÜRE, DIE DEN SPEZIELLEN EINSATZ FARBIGEN PAPIERS VON GILBERT PAPER DEMONSTRIERT. THEMA: DIE MACHT VON DRUCK UND PAPIER. (USA)

▲ 212-216 «LE POUVOIR DU PAPIER ET DE L'ENCRE»: D'UNE BROCHURE MONTRANT LES POSSIBILITÉS GRAPHIQUES QU'OFFRENT LES PAPIERS COLORÉS DE GILBERT PAPER. (USA)

■ 217 NEW SWATCH BOOKS FOR THE FRENCH PAPER COMPANY'S FIVE UPDATED PAPER LINES. (USA)

● 217 NEUE MUSTERBÜCHER DER FRENCH PAPER COMPANY FÜR FÜNF PAPIERSORTEN. (USA)

▲ 217 LIVRES D'ÉCHANTILLONS POUR CINQ SORTES DE PAPIERS DE LA FRENCH PAPER COMPANY. (USA)

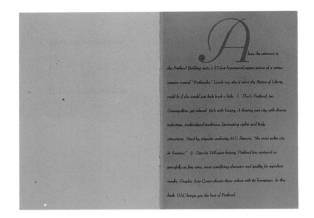

ART DIRECTOR:
KIT HINRICHS
DESIGNERS:
KIT HINRICHS
BELLE HOW
PHOTOGRAPHERS:
BARRY ROBINSON
TERRY HEFFERNAN
GARY BRAASCH
ARTISTS:
GARY OVERACRE
WILL NELSON
COPYWRITER:
DELPHINE HIRASUNA
AGENCY:
PENTAGRAM DESIGN
CLIENT:
GRAPHIC ARTS
CENTER
■ 218-225

■ 218-225 THE GRAPHIC ARTS CENTER OF PORTLAND SHARES THE VALUES OF ITS HOMETOWN, WHICH HAS "MATURED GRACEFULLY AS FINE WINE, NEVER SACRIFICING CHARACTER AND QUALITY FOR EXPEDIENT RESULTS." SHOWN ARE SPREADS AND THE COVER OF A PROMOTIONAL BROCHURE WITH ITS ENVELOPE UNFOLDED. THE ILLUSTRATIONS SERVE AS AN EXAMPLE OF THE PRINT QUALITY OFFERED BY THIS COMPANY AND AT THE SAME TIME THEY INFORM ABOUT ALL THE PLEASANT ASPECTS OF THIS "CITY OF ROSES". (USA)

● 218-225 DAS GRAPHIC ARTS CENTER VON PORT-LAND, OREGON, HAT SICH DIE WERTE DIESER STADT, DIE «WIE EIN GUTER WEIN GEREIFT IST, OHNE DEN CHARAKTER ZUGUNSTEN SCHNELLER ERGEBNISSE AUFZUGEBEN», ZU EIGEN GEMACHT. GEZEIGT SIND BESPIELE DER DOPPELSEITEN UND DER UMSCHLAG DER PROMOTIONSBROSCHÜRE MIT GEÖFFNETEM COUVERT. DIE ILLUSTRATIONEN DIE-NEN ALS BEISPIEL DER VON DER FIRMA ANGEBOTE-NEN DRUCKQUALITÄT UND INFORMIEREN ÜBER DIE ANNEHMLICHKEITEN DIESER «ROSENSTADT». (USA)

▲ 218-225 LE GRAPHIC ARTS CENTER DE PORTLAND, DANS L'OREGON, A ADOPTÉ LES VALEURS DE CETTE VILLE QUI «A MÛRI COMME UN BON VIN, SANS PERDRE DE SON CARACTÈRE AU PROFIT DE RÉSUL-TATS SPECTACULAIRES». ICI, ON PEUT VOIR DES EXEMPLES DE DOUBLES PAGES ET LA COUVERTURE DE CETTE BROCHURE PROMOTIONNELLE AVEC SON ENVELOPPE OUVERTE. LES IMAGES ILLUSTRENT LA QUALITÉ D'IMPRESSION DES PUBLICATIONS DU GRAPHIC ARTS CENTER ET INFORMENT SUR LES AGRÉMENTS DE LA «VILLE DES ROSES». (USA)

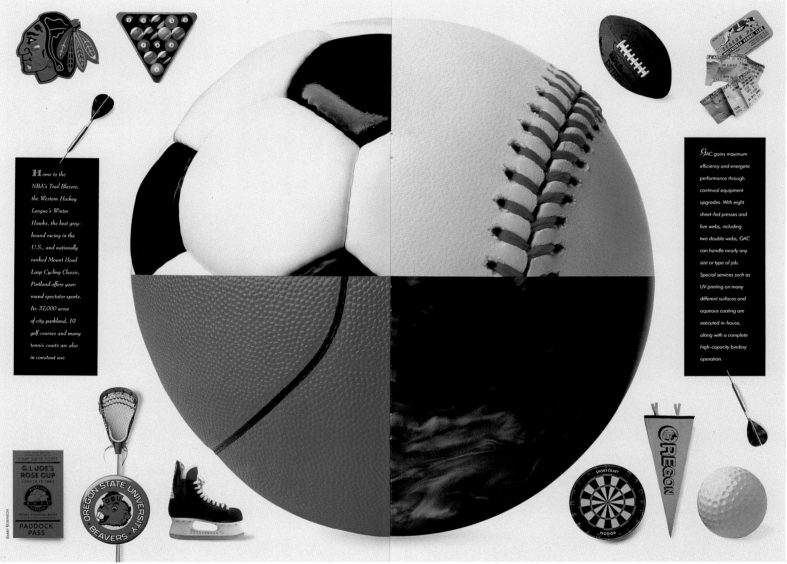

Home to the NBA's Trail Blazers, the Western Hockey League's Winter Hawks, best grey-hound racing in the U.S., and nationally ranked Mount Hood Loop Cycling Classic, Portland offers year-round spectator sports. Its 37,000 acres of city parkland, 10 golf courses and many tennis courts are also in constant use.

GAC gains maximum efficiency and energetic performance through continual equipment upgrades. With eight sheet-fed presses and five webs, including two double webs, GAC can handle nearly any size or type of job. Special services such as UV printing on many different surfaces and aqueous coating are executed in-house, along with a complete high-capacity bindery operation.

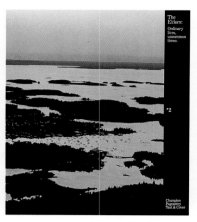
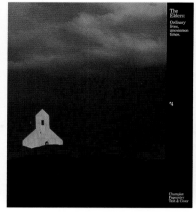
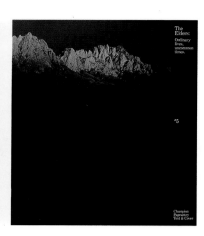

The Elders: Ordinary lives, uncommon times.

Champion Pageantry Text & Cover

#1 #2 #4 #5

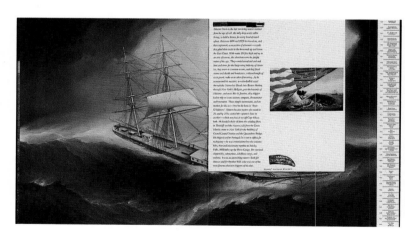

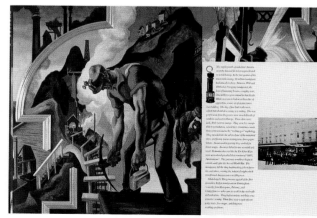

INVEST IN VICTORY LIBERT[Y]

There were no child labor laws. Children aged eight worked a 60-hour week sorting slate from the coal and were paid $1 to $5.

"Each family would do for itself. You see, there were about 220 families in the camp — each one would have five or so people that worked and washed the coal. The man next to me his son was working with him — they'd just started and a piece of rock fell down and caught the son and mashed him. His daddy was loading and the rock caught him in the car and about broke Joe in half, by the hip. And the son was under the rock. Me and another two men had to try and move the car and get the men out of there. I had a piece of wood and I tried to lift it up and it just broke. They gave a place for him to be buried in the Jewish cemetery on 11th Avenue. The father was crippled. He must have left Birmingham. I never saw him again. I decided to stop — the mine."

Pageantry" Text Smooth, White/100 lb.

ART DIRECTOR:
RICHARD HESS
DESIGNER:
KATHLEEN HOHL-
PHILLIPS
PHOTOGRAPHER:
DMITRI KASTERINE
ARTIST:
VARIOUS
COPYWRITERS:
JO DURDEN-SMITH
RICHARD HESS
AGENCY:
HESS & HESS
CLIENT:
CHAMPION
INTERNATIONAL
■ 226-236

■ 226-236 COVERS AND SPREADS FROM A SERIES OF PUBLICATIONS OF CHAMPION INTERNATIONAL UNDER THE TITLE OF "THE ELDERS: ORDINARY LIVES, UNCOMMON TIMES." FROM LEFT TO RIGHT AND TOP TO BOTTOM: THE BADLANDS; SOUTH DAKOTA; COASTAL ISLANDS, MAINE; ALABAMA LANDSCAPE; TWO SPREADS ON NATIVE AMERICANS; THE STORY OF THE LAST SURVIVING MASTER MARINER; WORLD WAR I; IMMIGRANTS; THE AGE OF COAL AND STEEL. SMALLER SIZE BOOKLETS INSERTED IN THE CENTERFOLD CONTAIN THE STORIES RELATED TO THE LARGE-FORMAT ILLUSTRATIONS. (USA)

● 226-236 UMSCHLÄGE UND DOPPELSEITEN AUS EINER PUBLIKATIONSREIHE DES PAPIERHERSTEL-LERS CHAMPION: »DIE ALTEN: GEWÖHNLICHE LEBEN IN UNGEWÖHNLICHEN ZEITEN«. V.L.N.R. UND V.O.N.U. THE BADLANDS, SOUTH DAKOTA; INSELN VOR MAINE; LANDSCHAFT IN ALABAMA; ZWEI DOPPELSEITEN ÜBER INDIANER; DIE GESCHICHTE DES LETZTEN MEISTERS DER SEGELSCHIFFE; DER 1. WELTKRIEG; IMMIGRANTEN; DAS ZEITALTER VON KOHLE UND STAHL. IM MITTELBUND SIND KLEINERE BROSCHÜREN EINGEHEFTET. SIE ENTHALTEN DIE GESCHICHTEN ZU DEN ILLUSTRATIONEN. (USA)

▲ 226-236 D'UNE SÉRIE DE PUBLICATIONS POUR LES PAPIERS CHAMPION, INTITULÉES «LES ANCIENS: DES VIES ORDINAIRES À UNE ÉPOQUE EXTRAORDINAIRE». DE G. À DR. ET DE HAUT EN BAS: THE BADLANDS, DAKOTA DU SUD; ÎLES CÔTIÈRES DU MAINE; PAYSAGE D'ALABAMA; DEUX DOUBLES PAGES SUR LES INDIENS; L'HISTOIRE DU DERNIER CAPITAINE AU LONG COURS D'UN GRAND VOILIER; LA PREMIÈRE GUERRE MONDIALE; DES IMMIGRANTS; L'ÂGE DU CHARBON ET DE L'ACIER. DE PETITES BROCHURES ENCARTÉES AU MILIEU RELATENT DES FAITS EN RAPPORT AVEC LES ILLUSTRATIONS. (USA)

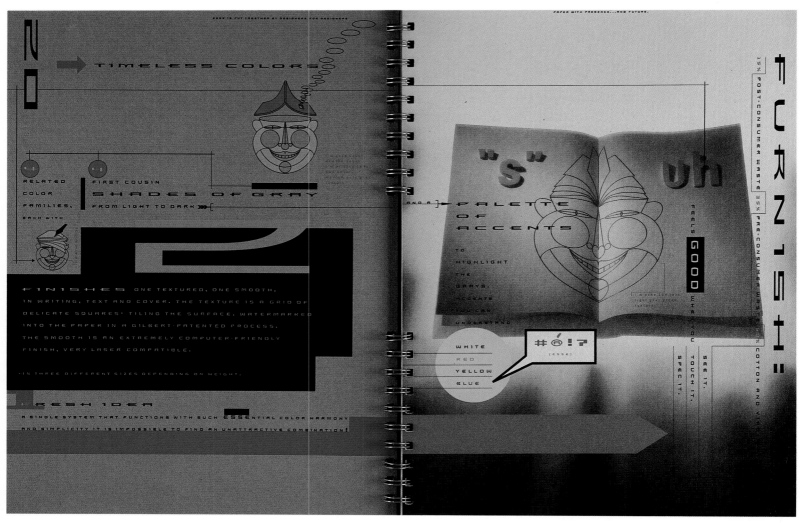

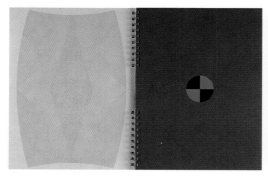
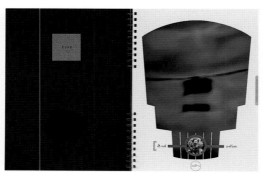
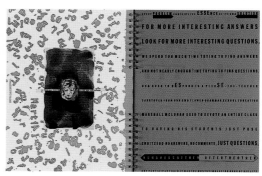

ART DIRECTOR:
RICK VALICENTI
DESIGNERS:
RICK VALICENTI
MICHAEL
GIAMMANCO
ARTIST:
CORINNE PFISTER
COPYWRITER:
TODD LIEF
AGENCY:
THIRST
CLIENT:
GILBERT PAPER
■ 237-244

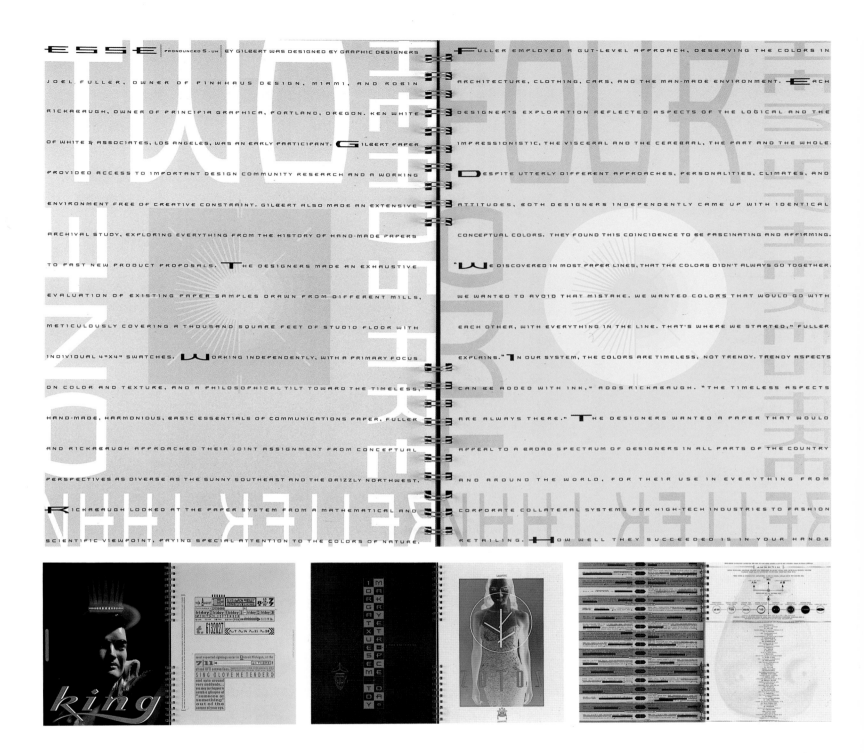

ESSE (PRONOUNCED S-UH) BY GILBERT WAS DESIGNED BY GRAPHIC DESIGNERS JOEL FULLER, OWNER OF PINKHAUS DESIGN, MIAMI, AND ROBIN RICKABAUGH, OWNER OF PRINCIPIA GRAPHICA, PORTLAND, OREGON. KEN WHITE OF WHITE & ASSOCIATES, LOS ANGELES, WAS AN EARLY PARTICIPANT. GILBERT PAPER PROVIDED ACCESS TO IMPORTANT DESIGN COMMUNITY RESEARCH AND A WORKING ENVIRONMENT FREE OF CREATIVE CONSTRAINT. GILBERT ALSO MADE AN EXTENSIVE ARCHIVAL STUDY, EXPLORING EVERYTHING FROM THE HISTORY OF HAND-MADE PAPERS TO PAST NEW PRODUCT PROPOSALS. THE DESIGNERS MADE AN EXHAUSTIVE EVALUATION OF EXISTING PAPER SAMPLES DRAWN FROM DIFFERENT MILLS, METICULOUSLY COVERING A THOUSAND SQUARE FEET OF STUDIO FLOOR WITH INDIVIDUAL 4"X4" SWATCHES. WORKING INDEPENDENTLY, WITH A PRIMARY FOCUS ON COLOR AND TEXTURE, AND A PHILOSOPHICAL TILT TOWARD THE TIMELESS, HAND-MADE, HARMONIOUS, BASIC ESSENTIALS OF COMMUNICATIONS PAPER, FULLER AND RICKABAUGH APPROACHED THEIR JOINT ASSIGNMENT FROM CONCEPTUAL PERSPECTIVES AS DIVERSE AS THE SUNNY SOUTHEAST AND THE DRIZZLY NORTHWEST. RICKABAUGH LOOKED AT THE PAPER SYSTEM FROM A MATHEMATICAL AND SCIENTIFIC VIEWPOINT, PAYING SPECIAL ATTENTION TO THE COLORS OF NATURE.

FULLER EMPLOYED A GUT-LEVEL APPROACH, OBSERVING THE COLORS IN ARCHITECTURE, CLOTHING, CARS, AND THE MAN-MADE ENVIRONMENT. EACH DESIGNER'S EXPLORATION REFLECTED ASPECTS OF THE LOGICAL AND THE IMPRESSIONISTIC, THE VISCERAL AND THE CEREBRAL, THE PART AND THE WHOLE. DESPITE UTTERLY DIFFERENT APPROACHES, PERSONALITIES, CLIMATES, AND ATTITUDES, BOTH DESIGNERS INDEPENDENTLY CAME UP WITH IDENTICAL CONCEPTUAL COLORS. THEY FOUND THIS COINCIDENCE TO BE FASCINATING AND AFFIRMING. "WE DISCOVERED IN MOST PAPER LINES, THAT THE COLORS DIDN'T ALWAYS GO TOGETHER. WE WANTED TO AVOID THAT MISTAKE. WE WANTED COLORS THAT WOULD GO WITH EACH OTHER, WITH EVERYTHING IN THE LINE. THAT'S WHERE WE STARTED," FULLER EXPLAINS. "IN OUR SYSTEM, THE COLORS ARE TIMELESS, NOT TRENDY. TRENDY ASPECTS CAN BE ADDED WITH INK," ADDS RICKABAUGH. "THE TIMELESS ASPECTS ARE ALWAYS THERE." THE DESIGNERS WANTED A PAPER THAT WOULD APPEAL TO A BROAD SPECTRUM OF DESIGNERS IN ALL PARTS OF THE COUNTRY AND AROUND THE WORLD, FOR THEIR USE IN EVERYTHING FROM CORPORATE COLLATERAL SYSTEMS FOR HIGH-TECH INDUSTRIES TO FASHION RETAILING. HOW WELL THEY SUCCEEDED IS IN YOUR HANDS.

■ 237-244 SPREADS FROM A PROMOTIONAL SPIRAL-BOUND BOOK FOR GILBERT PAPER INTRODUCING ITS NEW "ESSE" PAPER TO THE DESIGN WORLD. BEING AWARE OF THE GRAPHIC DESIGNER'S INCREASINGLY AUTHORITATIVE VOICE IN THE CLIENT'S MARKETING DECISIONS, THE COMPANY DECIDED TO PRESENT THIS NEW RECYCLED PAPER SYSTEM TO THE INDUSTRY. IT ASSIGNED A LEADING DESIGN FIRM TO EXPLORE IT BY MEANS OF THE CATALOG. (USA)

● 237-244 AUS EINEM KATALOG FÜR GILBERT PAPER, MIT DEM DER DESIGN-BRANCHE DIE NEUE PAPIERQUALITÄT «ESSE» VORGESTELLT WIRD. DIE FIRMA WAR SICH DES BEDEUTENDEN EINFLUSSES DER GRAPHIK-DESIGNER AUF DIE PAPIERWAHL IHRER AUFTRAGGEBER BEWUSST UND BESCHLOSS DESHALB, DAS NEUE UMWELT-PAPIER DURCH EINE DER BEKANNTESTEN DESIGNFIRMEN IN DEM KATALOG AUSPROBIEREN ZU LASSEN. (USA)

▲ 237-244 D'UN CATALOGUE À RELIURE SPIRALE AU MOYEN DUQUEL GILBERT PAPER PRÉSENTE AUX PROFESSIONNELS LE PAPIER «ESSE». CONSCIENTE DE L'IMPORTANCE DU CHOIX DU DESIGNER GRA-PHIQUE, CETTE FIRME A DÉCIDÉ DE FAIRE TESTER LA QUALITÉ DE CE NOUVEAU PAPIER RECYCLÉ, INVITANT L'UN DES STUDIOS DE DESIGN LES PLUS CONNUS À CONCEVOIR SON CATALOGUE EN EXPÉRI-MENTANT LES POSSIBILITÉS DE CE PAPIER. (USA)

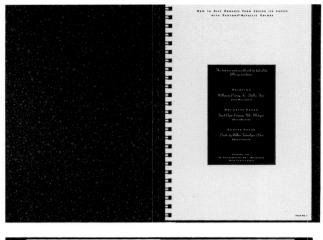

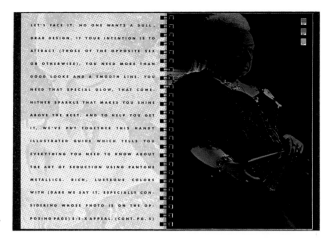

ART DIRECTORS:
CHARLES S.
ANDERSON
DAN OLSON
DESIGNERS:
CHARLES S.
ANDERSON
HALEY JOHNSON
DAN OLSON
ARTISTS:
CHARLES S.
ANDERSON
RANDALL DAHLK
DAN OLSON
COPYWRITER:
LISA PEMRICK
AGENCY:
CHARLES S.
ANDERSON DESIGN
CLIENT:
PANTONE, INC.
■ 245-252

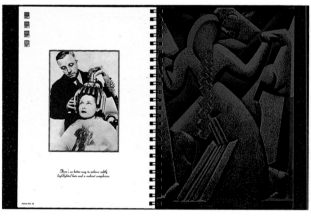

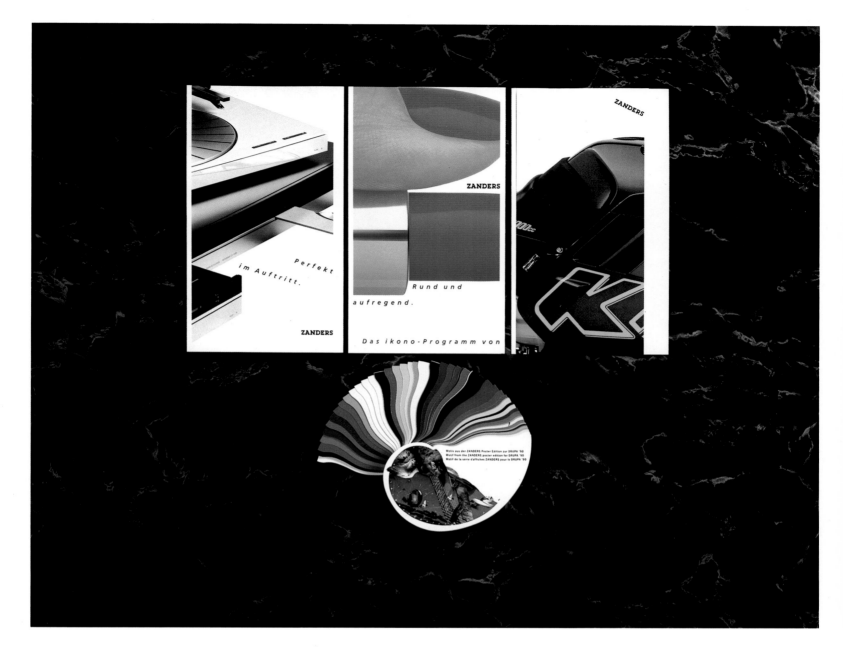

ART DIRECTORS:
TON VAN BRAGT
HÉLÉNE BERGMANS
MARC VAN
BOKHOVEN

DESIGNER:
UWE LOESCH

PHOTOGRAPHERS:
DIOR
HEINER SCHMITZ
LEX VAN PIETERSON

COPYWRITERS:
UWE LOESCH
PETRA ZIMMERMANN

AGENCY:
STUDIO DUMBAR

CLIENT:
ZANDERS
FEINPAPIERE AG

■ 253

■ 245-252 THIS PANTONE METALLIC BOOK WAS DESIGNED TO PROMOTE NEW METALLIC INKS AND UNIQUE PRINTING TECHNIQUES. IT IS SPIRAL-BOUND AND COMES IN A JACKET. ITS TITLE EXPLAINS ALL: "HOW TO KEEP ROMANCE FROM LOSING ITS LUSTER." (USA)

■ 253 COVERS OF FOLDERS TO BE INSERTED IN TRADE MAGAZINES OF THE COMMUNICATIONS INDUSTRY. THEY ARE MEANT TO DEMONSTRATE THE HIGH QUALITY OF IKONO PAPER. THE SPECIAL SAMPLER WITH A MOTIF OF THE ZANDERS POSTER EDITION WAS CREATED FOR A TRADE FAIR. (GER)

● 245-252 DIESES «METALL-BUCH» VON PANTONE STELLT NEUE METALLISCHE DRUCKFARBEN UND EINZIGARTIGE DRUCKTECHNIKEN VOR. ES IST SPIRALGEBUNDEN UND STECKT IN EINEM SCHUTZUM-SCHLAG. DER VIELSAGENDE TITEL: «WIE ROMANZEN IHREN GLANZ BEHALTEN.» (USA)

● 253 ALS BEILAGEN IN FACHZEITSCHRIFTEN KONZI-PIERTE PROSPEKTE, MIT DENEN DIE QUALITÄT DES IKONO-PAPIERS DEMONSTRIERT WERDEN SOLL. DAS SPEZIELLE MUSTERBUCH MIT EINEM MOTIV DER ZANDERS POSTER EDITION WURDE FÜR DIE DRUPA ANGEFERTIGT. (GER)

▲ 245-252 «POUR QUE LES ROMANCES NE PERDENT PAS DE LEUR LUSTRE»: CE PETIT LIVRE À RELIURE SPIRALE PRÉSENTE LES NOUVELLES COULEURS MÉTALLIQUES PANTONE ET DES TECHNIQUES D'IM-PRESSION SPÉCIALES. IL EST RECOUVERT D'UNE JAQUETTE. (USA)

▲ 253 CES PROSPECTUS INSÉRÉS DANS DES REVUES PROFESSIONNELLES DÉMONTRENT LA QUALITÉ DU PAPIER «IKONO» DE ZANDERS. LE NUANCIER RE-PREND UN MOTIF DE LA SÉRIE D'AFFICHES ZAN-DERS. IL A ÉTÉ RÉALISÉ POUR UNE FOIRE COMMER-CIALE, LA DRUPA'90. (GER)

ART DIRECTOR:
DREW CRONENWETT
DESIGNER:
DREW CRONENWETT
PHOTOGRAPHER:
GREG GLASS
AGENCY:
GRAPHICA, INC.
CLIENT:
DAYTON CONTEMPO-
RARY DANCE
COMPANY
■ 254

ART DIRECTOR:
MICHAEL PATRICK
CRONAN
DESIGNER:
MICHAEL PATRICK
CRONAN
PHOTOGRAPHERS:
MICHAEL CRONAN
NEIL HOFFMAN
TERRY LORANT
JOEL PULIATTI
AGENCY:
CRONAN DESIGN
CLIENT:
CALIFORNIA
COLLEGE OF ARTS
AND CRAFTS
▶■ 256-262

In the fall of 1824, three dusty youths on horseback clattered into Lexington looking for Robert Hamilton Bishop, vice-president of a small Kentucky college. Bishop welcomed them but said he would not be there much longer. "I am going over the river," he explained, "to establish a college in the woods of Ohio." . . .

The Campaign for Miami University

ART DIRECTORS:
FRANK ANELLO
ANN LEPLY
COPYWRITER:
LIZANN HILLS
AGENCY:
LIPMAN HEARNE
CLIENT:
MIAMI UNIVERSITY
■ 255

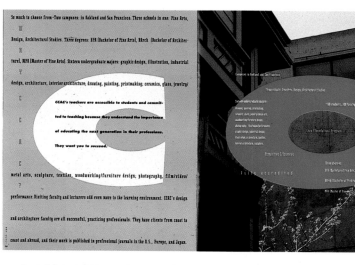

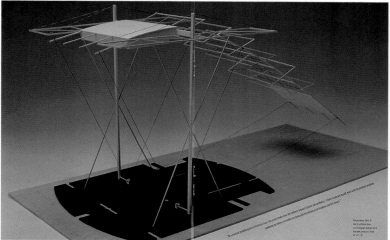

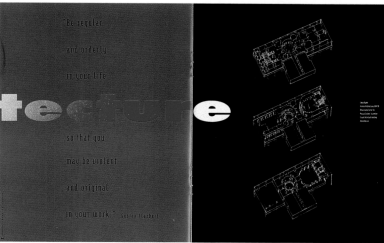

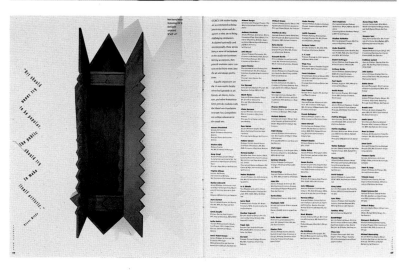

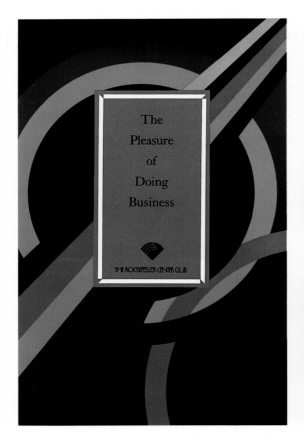

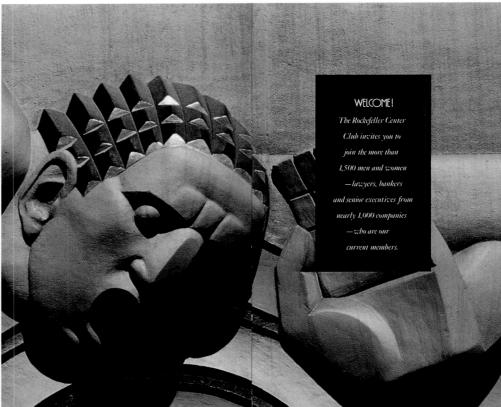

ART DIRECTOR:
MILTON GLASER
DESIGNERS:
MILTON GLASER
CHI-MING KAN
SUZANNE ZUMPANO
ARTIST:
MILTON GLASER
STYLIST:
MILTON GLASER
COPYWRITER:
IRENA CHALMERS
INC.
AGENCY:
MILTON GLASER, INC.
CLIENT:
THE ROCKEFELLER
CENTER CLUB
■ 263, 264

ART DIRECTOR:
FRANZ HOCHWARTER
DESIGNER:
SYLVIA DANZINGER
PHOTOGRAPHER:
BENE ARCHIV
(PAUSCH)
AGENCY:
DEMNER & MERLICEK
CLIENT:
BENE BÜROMÖBEL
▶■ 265

■ 263, 264 A SMALL BROCHURE DESIGNED LIKE A PRECIOUS PAPERBACK BOOK TO ENCOURAGE PEOPLE TO JOIN THE ROCKEFELLER CLUB. THE FIRST SPREAD SHOWS A DETAIL OF THE BUILDING. (USA)

■ 265 INVITATION ON THE OCCASION OF THE 200TH ANNIVERSARY OF BENE, A FURNITURE MANUFACTURER. SHOWN IS THE NEW ADMINISTRATIVE BUILDING, DESIGNED BY LAURIDS ORTNER. (AUT)

● 263, 264 EINE KLEINE BROSCHÜRE, WIE EIN WERTVOLLES TASCHENBUCH GESTALTET, WIRBT FÜR DEN ROCKEFELLER CLUB. DIE ERSTE DOPPELSEITE ZEIGT EIN DETAIL DES GEBÄUDES. (USA)

● 265 EINLADUNG AUS ANLASS DES 200JÄHRIGEN BESTEHENS VON BENE, EINEM MÖBELHERSTELLER. GEZEIGT IST DAS NEUE VERWALTUNGSGEBÄUDE, ENTWORFEN VON LAURIDS ORTNER. (AUT)

▲ 263, 264 CETTE BROCHURE CONÇUE COMME UN PETIT LIVRE LUXUEUX INVITE À DEVENIR MEMBRE DU ROCKEFELLER CLUB. LA PREMIÈRE DOUBLE PAGE MONTRE UN DÉTAIL DU BÂTIMENT. (USA)

▲ 265 COUVERTURE D'UNE INVITATION POUR LE 200E ANNIVERSAIRE DU FABRICANT DE MEUBLES BENE. ON Y VOIT LE NOUVEAU SIÈGE ADMINISTRATIF DE LA FIRME, DESSINÉ PAR LAURIDS ORTNER. (AUT)

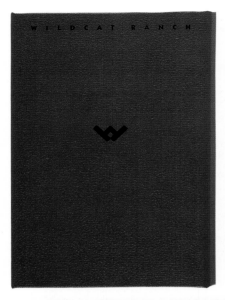

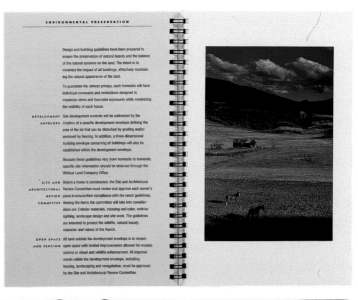

■ 266-269 THE RANCH AND FIELD GUIDE BROCHURES FOR WILDCAT RANCH (AN EXCLUSIVE RESIDENTIAL DEVELOPMENT NEAR ASPEN, COLORADO) COME IN A LINEN-LINED FOLDER. THEY INFORM ON FLORA AND FAUNA IN THIS AREA WHICH IS A WILDLIFE RESERVE OFFERING A SPECIAL QUALITY OF LIVING. (USA)

■ 270-274 PROMOTION FOR THE FIRST MARKET TOWER AT 525 MARKET STREET IN THE HEART OF SAN FRANCISCO'S FINANCIAL DISTRICT. THE SMALL FOLDER INFORMS ABOUT A NEW TENANT OF AN ENTIRE FLOOR, THE LARGE BROCHURE PRESENTS THE BUILDING. (USA)

● 266-269 ZWEI SPIRALGEBUNDENE BROSCHÜREN IN EINER KUNSTLEDERMAPPE MIT LEINENFUTTER INFORMIEREN ÜBER DIE FLORA UND FAUNA DER WILDCAT RANCH, EINEM NATURSCHUTZGEBIET IN DER NÄHE VON ASPEN. ES WIRD GLEICHZEITIG EIN EXKLUSIVES WOHNGEBIET ANGEBOTEN. (USA)

● 270-274 WERBUNG FÜR EINEN NEUEN WOLKEN-KRATZER AN DER 525 MARKET STREET IM HERZEN DES FINANZVIERTELS VON SAN FRANCISCO. DER KLEINE PROSPEKT INFORMIERT ÜBER DEN NEUEN MIETER EINES GANZEN STOCKWERKS, DER GRÖSSE-RE ZEIGT DAS GEBÄUDE. (USA)

▲ 266-269 DEUX BROCHURES SUR LA FLORE ET LA FAUNE DE WILDCAT RANCH, UNE RÉSERVE SITUÉE PRÈS D'ASPEN, DANS LE COLORADO, SONT PRÉSEN-TÉES DANS UNE CHEMISE À RABAT CARTONNÉE, RELIÉE CUIR ET TOILE. CE LIEU OFFRE ÉGALEMENT DES ZONES RÉSIDENTIELLES. (USA)

▲ 270-274 INVITATION À UNE MANIFESTATION CULTURELLE ET BROCHURE PRÉSENTANT LA FIRST MARKET TOWER, UNE TOUR COMMERCIALE SITUÉE DANS LE CENTRE DU QUARTIER FINANCIER DE SAN FRANCISCO. LE CHIFFRE 525 CORRESPOND AU NUMÉRO DE LA RUE. (USA)

ART DIRECTORS:

CHRIS HILL

SEAN PATRICK

DESIGNERS:

DOUG ALEXANDER

CHRIS HILL

LAURA MENEGAZ

PHOTOGRAPHERS:

K.D. MCGRAW

ROBERT MILLMAN

COPYWRITER:

SEAN PATRICK

AGENCY:

THE IMPACT GROUP

AGENCY

CLIENT:

WILDCAT LAND CO.

◄■ 266-269

ART DIRECTOR:

BILL CAHAN

DESIGNER:

TALIN GUREGHIAN

PHOTOGRAPHER:

DAVID PETERSON

AGENCY:

CAHAN & ASSOC.

CLIENT:

TISHMAN SPEYER

PROPERTIES

■ 270-274

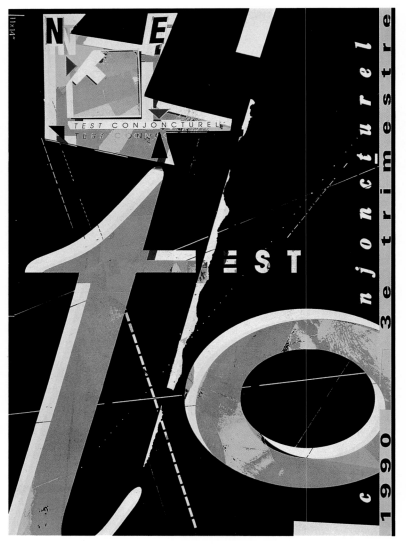

ART DIRECTOR:
ERIC SCHNEIDER
DESIGNER:
YVES ROTACH
AGENCY:
AGENCE SCHNEIDER
CLIENT:
CHAMBRE NEU-
CHATELOISE DU
COMMERCE ET
DE L' INDUSTRIE
■ 275

ART DIRECTOR:
BOB BURNS
DESIGNER:
BOB BURNS
ARTIST:
MICHAEL CRUMPTON
COPYWRITERS:
RENÉ DELBAR
NORBERT FLORENDO
ANN ROBINSON
AGENCY:
BURNS, CONNACHER
& WALDRON
CLIENT:
AGFA CORPORATION
■ 276

ART DIRECTOR:
BOB MANLEY
DESIGNERS:
BRENT CROXTON
GARY KOEPKE
PHOTOGRAPHER:
STEVE MARSEL
AGENCY:
ALTMAN & MANLEY
CLIENT:
AGFA CORPORATION
▶■ 277-282

■ 275 COVER OF A PUBLICATION CONCERNED WITH AN EXAMINATION OF ECONOMIC TRENDS IN SWITZERLAND. IT IS PUBLISHED BY THE CHAMBER OF COMMERCE OF NEUCHÂTEL. (USA)

■ 276 THIS SMALL-FORMAT BOOKLET PUBLISHED BY AGFA COMPUGRAPHIC IS CONCERNED WITH THE DEVELOPMENTS OF TYPOGRAPHIC SYSTEMS TECHNOLOGY. (USA)

■ 277-282 THIS BROCHURE PRESENTS THE AGFA POSTSCRIPT TYPE COLLECTION. IT STARTS WITH AN A ON THE COVER AND ENDS WITH AN X ON THE LAST SPREAD. ITS MOTTO IS THAT ALL LETTERS ARE DERIVED FROM ORGANIC SHAPES. (USA)

● 275 UMSCHLAG EINER PUBLIKATION DER HANDELS-KAMMER DES SCHWEIZER KANTONS NEUENBURG ÜBER DIE KONJUNKTURENTWICKLUNG IN DER SCHWEIZ, EINE STUDIE DER ETH ZÜRICH. (SWI)

● 276 MIT DIESER KLEINFORMATIGEN BROSCHÜRE INFORMIERT AGFA COMPUGRAPHIC ÜBER DIE TECH-NOLOGISCHE ENTWICKLUNG AUF DEM GEBIET DER COMPUTERSCHRIFTEN. (USA)

● 277-282 DIESE GROSSFORMATIGE BROSCHÜRE BEGINNT MIT EINEM A AUF DEM UMSCHLAG UND ENDET MIT EINEM X AUF DER LETZTEN DOPPEL-SEITE. SIE PRÄSENTIERT DIE POSTSCRIPT-COMPU-TERSCHRIFTEN VON AGFA. (USA)

▲ 275 COUVERTURE D'UNE PUBLICATION DE LA CHAMBRE DE COMMERCE NEUCHÂTELOISE. ELLE CONTIENT LE RÉSULTAT D'UNE ENQUÊTE SUR LA CROISSANCE DE L'ÉCONOMIE SUISSE. (SWI)

▲ 276 DANS CETTE BROCHURE DE PETIT FORMAT, AGFA COMPUGRAPHIC DONNE UNE INFORMATION SUR LES NOUVEAUTÉS TECHNOLOGIQUES DANS LE SECTEUR DU TRAITEMENT DE TEXTE. (USA)

▲ 277-282 CETTE BROCHURE GRAND FORMAT D'AGFA COMMENCE PAR UN «A» EN COUVERTURE ET SE TERMINE PAR UN «X» SUR LA DERNIÈRE DOUBLE PAGE. ELLE PRÉSENTE LE CATALOGUE DES CARACTÈRES INFORMATISÉS DISPONIBLES. (USA)

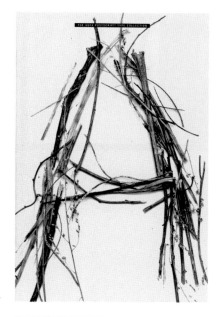

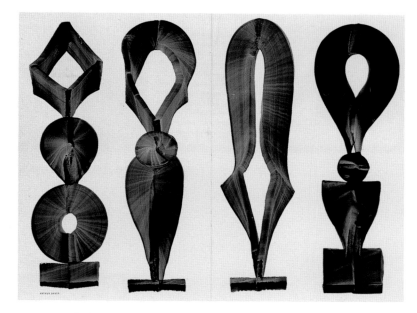

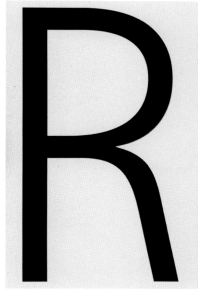

ROTIS

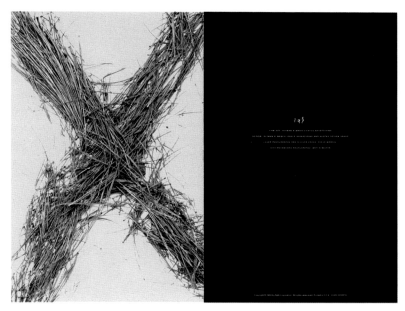

ART DIRECTOR:

TOM LEWIS

ARTIST:

DENNIS GILLASPY

AGENCY:

TOM LEWIS, INC.

CLIENT:

AIGA SAN DIEGO

▶■ 284

ART DIRECTORS:

DIDI KATONA

JOHN PYLYPCZAK

DESIGNERS:

SCOTT CHRISTIE

JOHN PYLYPCZAK

PHOTOGRAPHER:

KAREN LEVY

STUDIO:

CONCRETE DESIGN

COMMUNICATIONS

CLIENT:

AREA

▲▶■ 283, 285

■ 283, 285 "TO THE AGE ITS ART, TO THE ART ITS FREEDOM"—THIS MOTTO OF THE VIENNA SECESSION IS THE LEADING THEME OF THIS LEPORELLO FOLDER AND THE UNFOLDED POSTER INTRODUCING THE "SECESSION" FURNITURE LINE. (CAN)

■ 284 COVER OF A CATALOG FOR AN EXHIBITION OF POSTER ART IN THE SOVIET UNION: "A WINDOW INTO SOVIET LIFE." (USA)

● 283, 285 «DER ZEIT IHRE KUNST, DER KUNST IHRE FREIHEIT», DAS MOTTO DER WIENER SEZESSION IST DAS LEITMOTIV DIESES LEPORELLO-PROSPEKTS UND DES PLAKATES FÜR DIE EINFÜHRUNG DER NEUEN MÖBELLINIE «SECESSION». (CAN)

● 284 UMSCHLAG EINES KATALOG FÜR EINE AUS-STELLUNG SOWJETISCHER PLAKATE IN DEN USA: «EIN FENSTER ZUR SOWJETUNION.» (USA)

▲ 283, 285 «À CHAQUE ÂGE SON ART, À L'ART LA LIBERTÉ»: CE LEITMOTIV DE LA SÉCESSION VIEN-NOISE EST LE THÈME DE CE DÉPLIANT EN ACCOR-DÉON ET DE L'AFFICHE POUR LE LANCEMENT DE LA LIGNE DE MEUBLES «SÉCESSION». (CAN)

▲ 284 COUVERTURE DU CATALOGUE D'UNE EXPOSI-TION D'AFFICHES SOVIÉTIQUES AUX USA: «FENÊTRE OUVERTE SUR L'UNION SOVIÉTIQUE». (USA)

SECE SSION LINE

"THERE IS NO PAST TO LONG FOR THERE IS ONLY AN ETERNAL NEWNESS SHAPED BY ELEMENTS EXTENDED FROM THE PAST AND GENUINE LONGING MUST ALWAYS BE PRODUCTIVE CREATE SOMETHING NEW AND BETTER."
GOETHE 1749-1832

THE MOTTO OF THE VIENNA SECESSION 1889

"DER ZEIT IHRE KUNST DER KUNST IHRE FREIHEIT... TO THE AGE ITS ART TO THE ART ITS FREEDOM"

"ALL MODERN CREATIONS MUST CORRESPOND TO THE NEW MATERIALS AND DEMANDS OF THE PRESENT IF THEY ARE TO SUIT MODERN MAN." OTTO WAGNER 1841-1918

WIES NERH AGER

THE SECESSION LINE DESIGNED BY ADOLF KRISCHANITZ MANUFACTURED IN AUSTRIA BY WIESNER HAGER AVAILABLE AT AREA 334 KING ST. EAST TORONTO ONTARIO CANADA M5A 1K8 TELEPHONE 416·367·5850

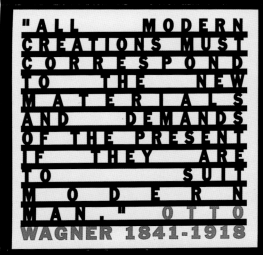

ART DIRECTOR:
TAKU SATOH
DESIGNER:
TAKU SATOH
PHOTOGRAPHER:
MEGUMU WADA
CLIENT:
TAKU SATOH DESIGN
OFFICE CO. LTD.
■ 286-297

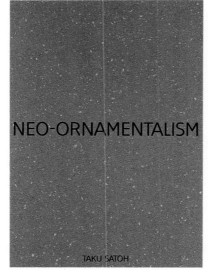

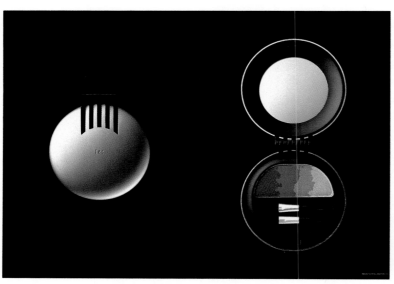

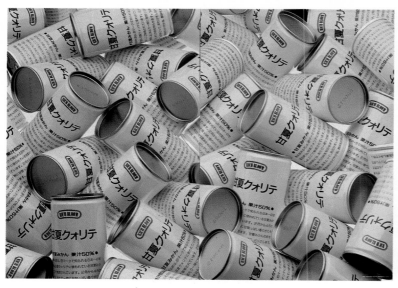

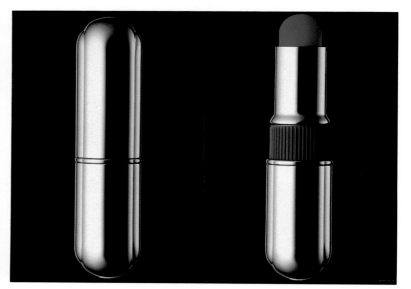

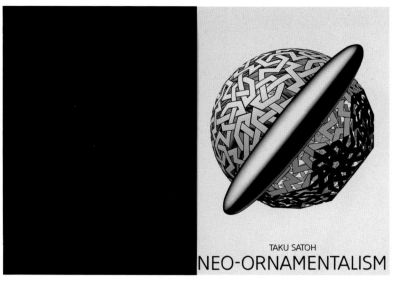

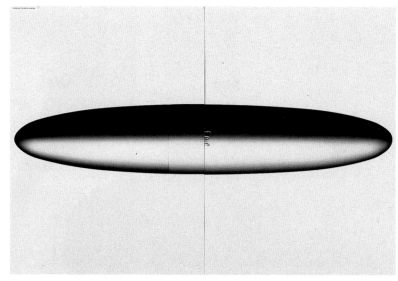

TAKU SATOH
NEO-ORNAMENTALISM

■ 286-297 FROM A PROMOTIONAL BROCHURE OF THE TAKU SATOH DESIGN OFFICE. OPPOSITE PAGE: THE COVER AND THREE SPREADS WITH EXAMPLES OF THE FEC COSMETICS LINE FOR MAX FACTOR; CANS FOR A CHINESE CITRUS JUICE; ROUGE FOR KANEBO; THIS PAGE: THE TITLE SPREAD; LIPSTICK FOR MAX FACTOR; BOXES FOR NITTOH TEABAGS; FRONT AND BACK OF A COFFEE TIN; A COMPUTER-GENERATED SPHERIC DESIGN CALLED T.S. COSMOS. (JPN)

● 286-297 AUS EINER WERBEBROSCHÜRE DES TAKU SATOH DESIGN OFFICE. GEGENÜBER V.L.N.R. UND V.O.N.U.: UMSCHLAG UND DREI DOPPELSEITEN MIT KOSMETIKPRODUKTEN FÜR MAX FACTOR; DOSEN FÜR DEN SAFT EINER CHINESISCHEN ZITRUSFRUCHT; LIPPENSTIFT FÜR KANEBO; DIESE SEITE: DIE TITEL-SEITE, LIPPENSTIFT FÜR MAX FACTOR; VERPACKUNG FÜR TEEBEUTEL, KAFFEEDOSE, «SPHÄRISCHES» (COMPUTER)-DESIGN. (JPN)

▲ 286-297 D'UNE BROCHURE DU STUDIO DE DESIGN TAKU SATOH. CI-CONTRE, DE G.À DR. ET DE HAUT EN BAS: COUVERTURE ET TROIS DOUBLES PAGES AVEC PRODUITS COSMÉTIQUES MAX FACTOR; BOÎTES D'UN JUS DE FRUIT FAIT À PARTIR D'UNE SORTE DE CITRON JAPONAIS; ROUGE À LÈVRES KANEBO. SUR CETTE PAGE: ROUGE À LÈVRES MAX FACTOR; POUR DU THÉ JAPONAIS; BOÎTE DE CAFÉ; «COSMOS», DESIGN SPHÉRIQUE CRÉÉ SUR ORDINATEUR. (JPN)

ART DIRECTOR:
MICHAEL VANDERBYL
DESIGNER:
MICHAEL VANDERBYL
AGENCY:
VANDERBYL DESIGN
CLIENT:
OAKLAND MUSEUM
■ 298

ART DIRECTOR:
WOODY PIRTLE
DESIGNER:
WOODY PIRTLE
AGENCY:
PENTAGRAM DESIGN
▼■ 299-302

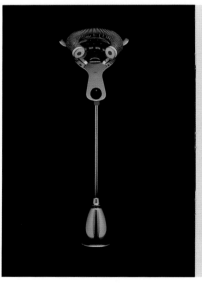

∧ Memphis

< Bowzer

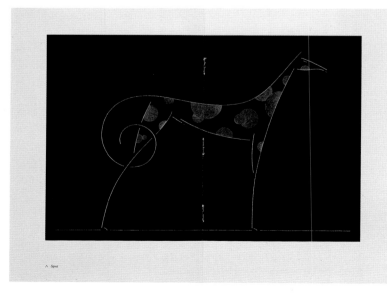

∧ Spot

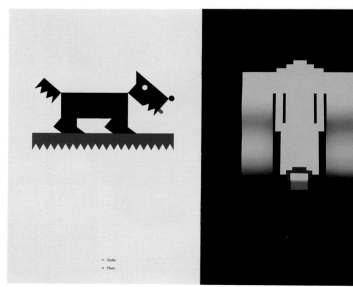

∧ Spike

> Pluto

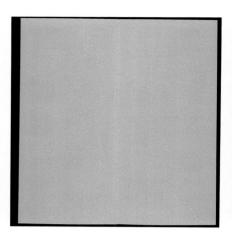

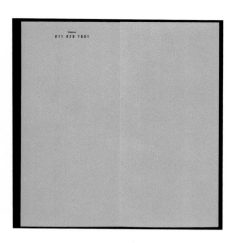

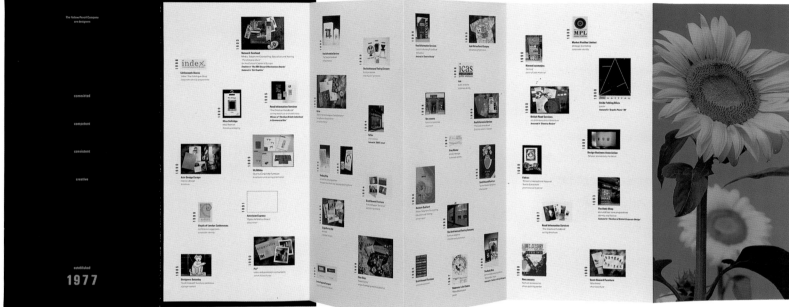

ART DIRECTOR:
ANDY EWAN
DESIGNERS:
ANDY EWAN
NICOLA PENNY
CLIENT:
THE YELLOW PENCIL
COMPANY
■ 303-307

■ 298 COVER OF A BROCHURE AS PART OF THE CORPORATE IDENTITY DESIGN SYSTEM FOR THE OAKLAND MUSEUM. (USA)

■ 299-302 "K 9—A TRIBUTE TO MAN'S BEST FRIEND" IS A SELF-PROMOTIONAL BROCHURE FOR PENTAGRAM DESIGN. SHOWN ARE THE COVER AND THE FIRST PAGE WITH DOG ADVERTISEMENTS AS WELL AS SPREADS PRESENTING "BOOZER" (BAR IMPLEMENTS); "MEMPHIS" (COLORED PENCIL ON PAPER); "SPOT" (COLORED PENCIL ON PAPER); "SPIKE" (COLORED PAPER) AND "PLUTO" (CUT PAPER). (USA)

■ 303-307 A PROMOTIONAL PIECE FOR THE YELLOW PENCIL DESIGN COMPANY. SHOWN ARE THE COVER, THE OPENED FOLDER, THE YELLOW BACK OF THE LEPORELLO AND THE FRONT OF THE LEPORELLO UNFOLDED SHOWING EXAMPLES OF THE COMPANY'S WORK. (USA)

● 298 UMSCHLAG EINER BROSCHÜRE ALS TEIL EINES CORPORATE IDENTITY-DESIGNSYSTEMS FÜR DAS OAKLAND MUSEUM. (USA)

● 299-302 «K 9 – EIN TRIBUT AN DEN BESTEN FREUND DES MENSCHEN.» EIGENWERBUNG DER DESIGNFIRMA PENTAGRAM. HIER DER UMSCHLAG MIT DER ERSTEN SEITE, DIE HUNDEINSERATE ENTHÄLT, SOWIE DOPPELSEITEN MIT «BOOZER» (METALL); MEMPHIS (FARBSTIFT AUF PAPIER); «SPOT» (FARBSTIFT AUF PAPIER); «SPIKE» (FARBIGES PAPIER); «PLUTO» (SCHERENSCHNITT). (USA)

● 303-307 EIGENWERBUNG DES DESIGNSTUDIOS THE YELLOW PENCIL COMPANY. GEZEIGT SIND DER UMSCHLAG, TEILE DER GELBEN RÜCKSEITE DES LEPORELLOS, DER GEÖFFNETE UMSCHLAG MIT DER ERSTEN SEITE DES LEPORELLOS UND EINE GESAMTANSICHT. (USA)

▲ 298 COUVERTURE D'UNE BROCHURE FAISANT PARTIE DU SYSTÈME D'IDENTITÉ CORPORATE DU MUSÉE D'OAKLAND. (USA)

▲ 299-302 «K 9 – UN TRIBUT AU MEILLEUR AMI DE L'HOMME»: BROCHURE AUTOPROMOTIONNELLE DE PENTAGRAM. ON VOIT ICI LA COUVERTURE AVEC LA PREMIÈRE PAGE, REMPLIE DE PETITES ANNONCES POUR CHIENS, ET QUELQUES DOUBLES PAGES: «BOOZER» (MÉTAL), «MEMPHIS» ET «SPOT» (CRAYONS DE COULEURS SUR PAPIER), «SPIKE» (PAPIER COLORÉ), «PLUTO» (DÉCOUPAGE). (USA)

▲ 303-307 AUTOPROMOTION DU STUDIO DE DESIGN THE YELLOW PENCIL COMPANY. ON VOIT ICI LA COUVERTURE, LE VERSO TOUT JAUNE DU DÉPLIANT EN ACCORDÉON, LA COUVERTURE OUVERTE AVEC LA PREMIÈRE PAGE DU DÉPLIANT ET UNE VUE D'ENSEMBLE DU DÉPLIANT OUVERT. (USA)

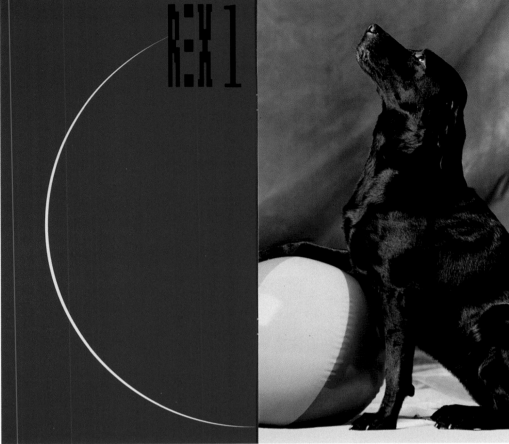

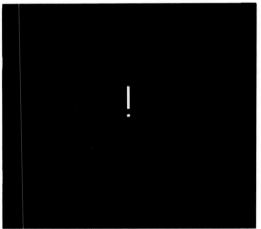

ART DIRECTORS:
LISA ASHWORTH
JOEL FULLER
DESIGNER:
LISA ASHWORTH
PHOTOGRAPHER:
MICHAEL DAKOTA
COPYWRITER:
FRANK CUNNINGHAM
STYLISTS:
LISA ASHWORTH
IRENE DAKOTA
AGENCY:
PINKHAUS
CLIENT:
REX THREE
■ 308, 309

ART DIRECTOR:
ROBERT APPLETON
DESIGNER:
ROBERT APPLETON
AGENCY:
APPLETON DESIGN
CLIENT:
AGFA CORPORATION
◄■ 310

■ 308, 309 "REX THREE, A DESIGNER'S BEST FRIEND". COVER AND SPREAD FROM A BROCHURE TO ANNOUNCE A NEW CORPORATE LOGO AND A NEW LOCATION OF A PRINTING COMPANY. (USA)

■ 310 COVER OF A BROCHURE PRESENTING THREE DIFFERENT PHOTOGRAPHERS WHO ALL WORK WITH AGFA FILM MATERIAL. (USA)

■ 311-316 THIS BOOK WAS DEVELOPED TO ANNOUNCE THE MERGER OF THE MICHAEL PETERS GROUP AND THE DUFFY GROUP AND TO PROMOTE THE "NEW" POSSIBILITIES IN THEIR DESIGN ABILITIES TO KEY CLIENTS IN THE US AND UK. THE BOOK OPENS FROM TWO SIDES AND IS DIVIDED IN TWO PARTS. ONE SHOWS AMERICA AS SEEN THROUGH THE EYES OF THE BRITISH MICHAEL PETERS GROUP, THE OTHER PRESENTS BRITAIN AS SEEN BY THE AMERICAN DUFFY GROUP. (GBR/USA)

● 308, 309 «REX THREE, DER BESTE FREUND DES DESIGNERS.» MIT DIESER BROSCHÜRE WIRD ÜBER EIN NEUES LOGO UND DIE NEUE ADRESSE EINES DRUCKERS INFORMIERT. (USA)

● 310 UMSCHLAG EINER BROSCHÜRE, IN DER DREI PHOTOGRAPHEN VORGESTELLT WERDEN, DIE MIT AGFA-FILMEN PHOTOGRAPHIEREN. (USA)

● 311-316 DIESES BUCH SOLL ÜBER DEN ZUSAM-MENSCHLUSS DER DESIGN-FIRMEN MICHAEL PETERS GROUP UND DER DUFFY GROUP INFORMIEREN UND DEN KUNDEN DAS NEUE DESIGN-POTENTIAL DEMON-STRIEREN. DAS BUCH BESTEHT AUS ZWEI TEILEN UND LÄSST SICH VON ZWEI SEITEN ÖFFNEN. EIN TEIL ZEIGT AMERIKA, MIT DEN AUGEN DER BRITI-SCHEN MICHAEL PETERS GROUP GESEHEN, DER ANDERE GROSSBRITANNIEN, WIE ES DIE AMERI-KANISCHE DUFFY GROUP SIEHT. (GBR/USA)

▲ 308, 309 «REX THREE, LE MEILLEUR AMI DU DESIGNER»: COUVERTURE ET DOUBLE PAGE D'UNE BROCHURE INFORMANT DU NOUVEAU LOGO ET DE LA NOUVELLE ADRESSE D'UNE IMPRIMERIE. (USA)

▲ 310 COUVERTURE D'UNE BROCHURE DANS LAQUELLE SONT PRÉSENTÉS TROIS PHOTOGRAPHES QUI TRAVAILLENT SUR DES PELLICULES AGFA. (USA)

▲ 311-316 CE LIVRE ANNONCE LA FUSION DES STUDIOS DE DESIGN MICHAEL PETERS GROUP ET DUFFY DESIGN ET PRÉSENTE AUX CLIENTS LES POSSIBILITÉS CRÉATRICES DE LA NOUVELLE FIRME. LE LIVRE COMPORTE DEUX PARTIES ET PEUT S'OUVRIR DE DEUX CÔTÉS. DANS L'UNE, L'AMÉRIQUE EST VUE AU TRAVERS DES YEUX DU STUDIO ANGLAIS MICHAEL PETERS GROUP; DANS L'AUTRE, LA GRANDE-BRETAGNE EST INTERPRÉTÉE PAR LE STUDIO AMÉRICAIN DUFFY DESIGN. (GBR/USA)

ART DIRECTORS:

THE DUFFY DESIGN
GROUP/
MICHAEL PETERS
GROUP

DESIGNERS:

JOE DUFFY

GARRICK HAMM

HALEY JOHNSON

GLENN TUTSSEL

SHARON WERNER

ARTISTS:

WARREN MAILL

JAMES MARSCH

ANDREW DAVIDSON

RICK KLOVSTAD

COPYWRITER:

CHUCK CARLSON

AGENCY:

THE DUFFY DESIGN
GROUP

CLIENTS:

THE DUFFY DESIGN
GROUP/MICHAEL
PETERS GROUP

■ 311-316

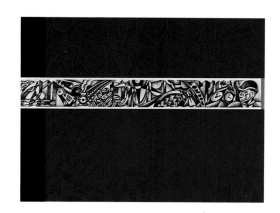

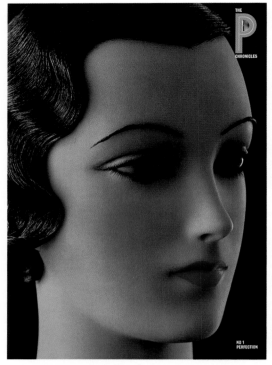

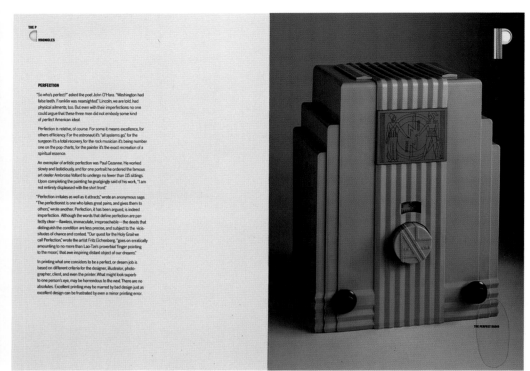

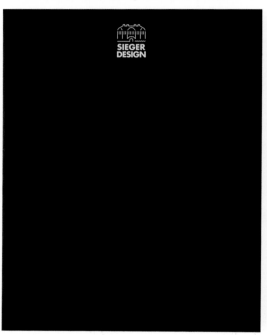

SCALA
BAGS AND SUITCASES 1989

BOLERO
TABLE LAMP FOR PEILL + PUTZLER 1989

■ 317-320 PERFECTION IS THE SUBJECT OF THIS PROMOTIONAL BROCHURE FOR THE PRINTING COMPANY IVY HILL CORPORATION. THE "PERFECT" MANNEQUINS, FEMALE AND MALE, ARE SHOWN ON THE FRONT AND THE BACK COVER. THE SPREADS PRESENT THE "PERFECT" RADIO AND THE "PERFECT" CAR AND MOTORCYCLE. THE BROCHURE IS TO DEMONSTRATE THE PRINTING QUALITY. (USA)

■ 321-324 THIS SELF-PROMOTIONAL PIECE FOR THE SIEGER DESIGN COMPANY CONSISTS OF A BLACK CARDBOARD SLIPCASE WITH A WHITE BOX, A BOOKLET AND POSTCARDS FEATURING THE DESIGNS OF THE COMPANY. SHOWN ARE A BAG, A TABLE LAMP, A DOOR HANDLE, AND A STANDARD LAMP. (GER)

● 317-320 PERFEKTION IST DAS THEMA DIESER EIGENWERBUNGSBROSCHÜRE EINER DRUCKEREI. VORDER- UND RÜCKSEITE ZEIGEN EIN WEIBLICHES UND EIN MÄNNLICHES GESICHT VON «PERFEKTEN» SCHAUFENSTERPUPPEN. AUF DEN ABGEBILDETEN DOPPELSEITEN DAS «PERFEKTE» RADIO UND DAS «PERFEKTE» AUTO UND MOTORRAD ALS BEISPIELE GUTER DRUCKQUALITÄT. (USA)

● 321-324 EIGENWERBUNG VON SIEGER DESIGN. DER SCHWARZE KARTONSCHUBER ENTHÄLT EINE WEISSE KARTONBOX MIT KLEINEM PROSPEKT UND KARTEN MIT DEN PRODUKTEN. GEZEIGT SIND EINE SCHULTERTASCHE, EINE TISCHLEUCHTE, EIN TÜRDRÜCKER UND EINE STANDLEUCHTE. (GER)

▲ 317-320 LA PERFECTION EST LE THÈME DE CETTE BROCHURE AUTOPROMOTIONNELLE D'UNE IMPRIMERIE. LES VISAGES DU MANNEQUIN «PARFAIT» SONT MONTRÉS EN COUVERTURE, AU RECTO LA FEMME, AU VERSO L'HOMME. LES DOUBLES PAGES MONTRENT ICI LA RADIO ET LA MOTO «PARFAITES». IL S'AGISSAIT DE DÉMONTRER LA QUALITÉ D'IMPRESSION DES IMAGES. (USA)

▲ 321-324 AUTOPROMOTION DE SIEGER DESIGN. L'ENVELOPPE DE CARTON NOIR RENFERME UNE BOÎTE BLANCHE AVEC UN PETIT PROSPECTUS ET LES CARTES PRÉSENTANT LES PRODUITS. ICI, UN SAC EN BANDOULIÈRE, UNE LAMPE DE TABLE, UNE POIGNÉE DE PORTE ET UNE LAMPE À PIED. (GER)

SO 8820
DOOR HANDLE FOR OGRO 1989

BIRD
STANDARD LAMP FOR GKS-LEUCHTEN 1989

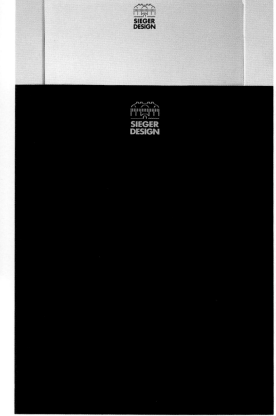

ART DIRECTOR:

SEYMOUR CHWAST

DESIGNER:

GREG SIMPSON

PHOTOGRAPHER:

ED SPIRO

COPYWRITER:

STEVE HELLER

AGENCY:

THE PUSHPIN GROUP

CLIENT:

IVY HILL CORP.

■ 317-320

ART DIRECTOR:

DIETER SIEGER

PHOTOGRAPHER:

ACA STUDIO

AGENCY:

SIEGER DESIGN

■ 321-324

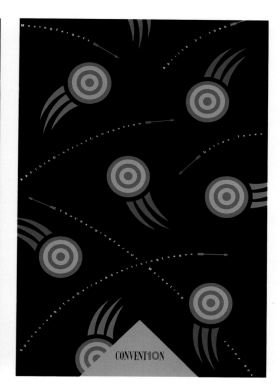

ART DIRECTOR:
MARK JOHNSON
DESIGNER:
MARK JOHNSON
COPYWRITER:
BILL MILLER
AGENCY:
FALLON MCELLIGOTT
CLIENT:
FALLON MCELLIGOTT
◄■ 325

ART DIRECTOR:
RICK EIBER
CLIENT:
RICK EIBER DESIGN
■ 326

ART DIRECTOR:
SCOTT PARAMSKI
DESIGNER:
SCOTT PARAMSKI
PHOTOGRAPHER:
TOM RYAN
AGENCY:
PETERSON & CO.
CLIENT:
AMERICAN SOCIETY
OF MAGAZINE
PHOTOGRAPHERS
■ 327

ART DIRECTOR:
JOHN SWIETER
DESIGNERS:
PAUL MUNSTERMAN
JOHN SWIETER
JIM VOGEL
AGENCY:
SWIETER DESIGN
CLIENT:
AMERICAN
ADVERTISING
FEDERATION
■ 328

■ 325 THE PURPOSE OF THIS BUSINESS MAILER FROM FALLON MCELLIGOTT TO ROLLERBLADE WAS TO WIN THEIR ADVERTISING ACCOUNT. THE BOX IS SHOWN CLOSED AND OPENED PRESENTING THE NEW ROLLERBLADE BOOT. (USA)

■ 326 COVER OF A SELF-PROMOTIONAL BROCHURE FOR RICK EIBER DESIGN = RED. (USA)

■ 327 COVER WITH CUT-OUTS FOR THE ASMP DIRECTORY OF PHOTOGRAPHERS. (USA)

■ 328 COVER OF A BROCHURE FOR THE TENTH CONVENTION OF THE AMERICAN ADVERTISING FEDERATION. THE MOTIF IS REPEATED ON ALL CONVENTION MATERIALS. (USA)

● 325 MIT DIESER WERBESENDUNG BIETET SICH FALLON MCELLIGOTT BEI ROLLERBLADE ALS GEEIGNETE WERBEAGENTUR FÜR DIE NEUEN ROLLSCHUHE AN. DIE BOX IST GESCHLOSSEN UND GEÖFFNET MIT DEM ROLLSCHUH GEZEIGT. (USA)

● 326 UMSCHLAG EINER EIGENWERBUNGSBROSCHÜRE FÜR RICK EIBER DESIGN, KURZ RED. (USA)

● 327 UMSCHLAG MIT AUSSTANZUNGEN FÜR EIN VERZEICHNIS DER ASMP-PHOTOGRAPHEN. (USA)

● 328 UMSCHLAG EINER BROSCHÜRE FÜR DIE 10. KONFERENZ DER AMERICAN ADVERTISING FEDERATION. DAS MOTIV WIRD AUF DEN GESAMTEN TAGUNGSUNTERLAGEN WIEDERHOLT. (USA)

▲ 325 FALLON MCELLIGOT SE PRÉSENTE À ROLLERBLADE COMME L'AGENCE IDÉALE POUR LES NOUVEAUX PATINS À ROULETTES EN ENVOYANT CE CADEAU PROMOTIONNEL PAR LA POSTE. ON VOIT ICI LA BOÎTE FERMÉE ET SON CONTENU. (USA)

▲ 326 COUVERTURE DE LA BROCHURE AUTOPROMOTIONNELLE DE RICK EIBER DESIGN, «R.E.D.». (USA)

▲ 327 COUVERTURE AVEC MOTIFS EN DÉCOUPE POUR UN ANNUAIRE DES PHOTOGRAPHES DE L'ASMP. (USA)

▲ 328 COUVERTURE D'UNE BROCHURE POUR LA 10E CONFÉRENCE DE L'AMERICAN ADVERTISING FEDERATION. LE MOTIF SE RÉPÈTE SUR TOUTE LA DOCUMENTATION DE CE CONGRÈS. (USA)

THE NEW FRONTIER

Salt Lake City's cultural heritage dates back more than 2,000 years when the first Native American Indians entered the Salt Lake Valley. They lived off the abundant land and etched the history of their survival on the canyon walls. The people who followed learned much from these early inhabitants, and found in Salt Lake City a virgin territory rich in resources and the promise of a better tomorrow. The ideal that inspired each passing generation was, and is, the frontier. Both a place and a philosophy, the frontier is an alluring blend of beauty and danger that shaped the lives of our ancestors and contributed in who we are today. Now, as the 20th century draws to a close, we stand on the edge of a new frontier—a new age in which anything and everything is possible. Our spirit is fresh, our outlook new. Our economy is strong and diverse,

our people young, highly educated and innovative. Our cultural and artistic achievements unparalleled in the region. Celebrating the Winter Games in Salt Lake City will help us open this New Frontier. The Winter Games will allow us to welcome the world to our city, to advance the Olympic Movement, to embrace its ideals and offer its spirit as a lasting legacy to our children. We have much to offer in return: an impressive natural setting, all the amenities of a modern city, and an enthusiastic community experienced at hosting international sporting events. Salt Lake City is a young city whose desire and preparedness to host the Winter Games is unsurpassed. United in the true spirit of the Olympics, we invite the people of the world to take the final step with us into the New Frontier.

LE NOUVEL OUEST

L'héritage culturel de Salt Lake City remonte à plus que 2 000 ans lorsque les autochtones américains sont entrés dans la vallée du Lac Salt. Ces indiens qui ont gravé leur histoire sur les roches des canyons, vivaient de l'abondance de la terre. À la recherche d'un meilleur lendemain, ceux qui les ont suivis ont beaucoup appris de ces peuples primitifs. Ils ont trouvé ici un territoire à la fois vierge et riche. L'idéal qui a inspiré les générations d'êtres si déjà c'est l'Ouest: à la fois un lieu et une philosophie, l'Ouest est ce mélange séduisant de beauté et de danger, qui a façonné la vie de nos ancêtres et qui a contribué à ce que nous sommes. À l'heure actuelle, alors que le 20ème siècle s'estompe, nous nous tenons au seuil d'une ère nouvelle, à l'aube d'un âge où tout est possible. Notre esprit a la fraîcheur des perspectives nouvelles, notre économie

est saine et diversifiée, notre peuple jeune et instruit. Nos réalisations artistiques et culturelles sont sans égal dans la région. Célébrer les Jeux d'Hiver Olympiques nous aidera à pénétrer ce Nouvel Ouest. Les Jeux d'Hiver nous conféreront l'honneur d'accueillir le monde et nous permettront de promouvoir le Mouvement Olympique, d'embrasser ses idéaux et de léguer un esprit à nos enfants. Nous avons beaucoup à offrir en échange : un cadre naturel impressionnant, les commodités d'une ville moderne, et une population enthousiaste, adepte à accueillir des épreuves inter-nationales. Salt Lake City, ville ardente, désire ardemment accueillir les Jeux d'Hiver et s'y prépare. Animés par le véritable Idéal Olympique, nous invitons les gens du monde entier à faire le premier pas avec vous vers le Nouvel Ouest.

SPEED SKATING
PATINAGE DE VITESSE

Centuries ago, when early skaters raced down frozen streams on skate blades made of bone, speed skating races were as fascinating to watch as they were to perform. The same is true today, and speed skating competitions at the Salt Lake Speed Skating Oval are sure to offer the same thrill and excitement to spectators at the Olympic Winter Games. The oval is conveniently located next to the Olympic Village, just a ten-minute drive from the center of the city. The facility, which is easily accessible, is adjacent to an Olympic-size ice rink. A new addition to the Olympic Winter program, short track speed skating has quickly earned a wide audience due to its fast-paced action and intricate strategies. Finals for short track speed skating will be held at the Salt Lake Sports Arena. The Salt Lake Speed Skating Oval will be the centerpiece of a plan to stimulate interest among children in this exhilarating sport, and will stand as a lasting legacy of Olympism long after the Winter Games are away.

Il y a bien des siècles, alors que les premiers patineurs dévalaient les rivières gelées, sur des patins fabriqués en os, les courses étaient aussi fascinantes pour les spectateurs que pour les participants. Il en va de même aujourd'hui, et les compétitions à l'Anneau de Patinage de Vitesse de Salt Lake City sont sûres d'offrir les mêmes émotions et passions à tout spectateur des Jeux Olympiques d'Hiver. La patinoire proposée est située près du Village Olympique, à dix minutes de conduite. Adjacente à un autre patinoire pour le patinage de vitesse sur piste courte, elle est aisément accessible. Une nouvelle addition au programme des Jeux d'Hiver, le patinage de vitesse sur piste courte a conquis une grande audience par son action rapide et ses stratégies compliquées. L'Arène de Patinage de Vitesse de Salt Lake City constituera le point focal d'un plan visant à stimuler l'intérêt des enfants dans ce sport discrétionnel, et perpétuera l'Héritage Olympique bien longtemps après la fin des Jeux d'Hiver.

SPEED SKATING
PATINAGE DE VITESSE

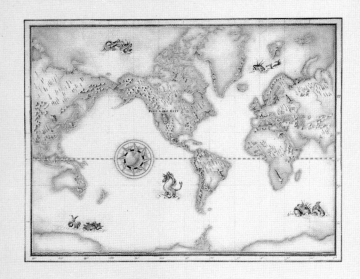

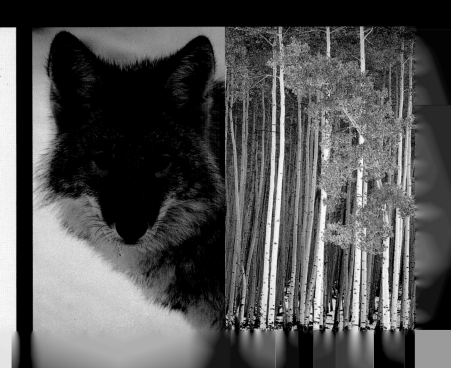

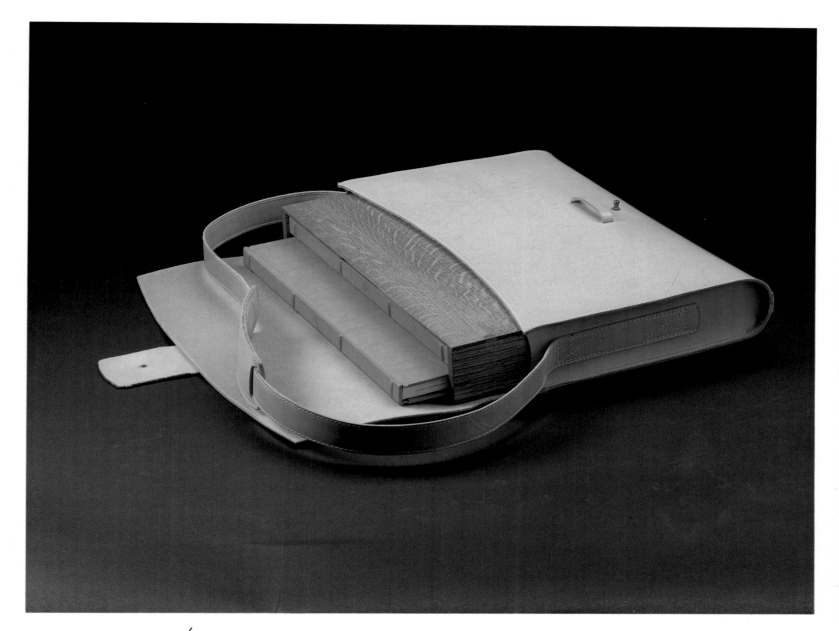

ART DIRECTOR:
ADRIAN PULFER
DESIGNERS:
ADRIAN PULFER
JEFF STREEPER
PHOTOGRAPHERS:
TOM TILL
NORMAN MAUSKOPF
KENT MILES
DAVID LEACH
JOHN P. GEORGE
JOHN TELFORD

ILLUSTRATORS:
MCRAY MAGLEBY
RICHARD HULL
COPYWRITER:
KEVIN RYAN
AGENCY:
PENNA, POWERS,
CUTTING & HAYNES
CLIENT:
SALT LAKE CITY
WINTER OLYMPIC
BID COMMITTEE
■ 329-335

■ 329-335 DOUBLE SPREADS FROM THE DOCUMENTS BELONGING TO SALT LAKE CITY'S APPLICATION TO HOST THE OLYMPIC WINTER GAMES IN 1998. THE TWO BOOKS ARE BOUND IN BUCKSKIN LEATHER AND COME IN AN OAK SLIPCASE WITH LEATHER SADDLE-BAG. THEY TOTAL ABOUT 280 PAGES AND HAVE OVER 110 PHOTOGRAPHS AND ILLUSTRATIONS. BOOK ONE IS THE ROMANCE BOOK, BOOK TWO THE TECHNICAL. THE 150 SETS TOOK SIX MONTHS TO COMPLETE AND THEY WERE DELIVERED TO THE INTERNATIONAL OLYMPIC COMMITTEE MEMBERS THROUGHOUT THE WORLD. (USA)

● 329-335 DOPPELSEITEN AUS DER DOKUMENTATION FÜR SALT LAKE CITYS BEWERBUNG ALS AUSTRA-GUNGSORT DER OLYMPISCHEN WINTERSPIELE 1998. ES HANDELT SICH UM ZWEI LEDERGEBUNDENE BÜCHER MIT EINEM SCHUBER AUS EICHENHOLZ UND EINER LEDERNEN SATTELTASCHE. DIE INSGESAMT 280 SEITEN ENTHALTEN 110 ILLUSTRATIONEN. BAND EINS BETRIFFT DIE EMOTIONALEN, BAND ZWEI DIE TECHNISCHEN ASPEKTE. DIE INSGESAMT 150 EXEM-PLARE, DEREN HERSTELLUNG SECHS MONATE DAUERTE, WURDEN AN DIE MITGLIEDER DES OLYM-PISCHEN KOMITEES VERTEILT. (USA)

▲ 329-335 DOUBLES PAGES DE LA DOCUMENTATION POUR LA CANDIDATURE DE SALT LAKE CITY AUX JEUX OLYMPIQUES D'HIVER 1998. DEUX LIVRES RELIÉS CUIR SONT PRÉSENTÉS DANS UN ÉTUI EN CHÊNE AVEC UNE SACOCHE EN CUIR. ILS COMPOR-TENT EN TOUT 280 PAGES ET 110 ILLUSTRATIONS. LE PREMIER VOLUME EST CONSACRÉ AUX ASPECTS ÉMOTIONNELS DE L'ENTREPRISE, LE DEUXIÈME AUX QUESTIONS TECHNIQUES. IL A FALLU SIX MOIS POUR PRODUIRE LES 150 EXEMPLAIRES QUI ONT ÉTÉ ENVOYÉS AUX MEMBRES DU COMITÉ INTERNATIONAL OLYMPIQUE DU MONDE ENTIER. (USA)

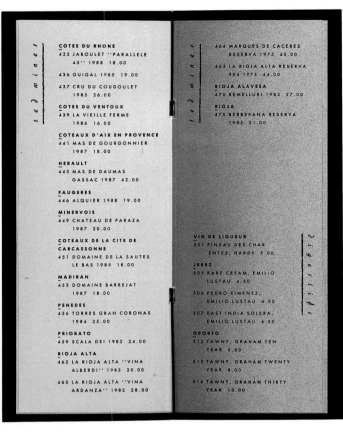

VIN BLANC · VIN · ROUGE · BOISSONS

ted wines		ted wines		ligeurs

COTES DU RHONE
435 JABOULET "PARALLELE
45'' 1988 18.00
436 GUIGAL 1985 19.00
437 CRU DU COUDOULET
1985 26.00
COTES DU VENTOUX
439 LA VIEILLE FERME
1986 16.00
COTEAUX D'AIX EN PROVENCE
441 MAS DE GOURGONNIER
1987 18.00
HERAULT
443 MAS DE DAUMAS
GASSAC 1987 42.00
FAUGERES
446 ALQUIER 1988 19.00
MINERVOIS
449 CHATEAU DE PARAZA
1987 20.00
COTEAUX DE LA CITE DE
CARCASSONNE
451 DOMAINE DE LA SAUTES
LE BAS 1988 18.00
MADIRAN
453 DOMAINE BARREJAT
1987 18.00
PENEDES
456 TORRES GRAN CORONAS
1984 25.00
PRIORATO
459 SCALA DEI 1982 24.00
RIOJA ALTA
462 LA RIOJA ALTA ''VINA
ALBERDI'' 1985 20.00
463 LA RIOJA ALTA ''VINA
ARDANZA'' 1982 28.00

464 MARQUES DE CACERES
RESERVA 1975 40.00
465 LA RIOJA ALTA RESERVA
904 1975 44.00
RIOJA ALAVESA
470 REMELLURI 1983 27.00
RIOJA
475 BERBERANA RESERVA
1985 21.00

VIN DE LIQUEUR
501 PINEAU DES CHAR
ENTES, HARDY 5.00
JEREZ
505 RARE CREAM, EMILIO
LUSTAU 4.50
506 PEDRO XIMENEZ,
EMILIO LUSTAU 4.50
507 EAST INDIA SOLERA,
EMILIO LUSTAU 4.50
OPORTO
512 TAWNY, GRAHAM TEN
YEAR 5.00
513 TAWNY, GRAHAM TWENTY
YEAR 8.00
514 TAWNY, GRAHAM THIRTY
YEAR 10.00

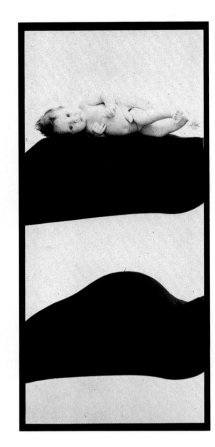

ART DIRECTOR:
SHARON WERNER
DESIGNER:
SHARON WERNER
AGENCY:
THE DUFFY DESIGN
GROUP
CLIENT:
D'AMICO &
PARTNERS
▲■ 336, 337

ART DIRECTOR:
SEAN BUTCHER
DESIGNER:
SEAN BUTCHER
AGENCY:
SEAN BUTCHER
■ 339

DESIGNER:
PETER BLANK
PHOTOGRAPHER:
BETSY CAMERON
AGENCY:
ALFSTAD BLANK
GROUP
▲■ 338

CREATIVE DIRECTORS:
JEFF LARAMORE
DAVID YOUNG
ART DIRECTOR:
MARK BRADLEY
COPYWRITER:
DAVID YOUNG
AGENCY:
YOUNG & LARAMORE
CLIENT:
WILHELM
CONSTRUCTION
■ 340

■ 336, 337 MENU FOR AZUR, AN UP-SCALE FRENCH RESTAURANT IN MINNEAPOLIS. IT WAS TO BE REFLECTIVE OF THE INTERIORS AND THE INNOVATIVE APPROACH TO FOOD PREPARATION. THE IRREGULAR CUT-OUTS ON THE COVER LOOK HAND-MADE. (USA)

■ 338 WITH THIS PHOTOGRAPH OF "BEFORE" AND "AFTER" A PHOTOGRAPHER ANNOUNCES THE BIRTH OF HER DAUGHTER. (USA)

■ 339 SELF-PROMOTION OF THE DESIGNER SEAN BUTCHER. IT IS SHOWN OPENED AND IN ITS ENVELOPE. COPY AND PROMOTION PIECE ARE A HUMOROUS ALLUSION TO THE FAMILY NAME. (GBR)

■ 340 DESIGN AND MATERIALS OF THIS THREE-DIMENSIONAL INVITATION BY A CONSTRUCTION COMPANY ARE REFLECTIVE OF THE ARCHITECTURE OF A RECENTLY FINISHED MUSEUM. (USA)

● 336, 337 MENU-KARTE FÜR EIN FRANZÖSISCHES RESTAURANT IN MINNEAPOLIS. DIE KARTE SOLLTE DER INNENAUSSTATTUNG UND DER INNOVATIVEN KÜCHE ENTSPRECHEN. DIE AUSSTANZUNGEN AUF DEM UMSCHLAG WIRKEN HANDGEMACHT. (USA)

● 338 MIT DIESER DARSTELLUNG VON «VORHER» UND «NACHHER» GIBT EINE PHOTOGRAPHIN DIE GEBURT IHRER TOCHTER BEKANNT. (USA)

● 339 EIGENWERBUNG, GEÖFFNET UND GESCHLOSSEN, FÜR DEN DESIGNER SEAN BUTCHER. TEXT UND MESSER SIND EINE HUMORVOLLE ANSPIELUNG AUF DEN FAMILIENNAMEN (METZGER). (GBR)

● 340 DESIGN UND MATERIAL DIESER DREIDIMENSIONALEN EINLADUNG EINES BAUUNTERNEHMENS REFLEKTIEREN DIE ARCHITEKTUR EINES KÜRZLICH FERTIGGESTELLTEN MUSEUMS. (USA)

▲ 336, 337 CARTE D'UN RESTAURANT SÉLECT DE MINNEAPOLIS. À G., LA COUVERTURE AVEC CERCLES DÉCOUPÉS À L'EMPORTE-PIÈCE. MENUS ET CARTES DES VINS ÉVOQUENT LA DÉCORATION ET L'INNOVATION CULINAIRE DE CE RESTAURANT. (USA)

▲ 338 CARTE ANNONÇANT LA NAISSANCE DE LA FILLE D'UNE PHOTOGRAPHE: LE CORPS DE LA MÈRE A ÉTÉ PHOTOGRAPHIÉ «AVANT» ET «APRÈS». (USA)

▲ 339 AUTOPROMOTION D'UN DESIGNER: LE COUTEAU DE BOUCHER MINIATURE EST UNE ALLUSION AU NOM DE FAMILLE DE SEAN BUTCHER, GRAVÉ SUR LA LAME, AVEC SON NUMÉRO DE TÉLÉPHONE. (GBR)

▲ 340 INVITATION À UN GALA D'UNE ENTREPRISE DE CONSTRUCTION, TENU DANS UN MUSÉE RÉCEMMENT CONSTRUIT. LE DESIGN ET LES MATÉRIAUX RAPPELLENT L'ARCHITECTURE. (USA)

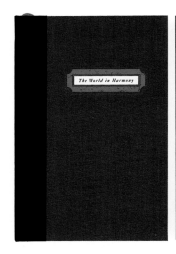

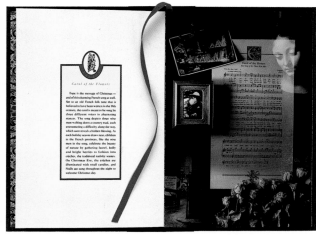

ART DIRECTOR:
ROBERT MILES
RUNYAN
DESIGNER:
LARRY LONG
COPYWRITER:
LARRY LONG
AGENCY:
RUNYAN HINSCHE
ASSOCIATES
CLIENT:
RUNYAN HINSCHE
ASSOCIATES
◀■ 341

ART DIRECTOR:
RICHARD M. SEMAN
DESIGNER:
RICHARD M. SEMAN
PHOTOGRAPHER:
WALT SENG
STYLIST:
THE OBJECT WORKS
AGENCY:
SEMAN DESIGN
GROUP
▶■ 345

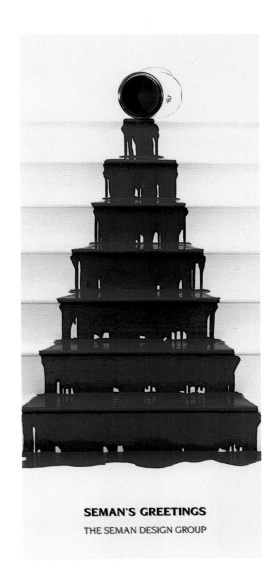

ART DIRECTOR:
DAVID CARTER
DESIGNER:
DAVID CARTER
PHOTOGRAPHER:
KLEIN AND WILSON
COPYWRITER:
MARSHA COBURN
AGENCY:
DAVID CARTER
GRAPHIC DESIGN
ASSOCIATES
CLIENT:
DAVID CARTER
GRAPHIC DESIGN
ASSOCIATES
■ 342-344

■ 341 THIS HOLIDAY GREETING CARD IS BASED ON A GUESSING GAME: NO L = NOËL, FRENCH WORD FOR CHRISTMAS. (USA)

■ 342-344 A SMALL BOOK SENT OUT BY A DESIGN STUDIO AS CHRISTMAS GIFT. THE BOOK TELLS THE STORY OF THE CHRISTMAS CAROLS. SHOWN ARE THE COVER, ITS INSIDE AND A SPREAD. (USA)

■ 345 A CHRISTMAS CARD OF A DESIGN STUDIO. EACH YEAR THE VISUAL IS AN ABSTRACT SHAPE OF A CHRISTMAS TREE. THIS TIME, GREEN PAINT WAS POURED DOWN A STAIRWAY. (USA)

● 341 DIESE WEIHNACHTSKARTE BASIERT AUF EINEM RATESPIEL: «NO L» (KEIN L) ENTSPRICHT DEM FRAN- ZÖSISCHEN «NOËL». (USA)

● 342-344 EIN KLEINES BUCH, DAS VON EINEM DESIGN-STUDIO ALS WEIHNACHTSGESCHENK VER- SCHICKT WURDE. ES ERZÄHLT DIE GESCHICHTE DER WEIHNACHTSLIEDER. (USA)

● 345 WEIHNACHTSGRUSS EINER DESIGN-FIRMA, DIE JEDES JAHR DEN BAUM ZUM THEMA HAT. DIESES MAL WURDE FARBE ÜBER TREPPENSTUFEN GEGOSSEN, UM DIE FORM DES BAUMES DARZUSTELLEN. (USA)

▲ 341 CETTE CARTE DE NOËL REPOSE SUR UNE DEVINETTE: IL N'Y A PAS DE «L», CE QUI EN ANGLAIS SE PRONONCE «NO L». (USA)

▲ 342-344 «LE MONDE EN HARMONIE»: PETIT LIVRE AUTOPROMOTIONNEL D'UN DESIGNER, ENVOYÉ COMME CADEAU DE NOËL. ON Y RACONTE L'HISTOIRE DES CHANTS DE NOËL. (USA)

▲ 345 CARTE DE NOËL D'UN STUDIO DE DESIGN FAISANT PARTIE D'UNE SÉRIE BASÉE SUR LA FORME TRIANGULAIRE DU SAPIN. LA FORME A ÉTÉ PEINTE SUR UN ESCALIER. (USA)

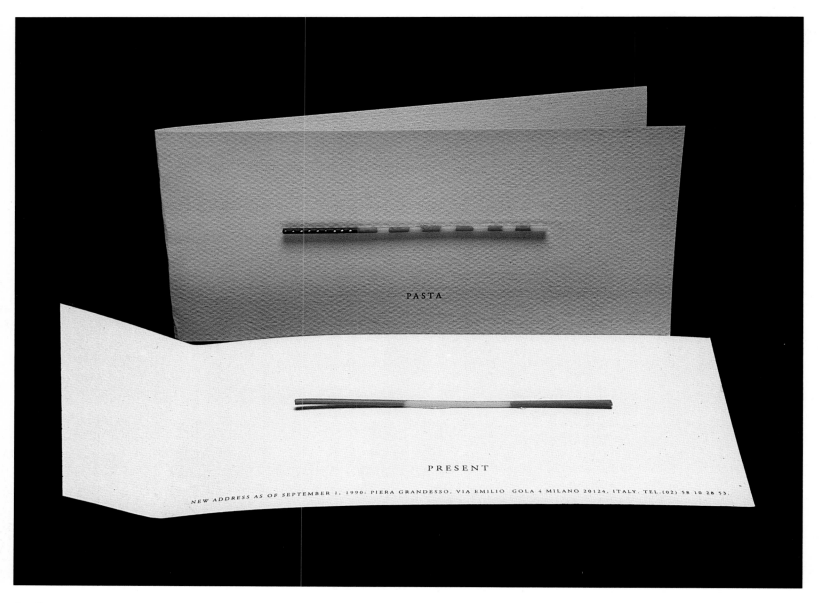

PASTA

PRESENT

NEW ADDRESS AS OF SEPTEMBER 1, 1990: PIERA GRANDESSO, VIA EMILIO GOLA 4 MILANO 20124, ITALY. TEL. (02) 58 10 28 53.

ART DIRECTOR:

TERRY DOBSON

DESIGNER:

TERRY DOBSON

STYLIST:

PIERA GRANDESSO

■ 346

ART DIRECTOR:

SIGRID UIBERREITHER

DESIGNER:

SIGRID UIBERREITHER

COPYWRITER:

JÖRG UI

AGENCY:

UI-IDEEN

CLIENT:

ATELIER 2000

FOTOGMBH

■ 347

■ 346 WITH THIS CARD A DESIGNER ANNOUNCES THAT HE WILL RETURN TO ITALY AFTER A FOUR YEARS' STAY IN THE UNITED STATES. (USA)

■ 347 A DIRECT MAIL PROMOTION ANNOUNCING THE OPENING OF A PHOTOSTUDIO. NAME AND ADDRESS ARE INDICATED ON THE FILM. (AUT)

● 346 MIT DIESER KARTE GIBT EIN DESIGNER SEINE RÜCKKEHR NACH ITALIEN BEKANNT, NACHDEM ER VIER JAHRE IN DEN USA VERBRACHT HAT. (USA)

● 347 WERBESENDUNG IN FORM EINER FILMROLLE ZUR ERÖFFNUNG EINES PHOTOSTUDIOS. NAME UND ANSCHRIFT STEHEN AUF DEM FILM. (AUT)

▲ 346 CARTE ANNONÇANT LE DÉPART D'UN DESIGNER ITALIEN QUI, APRÈS AVOIR TRAVAILLÉ QUATRE ANS AUX USA, RETOURNE DANS SON PAYS. (USA)

▲ 347 ANNONCE DE L'OUVERTURE D'UN STUDIO DE PHOTOGRAPHIE. SUR LA PELLICULE FIGURENT LE NOM ET L'ADRESSE DU STUDIO. (AUT)

EDITORIAL DESIGN

REDAKTIONELLES DESIGN

DESIGN DE PÉRIODIQUES

’CON NOR

O'Connor has emerged as the decade's first new superstar

PHOTOGRAPHS BY ANDREW MACPHERSON

HAMMER TIME

America's most popular rapper is also a demanding taskmaster · By Jeffrey Ressner

PHOTOGRAPH BY FRANK W. OCKENFELS 3

ROLLING STONE, SEPTEMBER 6TH, 1990 · 47

ART DIRECTOR:
FRED WOODWARD
PHOTOGRAPHY DIRECTOR:
LAURIE KRATOCHVIL
DESIGNERS:
FRED WOODWARD
GAIL ANDERSON
PHOTOGRAPHERS:
ANDREW
MACPHERSON
FRANK W.
OCKENFELS III
CLIENT:
ROLLING STONE
PUBLISHER:
STRAIGHT ARROW
PUBLISHERS
■ 348, 349

■ 348 DOUBLE SPREAD FROM ROLLING STONE MAGAZINE PRESENTING A PORTRAIT OF SINÉAD O'CONNOR, THE NEW SUPERSTAR OF THE MUSIC SCENE. (USA)

■ 349 INTRODUCTORY DOUBLE SPREAD TO AN ARTICLE IN ROLLING STONE ON AMERICA'S MOST POPULAR RAPPER, MC HAMMER, WHO IS SAID TO BE ALSO A DEMANDING TASKMASTER. (USA)

● 348 DOPPELSEITE AUS DER ZEITSCHRIFT ROLLING STONE MIT EINEM PORTRÄT DES NEUEN SUPER-STARS DER MUSIKSZENE SINÉAD O'CONNOR, EINE JUNGE FRAU, DIE VIEL DURCHGEMACHT HAT. (USA)

● 349 EINFÜHRENDE DOPPELSEITE ZU EINEM BEITRAG IN ROLLING STONE ÜBER DEN AMERIKANI-SCHEN RAPP-STAR MC HAMMER, DER EIN STRENGER ARBEITGEBER SEIN SOLL. (USA)

▲ 348 DOUBLE PAGE DU MAGAZINE ROLLING STONE PRÉSENTANT LE PORTRAIT DE LA NOUVELLE SUPERSTAR DE LA MUSIQUE, SINÉAD O'CONNOR, UNE JEUNE FEMME AU PASSÉ MOUVEMENTÉ. (USA)

▲ 349 DOUBLE PAGE INTRODUISANT UNE INTERVIEW DU RAPPER LE PLUS POPULAIRE D'AMÉRIQUE, MC HAMMER, PUBLIÉE DANS LE MAGAZINE ROLLING STONE. (USA)

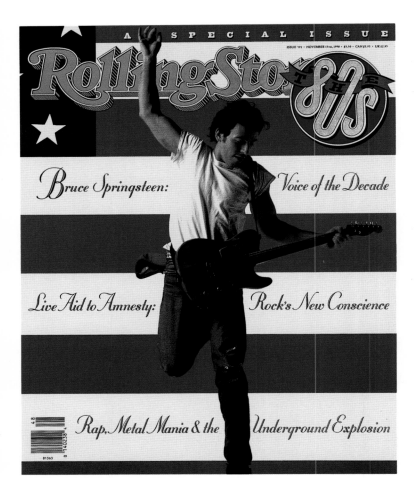

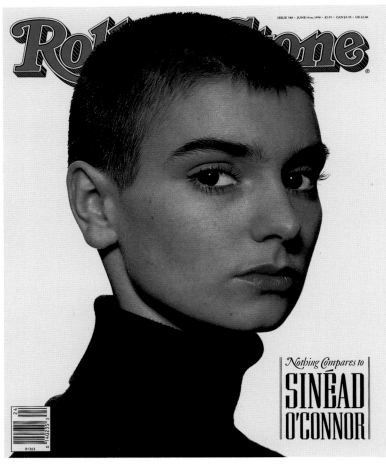

■ 350, 351 TWO COVERS OF *ROLLING STONE*
MAGAZINE: AT LEFT, BRUCE SPRINGSTEEN, THE
VOICE OF THE DECADE, FOR A SPECIAL ISSUE
DEDICATED TO THE EIGHTIES; AT RIGHT, A POR-
TRAIT OF THE UNIQUE SINÉAD O'CONNOR, THE NEW
STAR OF THE MUSIC SCENE. (USA)

■ 352-355 FOUR EXAMPLES OF DOUBLE SPREADS
FROM *ROLLING STONE* MAGAZINE. FROM LEFT TO
RIGHT: FOR AN ARTICLE ON SAXOPHONE PLAYER
SONNY ROLLINS, "THE TITAN OF JAZZ"; INTRODUC-
ING AN EXCERPT OF A BOOK ON THE INNER
WORKINGS OF HOLLYWOOD; FOR A STORY ON NOW
FAMOUS PRODUCER/FILM STAR KEVIN COSTNER. THE
ARROW IS TAKEN UP AS CONSTANT ELEMENT AS A
REFERENCE TO HIS EPIC WESTERN *DANCES WITH
WOLVES* WHICH WON HIM SEVEN OSCARS; INTRO-
DUCTORY SPREAD WITH PORTRAIT OF TECHNO POP
IDOLS DEPECHE MODE. (USA)

● 350, 351 ZWEI UMSCHLÄGE DER ZEITSCHRIFT
ROLLING STONE: LINKS BRUCE SPRINGSTEEN – DIE
STIMME DER ACHTZIGER JAHRE – AUF DEM TITEL
EINER SONDERNUMMER ÜBER DAS VERGANGENE
JAHRZEHNT; RECHTS EIN PORTRÄT DER «UNVER-
GLEICHLICHEN» SINÉAD O'CONNOR. (USA)

● 352-355 VIER BEISPIELE VON DOPPELSEITEN AUS
DER ZEITSCHRIFT *ROLLING STONE*. VON LINKS NACH
RECHTS: FÜR EINEN ARTIKEL ÜBER DEN BERÜHMTEN
SAXOPHONISTEN SONNY ROLLINS, DEN «TITANEN
DES JAZZ»; EIN AUSZUG AUS EINEM BUCH ÜBER
DAS, WAS HINTER DEN KULISSEN HOLLYWOODS
PASSIERT; FÜR EIN PORTRÄT DES FÜR SEINEN FILM
DANCES WITH WOLVES MIT SIEBEN OSCARS
AUSGEZEICHNETEN KEVIN COSTNER. DER PFEIL,
EINE ANSPIELUNG AUF SEINEN FILM, DIENT ALS
KONSTANTES GRAPHISCHES ELEMENT; PORTRÄT DER
TECHNO-POP-IDOLE DEPECHE MODE. (USA)

▲ 350, 351 DEUX COUVERTURES DU MAGAZINE
ROLLING STONE: À GAUCHE, LE CHANTEUR BRUCE
SPRINGSTEEN, «LA VOIX DE LA DÉCADE», POUR UN
NUMÉRO SPÉCIAL CONSACRÉ AUX ANNÉES 80; À
DROITE, GROS PLAN SUR «L'INCOMPARABLE SINÉAD
O'CONNOR». (USA)

▲ 352-355 QUATRE EXEMPLES DE DOUBLES PAGES
DU MAGAZINE *ROLLING STONE*. DE G. À DR.: D'UN
ARTICLE CONSACRÉ AU SAXOPHONISTE SONNY
ROLLINS, «LE TITAN DU JAZZ»; PRÉSENTATION D'UN
EXTRAIT D'UN LIVRE QUI DÉPEINT CE QUI SE PASSE
DERRIÈRE LES COULISSES D'HOLLYWOOD; UN
PORTRAIT DE KEVIN COSTNER, DONT LE FILM,
DANCES WITH WOLVES A REÇU PLUSIEURS OSCARS
(LA FLÈCHE, UNE ALLUSION À SES FILMS, EST
UTILISÉE COMME ÉLÉMENT DE COMPOSITION
GRAPHIQUE); UN PORTRAIT DU GROUPE DEPECHE
MODE, «IDOLES DU TECHNO-POP». (USA)

ART DIRECTOR:
FRED WOODWARD
PHOTOGRAPHY DIRECTOR:
LAURIE KRATOCHVIL
DEPUTY ART DIRECTOR:
GAIL ANDERSON
DESIGNERS:
FRED WOODWARD
DEBRA BISHOP
CATHERINE
GILMORE-BARNES
GAIL ANDERSON
PHOTOGRAPHERS:
ANNIE LEIBOVITZ
ANDREW
MACPHERSON
BRUCE WEBER
KURT MARKUS
JOHN STODDART
ARTIST:
SANDRA HENDLER
LETTERER:
JONATHAN HOEFLER
CLIENT:
ROLLING STONE
PUBLISHER:
STRAIGHT ARROW
PUBLISHERS
■ 350-355

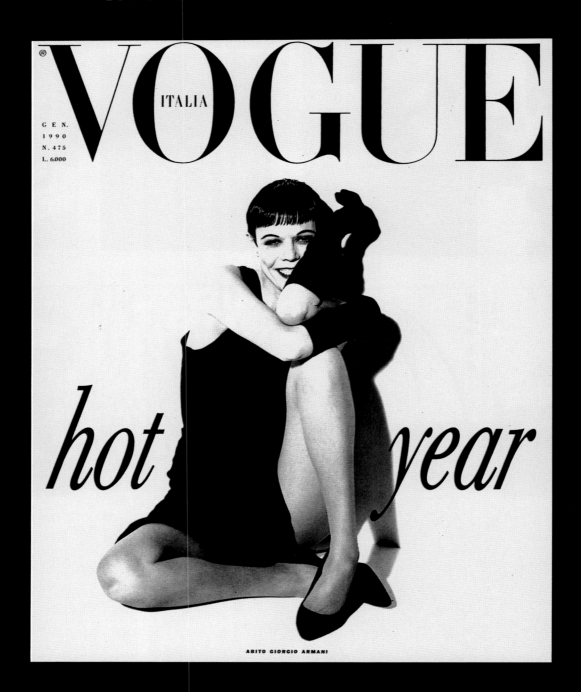

GEN.
1990
N. 475
L. 6.000

ABITO GIORGIO ARMANI

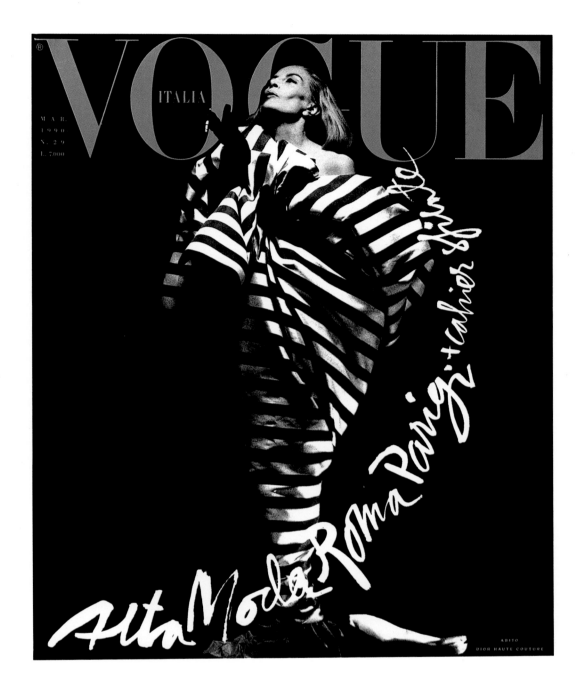

ART DIRECTOR:
JUAN GATTI
PHOTOGRAPHERS:
STEVEN MEISEL
ALBERT WATSON
CLIENT:
VOGUE ITALIA
PUBLISHER:
EDIZIONE CONDÉ
NAST S.P.A.
■ 356, 357

■ 356, 357 TWO COVERS OF *VOGUE ITALIA*, BOTH IN BLACK AND WHITE, WHICH IS TYPICAL FOR CONTEMPORARY FASHION PHOTOGRAPHY IN EUROPE. OPPOSITE PAGE: A DRESS BY GIORGIO ARMANI; THIS PAGE: FOR AN ISSUE ON HAUTE COUTURE IN ROME AND PARIS WITH A SUPPLEMENT ON THE FASHION SHOWS. (ITA)

● 356, 357 ZWEI UMSCHLÄGE FÜR DIE ZEITSCHRIFT *VOGUE ITALIA*. DIE SCHWARZWEISSPHOTOGRAPHIE ENTSPRICHT DEM GEGENWÄRTIGEN TREND IN DER DARSTELLUNG VON MODE. GEGENÜBER: «EIN HEISSES JAHR»; DIESE SEITE: FÜR EINE AUSGABE ÜBER DIE HAUTE COUTURE IN ROM UND PARIS, MIT EINER BEILAGE ÜBER DIE MODESCHAUEN. (ITA)

▲ 356, 357 DEUX COUVERTURES DE *VOGUE ITALIA*. LES PHOTOS EN NOIR ET BLANC SONT CARACTÉRISTIQUES DE LA PHOTOGRAPHIE DE MODE CONTEMPORAINE EN EUROPE. PAGE CI-CONTRE: «UNE ANNÉE TORRIDE»; CI-DESSUS: NUMÉRO CONSACRÉ À LA HAUTE COUTURE À ROME ET PARIS, AVEC SUPPLÉMENT DÉFILÉS DE COLLECTIONS. (ITA)

M

MINI ABITI MAXI ACCESSORI

Una sfilata, quella di Christian Lacroix, assolutamente all'avanguardia. Dove ricami e decori definiscono uno stile prezioso e glamorous allo stesso tempo. Nella pagina accanto. Grande cappello di paglia color oro e bijoux, Christian Lacroix Haute Couture. Scarpe con décor di piume, Sidonie Larizzi per Christian Lacroix. Styling Carlyne Cerf.

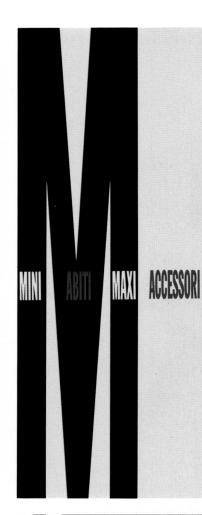

309

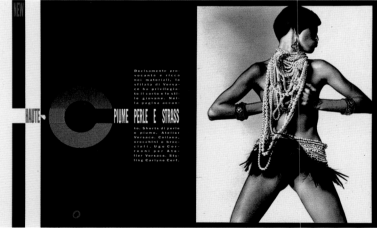

NEW HAUTE PIUME PERLE E STRASS

Decisamente provocante e ricca nei materiali, la sfilata di Versace ho privilegia to il corto e lo stile giovane. Nella pagina accanto. Shorts di perle e piume, Atelier Versace. Collant, orecchini e bracciali, Ugo Correnni per Atelier Versace. Styling Carlyne Cerf.

ART DIRECTOR:
JUAN GATTI
PHOTOGRAPHERS:
STEVEN MEISEL
ALBERT WATSON
CLIENT:
VOGUE ITALIA
PUBLISHER:
EDIZIONE CONDÉ
NAST S.P.A.
■ 358-360

ART DIRECTOR:
MANFRED NEUSSL
DESIGNER:
RALF GOTTSCHALL
PHOTOGRAPHERS:
GEORG VALERIUS
NACASA &
PARTNERS INC.
THOMAS DELBECK
MARKUS TEDES-
KINO
CLIENT:
AMBIENTE
PUBLISHER:
BURDA VERLAG
▶■ 361-363

KULT & KUNST

IM KANADISCHEN OTTAWA ENTSTANDEN DIE SPEKTAKULÄRSTEN NEUEN MUSEEN AMERIKAS: EIN SPANNUNGSREICHER DIALOG ZWISCHEN KULTUREN UND BAUSTILEN

MUSEUM OF CIVILIZATION

Wie eine indianische Maske: der Haupteingang des gerade eröffneten «Museum of Civilization», gebaut von Architekt Douglas Cardinal

167

PALAZZO

IN DER VORSTADT-PRÄRIE VON CHICAGO

LAND-FESTUNG FÜRS STADT-KAPITAL: IN CHICAGOS SUBURBIA PFLANZTE STANLEY TIGERMAN EIN ÜBERRASCHENDES GEWÄCHS. SEIN BACKSTEIN-HYBRIDE IST EINE POINTENREICHE HOMMAGE AN DIE ARCHITEKTUR-GESCHICHTE

■ 358-360 SPREADS FROM *VOGUE ITALIA*. FROM TOP TO BOTTOM AND FROM LEFT TO RIGHT: ACCESSORIES BY CHRISTIAN LACROIX UNDER THE TITLE: "TINY DRESS, BIG ACCESSORIES"; FEATHERS, BEADS AND ARTIFICIAL JEWELRY IN THE VERSACE COLLECTION; THE "BUBBLE FASHION" (AT LEFT THE BUBBLE HOUSE IN CHICAGO). (ITA)

■ 361-363 THREE DOUBLE SPREADS OF THE MAGAZINE *AMBIENTE*. ABOVE THE MAIN ENTRANCE OF THE MUSEUM OF CIVILIZATION BUILT BY DOUGLAS CARDINAL IN OTTAWA, BELOW LEFT THE DISCO BAR "CRONOS" IN TOKYO REMINISCENT OF A BUNKER AND AT RIGHT A PALAZZO IN CHICAGO, A PINPOINTED HOMAGE TO THE HISTORY OF ARCHITECTURE. (GER)

● 358-360 DOPPELSEITE AUS VOGUE ITALIA. V.O.N.U. UND V.L.N.R.: ACCESSOIRES VON CHRISTIAN LACROIX: MINI-DRESS, MAXI-ACCESSSOIRES"; FEDERN, PERLEN UND STRASS IN DER VERSACE-KOLLEKTION; DIE «AUFGEBLASENE MODE» (BUBBLE FASHION) – LINKS EIN DETAIL DES BUBBLE-HAUSES IN CHICAGO. (ITA)

● 361-363 DREI DOPPELSEITEN AUS DER ZEITSCHRIFT *AMBIENTE*. ZUOBERST: DER HAUPTEINGANG DES MUSEUM OF CIVILISATION IN OTTOWA, VON DOUGLAS CARDINAL GEBAUT; DARUNTER ATOMBUNKER-ÄSTHETIK: DIE DISCOBAR «CRONOS» IN TOKIO, RECHTS EIN PALAZZO IN CHICAGO, EINE POINTENREICHE HOMMAGE AN DIE ARCHITEKTUR-GESCHICHTE. (GER)

▲ 358-360 DOUBLES PAGES DE *VOGUE ITALIA*. DE HAUT EN BAS ET DE G. À DR.: PRÉSENTATION DES ACCESSOIRES CHRISTIAN LACROIX SOUS LE TITRE «HABITS MINI, ACCESSOIRES MAXI»; REPORTAGE SUR LES POINTS FORTS DE LA COLLECTION GIANNI VERSACE; LA «MODE-BULLE» AVEC, À GAUCHE, UN HUBLOT DE LA BUBBLE HOUSE DE CHICAGO. (ITA)

▲ 361-363 TROIS DOUBLES PAGES DU MAGAZINE *AMBIENTE*. EN HAUT: L'ENTRÉE DU «MUSÉE DE LA CIVILISATION» D'OTTAWA ILLUSTRANT UN ARTICLE SUR L'ARCHITECTURE DES MUSÉES. EN BAS: LE DISCO-BAR «CRONOS» À TOKYO, EXEMPLE DE L'ARCHITECTURE DE BUNKER; UN PALAZZO DANS LA BANLIEUE DE CHICAGO, HOMMAGE À L'HISTOIRE DE L'ARCHITECTURE. (GER)

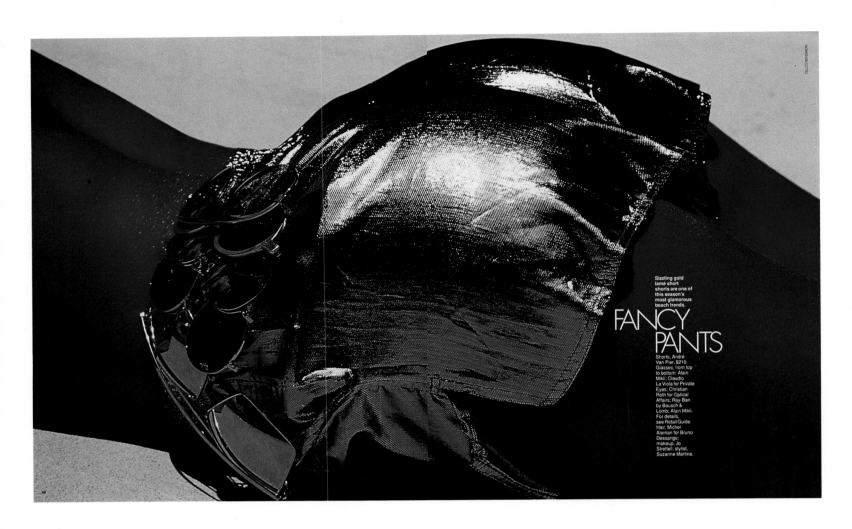

GILLES BENSIMON

Sizzling gold lamé short shorts are one of this season's most glamorous beach trends.

FANCY PANTS

Shorts, André Van Pier, $210. Glasses, from top to bottom: Alain Mikli; Claudio La Viola for Private Eyes; Christian Roth for Optical Affairs; Ray-Ban by Bausch & Lomb; Alain Mikli. For details, see Retail Guide. Hair, Michel Aleman for Bruno Dessange; makeup, Jo Strettell; stylist, Suzanne Martine.

■ 364-370 SPREADS FROM *ELLE* MAGAZINE. THIS PAGE: THE SEASON'S MOST GLAMOROUS BEACH TRENDS; OPPOSITE FROM LEFT TO RIGHT: VARIOUS FANNY BAGS; FASHION IN BRIGHT COLORS AND IN BOLD GRAPHIC STYLE; BEADED WONDERS FOR THE EVENING; SEXY FUN CLOTHES AND HULA-HOOP HANDBAGS; SUNNY SURF SIRENS WITH FASHIONABLE SCALES; A UNITARD SWIMSUIT WITH CAP, FOR SERIOUS SWIMMERS ONLY. (USA)

● 364-370 DOPPELSEITE AUS *ELLE*. DIESE SEITE: GLÄNZENDE SHORTS FÜR DEN STRAND; GEGENÜBER V.L.N.R.: VERSCHIEDENE GÜRTELTASCHEN; KRÄFTI-GE FARBEN UND MUSTER; BESTICKTE WUNDER FÜR DEN FESTLICHEN ABEND; MODE, DIE SPASS MACHT, MIT HANDTASCHEN AM HULA-HOOP-REIFEN; SIRENEN MIT GLÄNZENDEN SCHUPPEN AUS PAILLETTEN; EIN EINTEILER MIT BADEKAPPE – NUR FÜR DIE ERNST-HAFTE SCHWIMMERIN. (USA)

▲ 364-370 DOUBLES PAGES DE *ELLE*. CI-DESSUS: D'UN ARTICLE SUR LES SHORTS FANTAISIE; MODÈLE EN LAMÉ D'ANDRÉ VAN PIER. CI-CONTRE, DE HAUT EN BAS ET DE G. À DR.: LES SACS-CEINTURES, QUI ASSOCIENT FORME, FONCTION ET MODE; «VIVRE EN COULEURS»; ACCESSOIRES ET ROBES POUR ALLER DANSER; TENUES SPORTIVES ET SACS HULA-HOOP; «SIRÈNES PAILLETÉES»; MAILLOT DE BAIN POUR NAGEUSE DE COMPÉTITION. (USA)

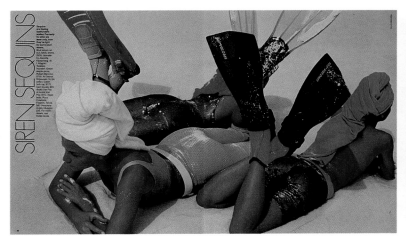

PUBLICATION DIRECTOR:

RÉGIS PAGNIEZ

ART DIRECTOR:

OLIVIA BADRUTT-

GIRON

PHOTOGRAPHERS:

GILLES BENSIMON

TOSCANI

TYEN

STYLISTS:

SUZANNE MARTINE

LÉNA KORDIC

FANNY PAGNIEZ

LOREN LANEY

CLIENT:

ELLE

PUBLISHER:

HACHETTE

MAGAZINES, INC.

■ 364-370

■ 371-375 COVER AND DOUBLE SPREADS FROM THE WOMEN'S MAGAZINE *MIRABELLA*. THIS PAGE AT RIGHT: THE NEW FUR FASHION, A BLANKET COAT AND A BOLERO JACKET; OPPOSITE: FASHION AS THE "SIGNS OF TIMES"; 18K-GOLD CUFFS INSPIRED BY NATURE AND ARCHITECTURE; "SPECIAL EFFECTS" - THE INITIALS STAND FOR THE FASHION DESIGNERS, THE Y FOR YVES SAINT LAURENT AND THE V FOR VALENTINO. (USA)

● 371-375 UMSCHLAG UND DOPPELSEITEN AUS DER ZEITSCHRIFT *MIRABELLA*. DIESE SEITE UNTEN RECHTS: DIE NEUE PELZMODE, EIN UMHANG UND EINE BOLERO-JACKE. GEGENÜBER: MODE ALS «ZEICHEN DER ZEIT»; 18KARÄTIGE GOLD ARMBÄN-DER, VON DER NATUR UND DER ARCHITEKTUR INSPIRIERT; «SPEZIELLE EFFEKTE» – DIE BUCH-STABEN BEZEICHNEN DIE COUTURIERS: Y FÜR YVES SAINT LAURENT UND V FÜR VALENTINO. (USA)

▲ 371-375 COUVERTURE ET DOUBLES PAGES DU MAGAZINE FÉMININ *MIRABELLA*. CI-DESSOUS, À DR.: LES NOUVEAUX MODÈLES DE FOURRURES. CI-CONTRE, DE HAUT EN BAS: LES DÉTAILS QUI FONT DE LA MODE «LE SIGNE DES TEMPS»; BRACELETS INSPIRÉS PAR LA NATURE ET L'ARCHITECTURE; «EFFETS SPÉCIAUX»: LES LETTRES DÉSIGNENT LES COUTURIERS, Y POUR YVES SAINT LAURENT ET V POUR VALENTINO. (USA)

SHEARED MUSKRAT, WRAP "BLANKET" COAT, GIORGIO DI SANT'ANGELO FOR ROBERT SIDNEY FURS. MORE INFO, LAST PAGES.

BOLERO-STYLE JACKET IN SHEARED, DYED BEAVER, GEOFFREY BEENE FOR GOLDIN-FELDMAN. MORE INFO, LAST PAGES.

ART DIRECTOR:

KAREN LEE GRANT

DESIGNERS:

KAREN LEE GRANT

ANDRZEJ JANERKA

PHOTOGRAPHERS:

GUZMAN

TIMOTHY GREEN-

FIELD-SANDERS

JOSE PICAYO

WILLIAM LAXTON

PUBLISHER:

MIRABELLA

■ 371-375

AUGUST 1990
MIRABELLA

signals

2

The catsuit cut out for night: sleek, strapless, velvet—worn with a lace bolero

EACH SEASON THERE ARE CERTAIN LOOKS THAT STAND OUT FROM THE PACK AND DETERMINE THE TRENDS—A BRIGHT COAT, A SHINY SHOE, AN UNUSUAL ACCESSORY. IN FASHION, THEY'RE THE SIGNS OF THE TIMES...

A removable "harness" ornament puts a twist on a classic wool jumpsuit

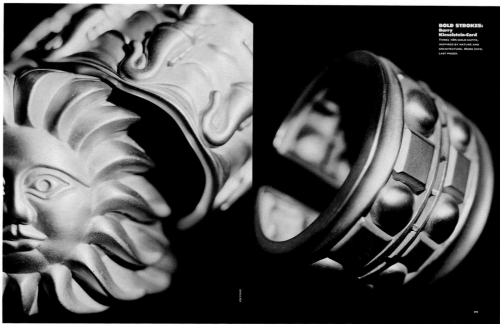

BOLD STROKES: Barry Kieselstein-Cord Three 18K-gold cuffs, inspired by nature and architecture. More info, last pages.

SPECIAL EFFECTS Yves Saint Laurent haute couture silk-chiffon dress with empire waistline, narrow sleeves, and straight skirt slit to the waist. More info, last pages.

SPECIAL EFFECTS Valentino haute couture column dress of plissé silk mousseline with concealed side slit. More info, last pages.

CREATIVE DIRECTOR:
LESLEY VINSON

DESIGNER:
LESLEY VINSON

PHOTOGRAPHER:
STEVE MELNICK

ILLUSTRATOR:
HARRY ROOLAART

PUBLISHER:
DETAILS

◄■ 376

ART DIRECTOR:
JEROLD SMOKLER

PHOTOGRAPHER:
JEAN-BAPTISTE
MONDINO

CLIENT:
HARPER'S BAZAAR

PUBLISHER:
THE HEARST
CORPORATION

■ 377

ART DIRECTOR:
ERIC COLMET DAAGE

PHOTOGRAPHER:
ELLEN VON UNWERTH

PUBLISHER:
PHOTO

■ 378

PUBLICATION DIRECTOR:
RÉGIS PAGNIEZ

ART DIRECTOR:
ROBERTO BURRONI

PHOTOGRAPHER:
GILLES BENSIMON

CLIENT:
ELLE

PUBLISHER:
HACHETTE
MAGAZINES, INC.

■ 379

■ 376 COVER OF THE MONTHLY MAGAZINE *DETAILS*. THE BLUE STRANDS OF HAIR HAVE BEEN PAINTED ON THE PHOTO. (USA)

■ 377 BREATHLESS MADONNA ON THE COVER OF *HARPER'S BAZAAR* LISTING ALL THE HOT SUMMER SUBJECTS OF THE JUNE ISSUE. (USA)

■ 378 COVER OF AN ISSUE OF FRENCH *PHOTO* MAGAZINE, DEDICATED TO ADVERTISING AND ITS STARS, HERE CLAUDIA SCHIFFER. (FRA)

■ 379 COVER OF THE US EDITION OF *ELLE* MAGAZINE: THE MAIN SUBJECTS OF THIS ISSUE ARE EMPLOYED AS GRAPHIC ELEMENTS. (USA)

● 376 UMSCHLAG DER MONATSZEITSCHRIFT *DETAILS*. DIE BLAUEN HAARSTRÄHNEN SIND AUF DAS PHOTO GEMALT. (USA)

● 377 MADONNA AUF DEM UMSCHLAG VON *HARPER'S BAZAAR*. LUXUS, SEX, MEER UND SONNE SIND DIE HAUPTTHEMEN DIESER SOMMERAUSGABE. (USA)

● 378 UMSCHLAG VON EINER AUSGABE VON *PHOTO*, DIE DER WERBUNG UND IHREN STARS GEWIDMET IST; HIER CLAUDIA SCHIFFER. (FRA)

● 379 UMSCHLAG DER AMERIKANISCHEN AUSGABE VON *ELLE*. DIE HAUPTTHEMEN DER NUMMER SIND ALS GRAPHISCHE ELEMENTE EINGESETZT. (USA)

▲ 376 COUVERTURE DU MAGAZINE MENSUEL *DETAILS*. LES REFLETS COLORÉS DE LA CHEVELURE ONT ÉTÉ PEINTS SUR LA PHOTO. (USA)

▲ 377 MADONNA EN COUVERTURE DU NUMÉRO SPÉCIAL ÉTÉ 1990 DE *HARPER'S BAZAAR*. LUXE, SEXE, MER ET SOLEIL EN SONT LES THÈMES. (USA)

▲ 378 COUVERTURE D'UN NUMÉRO DU MAGAZINE *PHOTO* CONSACRÉ À LA PUBLICITÉ ET À SES STARS, ICI CLAUDIA SCHIFFER. (FRA)

▲ 379 COUVERTURE DE L'ÉDITION AMÉRICAINE DE *ELLE*: LES RUBRIQUES DE CE NUMÉRO SONT UTILISÉES COMME ÉLÉMENT GRAPHIQUE. (USA)

FICTION by Margaret Atwood

THE AGE OF LEAD

**JANE LEARNED THERE
WERE CONSEQUENCES AFTER ALL, BUT
CONSEQUENCES TO THINGS
YOU DIDN'T EVEN KNOW YOU'D DONE.
LOOK AT WHAT HAPPENED
TO THE SAILOR IN THE PERMAFROST**

Sidney Poitier

"I'm 63 years old and I've spent most of my life chasing dollars," Sidney Poitier said. "We spend most of our lives searching for answers in terms of money, job, position. Then there comes a time for some of us, and luckily it has come for me, when we can explore just for the sake of knowing."

He answers his car around the cluster of palm trees in his circular driveway. Crisp and elegant, perfectly pressed in a light-gray double-breasted suit with a red print tie and red pocket handkerchief, in tasseled black loafers, he was driving from Beverly Hills to a lunch at Columbia Pictures. At the bottom of the driveway he braked, pressed a button, and the electronically controlled steel gates swung slowly open. After he drove through, the gates closed silently behind the car—concise symbolism for the private man who lives behind these high walls in a house invisible from the street, a man who is known mostly through his screen image. He's never had a press agent. "I prefer to be out of the limelight," he says. "I don't do many interviews, because they rarely get beyond color. If I'm going to do an interview, I want to take it on the level of 'Who is this guy?'"

"This guy" is marking his 40th anniversary in films this year, as actor, producer, director, and social symbol. He is a novelist—his book isn't finished, isn't yet titled but is already sold to Knopf. He is a born-again feminist, an environmentalist, a man of primary contradictions: tight self-discipline controlling a violent strain that has been fueled by racism (he was stalked by the Klan twice, as a teenager and as a grown man) and by the stupidity of blacklisting. A man who on screen was a paragon of virtue, a man who in real life reveled in late-night card games and bedroom adventures (especially after he ventured beyond the missionary position with a poker-playing schoolteacher in Baltimore).

Poitier grew up on Cat Island in the Bahamas. His parents, Reginald and Evelyn, were tomato farmers. Poitier is an American citizen by accident, born in Miami while his parents were there on a tomato-selling trip, on February 20, 1927. The house he grew up in had no electricity, no running water, and his mother baked bread in a wood-fired oven outdoors. At 16 he went to New York, washed dishes and plucked chickens to live, and found his way to the American Negro Theatre. Criticized for being inarticulate, he bought a radio and taught himself to speak by repeating whatever he heard: news, weather, *Lux Presents Hollywood*. From these beginnings he built a career that is studded with landmark films, and he won the 1963 Academy Award for best actor in *Lilies of the Field*.

To this day his speech is so meticulous that a listener can hear the punctuation—not just the periods and the commas but the semicolons. While learning to speak, Poitier found a voice—sometimes earthy, as revealed in his autobiography, *This Life*, and sometimes so flowery ("The cape of history swirled across my shoulders") that his best friend, Harry Belafonte, tells him, "Don't recite the Constitution to me!" His language is so crucial to his character that when he and Belafonte disagreed on the arrangements for Martin Luther King, Jr.'s, funeral, they didn't speak for two years, and then it was Belafonte who broke the silence. "Sidney loves control," Belafonte says now. "When I first met him, he was very angry—it came from a lot of hurt—and he still has that anger."

Anger was just one of the burdens he brought to nine years of psychoanalysis—four or five times a week, from 1961 to 1970. Unhappily married, he was caught up in—and publicly criticized for—a long, troubled romance with Diahann Carroll. When he built a house in Nassau for his parents, his mother continued to bake bread in an outdoor oven. She died three months before he won his Oscar. As the only black actor making a living in movies,

By JOAN BARTHEL   **161**

A tool of high romance and incredible efficiency, the Leica has recorded some of the most memorable

THE

images of the past century. Photographers continue to rhapsodize over the camera, a thing of beauty equally prized these days by collectors

BEHOLDER

You might have thought that the whole point was the photographs. After all, two of the most memorable images of the 20th century—Robert Capa's Loyalist soldier falling in the Spanish Civil War and Alfred Eisenstaedt's U.S. sailor spontaneously kissing a girl in Times Square on V.J. Day—were taken with Leicas. Leica photographs were everywhere during the fabled age of photojournalism, the '30s to the '60s, when our images of the world came to us so powerfully, in stills and black-and-white, and with no "voice-over." *Life* magazine's finest—Andreas Feininger, Eugene Smith, Henri Cartier-Bresson, David Douglas Duncan, as well as Eisenstaedt and the Capa brothers—preferred the Leica. And for years the only 35mm cameras that *National Geographic* photographers used for color pictures were Leicas. The camera was only a tool—as a great racing yacht is a tool, or the finest thoroughbred—but it was a tool of high romance and incredible efficiency, the expert's pride, the amateur's badge of merit.

Some of the world's greatest photographers still use the Leica, still speak of it with awe and affection. These days, however, many Leicas are bought and sold not for the photographs they produce but for their sentimental or investment value. Like the classic cars gleaming immaculately in private garages, like the vintage wines moving from auction house to cellar to auction house but never from goblet to gullet, Leicas today no longer function primarily in an active world of use. They have become commodities of contemplation—"collectibles."

Today most Leicas sell secondhand for more than they cost new, even adjusting for inflation. The two M4 bodies I bought in 1968 for $288 each are now worth $600 to $1,000 apiece. Other models are valued in the thousands or higher. Moreover, the company now deliberately produces some limited editions for the collectibles market. Last year a brand-new, platinum-plated M6 was auctioned off at Christie's for about $38,000 to benefit the World Wildlife Fund. ▷

By DANIEL GROTTA

DESIGN DIRECTOR:
RON ALBRECHT
ART DIRECTORS:
JEANNE ARNOLD
KAREN WELLS
VERLANDER
ASSOCIATE ART
DIRECTORS:
KAREN WELLS
VERLANDER
STEPHEN WEBSTER
PHOTOGRAPHERS:
GREG WATERMAN
ANDREW ECCLES
RICHARD PIERCE
PUBLISHER:
LEAR'S
◀■ 380-382

ART DIRECTOR:
GARY KOEPKE
DESIGNER:
GARY KOEPKE
PHOTOGRAPHER:
STEVE MARSEL
AGENCY:
REDGATE
COMMUNICATIONS
KOEPKE DESIGN
PUBLISHER:
BULL HN WORLDWIDE
■ 383

GLOBAL

A VISION OF WORLD BUSINESS

MARCH 1990 PREMIER ISSUE

■ 380-382 DOUBLE SPREADS FROM LEAR'S MAGA-ZINE. FROM TOP TO BOTTOM: INTRODUCTION TO A FICTION STORY INSPIRED BY THE DISCOVERY OF THE TOTALLY INTACT BODY OF JOHN TORRINGTON, MEMBER OF THE FRANKLIN EXPEDITION IN SEARCH OF A SHIPPING ROUTE IN THE NORTH OF CANADA. LIKE HIS COMPANIONS, HE DIED OF POISONING CAUSED BY THE TINS; PORTRAIT OF ACTOR SIDNEY POITIER; INTRODUCTION TO AN ARTICLE ON THE LEICA, THE CAMERA THAT IS HELD IN GREAT ES-TEEM BY PHOTOGRAPHERS AND COLLECTORS. (USA)

■ 383 COVER OF THE FIRST ISSUE OF GLOBAL, A QUARTERLY PUBLICATION SPONSORED BY BULL. THE ILLUSTRATION VISUALIZES THE TARGET: TO PROVIDE ITS READERS WITH A VISION OF WORLD BUSINESS. (USA)

● 380-382 DOPPELSEITEN AUS LEAR'S MAGAZINE, V.O.N.U.: FÜR EINE ERDACHTE GESCHICHTE, DIE DURCH DEN FUND DES INTAKTEN LEICHNAMS DES MATROSEN JOHN TORRINGTON INSPIRIERT WURDE. ER NAHM AN DER FRANKLIN-EXPEDITION IM NORDEN KANADAS TEIL UND STARB WIE ALLE TEILNEHMER DURCH EINE VON KONSERVENDOSEN VERURSACHTE VERGIFTUNG; DER SCHAUSPIELER SIDNEY POITIER; EINFÜHRUNG ZU EINEM ARTIKEL ÜBER DIE LEICA, DIE NOCH IMMER VON PHOTOGRAPHEN UND SAMM-LERN HOCH GESCHÄTZT WIRD. (USA)

● 383 UMSCHLAG DER ERSTEN AUSGABE VON GLOBAL, EINER VON BULL GESPONSERTEN ZEIT-SCHRIFT. DIE ILLUSTRATION VERDEUTLICHT IHR ZIEL: IHREN LESERN EINE VORSTELLUNG INTER-NATIONALER GESCHÄFTE ZU GEBEN. (USA)

▲ 380-382 TROIS DOUBLES PAGES DU MAGAZINE LEAR'S. DE HAUT EN BAS: POUR UNE NOUVELLE INTITULÉE «L'ÂGE DU PLOMB», INSPIRÉE PAR LA DÉCOUVERTE DU CORPS INTACT DU MARIN JOHN TORRINGTON, MEMBRE DE L'EXPÉDITION FRANKLIN AU PÔLE NORD, QUI, COMME SES COMPAGNONS, MOURUT D'UN EMPOISONNEMENT DÛ AUX BOÎTES DE CONSERVE; PORTRAIT DE L'ACTEUR SIDNEY POITIER; POUR UN ARTICLE SUR LE LEICA, APPAREIL PHOTO TOUJOURS FORT PRISÉ ET OBJET DE COLLECTION. (USA)

▲ 383 COUVERTURE DU PREMIER NUMÉRO DE GLOBAL, UNE PUBLICATION TRIMESTRIELLE SPON-SORISÉE PAR BULL. L'IMAGE VISUALISE L'OBJECTIF DE LA REVUE: DONNER UNE VISION DU MONDE INTERNATIONAL DES AFFAIRES. (USA)

■ 384, 385 TWO COVERS OF THE CULTURAL MAGA-ZINE *TRANSATLANTIK*. AT LEFT, AN ISSUE ON THE CULTURAL SEPARATION OF GERMANY; AT RIGHT: "BEWARE OF THE DOG", A REFERENCE FEATURE BY PETER HACKS ON THE MEDIA. (GER)

■ 386-389 COVER AND SPREADS OF THE *FRANKFUR-TER ALLGEMEINE MAGAZIN*. 386: DIRK ASCHMONEIT, A TRIATHLON ATHLETE, WHO IS TRYING TO BE NUMBER ONE IN THIS DISCIPLINE; *387, 389* DISTORTED OR TRUE FACES—THE MANY ASPECTS OF THE HUMAN PERSONALITY SHOWN WITH THE HELP OF THE CAMERA. *388*: THE BROTHERS PAOLO AND VITTORIO TAVIANI, WHO WORK IN PERFECT HAR-MONY WHEN THEY PRODUCE AND DIRECT A FILM WHICH IS A PHENOMENON IN THIS INDUSTRY. (GER)

● 384, 385 ZWEI UMSCHLÄGE DER ZEITSCHRIFT *TRANSATLANTIK*. LINKS EINE AUSGABE ÜBER DIE KULTURELLE TEILUNG DEUTSCHLANDS; RECHTS EINE ANSPIELUNG AUF EINEN ARTIKEL VON PETER HACKS ÜBER DIE MEDIENKULTUR. (GER)

● 386-389 UMSCHLAG UND DOPPELSEITEN AUS DEM *FRANKFURTER ALLGEMEINE MAZAGIN*. 386: DIRK ASCHMONEIT, DER DIE NUMMER EINS DER TRIATHLE-TEN WERDEN MÖCHTE. 387, 389: VERZERRTE ODER WAHRE GESICHTER, VERSCHIEDENE FACETTEN DER PERSÖNLICHKEIT WERDEN MIT HILFE DES OBJEK-TIVS SICHTBAR GEMACHT. 388: DIE BRÜDER PAOLO UND VITTORIO TAVIANI, ZWISCHEN DENEN VOLL-KOMMENE KOMPLIZITÄT HERRSCHT, WENN SIE EINEN FILM DREHEN. (GER)

▲ 384, 385 COUVERTURES DU MAGAZINE CULTUREL *TRANSATLANTIK*. À GAUCHE, NUMÉRO CONSACRÉ AU CLIVAGE CULTUREL DE L'ALLEMAGNE RÉUNIFIÉE; À DROITE, «ATTENTION, CHIEN MÉCHANT», ARTICLE DE PETER HACKS AU SUJET DES MÉDIAS. (GER)

▲ 386-389 COUVERTURE ET DOUBLES PAGES DU *FRANKFURTER ALLGEMEINE MAGAZIN*. 386: DIRK ASCHMONEIT, QUI ASPIRE À DEVENIR LE NUMÉRO 1 DU TRIATHLON; 387, 389: DEUX VISAGES SOUMIS AUX DÉFORMATIONS DE L'OBJECTIF D'UN APPAREIL PERMETTANT DE PHOTOGRAPHIER TOUTES LES FACES D'UN SUJET, ICI, LE BIBLIOTHÉCAIRE JOHN EASTERBY ET LE NAGEUR DUNCAN GOODHEW; 388: PORTRAIT DES FRÈRES TAVIANI, CINÉASTES TRAVAILLANT EN PARFAITE COMPLICITÉ. (GER)

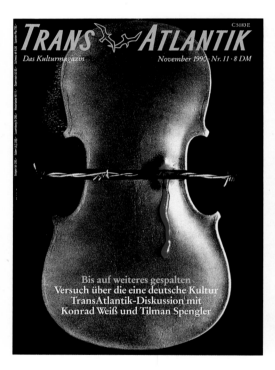

ART DIRECTOR:
RAINER WÖRTMANN
DESIGNER:
MARLIES BOCHERT
ARTISTS:
OTTO DRESSLER
HEINZ EDELMANN
PUBLISHER:
TRANSATLANTIK
■ 384, 385

ART DIRECTOR:
HANS-GEORG
POSPISCHIL
PHOTOGRAPHERS:
WOLFGANG
WESENER
CHRIS STEELE-
PERKINS
LILIAN BIRNBAUM
CLIENT:
FRANKFURTER ALL-GEMEINE MAGAZIN
■ 386-389

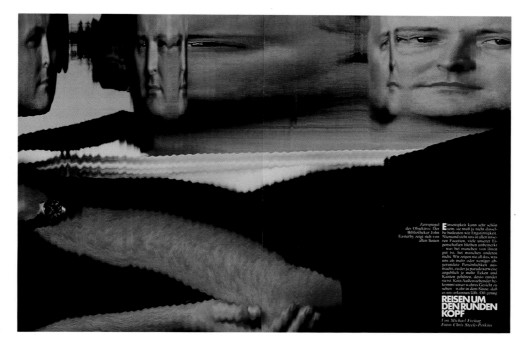

Zerrspiegel des Objektivs: Der Bibliothekar John Easterby zeigt sich von allen Seiten

Einsamkeit kann sehr schön sein, sie muß ja nicht dasselbe bedeuten wie Einsamkeit. Niemand sieht uns in allen inneren Facetten, viele unserer Eigenschaften bleiben unbemerkt – was bei manchen von ihnen gut ist, bei manchen anderen nicht. Wir zeigen nie all das, was uns als mehr oder weniger abgerundete Persönlichkeit ausmacht; zu der ja paradoxerweise angeblich je mehr Ecken und Kanten gehören, desto runder sie ist. Kein Außenstehender bekommt unser wahres Gesicht zu sehen – wahr in dem Sinne, daß es sein erkennen läßt. Oft genug

REISEN UM DEN RUNDEN KOPF

Von Michael Freitag
Fotos Chris Steele-Perkins

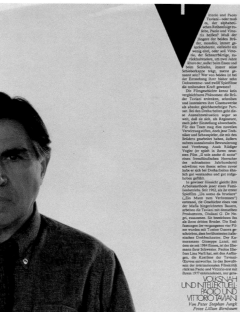

Vittorio und Paolo Taviani – oder muß es, der alphabetischen Reihenfolge zuliebe, Paolo und Vittorio heißen? Muß der jüngere der beiden Brüder, mondän, immer gesprächsbereit, vielleicht ein wenig eitel, oder soll Vittorio, der Schnurrbärtige, zurückhaltendere, um zwei Jahre ältere der, außer beim Essen und beim Schlafen, immer seine Schieberkappe trägt, zuerst genannt sein? Wer von beiden ist bei der Entstehung ihrer bisher zehn Dokumentar- und zwölf Spielfilme die treibende Kraft gewesen?

Die Filmgeschichte kennt kein vergleichbares Phänomen: die Brüder Taviani erdenken, schreiben und inszenieren ihre Cineastwerke als absolut gleichberechtigte Partner. Bei den Dreharbeiten geht diese Ausnahmesituation sogar so weit, daß sie sich, als Regisseure, nach jeder Einstellung abwechseln. Für das Team mag dies zuweilen Verwirrung stiften, doch jene Techniker und Schauspieler, die mit den Brüdern gearbeitet haben, äußern nahezu ausnahmslos Bewunderung und Verehrung. Auch Rüdiger Vogler (er spielt in ihrem neuesten Film „Il sole anche di notte" einen fremdländischen Herrscher des achtzehnten Jahrhunderts) schwärmt von ihnen: selten zuvor habe er sich bei Dreharbeiten ähnlich gut verstanden und gut aufgehoben gefühlt.

In gewisser Hinsicht gleicht ihre Arbeitsmethode jener eines Familienbetriebs. Seit 1962, als ihr erster Spielfilm „Un uomo da bruciare" („Ein Mann zum Verbrennen") entstand, die Geschichte eines von der Mafia hingerichteten Bauern, arbeiten die Taviani mit demselben Produzenten, Giuliani G. De Negri, zusammen. Sie bezeichnen ihn als ihren dritten Bruder. Die Endfassungen der vergangenen vier Filme wurden mit Tonino Guerra geschrieben, dem berühmtesten italienischen Drehbuchautor. Der Kameramann Giuseppe Lanci, mit dem sie seit 1984 filmen, ist der Ehemann ihrer Schwester. Paolos Ehefrau Lina Nerli hat, seit den Anfängen, die Kostüme der Taviani-Œuvres entworfen. In das Bewußtsein der internationalen Filmkritik rückten Paolo und Vittorio erst mit ihrem 1977 entstandenen, nur gera-

Zwei Brüder – ein Kunstwerk. Wenn Paolo- und Vittorio Taviani einen Film drehen, herrscht vollkommene Komplizität zwischen ihnen. Die Harmonie läßt sie wie zwei Erbauer einer Kathedrale erscheinen

VOLKSNAH UND INTELLEKTUELL: PAOLO UND VITTORIO TAVIANI

Vom Peter Stephan Jungk
Fotos Lillian Birnbaum

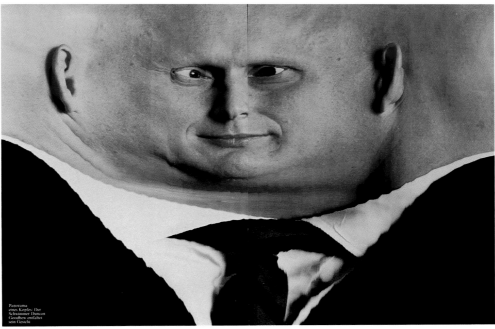

Panorama eines Kopfes: Der Schwimmer Duncan Goodhew entfaltet sein Gesicht

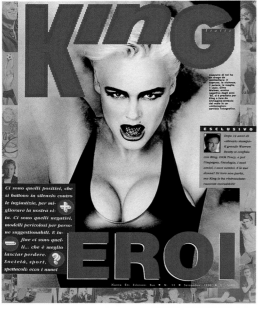

ART DIRECTOR:
DON MORRIS
DESIGNERS:
DON MORRIS
RICHARD FERRETTI
SUSAN FOSTER
PHOTOGRAPHER:
PETER MAUSS
CLIENT:
METROPOLITAN HOME
PUBLISHER:
MEREDITH CORP.
▲■ 390, 391

ART DIRECTORS:
MARIA PIA COPPIN
MARTINA COZZI
PHOTOGRAPHERS:
WAYNE MASER
ALBERTO TOLOT
COPYWRITER:
FRANCESCA NOCERINO
CLIENT:
KING
PUBLISHER:
NUOVA ERI-EDIZIONI
RAI
■ 392, 393

DESIGN DIRECTOR:
MICHAEL BROCK
ART DIRECTOR:
MICHAEL BROCK
DESIGNER:
MICHAEL BROCK
PHOTOGRAPHERS:
PAUL JASMIN
GEORGE HOLZ
STYLISTS:
KATE HARRINGTON
SHEA
DENISE TERESE
SOLIS
AGENCY:
MICHAEL BROCK
DESIGN
PUBLISHER:
L.A. STYLE
▲
▶■ 394, 395

ART DIRECTOR:
HANS VAN
BLOOMESTEIN
DESIGNERS:
LOUIS VOOGT
TINY LAARAKKER
PHOTOGRAPHERS:
ALAN DAVID-TU
MARC BORTHWICK
PUBLISHER:
AVENUE
▶■ 396, 397

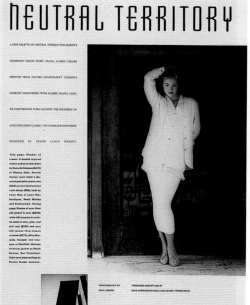

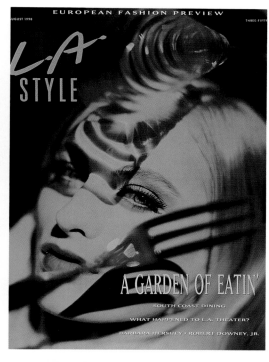

■ 390, 391 COVER OF AN ISSUE OF *METROPOLITAN HOME* MAGAZINE DEDICATED TO CONTEMPORARY DESIGN AND A SPREAD SHOWING HOW ARCHITECT HENRY MYERBERG TRANSLATED FRENCH ARCHITECT JEAN PROUVÉ'S DESIGN INTO HIS OWN DYNAMIC STYLE. HE USED CONCRETE FOR THIS HOUSE. (USA)

■ 392, 393 COVER AND SPREAD FROM *KING* MAGAZINE ON THE SUBJECT OF HEROES, SYMBOLIZED BY THE PROVOCATIVE POSES OF MADONNA. (ITA)

■ 394 FASHION'S PALETTE OF NEUTRAL TONES PHOTOGRAPHED IN THE CHARLES ENNIS HOUSE DESIGNED BY FRANK LLOYD WRIGHT. SPREAD FROM *L.A. STYLE* MAGAZINE. (USA)

■ 395 EATING IS THE SUBJECT OF THIS COVER OF *L.A. STYLE*. (USA)

■ 396, 397 THIS SPREAD FROM *AVENUE* DEALS WITH THE DANGERS OF SUNBATHING. THE THEME OF THE COVER IS THE ENHANCEMENT OF THE SKIN THROUGH FASHION. (NLD)

● 390, 391 DER UMSCHLAG DIESER AUSGABE VON *METROPOLITAN HOME* IST DEM EINFLUSS DES DESIGNS GEWIDMET. DIE DOPPELSEITE ZEIGT BAUTEN VON HENRY MYERBERG, DIE VON DEM FRANZÖSISCHEN ARCHITEKTEN JEAN PROUVÉ INSPIRIERT WURDEN. (USA)

● 392, 393 UMSCHLAG UND DOPPELSEITE VON *KING* ZUM THEMA IDOLE, DIE DURCH MADONNA IN PROVOKATIVEN POSEN SYMBOLISIERT WERDEN. (ITA)

● 394 NEUTRALE FARBEN KLASSISCHER MODE, PHOTOGRAPHIERT IM CHARLES ENNIS HOUSE VON FRANK LLOYD WRIGHT. DOPPELSEITE AUS DER ZEITSCHRIFT *L.A. STYLE*. (USA)

● 395 ESSEN IST DAS THEMA DIESES UMSCHLAG VON *L.A. STYLE*. (USA)

● 396, 397 DIESE DOPPELSEITE AUS *AVENUE* BEFASST SICH MIT DEM SONNENBADEN, DER UMSCHLAG BEZIEHT SICH AUF DIE BETONUNG DER HAUT DURCH DIE MODE. (NLD)

▲ 390, 391 COUVERTURE D'UN NUMÉRO DU MAGAZINE *METROPOLITAN HOME* CONSACRÉ AUX PERSONNALITÉS ET AUX GRANDES OPTIONS DU DESIGN D'AUJOURD'HUI. SUR LA DOUBLE PAGE, ON VOIT DES BÂTIMENTS D'HENRY MYERBERG, INSPIRÉS DE L'ARCHITECTURE DE JEAN PROUVÉ. (USA)

▲ 392, 393 COUVERTURE ET DOUBLE PAGE DU MAGAZINE *KING* SUR LE THÈME DES HÉROS, SYMBOLISÉS DE MANIÈRE PROVOCATRICE PAR MADONNA. (ITA)

▲ 394 DOUBLE PAGE DU MAGAZINE *L.A. STYLE* SUR LE THÈME DES COULEURS NEUTRES DANS LA MODE. LES PHOTOS ONT ÉTÉ PRISES DANS LA CHARLES ENNIS HOUSE DE FRANK LLOYD WRIGHT. (USA)

▲ 395 LA GASTRONOMIE EST LE SUJET DE CETTE COUVERTURE DE *L.A. STYLE*. (USA)

▲ 396, 397 COUVERTURE D'UN NUMÉRO DE *AVENUE* CONSACRÉ À UNE MODE QUI MET L'ACCENT SUR LA PEAU. DOUBLE PAGE SUR LES BAINS DE SOLEIL ET LES DANGERS DU BRONZAGE POUR LA PEAU. (NLD)

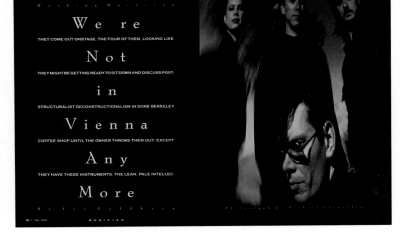

ART DIRECTOR:
MATTHEW DRACE
DESIGNER:
MATTHEW DRACE
PHOTOGRAPHER:
DAVID PETERSON
PUBLISHER:
SAN FRANCISCO
FOCUS
▲■ 398

ART DIRECTOR:
D.J. STOUT
DESIGNER:
D.J. STOUT
PHOTOGRAPHER:
BRIAN BARNAUD
PUBLISHER:
TEXAS MONTHLY
■ 399

ART DIRECTOR:
ANNELISE RAZZINI
DESIGNER:
ANNELISE RAZZINI
PHOTOGRAPHER:
CARLO BELLINCAMPI/
LOOK PHOTO
CLIENT:
MODA
PUBLISHER:
NUOVA ERI EDIZIONI
RAI
▲■ 400

ART DIRECTOR:
PATRICK MITCHELL
DESIGNER:
PATRICK MITCHELL
PHOTOGRAPHER:
MICHAEL LLEWELLYN
PUBLISHER:
BILLBOARD
■ 401

MY BEAUTIFUL BALLOONIST

What happens when the hero of your youth grows older— and you do too?

by Jeanne Marie Laskas

Connie Wolf, 85, learned to soar above everyday life in balloons. She flew this $100,000 nylon bubble to celebrate the 200th anniversary of the Constitution.

ART DIRECTOR:
TOM BENTKOWSKI
DESIGNERS:
TOM BENTKOWSKI
MARTI GOLON
PHOTOGRAPHER:
DONNA FERRATO
CLIENT:
LIFE
PUBLISHER:
TIME, INC.
■ 402

■ 398 FROM AN ARTICLE ON THE DESIGNER ROBERT FILLER IN *SAN FRANCISCO FOCUS*. SHOWN IS A TELEVISION SET, A SUITCASE AND CHAIR FROM HIS JOURNEY OBJECT SERIES. HE ALSO PREFERS BLACK IN HIS OWN APARTMENT AS HE FEELS THAT IT DEFINES FUNCTIONS. (USA)

■ 399 INTRODUCTORY SPREAD FOR AN ARTICLE IN *TEXAS MONTHLY* ON SELF-MADE TRENDMONGER AND PUBLISHER ERIC KIMMEL. (USA)

■ 400 DOUBLE SPREAD FROM A FEATURE IN *MODA* ON ISABELLA FERRARI, AN AMBITIOUS AND DETERMINED ITALIAN ACTRESS, WHO SPEAKS HERE ABOUT HER PRIVATE LIFE. (ITA)

■ 401 INTRODUCTORY SPREAD FOR AN ARTICLE IN THE MAGAZINE *MUSICIAN* OFFERING AN INTIMATE LOOK AT THE NEW WAVE GROUP "THE KRONOS QUARTET". (USA)

■ 402 CONNIE WOLF, 85 YEARS OLD BALLOONIST, WITH THE BALLOON IN WHICH SHE FLEW TO CELEBRATE THE 200TH ANNIVERSARY OF THE CONSTITUTION, SPREAD FROM *LIFE* MAGAZINE. (USA)

● 398 AUS EINEM ARTIKEL ÜBER DEN DESIGNER ROBERT FILLER IN *SAN FRANCISCO FOCUS*. GEZEIGT SIND EIN VON IHM ENTWORFENER FERNSEH-APPARAT, KOFFER UND STUHL. SCHWARZ DOMINIERT IN SEINER WOHNUNG, WEIL ES, GEMÄSS FILLER, FUNKTIONEN HERVORHEBT. (USA)

● 399 EINFÜHRUNG ZU EINEM ARTIKEL IN *TEXAS MONTHLY* ÜBER ERIC KIMMEL, ENFANT TERRIBLE DER TEXANISCHEN VERLAGSSZENE. (USA)

● 400 DOPPELSEITE AUS DER ZEITSCHRIFT *MODA* MIT EINEM BEITRAG ÜBER DIE AMBITIÖSE UND ENTSCHLOSSENE ITALIENISCHE SCHAUSPIELERIN ISABELLA FERRARI. (ITA)

● 401 «WIR SIND NICHT MEHR IN WIEN.» EINFÜH-RENDE DOPPELSEITE ZU EINEM BEITRAG IN DER ZEITSCHRIFT *MUSICIAN* ÜBER DAS MODERNE STREICHQUARTETT KRONOS. (USA)

● 402 CONNIE WOLF, 85 JAHRE ALT, VOR DEM BAL-LON, MIT DEM SIE ANLÄSSLICH DER AMERIKANI-SCHEN 200-JAHR-FEIER EINEN FLUG UNTERNAHM. AUS EINEM ARTIKEL IN *LIFE*. (USA)

▲ 398 D'UN ARTICLE SUR LE DESIGNER ROBERT FILLER PARU DANS *SAN FRANCISCO FOCUS*. SON APPARTEMENT, TOUT EN NOIR ET BLANC, EST L'EXPRESSION MÊME DE SA PHILOSOPHIE, LE NOIR METTANT EN VALEUR LA FONCTION DES OBJETS. IL A CRÉÉ LA TV, LA VALISE ET LA CHAISE. (USA)

▲ 399 DOUBLE PAGE D'UN ARTICLE SUR ERIC KIMMEL, L'ENFANT TERRIBLE DE L'ÉDITION TEXANE, PUBLIÉ DANS *TEXAS MONTHLY*. (USA)

▲ 400 DOUBLE PAGE D'UN ARTICLE DE *MODA* SUR ISABELLA FERRARI, UNE ACTRICE ITALIENNE AMBITIEUSE ET DÉTERMINÉE QUI, INTERROGÉE SUR SA VIE PRIVÉE, RÉTABLIT LA VÉRITÉ. (ITA)

▲ 401 DOUBLE PAGE D'UN ARTICLE DU MAGAZINE *MUSICIAN* RELATANT UNE ENTREVUE AVEC LES QUATRE MUSICIENS DU GROUPE NEW WAVE, «THE KRONOS QUARTET». (USA)

▲ 402 CONNIE WOLF, 85 ANS, DEVANT LE BALLON AVEC LEQUEL ELLE A EFFECTUÉ UN VOL POUR LE 200E ANNIVERSAIRE DE LA CONSTITUTION AMÉRI-CAINE. D'UN ARTICLE PARU DANS *LIFE*. (USA)

DOSSIER

ART DIRECTOR:

RUEDI BAUR

DESIGNERS:

RUEDI BAUR

JULIETTE TIXADOR

AGENCY:

INTEGRAL CONCEPT

PUBLISHER:

BEAUX-ART

MAGAZINE

■ 403-406

ART DIRECTORS:

TAKE STUDIO

RAY NHER

CHRISTOF RABANUS

WOLFGANG KOWALL

SIBYLLE MENSINGA

PHOTOGRAPHERS:

TAKE STUDIO

YVONNE BARGSTÄDT

HANS CHRISTOPH

BRINKSCHMIDT

KEN HAAK

PUBLISHER:

PETER SCHULZ

FOERSTEN/

2029 MAGAZIN

▶■ 407-409

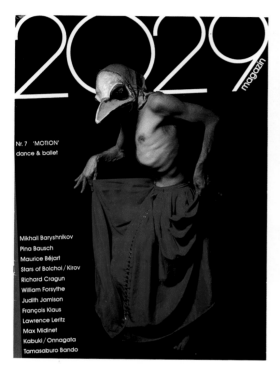

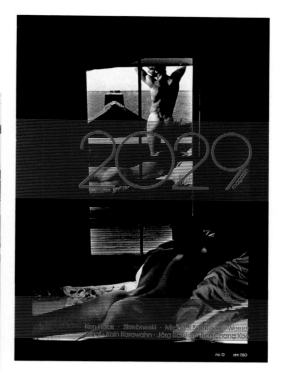

■ 403-406 DOUBLE SPREADS FROM THE REDESIGNED *BEAUX ARTS MAGAZINE*: "DAVID UNDRESSED," AN ARTICLE ON THE FRENCH PAINTER JACQUES LOUIS DAVID; "ARCHITECTS OF FREEDOM", INTRODUCTORY SPREAD FOR A COMMENT ON AN EXHIBITION OF ARCHITECTS FROM THE FRENCH REVOLUTIONARY PERIOD; THE PAINTING "LA NATIVITÉ" BY GEORGES DE LA TOUR FOR AN ARTICLE ON THE SALE OF WORKS OF ART; "UTOPIA IN CONCRETE" INTRODUCING AN ARTICLE ON ARCHITECTURE. (FRA)

■ 407-409 COVERS OF THREE ISSUES OF *2029 MAGAZIN*, EACH DEDICATED TO A PARTICULAR SUBJECT: DANCE AND BALLET; ARCHITECTURE AND DESIGN; MALE NUDE PHOTOGRAPHY. (GER)

● 403-406 AUS DEM NEU GESTALTETEN *BEAUX ARTS MAGAZINE*: «DAVID, ENTKLEIDET», ALS EINLEITUNG ZU EINEM ARTIKEL ÜBER DEN FRANZÖSISCHEN MALER J.L. DAVID; «ARCHITEKTEN DER FREIHEIT», EIN BERICHT ÜBER EINE AUSSTELLUNG VON ARCHITEKTEN AUS DER ZEIT FRANZÖSISCHEN REVOLUTION; DAS GEMÄLDE «LA NATIVITÉ» VON GEORGES DE LA TOUR ILLUSTRIERT EINEN ARTIKEL ÜBER DEN VERKAUF VON KUNSTWERKEN; «UTOPIE IN BETON», FÜR EINEN ARCHITEKTURARTIKEL. (FRA)

● 407-409 UMSCHLÄGE DER ZEITSCHRIFT *2029 MAGAZIN*, DIE JEWEILS EINEM THEMA GEWIDMET SIND: TANZ UND BALLETT; ARCHITEKTUR UND DESIGN UND MÄNNLICHE AKTPHOTOGRAPHIE. (GER)

▲ 403-406 DOUBLES PAGES DE *BEAUX-ARTS MAGAZINE*, QUI A FAIT L'OBJET D'UN RESTYLING. EN HAUT, OUVERTURE D'ARTICLE SUR LE DÉSHABILLÉ CHEZ DAVID. CI-DESSUS: D'UN ARTICLE SUR LES ARCHITECTES DE LA RÉVOLUTION, À L'OCCASION D'UNE EXPOSITION À L'ÉCOLE DES BEAUX-ARTS DE PARIS; «LA NATIVITÉ» DE GEORGES DE LA TOUR ILLUSTRE UN ARTICLE SUR LES VENTES D'ŒUVRES D'ART; PROJET FUTURISTE POUR UN ARTICLE SUR L'ARCHITECTURE EN BÉTON. (FRA)

▲ 407-409 COUVERTURES DE TROIS NUMÉROS DE *2029 MAGAZIN* CONSACRÉS AUX THÈMES SUIVANTS: DANSE ET BALLET, ARCHITECTURE ET DESIGN, LA PHOTOGRAPHIE DE NUS MASCULINS. (GER)

What a Bomber
A classic jacket takes flight

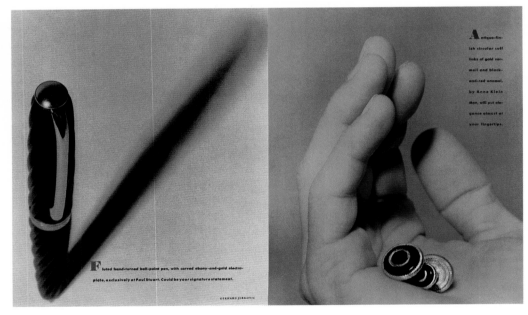

CREATIVE DIRECTOR:
DEREK UNGLESS
DESIGNERS:
DEREK UNGLESS
LUCY SISMAN
PHOTOGRAPHERS:
PAMELA HANSON
ALBERT WATSON
ISABEL SNYDER
BILL STEELE
TOM KASSER/
GAMMA LIAISON
PETA
ANDREW MAC-
PHERSON
WAYNE MASER
ARTIST:
JULIAN ALLEN
PUBLISHER:
DETAILS
▲■ 410-413

ART DIRECTOR:
TERRY KOPPEL
DESIGNER:
TERRY KOPPEL
PHOTOGRAPHERS:
MATTHEW ROLSTON
GERHARD JURKOVIC
CHRIS CRANCE
CLIENT:
ESQUIRE
PUBLISHER:
HEARST CORP.
■ 414-417

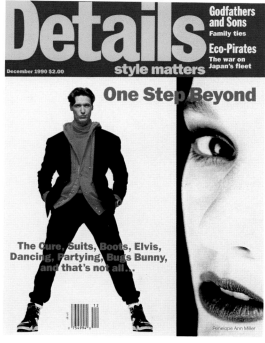

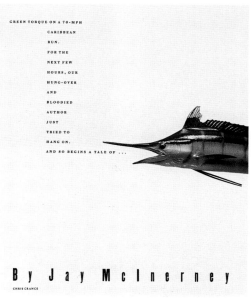

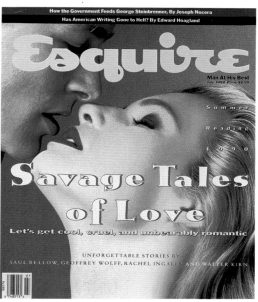

■ 410, 411 COVER OF THE JANUARY 1991 ISSUE OF *DETAILS* MAGAZINE WITH A YEAR-END WRAP-UP, AND A DOUBLE SPREAD SHOWING THE LATEST IN CLASSICAL JACKETS INCLUDING PRICE AND SHOP INFORMATION. (USA)

■ 412 SPREAD FROM *DETAILS* REPORTING (LEFT) ON THE NIGHT-VISION GOGGLES OF THE US ARMY'S TASK FORCE 160. TWENTY-EIGHT MEMBERS OF THE 160TH DIED IN CRASHES WHILE DEVELOPING THE NIGHT-VISION SYSTEM. THE GOGGLES ARE NOW ALSO EMPLOYED IN THE DRUG WAR, AND (RIGHT) ON TORTUROUS EXPERIMENTS WITH MONKEYS AND THEIR DEATH. (USA)

■ 413 COVER OF *DETAILS* MAGAZINE. (USA)

■ 414, 415 CONTROVERSIAL WRITER TOM WOLFE GRACING THE COVER OF *ESQUIRE* MAGAZINE. THE DOUBLE SPREAD PRESENTS SPECIAL ITEMS: A BALL POINT PEN AND ANTIQUE FINISH CIRCULAR CUFF LINKS. (USA)

■ 416, 417 INTRODUCTORY DOUBLE SPREAD TO A STORY AND THE COVER OF AN ISSUE OF *ESQUIRE* MAGAZINE. (USA)

● 410, 411 UMSCHLAG DER JANUAR 1991-AUSGABE DER ZEITSCHRIFT *DETAILS* MIT EINEM JAHRES-ÜBERBLICK. AUF DER DOPPELSEITE WERDEN DIE NEUSTEN VERSIONEN KLASSISCHER JACKEN GEZEIGT. (USA)

● 412 DOPPELSEITE AUS *DETAILS*. LINKS GEHT ES UM SPEZIELLE GLÄSER, DIE UNTER GROSSEN OPFERN FÜR DIE US ARMY ENTWICKELT WURDEN UND JETZT AUCH BEI DER DROGENFAHNDUNG EINGE-SETZT WERDEN, UM KLEINE FLUGZEUGE AM HIMMEL AUSZUMACHEN. RECHTS WIRD ÜBER GRAUSAME TIERVERSUCHE AN DREI AFFEN UND DEREN EUTHA-NISIERUNG BERICHTET. (USA)

● 413 UMSCHLAG DER ZEITSCHRIFT *DETAILS*. (USA)

● 414, 415 DER KONTROVERSE AUTOR TOM WOLFE AUF DEM UMSCHLAG DER ZEITSCHRIFT *ESQUIRE*. DIE DOPPELSEITE PRÄSENTIERT SPEZIELLE ARTIKEL: EIN HANDGEDRECHSELTER KUGELSCHREIBER UND MANSCHETTENKNÖPFE MIT ANTIK-FINISH. (USA)

● 416, 417 EINLEITENDE DOPPELSEITE ZU EINER GESCHICHTE ÜBER «GROSSE FISCHE» UND DER UMSCHLAG EINER AUSGABE VON *ESQUIRE*. (USA)

▲ 410, 411 COUVERTURE DU NUMÉRO DE JANVIER 1991 DU MAGAZINE *DETAILS*, COMPORTANT UN RAPPEL DE L'ANNÉE ÉCOULÉE ET DOUBLE PAGE PRÉSENTANT LES NOUVEAUX MODÈLES DE BLOU-SONS CLASSIQUES. (USA)

▲ 412 DOUBLE PAGE DU MAGAZINE *DETAILS* SUR LES EXPÉRIMENTATIONS: À GAUCHE, LA MISE AU POINT DE CES VERRES SPÉCIAUX PERMETTANT LES RAIDS AÉRIENS NOCTURNES A CAUSÉ LA MORT DE NOMBREUX PILOTES DANS LA PHASE DE TEST; À DROITE, L'ARTICLE ÉVOQUE LES EXPÉRIENCES CRUELLES AUXQUELLES FURENT SOUMIS TROIS SINGES, AVANT D'ÊTRE EUTHANASIÉS. (USA)

▲ 413 COUVERTURE DU MAGAZINE *DETAILS*. (USA)

▲ 414, 415 COUVERTURE ET DOUBLE PAGE DU MAGAZINE *ESQUIRE*. À G., L'ÉCRIVAIN-DANDY TOM WOLFE. A DR., PRÉSENTATION D'ARTICLES EXCLU-SIFS: UN STYLO-PLUME ÉBÈNE ET OR, ET BOUTONS DE MANCHETTE EN VERMEIL ET ÉMAIL. (USA)

▲ 416, 417 DOUBLE PAGE INTRODUISANT UN ARTICLE SUR LES GRANDS POISSONS ET COUVER-TURE D'UN NUMÉRO DU MAGAZINE *ESQUIRE*. (USA)

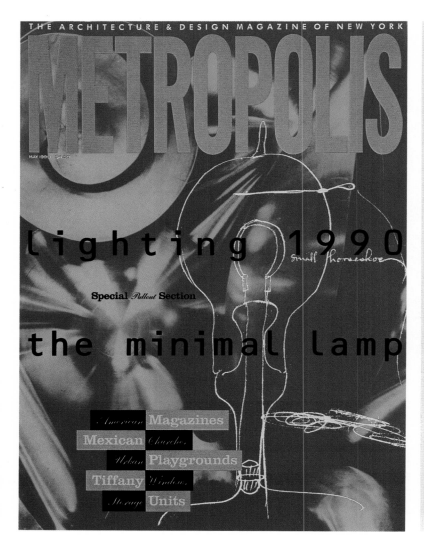

ART DIRECTOR:

JEFF CHRISTENSEN

CLIENT:

METROPOLIS

PUBLISHER:

BELLEROPHON

PUBLICATIONS, INC.

■ 418, 419

ART DIRECTOR:

CARL LEHMANN-HAUPT

PHOTOGRAPHER:

RICHARD BRYANT/

ARCAID

CLIENT:

METROPOLIS

PUBLISHER:

BELLEROPHON

PUBLICATIONS, INC.

►■ 420

flash

of the

spirit

the art lamp uses traditional materials

in richly inventive ways to give new

form to light. here's a look at

unbridled illumination.

68 METROPOLIS JUNE 1992

Left: Elle, floor lamp with table of nickel-plated brass, bubinga wood, and tinted glass by Luigi Blau for Woka Lamps Vienna; sold in New York by Modern Age and George Kovacs. Right: Custom-designed chandelier of steel and colored glass by Patrice Butler of Butler-Radice, London.

■ 418-420 COVER AND PAGES OF AN ISSUE OF *METROPOLIS*, A MAGAZINE ON DESIGN AND ARCHITECTURE. THE COVER ILLUSTRATION AND THE DOUBLE SPREAD REFER TO A SPECIAL ARTICLE ON LIGHTING, WHILE THE SINGLE PAGE SHOWS FRANK GEHRY'S VITRA DESIGN MUSEUM IN WEIL AM RHEIN, GERMANY. (USA)

● 418-420 UMSCHLAG UND SEITEN VON *METROPOLIS*, EINER ZEITSCHRIFT FÜR ARCHITEKTUR UND DESIGN. DIE UMSCHLAGILLUSTRATION UND DIE DOPPELSEITE GEHÖREN ZU EINEM SONDERBEITRAG ÜBER BELEUCHTUNG. DIE EINZELNE SEITE ZEIGT DAS VON FRANK GEHRY ENTWORFENE VITRA DESIGN MUSEUM IN WEIL AM RHEIN. (USA)

▲ 418-420 COUVERTURE ET PAGES INTÉRIEURES DE *METROPOLIS*, UN MAGAZINE DE DESIGN ET D'ARCHITECTURE. L'IMAGE DE COUVERTURE ET LA DOUBLE PAGE PROVIENNENT D'UN NUMÉRO CONSACRÉ À L'ÉCLAIRAGE. SUR LA PAGE SIMPLE, ON PEUT VOIR LE MUSÉE DU DESIGN VITRA DE WEIL AM RHEIN, ŒUVRE DE L'ARCHITECTE FRANK GEHRY. (USA)

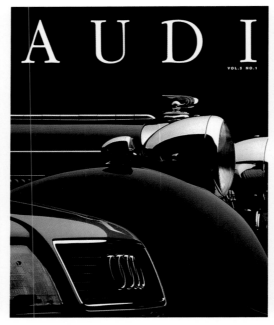

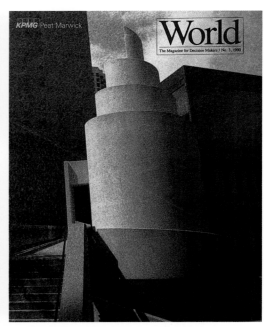

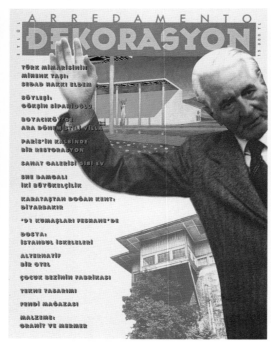

ART DIRECTOR:
ROBERT BEST
DESIGNERS:
ROBERT BEST
SYNDI BECKER
PHOTOGRAPHER:
LOUIS PSIHOYOS/
MATRIX
CLIENT:
NEW YORK
PUBLISHER:
MURDOCH
MAGAZINES
▲■ 421

ART DIRECTOR:
MILES ABERNETHY
DESIGNER:
MILES ABERNETHY
PHOTOGRAPHER:
RODNEY RASCONA
AGENCY:
SHR DESIGN
COMMUNICATIONS
CLIENT:
AUDI OF AMERICA
■ 422

ART DIRECTOR:
DONNA M. BONAVITA
DESIGNER:
DONNA M. BONAVITA
PHOTOGRAPHER:
ARTHUR MEYERSON
CLIENT:
WORLD
PUBLISHER:
KPMG PEAT MARWICK
▲
▲■ 423

ART DIRECTOR:
KIT HINRICHS
DESIGNERS:
TERRI DRISCOLL
KIT HINRICHS
PHOTOGRAPHER:
COMSTOCK, INC.
AGENCY:
PENTAGRAM DESIGN
CLIENT:
SKALD
PUBLISHER:
ROYAL VIKING LINE
■ 424

ART DIRECTOR:
BÜLENT ERKMEN
DESIGNER:
BÜLENT ERKMEN
AGENCY:
REKLAMEVI Y&R
CLIENT:
ARREDAMENTO
DEKORASYON
PUBLISHER:
BOYUT PUBLISHING
GROUP
▲
▲■ 425

ART DIRECTOR:
RICHARD HESS
DESIGNERS:
ELLIE EISNER
KATHLEEN HOHL-
PHILLIPS
AGENCY:
HESS & HESS
PUBLISHER:
AT&T
■ 426

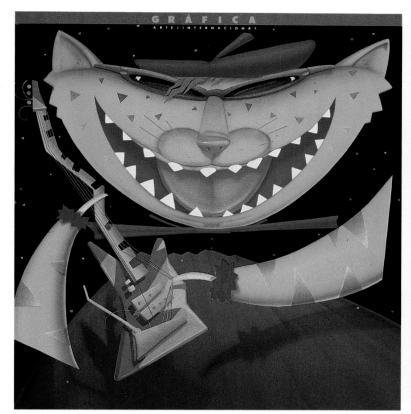

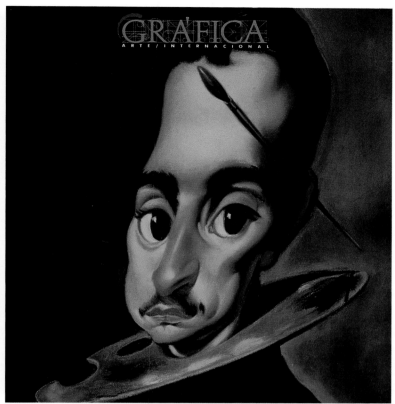

ART DIRECTOR:
OSWALDO MIRANDA
DESIGNER:
OSWALDO MIRANDA
ARTISTS:
BILL MAYER
RUBEM CARCAMO
AGENCY:
CASA DE IDÉIAS
CLIENT:
GRAFICA
■ 427, 428

■ 421 COVER OF A SPECIAL ISSUE OF *NEW YORK* MAGAZINE. THE HEADLINE ALLUDES TO THE TITLE OF THE FAMOUS BOOK SERIES "A DAY IN THE LIFE OF...". (USA)

■ 422 A VINTAGE AUDI, THE HORCH 853A OF THE LATE THIRTIES, ON THE COVER OF A CUSTOMER MAGAZINE OF AUDI OF AMERICA. (USA)

■ 423 COVER FOR *WORLD* ("THE MAGAZINE FOR DECISION MAKERS") RELATING TO AN ARTICLE ON THE FUTURE OUTLOOK OF DALLAS, TEXAS. (USA)

■ 424 AN ARTICLE ON AFRICA AND THE FACT THAT LIONS, UNLIKE MOST BIG CATS, TRAVEL AS PART OF A GROUP, BROUGHT THIS LION ON THE COVER OF THE MAGAZINE OF ROYAL VIKING LINE'S SKALD CLUB. (USA)

■ 425 COVER OF A TURKISH MAGAZINE ON ARCHITECTURE AND DESIGN. (TUR)

■ 426 COVER OF THE EMPLOYEE ANNUAL REPORT OF AT&T SHOWING PORTRAITS OF ITS STAFF. (USA)

■ 427, 428 COVERS OF THE GRAPHIC ARTS MAGAZINE *GRAFICA*. THE ONE AT LEFT REFERS TO A FEATURE ON ARTIST BILL MAYER, THE ONE AT RIGHT IS A HOMAGE TO VELASQUEZ. (BRA)

● 421 UMSCHLAG EINER SPEZIALAUSGABE DER ZEITSCHRIFT *NEW YORK*. DIE SCHLAGZEILE IST EINE ANSPIELUNG AUF DIE BUCHREIHE «A DAY IN THE LIFE OF...». (USA)

● 422 DETAIL EINES AUDIS, DES HORCH 853A AUS DEN SPÄTEN 30ER JAHREN, AUF DEM UMSCHLAG DER KUNDENZEITSCHRIFT VON AUDI OF AMERICA. (USA)

● 423 DIESER UMSCHLAG DER KUNDENZEITSCHRIFT VON KPMG PEAT MARWICK BEZIEHT SICH AUF EINEN BEITRAG ÜBER DIE ZUKUNFT VON DALLAS. (USA)

● 424 EIN BERICHT ÜBER AFRIKA UND DIE TATSACHE, DASS LÖWEN IN GRUPPEN ZIEHEN, WAS BEI GROSSKATZEN EHER DIE AUSNAHME IST, BRACHTE IHN AUF DIE TITELSEITE DIESER PUBLIKATION DER ROYAL VIKING LINE. (USA)

● 425 UMSCHLAG EINER TÜRKISCHEN ZEITSCHRIFT ÜBER ARCHITEKTUR UND DESIGN. (TUR)

● 426 UMSCHLAG DES JAHRESBERICHTES DER AT&T MIT PORTRÄTS DER MITARBEITER. (USA)

● 427, 428 UMSCHLÄGE DER GRAPHIKZEITSCHRIFT *GRAFICA*. SIE BEZIEHEN SICH AUF BEITRÄGE ÜBER DEN KÜNSTLER BILL MAYER UND DAS VELASQUEZ-GEDENKJAHR. (BRA)

▲ 421 COUVERTURE D'UN NUMÉRO SPÉCIAL DU MAGAZINE *NEW YORK* CONSACRÉ À LA VIE NOCTURNE DE CETTE VILLE. LE SLOGAN PLAGIE LA FORMULE: «A DAY IN THE LIFE OF...» (USA)

▲ 422 DÉTAIL D'UN MODÈLE AUDI DE LA FIN DES ANNÉES 30, LA HORCH 853A, EN COUVERTURE D'UN MAGAZINE PUBLIÉ PAR AUDI OF AMERICA. (USA)

▲ 423 CETTE COUVERTURE DU MAGAZINE *WORLD* SE RAPPORTE À UN ARTICLE SUR LE FUTUR DE LA VILLE DE DALLAS. (USA)

▲ 424 UN REPORTAGE SUR L'AFRIQUE ET LE FAIT QUE, CONTRAIREMENT AUX AUTRES FÉLINS, LES LIONS VIVENT EN GROUPE, ONT FOURNI LE MOTIF DE CETTE PAGE DE COUVERTURE DU MAGAZINE DE LA ROYAL VIKING LINE. (USA)

▲ 425 COUVERTURE D'UN MAGAZINE DE DÉCORATION INTÉRIEURE ET D'AMEUBLEMENT. (TUR)

▲ 426 «QUI SOMMES-NOUS?»: COUVERTURE DU JOURNAL D'ENTREPRISE DE AT&T. (USA)

▲ 427, 428 COUVERTURES DU MAGAZINE BIMENSUEL *GRAFICA*, L'UN (À G.) CONSACRÉ À L'ILLUSTRATEUR BILL MAYER ET L'AUTRE PUBLIÉ À L'OCCASION DE L'ANNIVERSAIRE DE LA MORT DE VELASQUEZ. (SPA)

BEACH CULTure

Bob Mould
Singing In the Rain

Anton Corbijn:
The Man Who Shot U–2

Brad Gerlach
Animal Magnetism

Mick Jones
On Apocalypse Beach

Special No-Emigre-Fonts
Issue

Punk Gods: Soul Surfers:
John Doe
Henry Rollins
Iggy Pop
Phranc
John Hiatt

Mazzy Star
Rising

Bathing Suits
Yesterday and Today

Wedge People

The Shred–
Where Attitude Meets
Altitude

Robert Ferrigno
Turned On

Henrik Drescher
Waste Deep

Road Tripping:
Baja
Austin
Santa Barbara
Diamond Head

The End of Summer

BEACH CULTure 1990

Water

david
The First Interview
lynch

sinéad
o'connor

art+music surf + skate
style+attitude

the day
manson
met the beach boy

the birth of
the endless
summer

ART DIRECTOR:

DAVID CARSON

DESIGNER:

DAVID CARSON

PHOTOGRAPHER:

ANTON CORBIJN

AGENCY:

CARSON DESIGN

CLIENT:

BEACH CULTURE

PUBLISHER:

SURFER

PUBLICATIONS

■ 429, 430

ART DIRECTOR:

AMILCARE PONCHIELLI

DESIGNER:

GUIDO TERRAGNI

PHOTOGRAPHER:

RALPH LOMBARD

CLIENT:

*CORRIERE DELLA
SERA*

PUBLISHER:

RCS EDITORIALE
QUOTIDIANI SPA

▶■ 431

■ 429, 430 TWO COVERS OF THE MAGAZINE *BEACH CULTURE*: AT LEFT "THE END OF SUMMER", AT RIGHT A SPECIAL SUMMER ISSUE ON THE THEME OF "WATER." (USA).

■ 431 COVER OF AN ISSUE OF THE SUNDAY SUPPLEMENT OF THE ITALIAN NEWSPAPER *CORRIERE DELLA SERA* WITH AN ARTICLE ON JERUSALEM, CITY TORN BETWEEN "HATE AND FAITH." (ITA).

● 429, 430 UMSCHLÄGE VON ZWEI AUSGABEN DER ZEITSCHRIFT *BEACH CULTURE*. LINKS «DAS ENDE DES SOMMERS», RECHTS FÜR EINE SONDERNUMMER ÜBER «WASSER». (USA)

● 431 UMSCHLAG EINER AUSGABE DER SONNTAGS-BEILAGE DES *CORRIERE DELLA SERA* MIT EINEM ARTIKEL ÜBER JERUSALEM, STADT ZWISCHEN «HASS UND GLAUBEN». (ITA)

▲ 429, 430 DEUX EXEMPLES DE COUVERTURES DU MAGAZINE *BEACH CULTURE*. À GAUCHE, «LA FIN DE L'ÉTÉ», À DROITE, UN NUMÉRO SPÉCIAL ÉTÉ SUR LE THÈME DE L'EAU. (USA)

▲ 431 COUVERTURE D'UN NUMÉRO DU SUPPLÉMENT DOMINICAL DU *CORRIERE DELLA SERA* COMPORTANT UN REPORTAGE SUR JÉRUSALEM, CITÉ DÉCHIRÉE «ENTRE LA HAINE ET LA FOI». (ITA)

7

CORRIERE DELLA SERA

RCS Editoriale Quotidiani

N. 41 - SUPPLEMENTO
DEL CORRIERE DELLA SERA
SPEDIZIONE IN ABBONAMENTO
POSTALE GRUPPO I/70

GERUSALEMME
TRA ODIO E FEDE

VENUS roamed about the boardwalk, feeling hopeless and more than a little annoyed with the sand in her shiny shoes.

A KINDLY old fortune teller took her aside and told her that soon she would meet a tall, dark, handsome stranger...an Aquarius no less. VENUS set out in search of her sole mate. SHE wondered

into the Sun Block a dark, smoky club at the waters edge where she would meet her destiny. "CAN I get you a Sea Breeze?" the voice said, in a language only they could understand.

"oh shit, I don't have any money." "TYPICAL," she thought, but dared not test fate. "MY name is Neptune, and I have come to rescue you...

ART DIRECTOR:

DEBBIE KLEIN

DESIGNER:

DEBBIE KLEIN

PHOTOGRAPHER:

KIMBERLY

HOLCOMBE

COPYWRITER:

SARA HOOTNICK

STYLIST:

COLLEEN GANON/

TEAM

CLIENT:

STUFF MAGAZINE

PUBLISHER:

ROBERT BIRNBAUM

◄■ 432

ART DIRECTOR:

KIT HINRICHS

DESIGNERS:

TERRI DRISCOLL

KIT HINRICHS

PIPER MURAKAMI

PHOTOGRAPHER:

STEVEN A. HELLER

COPYWRITER:

STUART FROLICK

AGENCY:

PENTAGRAM DESIGN

PUBLISHER:

ART CENTER

COLLEGE OF DESIGN

■ 433, 434

■ 432 BEACH FASHION FOR MEN PRESENTED ON THE SPREADS OF *STUFF* MAGAZINE. THE COPY TELLS ABOUT HOW VENUS SET OUT IN SEARCH OF HER SOULMATE, NEPTUNE. (USA)

■ 433, 434 A DOUBLE SPREAD OF THE LARGE-FORMAT MAGAZINE PUBLISHED BY THE ART CENTER COLLEGE OF DESIGN OF CALIFORNIA AND THE COVER OF THE SAME ISSUE WHICH CONTAINED AN ARTICLE ON KEITH HARING WHO SPENT THREE DAYS AT THE SCHOOL TO DO A MURAL. (USA).

● 432 BADEMODE FÜR MÄNNER, VORGESTELLT IN DER ZEITSCHRIFT *STUFF*. DER TEXT BERICHTET VON VENUS AUF DER SUCHE NACH IHREM EINZIGEN GEFÄHRTEN, NEPTUN. (USA)

● 433, 434 DOPPELSEITE AUS DER GROSSFORMA-TIGEN PUBLIKATION DES ART CENTER COLLEGE OF DESIGN UND UMSCHLAG DER GLEICHEN AUSGABE MIT EINEM PORTRÄT VON KEITH HARING, DER DREI TAGE IN DER SCHULE VERBRACHTE, UM EIN WAND-GEMÄLDE ANZUFERTIGEN. (USA)

▲ 432 DOUBLE PAGE DU MAGAZINE *STUFF* PRÉSENTANT DES MODÈLES DE MAILLOTS DE BAIN POUR HOMMES. LE TEXTE RACONTE L'HISTOIRE DE LA RENCONTRE ENTRE VÉNUS ET NEPTUNE. (USA)

▲ 433, 434 UNE DOUBLE PAGE DE LA REVUE GRAND FORMAT DU ART CENTER COLLEGE OF DESIGN ET LA COUVERTURE DE CE MÊME NUMÉRO QUI CONTENAIT UN REPORTAGE SUR KEITH HARING. LORS D'UNE VISITE DE TROIS JOURS DANS CETTE ÉCOLE, CE DERNIER EXÉCUTA UNE PEINTURE MURALE. (USA)

PORTFOLIO

2 PUBLIC FINANCE LEAD MAN-
AGES BOND OFFERING FOR
RECYCLED PAPER MILL
◦ NEW LONDON HEADQUAR-
TERS AT CANARY WHARF ◦
ANNUAL MEETING ◦ DAVID
MARCUS JOINS THE FIRM.

3 JOHN LAIRD IS THE NEW CHAIRMAN
AND CHIEF EXECUTIVE OFFICER OF
THE BOSTON COMPANY. HE HAS
SPENT HIS FIRST FEW MONTHS ON
THE JOB MEETING EMPLOYEES
AND CLIENTS AND DETERMINING
PRIORITIES.

NEWS FOR THE PEOPLE OF SHEARSON LEHMAN BROTHERS INC.

SEPTEMBER 1990

the natural resources group: the oil industry takes center stage

The Graceland Experience

Premiere Issue • Agency Growth Compromises Creativity

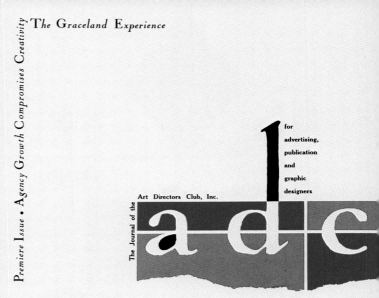

for
advertising,
publication
and
graphic
designers

The Journal of the   Art Directors Club, Inc.

1

a d c

Hall of Fame '89

LES FIGURES

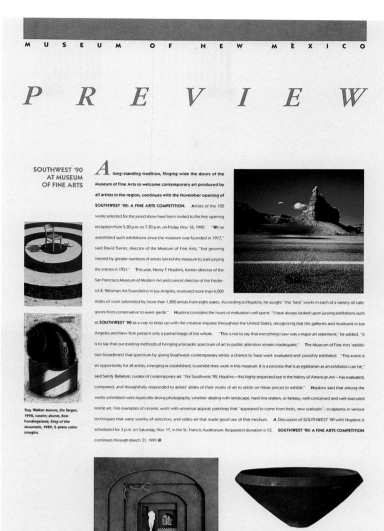

ART DIRECTOR:
DAVID BARNETT
DESIGNERS:
DAVID BARNETT
THEO FELS
ARTIST:
CHRIS GALL
PUBLISHER:
SHEARSON LEHMAN
BROTHERS
◄◄■ 435

ART DIRECTOR:
TERRY R. KOPPEL
DESIGNER:
TERRY R. KOPPEL
PHOTOGRAPHER:
GEOF KERN
CLIENT:
ART DIRECTORS
CLUB, INC.
PUBLISHER:
ESQUIRE
◄■ 436

ART DIRECTOR:
CINDY SCHNELL
DESIGNER:
CINDY SCHNELL
ARTIST:
KEVIN BURKE
AGENCY:
GRAPHICA, INC.
CLIENT:
NCR CORPORATION
■ 437

ART DIRECTOR:
HELEN MCCARTY
COPYWRITERS:
BEVERLY BECKER
CHERYL MITCHELL
AGENCY:
HELEN MCCARTY
CLIENT:
MUSEUM OF NEW
MEXICO
■ 438

■ 435 COVER PAGE OF A CORPORATE PUBLICATION OF SHEARSON LEHMAN BROTHERS INC. THE ILLUSTRATION REFERS TO AN ARTICLE ON THE OIL INDUSTRY. (USA)

■ 436 COVER OF THE FIRST ISSUE OF *ADC* MAGZINE, A NEW PUBLICATION OF THE ART DIRECTORS CLUB. THE SURREALISTIC PHOTOGRAPHY REFERS TO AN ARTICLE ON THE HALL OF FAME '89 AWARD WINNERS. (USA)

■ 437 COVER PAGE OF A NEWSLETTER PUBLISHED TWICE A YEAR BY THE NCR CORPORATION WITH THE AIM OF RECRUITING COLLEGE GRADUATES. (USA)

■ 438 COVER OF A JOURNAL PUBLISHED BY THE MUSEUM OF NEW MEXICO WITH INFORMATION ON ITS PROGRAM. PRESENTED HERE ARE SOME OF THE AWARDED WORKS OF ART OF A CONTEMPORARY ART COMPETITION IN THE REGION. (USA)

● 435 UMSCHLAG EINER FIRMENPUBLIKATION VON SHEARSON LEHMAN BROTHERS. DIE ILLUSTRATION BEZIEHT SICH AUF EINEN ARTIKEL ÜBER DIE ÖLINDUSTRIE. (USA)

● 436 DIE PREISTRÄGER DER HALL OF FAME 89 DES ART DIRECTORS CLUB SIND DAS THEMA DIESER SURREALISTISCHEN AUFNAHME AUF DEM UMSCHLAG DER ERSTEN AUSGABE VON ADC, EINER PUBLI-KATION DES ART DIRECTORS CLUB. (USA)

● 437 TITELSEITE EINES JOURNALS, DAS ZWEIMAL JÄHRLICH VON NRC CORP. HERAUSGEGEBEN WIRD UND UM ABSOLVENTEN VON COLLEGES WIRBT. (USA)

● 438 TITELSEITE EINER PUBLIKATION DES MUSEUM OF NEW MEXICO MIT INFORMATIONEN ÜBER VERAN-STALTUNGEN. HIER WERDEN EINIGE DER PRÄMIER-TEN WERKE EINES WETTBEWERBS FÜR KÜNSTLER DER REGION VORGESTELLT. (USA)

▲ 435 PAGE DE TITRE DU JOURNAL DE LA SOCIÉTÉ SHEARSON LEHMAN BROTHERS. L'ILLUSTRATION SE RAPPORTE À UN ARTICLE SUR L'INDUSTRIE PÉTROLIÈRE, AU CŒUR DE L'ACTUALITÉ. (USA)

▲ 436 COUVERTURE DU PREMIER NUMÉRO DE *ADC*, UNE NOUVELLE PUBLICATION DE L'ART DIRECTORS CLUB. LA PHOTO D'INSPIRATION SURRÉALISTE SE RAPPORTE À UN ARTICLE SUR LE HALL OF FAME 89 ET SES LAURÉATS. (USA)

▲ 437 CETTE PUBLICATION PERMET D'INFORMER LES ÉLÈVES DES COLLÈGES DES POSSIBILITÉS DE TRAVAIL OFFERTES PAR NRC CORP. (USA)

▲ 438 COUVERTURE DU JOURNAL DU MUSEUM OF NEW MEXICO, UNE PUBLICATION BIMENSUELLE QUI ANNONCE LE PROGRAMME DES MANIFESTATIONS, ICI, UNE EXPOSITION D'ŒUVRES D'ART MODERNE, SÉLECTIONNÉES PAR UN JURY. (USA)

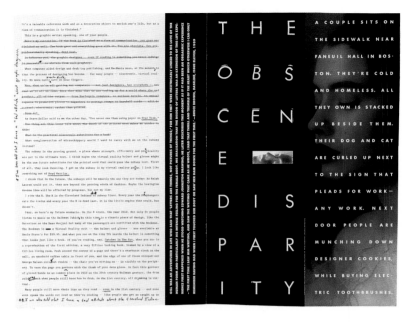

THE OBSCENE DISPARITY

A COUPLE SITS ON THE SIDEWALK NEAR FANEUIL HALL IN BOS-TON. THEY'RE COLD AND HOMELESS. ALL THEY OWN IS STACKED UP BESIDE THEM. THEIR DOG AND CAT ARE CURLED UP NEXT TO THE SIGN THAT PLEADS FOR WORK—ANY WORK. NEXT DOOR PEOPLE ARE MUNCHING DOWN DESIGNER COOKIES, WHILE BUYING ELEC-TRIC TOOTHBRUSHES.

schlang schlecht schlemazel
schlemiel schlep schleppy
schlock schlockmeister schlong
schlontz schloomp schlub
schmaltz schmancy schmatte
schmear schmear schmeck
schmegeggy schmendrick schmo
schmooz schmuck schmutz
schnockered schnook schnorrer
schnorrer schnozz schpritz
schtarker schtick schtoonk
schtup schvantz

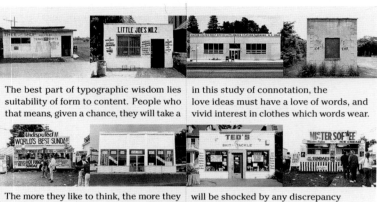

The best part of typographic wisdom lies suitability of form to content. People who that means, given a chance, they will take a in this study of connotation, the love ideas must have a love of words, and vivid interest in clothes which words wear.

The more they like to think, the more they between a lucid idea and a murky typesetting. will be shocked by any discrepancy

CREATIVE DIRECTOR:
TYLER SMITH
ART DIRECTOR:
BOB MANLEY
DESIGNERS:
GARY KOEPKE
TYLER SMITH
TIBOR KALMAN
PHOTOGRAPHERS:
STEVE MARSEL
GEORGE PETRAKES
TOM STRONG
ARTISTS:
PAULA SCHER
EDWARD FELLA
COPYWRITER:
BRUCE MACINTOSH
AGENCY:
ALTMAN & MANLEY
KOEPKE DESIGN
CLIENT:
AGFA
PUBLISHER:
AGFA COMPUGRAPHIC
■ 439-443

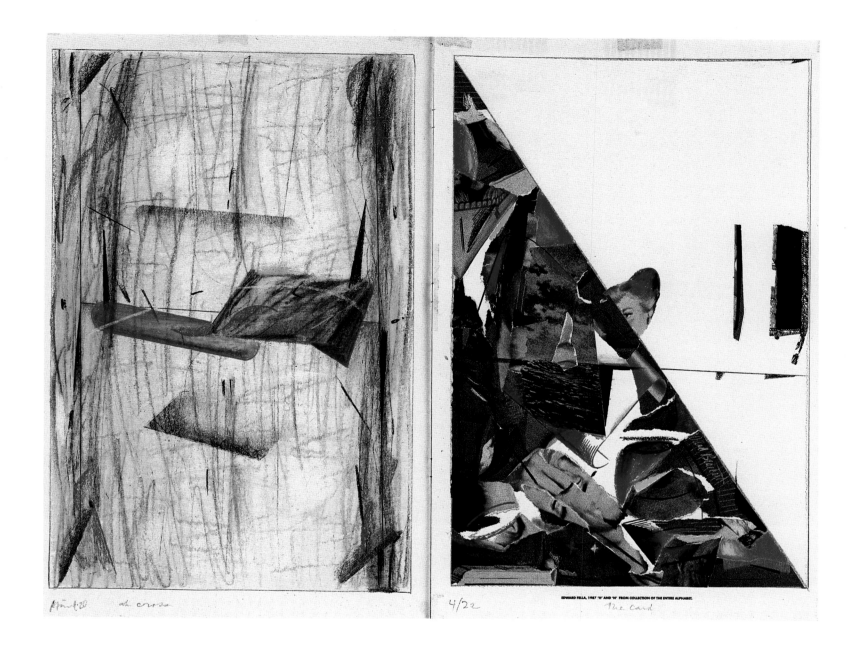

EDWARD FELLA, 1987 'H' AND 'N' FROM COLLECTION OF THE ENTIRE ALPHABET.

■ 439-443 COVER AND DOUBLE SPREADS OF THE FIRST ISSUE OF *TWENTY-SIX*, A JOURNAL ABOUT TYPE AND TYPOGRAPHY PUBLISHED QUARTERLY BY AGFA COMPUGRAPHIC. *440*: A MANUSCRIPT WITH NOTATIONS OF A SPEECH DELIVERED BY KARRIE JACOBS AT AN AIGA FORUM AND THE BEGINNING OF A NOVEL; *441*: A DICTIONARY OF YIDDISH FROM SCHLANG TO SCHVANTZ WITH A FULL PAGE ILLUS-TRATION BY PAULA SCHER; *442*: A TEXT BY BEATRICE WARDE ACCOMPANIED BY PHOTOGRAPHS OF TOM STRONG; *443*: THESE INTERPRETATIONS OF THE LETTERS "H" AND "N" DONE BY EDWARD FELLA IN 1987 ARE PART OF A COMPLETE ALPHABET. (USA)

● 439-443 UMSCHLAG UND DOPPELSEITEN VON *SECHSUNDZWANZIG*, DER ERSTEN AUSGABE EINER ZEITSCHRIFT ÜBER TYPOGRAPHIE, DIE VIERTEL-JÄHRLICH VON AGFA COMPUGRAPHIC HERAUS-GEGEBEN WIRD. *440*: DAS KORRIGIERTE MANU-SKRIPT EINES VORTRAGS VON KARRIE JACOBS AN EINER AIGA-TAGUNG; *441*: JIDDISCHE BEGRIFFE VON SCHLANG BIS SCHVANTZ UND EINE ILLUSTRATION VON PAULA SCHER; *442*: EIN TEXT VON BEATRICE WARDE MIT PHOTOS VON TOM STRONG; *443*: DIESE INTERPRETATIONEN DER BUCHSTABEN «H» UND «N», VON EDWARD FELLA 1987 ENTWORFEN, GEHÖREN ZU EINEM ALPHABET. (USA)

▲ 439-443 COUVERTURE ET DOUBLES PAGES DU PREMIER NUMÉRO DE *VINGT-SIX*, MAGAZINE TRIMES-TRIEL INTERNATIONAL D'AGFA COMPUGRAPHIC, CONSACRÉ À LA TYPOGRAPHIE ET À SES APPLICA-TIONS. *440*: TEXTE MANUSCRIT ANNOTÉ D'UNE CONFÉRENCE DE KARRIE JACOBS SUR L'AVENIR DU DESIGN GRAPHIQUE; *441*: UNE LISTE DE TERMES YIDDISH, ILLUSTRATION DE PAULA SCHER; *442*: UN TEXTE DE BEATRICE WARDE ACCOMPAGNE LES PHOTOS DE TOM STRONG; *443*: CES INTERPRÉ-TATIONS DES LETTRES «H» ET «N», RÉALISÉES PAR EDWARD FELLA EN 1987, FONT PARTIE D'UN ALPHABET. (USA)

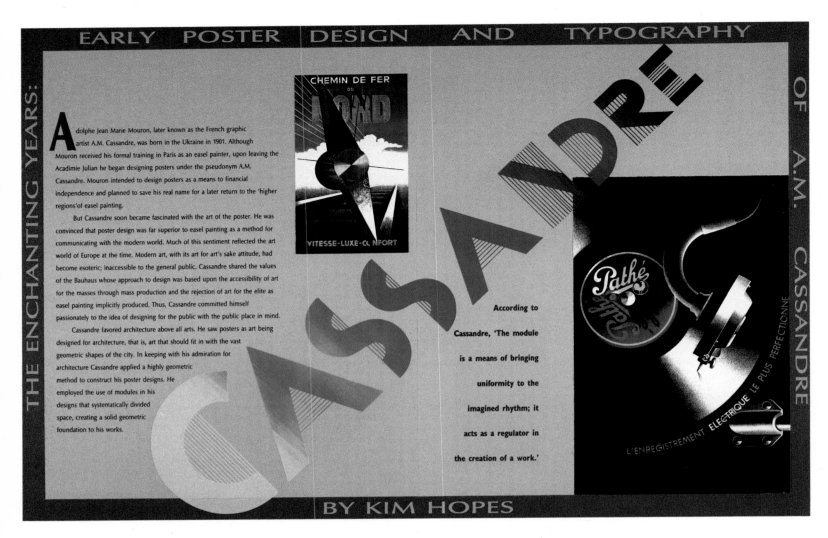

EARLY POSTER DESIGN AND TYPOGRAPHY OF A.M. CASSANDRE

THE ENCHANTING YEARS:

Adolphe Jean Marie Mouron, later known as the French graphic artist A.M. Cassandre, was born in the Ukraine in 1901. Although Mouron received his formal training in Paris as an easel painter, upon leaving the Académie Julian he began designing posters under the pseudonym A.M. Cassandre. Mouron intended to design posters as a means to financial independence and planned to save his real name for a later return to the 'higher regions' of easel painting.

But Cassandre soon became fascinated with the art of the poster. He was convinced that poster design was far superior to easel painting as a method for communicating with the modern world. Much of this sentiment reflected the art world of Europe at the time. Modern art, with its art for art's sake attitude, had become esoteric; inaccessible to the general public. Cassandre shared the values of the Bauhaus whose approach to design was based upon the accessibility of art for the masses through mass production and the rejection of art for the elite as easel painting implicitly produced. Thus, Cassandre committed himself passionately to the idea of designing for the public with the public place in mind.

Cassandre favored architecture above all arts. He saw posters as art being designed for architecture, that is, art that should fit in with the vast geometric shapes of the city. In keeping with his admiration for architecture Cassandre applied a highly geometric method to construct his poster designs. He employed the use of modules in his designs that systematically divided space, creating a solid geometric foundation to his works.

According to Cassandre, 'The module is a means of bringing uniformity to the imagined rhythm; it acts as a regulator in the creation of a work.'

BY KIM HOPES

DESIGNER:
KIM HOPES
COPYWRITER:
KIM HOPES
■ 444

ART DIRECTOR:
JIM BERTÉ
DESIGNER:
JIM BERTÉ
AGENCY:
ROBERT MILES
RUNYAN
& ASSOCIATES
CLIENT:
SOFTSEL COMPUTER
PRODUCTS, INC.
▶■ 445-449

■ 444 DOUBLE SPREAD FROM A BROCHURE ON POSTER ARTIST CASSANDRE, A PROJECT BY A GRAPHIC DESIGN STUDENT. (USA)

■ 445-449 PAGES AND COVER OF AN ANNUAL REPORT FOR SOFTSEL COMPUTER PRODUCTS ANNOUNCING THE FOUNDATION OF MERISEL, THE RESULT OF ITS MERGER WITH MICROAMERICA. THE ILLUSTRATION IS EMBOSSED. (USA)

● 444 DOPPELSEITE AUS EINEM KATALOG ÜBER DEN PLAKATKÜNSTLER CASSANDRE, EIN PROJEKT EINES GRAPHIK-DESIGN-STUDENTEN. (USA)

● 445-449 DOPPELSEITEN UND UMSCHLAG EINES JAHRESBERICHTES VON SOFTSEL COMPUTER PRODUCTS, INC., DER ÜBER EINEN ZUSAMMENSCHLUSS UND DIE DARAUS ENTSTEHENDE FIRMA MERISEL INFORMIERT. (USA)

▲ 444 DOUBLE PAGE D'UN PROJET DE BROCHURE SUR L'AFFICHISTE CASSANDRE, RÉALISÉ PAR UN ÉTUDIANT EN ART GRAPHIQUE. (USA)

▲ 445-449 PAGES INTÉRIEURES DU RAPPORT ANNUEL 1989 DE SOFTSEL COMPUTER PRODUCTS, UNE FIRME PRODUISANT DES LOGICIELS QUI VIENT DE FUSIONNER AVEC L'UN DES LEADERS DE LA DISTRIBUTION D'ORDINATEURS. (USA)

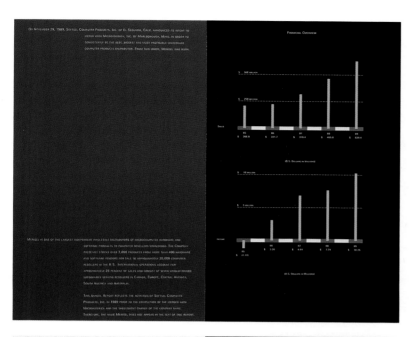

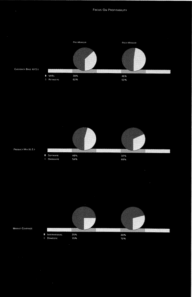

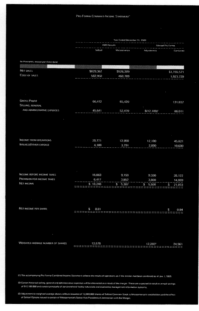

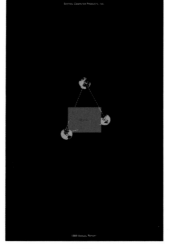

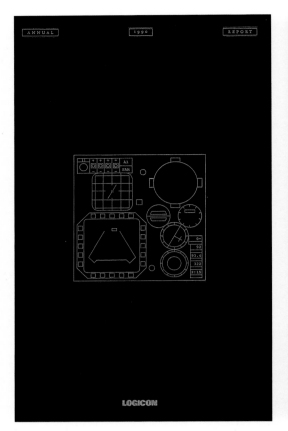

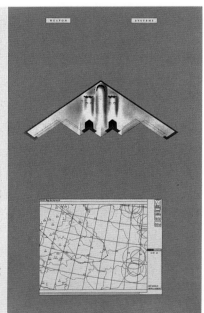

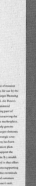

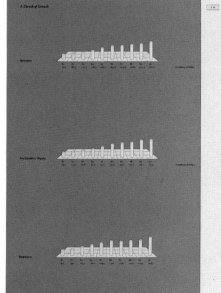

■ 450-453 COVER AND SPREADS FROM AN ANNUAL REPORT FOR LOGICON, A COMPANY WHICH PROVIDES ADVANCED TECHNOLOGY SYSTEMS AND SERVICES TO SUPPORT NATIONAL SECURITY, CIVIL AND INDUSTRIAL NEEDS. THE COMPANY HAS CONTRIBUTED TO THE DEVELOPMENT OF MISSION PLANNING SYSTEMS FOR THE US AIRFORCE AND A COMBAT SIMULATION PROGRAM FOR THE ARMY. (USA)

● 450-453 UMSCHLAG UND DOPPELSEITEN AUS EINEM JAHRESBERICHT FÜR LOGICON, EINE FIRMA, DIE HOCHENTWICKELTE ELEKTRONIK FÜR DIE LANDESVERTEIDIGUNG UND ZIVILE ZWECKE HERSTELLT. SIE BEFASST SICH U.A. MIT FLUGABWEHR- UND KAMPFSYSTEMEM FÜR DIE US-LUFTWAFFE SOWIE MIT DER ENTWICKLUNG VON SIMULATIONS-PROGRAMMEN FÜR DIE PILOTENAUSBILDUNG (USA)

▲ 450-453 COUVERTURE AVEC EFFET DE GAUFRAGE ET PAGES INTÉRIEURES DU RAPPORT ANNUEL 1990 DE LOGICON, UN SPÉCIALISTE DES SYSTÈMES INFORMATISÉS. CETTE ENTREPRISE A NOTAMMENT CONTRIBUÉ À LA MISE AU POINT DES NOUVEAUX AVIONS INDÉTECTABLES DE L'ARMÉE AMÉRICAINE ET PRODUIT LES PROGRAMMES DE SIMULATION DE VOL POUR LA FORMATION DES PILOTES. (USA)

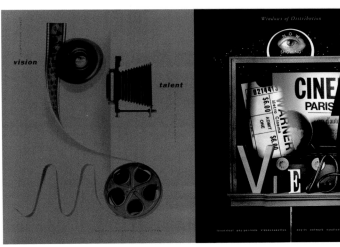

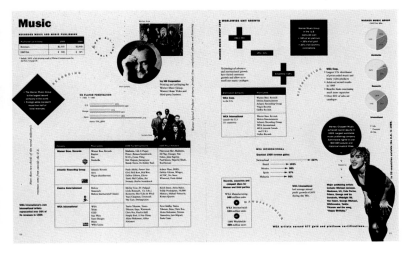

ART DIRECTOR:

JIM BERTÉ

DESIGNER:

JIM BERTÉ

ARTIST:

PAUL BICE, JR.

AGENCY:

ROBERT MILES

RUNYAN & ASSOC.

CLIENT:

LOGICON, INC.

◀■ 450-453

CREATIVE DIRECTORS:

AUDREY BALKIND

KENT HUNTER

DESIGNERS:

KENT HUNTER

RIKI SETHIADI

PHOTOGRAPHERS:

GEOF KERN

SCOTT MORGAN

CHRIS SANDERS

AGENCY:

FRANKFURT GIPS

BALKIND

CLIENT:

TIME WARNER INC.

■ 454-457

■ 454-457 COVER AND SPREADS FROM THE ANNUAL REPORT 1989 FOR TIME WARNER INC. THE NEW GIANT OF THE ENTERTAINMENT INDUSTRY. 455 AND 457 REFER TO THE RECORD AND MUSIC PUBLISHING BUSINESS; 456 IS ABOUT THE MOVIE PRODUCTION. THE USE OF FLUORESCENT COLORS EMPHASIZES AN AGGRESSIVE APPROACH AS TO DEVELOPMENT OF BUSINESS AND CREATE A FRESH, STRAIGHT-FORWARD IMAGE. LIKE THE COVER, CHAPTERS ARE INTRODUCED WITH "HOW" AND "WHO." (USA)

● 454-457 UMSCHLAG UND SEITEN AUS DEM JAHRES-BERICHT 1989 FÜR TIME WARNER INC, DEM NEUEN GIGANTEN DER UNTERHALTUNGSINDUSTRIE. 455 UND 457 BEZIEHEN SICH AUF DEN SCHALLPLATTEN- UND MUSIKVERLAGSBEREICH, 456 AUF DIE FILMPRO-DUKTION. DER EINSATZ VON FLUORESZIERENDEN FARBEN GIBT DEM BERICHT EINEN FRISCHEN, DIREKTEN CHARAKTER, UNTERSTÜTZT VON TITELN WIE »WARUM, «WIE» UND «WER», WELCHE DIE EINZELNEN KAPITEL EINLEITEN. (USA)

▲ 454-457 D'UN RAPPORT ANNUEL 1989 DE TIME WARNER INC., LEADER DE L'AUDIOVISUEL QUI PRÉSENTE SES ACTIVITÉS DANS LE DOMAINE DE LA MUSIQUE (455, 457) ET DU CINÉMA (456). L'EMPLOI DE COULEURS FLUO SOULIGNE LE TON DIRECT ET UNE POLITIQUE DE DÉVELOPPEMENT AGRESSIVE. LE CONCEPT DE GLOBALISATION EST DÉVELOPPÉ DANS CE RAPPORT QUI S'ARTICULE AUTOUR DES QUES-TIONS-CLÉS: «POURQUOI?» (SUR LA COUVERTURE), «COMMENT?» ET «QUOI?». (USA)

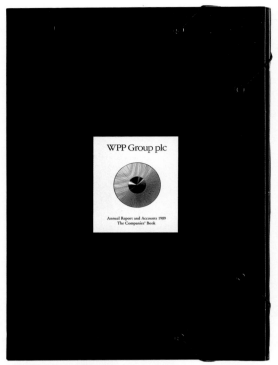

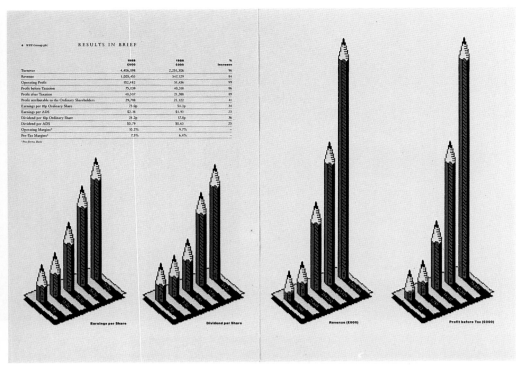

RESULTS IN BRIEF

	1989 £000	1988 £000	% Increase
Turnover	1,406,598	2,251,306	96
Revenue	1,005,453	547,129	84
Operating Profit	102,482	51,436	99
Profit before Taxation	75,039	40,318	86
Profit after Taxation	40,507	21,388	89
Profit attributable to the Ordinary Shareholders	29,788	21,122	41
Earnings per 10p Ordinary Share	73.0p	54.3p	34
Earnings per ADS	$2.16	$1.93	23
Dividend per 10p Ordinary Share	24.2p	17.8p	36
Dividend per ADS	$0.79	$0.63	25
Operating Margins*	10.2%	9.7%	–
Pre-Tax Margins*	7.5%	6.4%	–

*Pro-forma Basis

Earnings per Share   Dividend per Share   Revenue (£000)   Profit before Tax (£000)

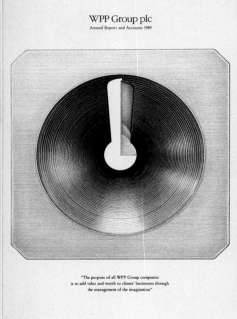

WPP Group plc
Annual Report and Accounts 1989

"The purpose of all WPP Group companies
is to add value and worth to clients' businesses through
the management of the imagination"

ART DIRECTOR:
DAVID FREEMAN
DESIGNERS:
PAUL BARLOW
LINDA WESTON

AGENCY:
SAMPSON TYRELL
CLIENT:
WPP GROUP PLC.
■ 458-460

■ 458-460 THE TOP OF A SHARPENED PENCIL ILLUSTRATES THE COVER OF A CARTON FOLDER AND A SHARPENER ITS BACK FLAP. THE FOLDER CONTAINS THE ANNUAL REPORT AND A BROCHURE INFORMING ON THE ACTIVITIES OF WPP GROUP PLC, A NEW ENTERPRISE IN THE COMMUNICATIONS AND ADVERTISING INDUSTRY. THE OPENED FOLDER REVEALS THE COVER OF THE ANNUAL REPORT. THE THEME OF THE PENCIL IS REPEATED THROUGHOUT AND IS ALSO USED FOR THE DIAGRAMS. (GBR)

● 458-460 EIN GESPITZTER BLEISTIFT AUF DER VORDERSEITE EINER KARTONMAPPE, DEREN HINTE-RE KLAPPE EIN ANSPITZER ILLUSTRIERT. SIE ENT-HÄLT EINEN JAHRESBERICHT UND EINE BROSCHÜRE, DIE ÜBER DIE AKTIVITÄTEN DER NEUEN WPP-GRUPPE FÜR KOMMUNIKATION UND WERBUNG INFOR-MIERT. DIE GEÖFFNETE MAPPE ZEIGT DEN UM-SCHLAG DES JAHRESBERICHTS. DER BLEISTIFT IST EIN KONSTANTES ELEMENT UND WIRD AUCH FÜR DIAGRAMME EINGESETZT. (GBR)

▲ 458-460 UN CRAYON EN COUPE ORNE LE RECTO ET UN AIGUISE-CRAYON LE RABAT INTÉRIEUR DE LA CHEMISE DE CARTON CONTENANT LE RAPPORT ANNUEL 1989 ET UNE BROCHURE PRÉSENTANT LES ACTIVITÉS DU GROUPE DE COMMUNICATION ET PUBLICITÉ WPP. EN BAS, LA CHEMISE DE PROTECTION OUVERTE ET LA COUVERTURE DU RAPPORT ANNUEL. LE THÈME DU CRAYON EST REPRIS DANS LES PAGES INTÉRIEURES, PAR EX. LES DIAGRAMMES. (GBR)

ILLUSTRATION

ILLUSTRATIONEN

ILLUSTRATION

ART DIRECTOR:
HANS-GEORG
POSPISCHIL
ILLUSTRATOR:
SEYMOUR CHWAST
PUBLISHER:
FRANKFURTER ALL-
GEMEINE MAGAZIN
■ 461

ART DIRECTORS:
DOUGLAS JOSEPH
RIK BESSER
DESIGNER:
DOUGLAS JOSEPH
ILLUSTRATOR:
STEVE JOHNSON
AGENCY:
BESSER JOSEPH
PARTNERS
CLIENT:
LINCOLN BANCORP
▶■ 462-465

■ 461 "HOW EASY WOULD THE FLIGHT FROM EGYPT HAVE BEEN HAD HUMANITY ALREADY KNOWN THE IDEAL MOTORCYCLE FOR CROSS-COUNTRY RIDES". THIS ILLUSTRATION WAS USED FOR AN ARTICLE IN THE FRANKFURTER ALLGEMEINE MAGAZIN DEDICATED TO THE MOTORCYCLE, WHICH WAS INVENTED IN 1885 BY GOTTLIEB DAIMLER. (GER)

■ 462-465 THESE FOUR ILLUSTRATIONS (OIL ON WATERCOLOR PAPER) ALL DEPICTING A SUBJECT LINKED TO SEAFARING AND WATERSPORTS WERE USED IN THE 1989 ANNUAL REPORT FOR LINCOLN BANCORP. (USA)

● 461 «WIE LEICHT WÄRE DIE FLUCHT AUS ÄGYPTEN GEWESEN, WENN DAS GELÄNDEGÄNGIGE ZWEIRAD SCHON HÄTTE HELFEN KÖNNEN.» DIESE ILLUSTRATION GEHÖRT ZU EINEM BEITRAG IM FRANKFURTER ALLGEMEINE MAGAZIN ÜBER DAS 1885 VON GOTTLIEB DAIMLER ENTWICKELTE MOTORRAD, DAMALS «REITWAGEN» GENANNT. (GER)

● 462-465 DIESE ILLUSTRATIONEN (ÖL AUF AQUARELLPAPIER), DIE ALLE MIT DEM WASSER BEZIEHUNGSWEISE DER SEEFAHRT ZU TUN HABEN, WURDEN IM JAHRESBERICHT 1989 DER LINCOLN BANCORP VERWENDET. (USA)

▲ 461 «COMME LA FUITE EN ÉGYPTE AURAIT ÉTÉ FACILE SI LES HOMMES AVAIENT DÉJÀ CONNU LA MOTO TOUT TERRAIN». CETTE ILLUSTRATION FIGURE DANS UN ARTICLE DU FRANKFURTER ALLGEMEINE MAGAZIN CONSACRÉ À LA MOTO, QUI FUT INVENTÉE EN 1885 PAR L'INGÉNIEUR ALLEMAND GOTTLIEB DAIMLER. (GER)

▲ 462-465 CES ILLUSTRATIONS QUI ONT POUR SUJET LA MER ET LA NAVIGATION ONT ÉTÉ PUBLIÉES DANS LE RAPPORT ANNUEL D'UNE BANQUE CALIFORNIENNE, LA LINCOLN BANCORP. PEINTURE À L'HUILE SUR PAPIER AQUARELLE. (USA)

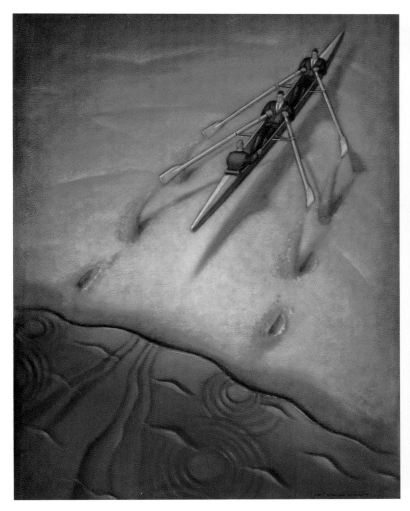

ILLUSTRATOR:

MARIE PLOTENA

■ 466

ART DIRECTOR:

KENNETH KRAFCHEK

DESIGNER:

BONO MITCHELL

ILLUSTRATOR:

ROBERT GIUSTI

CLIENT:

THE ILLUSTRATORS

CLUB OF WASHINGTON

■ 467

■ 466 "GALAXIE", A PERSONAL PEN AND INK DRAWING BY CZECHOSLOVAKIAN ARTIST MARIE PLOTENA. (CFR)

■ 467 THIS ILLUSTRATION WAS USED FOR THE COVER OF A BROCHURE ANNOUNCING A LECTURE SERIES ON THE SUBJECT OF "ILLUSTRATION AS COMMUNICATION." (USA)

● 466 «GALAXIE», EINE FREIE FEDERZEICHNUNG DER TSCHECHOSLOVAKISCHEN KÜNSTLERIN MARIE PLOTENA. (CFR)

● 467 DIESE ILLUSTRATION WURDE AUF DEM UMSCHLAG EINER BROSCHÜRE VERWENDET. SIE KÜNDIGT EINE VORTRAGSREIHE ZUM THEMA «ILLUSTRATION ALS KOMMUNIKATION» AN. (USA)

▲ 466 «GALAXIE», UN DESSIN À LA PLUME, ŒUVRE PERSONNELLE DE L'ARTISTE TCHÉCOSLOVAQUE MARIE PLOTENA. (CFR)

▲ 467 CETTE ILLUSTRATION ORNE LA COUVERTURE D'UNE BROCHURE ANNONÇANT UNE SÉRIE DE CONFÉRENCES SUR LE THÈME DE «L'ILLUSTRATION EN TANT QUE COMMUNICATION». (USA)

OPERATING INSTRUCTIONS

1. PLACE COFFEE PACK, SEAM DOWN IN BREW CUP
2. INSTALL SERVER AND BREW CUP IN COFFEE MACHINE
3. PULL BREW HANDLE DOWN TO STOP
4. PRESS ON/OFF SWITCH TO START COFFEE MACHINE
5. PRESS BREW, LIGHT INDICATES COFFEE IS BREWING
6. OPEN HANDLE WHEN BREW LIGHT IS OUT
7. REMOVE CUP AND DISPOSE OF USED COFFEE BAG

ON/OFF

BREW

HOT
PLATE
IS ON

WATER
IS
HOT

NO
WATER

LH

ART DIRECTOR:

HERMANN ROTH

ILLUSTRATOR:

PETER KRÄMER

CLIENT:

DEUTSCHE

LUFTHANSA AG

◀■ 468

DESIGNER:

MICHAEL DIAS

ILLUSTRATOR:

ODILE OUELLET

PUBLISHER:

TUNDRA BOOKS INC.

■ 469, 470

■ 468 AIRBRUSH ILLUSTRATION USED IN THE INFLIGHT MAGAZINE OF LUFTHANSA GERMAN AIRLINES FOR THE COLUMN "CHECK LIST", WHICH DEALS WITH MODERN FLIGHT TECHNIQUES. (GER)

■ 469, 470 TWO ILLUSTRATIONS FROM A BOOK ENTITLED "WHAT IF THE BUS DOESN'T COME." IT TELLS OF THE PRECAUTIONS A LITTLE GIRL AND A LITTLE BOY TAKE THE DAY BEFORE THEY GO TO SCHOOL FOR THE FIRST TIME. (CAN)

● 468 AIRBRUSH ILLUSTRATION FÜR DIE RUBRIK «CHECKLIST» IM «BORDBUCH», DEM INFLIGHT-MAGAZIN DER LUFTHANSA. DAS THEMA IST MODERNE FLUGTECHNIK. (GER)

● 469, 470 AUS EINEM BUCH MIT DEM TITEL: «UND WENN DER BUS NICHT KOMMT?» ES ERZÄHLT VON DEN VORSICHTSMASSNAHMEN, DIE EIN KLEINES MÄDCHEN UND EIN KLEINER JUNGE AM TAG VOR DEM ERSTEN SCHULBESUCH TREFFEN. (CAN)

▲ 468 ILLUSTRATION À L'AÉROGRAPHE POUR LA RUBRIQUE «CHECKLIST» DU MAGAZINE DE BORD DE LA LUFTHANSA. L'ARTICLE PARLAIT DE LA MODER-NITÉ DE LA TECHNIQUE DANS LES AVIONS. (GER)

▲ 469, 470 ILLUSTRATIONS TIRÉES D'UN LIVRE INTI-TULÉ «ET SI L'AUTOBUS NOUS OUBLIE», DESTINÉ AUSSI BIEN AUX ENFANTS QU'AUX ENSEIGNANTS. IL RACONTE LES PRÉPARATIFS DE DEUX ENFANTS LA VEILLE DU PREMIER JOUR DE CLASSE. (CAN)

ART DIRECTOR:
TINA ADAMEK
ILLUSTRATOR:
GARY KELLEY
PUBLISHER:
THE PHYSICIAN AND
SPORTSMEDICINE
■ 471

ART DIRECTOR:
NEIL STUART
DESIGNER:
NEIL STUART
ILLUSTRATOR:
JOHN JINKS
CLIENT:
PENGUIN USA
▶■ 472

■ 471 ILLUSTRATION FOR AN ARTICLE ENTITLED "GETTING TOUGH ON ANABOLIC STEROIDS: CAN WE WIN THE BATTLE?" IN THE MAGAZINE THE PHYSICIAN AND SPORTSMEDICINE. (USA)

■ 472 A CUBISTIC AIRBRUSH ILLUSTRATION (ACRYL) BY JOHN JINKS FOR THE COVER OF "THE AUTO-BIOGRAPHY OF MY BODY", A STORY ABOUT A MAN'S COMING OUT EMOTIONALLY AND SEXUALLY, WRITTEN BY DAVID GUY. (USA)

● 471 ILLUSTRATION FÜR EINEN ARTIKEL MIT DEM TITEL «STRENGERE KONTROLLE VON ANABOLIKA: KÖNNEN WIR DEN KAMPF GEWINNEN?» IN THE PHYSICIAN AND SPORTSMEDICINE. (USA)

● 472 AIRBRUSH-ILLUSTRATION (ACRYL) FÜR DEN UMSCHLAG EINES BUCHES MIT DEM TITEL «DIE AUTOBIOGRAPHIE MEINES KÖRPERS» ÜBER DAS EMOTIONALE UND SEXUELLE ERWACHEN EINES MANNES. (USA)

▲ 471 ILLUSTRATION POUR UN ARTICLE INTITULÉ «LE CONTRÔLE DES ANABOLISANTS: GAGNERONS-NOUS LA BATAILLE?», PARU DANS LE MAGAZINE THE PHYSICIAN AND SPORTMEDICINE. (USA)

▲ 472 ILLUSTRATION STYLISÉE POUR LA COUVER-TURE D'UN LIVRE S'INTITULANT: «L'AUTOBIOGRA-PHIE DE MON CORPS», QUI RACONTE L'ÉVEIL DE LA SEXUALITÉ D'UN HOMME. PEINTURE ACRYLIQUE À L'AÉROGRAPHE. (USA)

ART DIRECTOR:
HEINZ EDELMANN
DESIGNER:
ROBERT PÜTZ
ILLUSTRATOR:
RICHARD HESS
AGENCY:
ROBERT PÜTZ GMBH
CLIENT:
NIXDORF COMPUTER
CORPORATION
■ 473, 475

ART DIRECTOR:
GHOLAM-REZA
MOTAMEDI
ILLUSTRATOR:
AHMAD-REZA
DALVAND
CLIENT:
SAN'AT-E HAML-O
NAGHL MONTHLY
■ 474

ILLUSTRATOR:

THOMAS GATNARCZYK

■ 476

■ 473, 475 THE FIRST TRANSATLANTIC FLIGHT —WESTBOUND (1928) WITH HERMANN KÖHL, JAMES FITZMAURICE, GÜNTHER VON HÜNEFELD AND THE "BREMEN", AND EASTBOUND (1927) WITH CHARLES A. LINDBERGH AND "THE SPIRIT OF ST. LOUIS" (1927) —FOR INVITATIONS BY NIXDORF COMPUTERS. (GER)

■ 474 IRAN'S NATIONAL BUDGET—PEN AND INK DRAWING IN AN IRANIAN MONTHLY MAGAZINE. (IRN)

■ 476 WATERCOLOR AND CRAYON ILLUSTRATION FOR ECO'S "THE NAME OF THE ROSE". (GER)

● 473, 475 DIE ERSTEN FLÜGE ÜBER DEN ATLANTIK, 1928 VON OSTEN NACH WESTEN: HERMANN KÖHL, JAMES FITZMAURICE, GÜNTHER VON HÜNEFELD UND DIE «BREMEN» UND 1927 VON WESTEN NACH OSTEN: CHARLES A. LINDBERGH UND «THE SPIRIT OF ST. LOUIS» – FÜR EINLADUNGEN VON NIXDORF. (GER)

● 474 IRANS STAATSETAT – TUSCHZEICHNUNG FÜR EINE IRANISCHE MONATSZEITSCHRIFT. (IRN)

● 476 ZEICHNUNG, AQUARELL UND BLEISTIFT, FÜR UMBERTO ECOS «DER NAME DER ROSE». (GER)

▲ 473, 475 LES PREMIERS VOLS TRANSATLANTIQUES – HERMANN KÖHL, JAMES FITZMAURICE, GÜNTHER VON HÜNEFELD ET LE «BREMEN» (VOL EST-OUEST EN 1928); CHARLES LINDBERGH ET «THE SPIRIT OF ST. LOUIS» (VOL OUEST-EST EN 1927) – POUR DES INVITATIONS DE NIXDORF. (GER)

▲ 474 LE BUDGET DE L'ÉTAT IRANIEN – DESSIN À LA PLUME, PUBLIÉ DANS UN MAGAZINE MENSUEL. (IRN)

▲ 476 DESSIN CRAYON ET AQUARELLE ILLUSTRANT «LE NOM DE LA ROSE» D'UMBERTO ECO. (GER)

ART DIRECTOR:
RUDY HOGLUND
ILLUSTRATOR:
MARSHALL ARISMAN
CLIENT:
TIME MAGAZINE
◀■ 477

ILLUSTRATOR:
DANIEL SCHWARTZ
■ 478

■ 477 A PAINTING (OIL ON RAGBOARD) BY MARSHALL ARISMAN USED AS FULL-PAGE ILLUSTRATION FOR AN ARTICLE IN *TIME* MAGAZINE ON THE SUBJECT OF THE DEATH PENALTY. (USA)

■ 478 ACRYLIC PAINTING USED FOR THE SELF-PROMOTION MAILER OF NEW YORK ARTIST DANIEL SCHWARTZ. (USA)

● 477 BILD VON MARSHALL ARISMAN (ÖL AUF HART-FASERPLATTE), DAS IN DER ZEITSCHRIFT *TIME* ALS GANZSEITIGE ILLUSTRATION FÜR EINEN ARTIKEL ÜBER DIE TODESSTRAFE VERWENDET WURDE. (USA)

● 478 ALS EIGENWERBUNG DES NEW YORKER KÜNSTLERS DANIEL SCHWARTZ VERWENDETES BILD (ACRYL). (USA)

▲ 477 UNE PEINTURE DE MARSHALL ARISMAN (HUILE SUR CONTRE-PLAQUÉ) PUBLIÉE COMME ILLUSTRATION PLEINE PAGE D'UN ARTICLE DU MAGAZINE *TIME* SUR LA PEINE DE MORT. (USA)

▲ 478 PEINTURE ACRYLIQUE UTILISÉE COMME AUTOPROMOTION PAR L'ARTISTE NEW-YORKAIS DANIEL SCHWARTZ. (USA)

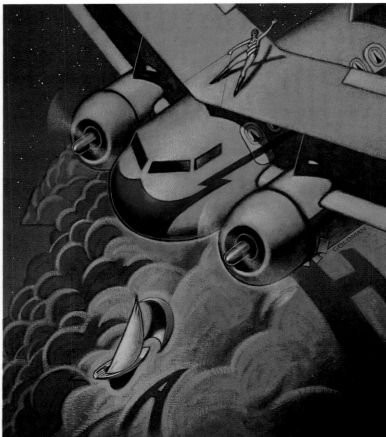

ART DIRECTOR:
BRUCE HOLDEMAN
ILLUSTRATOR:
BRUCE HOLDEMAN
AGENCY:
601 DESIGN
CLIENT:
NATIONAL CONFER-
ENCE OF STATE
LEGISLATURES
■ 479

ART DIRECTOR:
DON WELLER
DESIGNER:
DON WELLER
ILLUSTRATOR:
BART GOLDMAN
COPYWRITER:
CANDACE PEARSON
AGENCY:
THE WELLER INSTI-
TUTE FOR THE CURE
OF DESIGN INC.
CLIENT:
ALPHA GRAPHIX
■ 480

ART DIRECTOR:
JENNIFER PHILLIPS
DESIGNER:
JENNIFER PHILLIPS
ILLUSTRATOR:
BRAD HOLLAND
STUDIO:
BARTON GILLET
CLIENT:
NEW SCHOOL FOR
SOCIAL RESEARCH
■ 481

■ 479 THIS AIRBRUSH ILLUSTRATION, WHICH WAS USED ON THE COVER OF *STATE LEGISLATURES* MAGAZINE, REFERS TO AN ARTICLE ON "PARADIGMS OF POWER." IT TELLS OF HOW CERTAIN LEADERS CAME TO POWER AND STATES THAT LARGE POLITICAL MACHINES ARE OBSOLETE. (USA)

■ 480 THE COPY OF THIS AD FOR ALPHA GRAPHIX SPEAKS OF THE SOMETIMES ROCKY SEAS OF TYPESETTING THAT ARE SMOOTH SAILING FOR THIS COMPANY AND OF HOW THE "CUSTOMER'S VISION REACHES ITS DESTINATION WHEN HE DOCKS WHERE MAGIC CAN HAPPEN." (USA)

■ 481 FOUR NEARLY IDENTICAL MEN GUIDED BY A FLASHLIGHT ON THEIR WAY THROUGH A DARK LANDSCAPE—A PAINTING BY BRAD HOLLAND SHOWN ON A DOUBLE SPREAD OF A BROCHURE REPORTING ABOUT A NEW SCHOOL FOR SOCIAL RESEARCH IN NEW YORK. (USA)

● 479 DIESE AIRBRUSH-ILLUSTRATION FÜR DEN UMSCHLAG DES MAGAZINS *STATE LEGISLATURES* BEZIEHT SICH AUF EINEN ARTIKEL ÜBER «MUSTERBEISPIELE VON MACHT», DER DIE KARRIERE EINIGER POLITIKER UND GROSSE POLITISCHE SYSTEME UNTER DIE LUPE NIMMT. (USA)

● 480 IM TEXT DIESER ANZEIGE FÜR ALPHA GRAPHIX IST VON STÜRMISCHER SEE DIE REDE, DEREN WOGEN SICH FÜR DIE KUNDEN DIESES SCHRIFTSATZHERSTELLERS GLÄTTEN, UND VON VISIONEN DER KUNDEN, DIE MIT HILFE DIESER FIRMA WIRKLICHKEIT WERDEN. (USA)

● 481 VIER FAST IDENTISCHE MÄNNER, DIE IM LICHT VON TASCHENLAMPEN IHREN WEG DURCH EINE DUNKLE LANDSCHAFT SUCHEN. EIN BILD VON BRAD HOLLAND AUF DER DOPPELSEITE EINER BROSCHÜRE, IN DER ÜBER EINE NEUE SCHULE IN NEW YORK BERICHTET WIRD. (USA)

▲ 479 CETTE ILLUSTRATION À L'AÉROGRAPHE POUR LA COUVERTURE DU MAGAZINE *STATE LEGISLATURES* SE RAPPORTE À UN ARTICLE INTITULÉ «PARADIGMES DU POUVOIR», DANS LEQUEL ON EXAMINE LA CARRIÈRE DE CERTAINS POLITICIENS ET LES FAIBLESSES DES SYSTÈMES POLITIQUES. (USA)

▲ 480 DANS LE TEXTE DE CETTE ANNONCE POUR ALPHA GRAPHIX, IL EST QUESTION D'UNE MER AGITÉE DONT LES VAGUES, CAUSÉES PAR LES PROBLÈMES DE TYPOGRAPHIE, S'APAISENT GRÂCE À CE COMPOSITEUR-TYPOGRAPHE QUI SAIT RÉALISER LES RÊVES DE SES CLIENTS. (USA)

▲ 481 QUATRE HOMMES CHERCHENT LEUR ROUTE DANS L'OBSCURITÉ, À LA LUMIÈRE D'UNE LAMPE DE POCHE. CETTE IMAGE DE BRAD HOLLAND A ÉTÉ PUBLIÉE SUR DOUBLE PAGE DANS UNE BROCHURE QUI ÉVOQUE L'OUVERTURE D'UNE NOUVELLE ÉCOLE À NEW YORK. (USA)

ART DIRECTOR:
BALVIS RUBESS
ILLUSTRATOR:
BALVIS RUBESS
◀■ 482-485

ART DIRECTORS:
IVAN CHERMAYEFF
JANE CLARK
CHERMAYEFF
DESIGNER:
SEYMOUR CHWAST
ILLUSTRATOR:
SEYMOUR CHWAST

AGENCY:
THE PUSHPIN GROUP
CLIENT:
INTERNATIONAL
DESIGN CONFERENCE
OF ASPEN
■ 486

■ 482-485 EXAMPLES FROM AN UNPUBLISHED SERIES OF AIRBRUSH ILLUSTRATIONS BY AMOK RUNNING ON "THE SEVEN DEADLY SINS". FROM LEFT TO RIGHT: "LUST", "ENVY", "SLOTH", "PRIDE." (CAN)

● 482-485 AUS EINER UNVERÖFFENTLICHTEN SERIE VON AIRBRUSH-ILLUSTRATIONEN UNTER DEM TITEL «DIE SIEBEN TODSÜNDEN». V.L.N.R.: «WOLLUST», «NEID», «FAULHEIT», «STOLZ». (CAN)

▲ 482-485 D'UNE SÉRIE D'ILLUSTRATIONS INÉDITES, RÉALISÉES À L'AÉROGRAPHE, INTITULÉE «LES SEPT PÉCHÉS CAPITAUX». DE G. À DR.: «LUXURE», «ENVIE», «PARESSE», «ORGUEIL». (CAN)

■ 486 THE ILLUSTRATION WAS USED FOR THE COVER OF A BROCHURE FOR THE INTERNATIONAL DESIGN CONFERENCE OF ASPEN (IDCA) ON THE SUBJECT OF "GROWING BY DESIGN" AND FOR A PORTFOLIO OF ILLUSTRATORS PRODUCED FOR THE IDCA BY HALLMARK CARDS. (USA)

● 486 DIESE ILLUSTRATION DIENTE ALS UMSCHLAG EINER BROSCHÜRE FÜR DIE INTERNATIONAL DESIGN CONFERENCE IN ASPEN (IDCA) ÜBER DAS THEMA «DURCH DESIGN WACHSEN», UND SIE WAR TEIL EINER ILLUSTRATIONSMAPPE, DIE HALLMARK CARDS FÜR DIE IDCA ZUSAMMENSTELLTE. (USA)

▲ 486 CETTE ILLUSTRATION EST PARUE EN COUVER-TURE D'UNE BROCHURE POUR LA INTERNATIONAL DESIGN CONFERENCE D'ASPEN, SUR LE SUJET: «CROÎTRE GRÂCE AU DESIGN». ELLE FAISAIT PARTIE D'UN DOSSIER D'ILLUSTRATIONS DE HALLMARK CARDS POUR L'IDCA. (USA)

ILLUSTRATOR:

ROLF JANSSON

■ 487

ILLUSTRATOR:

WIESLAW SMETEK

PUBLISHER:

WILLEM DE LAAT

■ 488

■ 487 A PAINTER IN A SARDINE BOX, A GUACHE, ORIGINALLY DONE FOR THE COVER OF A BOOK ON ILLUSTRATION. (NOR)

■ 488 A PASTEL BY POLISH ARTIST WIESLAV SMETEK. (POL)

■ 489 ILLUSTRATION, ORIGINALLY COMMISSIONED BY THE BOSTON GLOBE MAGAZINE TO ILLUSTRATE A STORY ABOUT A WOMAN WHO WAS MISDIAGNOSED AS A SCHIZOPHRENIC IN HER YOUTH. IT WAS ALSO USED IN A BROCHURE TO ANNOUNCE A SMITHSONIAN LECTURE SERIES BY THE ARTIST. TECHNIQUE: OIL CRAYON ON PAPER WITH TAPE AND STAPLES (USA)

■ 490 "THE PARTY WAS OVER. COULD THE MARRIAGE SURVIVE THE DRIVE HOME?" THE FULL-PAGE ILLUSTRATION REFERS TO THIS EXCERPT OF A STORY (FICTION) IN ESQUIRE MAGAZINE. (USA)

● 487 EIN MALER IN EINER SARDINENBÜCHSE – GUACHE, DIE FÜR DEN UMSCHLAG EINES BUCHES ÜBER ILLUSTRATION VORGESEHEN WAR. (NOR)

● 488 EIN PASTELL DES POLNISCHEN KÜNSTLERS WIESLAV SMETEK. (POL)

● 489 FÜR EINE IM BOSTON GLOBE MAGAZINE ER-SCHIENENE GESCHICHTE EINER FRAU, BEI DER IN DER JUGEND IRRTÜMLICH SCHIZOPHRENIE DIAGNO-STIZIERT WURDE. DIE ILLUSTRATION WURDE AUCH IN EINER BROSCHÜRE FÜR EINE VORTRAGSREIHE DES KÜNSTLERS VERWENDET. ÖLKREIDE AUF PAPIER MIT KLEBSTREIFEN UND KLAMMERN.(USA)

● 490 «DIE PARTY WAR VORBEI. WÜRDE DIE EHE DIE HEIMFAHRT ÜBERLEBEN?» DIE GANZSEITIGE ILLU-STRATION BEZIEHT SICH AUF DIESEN AUSZUG AUS EINER KURZGESCHICHTE IN ESQUIRE. (USA)

▲ 487 UN PEINTRE DANS UNE BOÎTE DE SARDINES – ÉTUDE PERSONNELLE DE L'ARTISTE NORVÉGIEN ROLF JANSSON. (NOR)

▲ 488 UN PASTEL DE L'ARTISTE POLONAIS WIESLAV SMETEK. (POL)

▲ 489 ILLUSTRATION D'UN RÉCIT DU BOSTON GLOBE MAGAZINE RELATANT L'HISTOIRE D'UNE FEMME CHEZ LAQUELLE ON DIAGNOSTIQUA PAR ERREUR DANS L'ENFANCE UNE SCHIZOPHRÉNIE. CETTE IMAGE FUT REPRISE DANS UNE BROCHURE POUR DES CONFÉRENCES DE L'ARTISTE. CRAIES À L'HUILE SUR PAPIER, RUBAN ADHÉSIF ET AGRAFES. (USA)

▲ 490 «LA FÊTE ÉTAIT TERMINÉE. LE MARIAGE ALLAIT-IL SURVIVRE AU RETOUR EN VOITURE?»: CETTE ILLUSTRATION PLEINE PAGE A ÉTÉ RÉALISÉE POUR UNE NOUVELLE DU MAGAZINE ESQUIRE. (USA)

ILLUSTRATOR:
ANDRZEJ DUDZINSKI
ART DIRECTORS:
RONN CAMPISI
BONO MITCHELL
CLIENTS:
BOSTON GLOBE
MAGAZINE/
SMITHSONIAN
INSTITUTION
■ 489

ART DIRECTOR:
TERRY R. KOPPEL
DESIGNER:
TERRY R. KOPPEL
ILLUSTRATOR:
ANTHONY RUSSO
PUBLISHER:
ESQUIRE
■ 490

DESIGNER:
CARL W. RÖHRIG
ILLUSTRATOR:
CARL W. RÖHRIG
PUBLISHER:
PRO TERRA
◀■ 491

ART DIRECTOR:
YUKAKO HONDA
DESIGNER:
TAKAYOSHI NOMA
ILLUSTRATOR:
GUY BILLOUT
AGENCY:
DAI NIPPON PRINTING
CLIENT:
MATSUZAKI SHOJI
■ 492

ART DIRECTOR:
DIANA LAGUARDIA
DESIGNER:
AUDREY RAZGAITIS
ILLUSTRATOR:
GUY BILLOUT
PUBLISHER:
CONDE NAST
TRAVELER
■ 493

■ 491 "THE ANIMALS OF THE RAIN FOREST"—GROUP PORTRAIT IN MIXED MEDIA ON CARDBOARD FOR THE BOOK: "THE GARDEN OF EDEN MUST NOT DIE." (GER)

■ 492 THE DOVE OF PEACE KILLED BY A FIGHTER PLANE. THIS ILLUSTRATION ENTITLED "THE MARS WAR" WAS USED IN A 1990 CALENDAR ON THE THEME OF "THE UNIVERSE." (JPN)

■ 493 "WHERE TIME BEGINS", AN ILLUSTRATION (WATERCOLOR AND AIRBRUSH) FOR AN ARTICLE ON THE KINGDOM OF TONGA IN CONDÉ NAST TRAVELER MAGAZINE. (USA)

● 491 «DIE TIERE DES REGENWALDES», EIN GRUPPENPORTRÄT IN MISCHTECHNIK FÜR DAS BUCH «DER GARTEN EDEN DARF NICHT STERBEN». (GER)

● 492 DIE FRIEDENSTAUBE, VON EINEM KAMPFFLUGZEUG GETÖTET. DIESE ILLUSTRATION, «DER MARSKRIEG», STAMMT AUS EINEM KALENDER MIT DEM THEMA «DAS UNIVERSUM». (JPN)

● 493 «WO DIE ZEIT BEGINNT» – ILLUSTRATION (AQUARELL UND AIRBRUSH) FÜR EINEN ARTIKEL ÜBER DAS KÖNIGREICH TONGA IN DER ZEITSCHRIFT CONDÉ NAST TRAVELER. (USA)

▲ 491 «LES ANIMAUX DE LA FORÊT TROPICALE», ILLUSTRATION POUR LE LIVRE: «LE JARDIN D'ÉDEN NE DOIT PAS MOURIR.» (GER)

▲ 492 LA COLOMBE DE LA PAIX, ABATTUE PAR UN AVION DE COMBAT. CETTE ILLUSTRATION INTITULÉE «LA GUERRE DE MARS» ORNE UNE PAGE D'UN CALENDRIER SUR LE THÈME DE L'UNIVERS. (JPN)

▲ 493 «LÀ OÙ LE TEMPS COMMENCE»: ILLUSTRATION POUR UN ARTICLE SUR LE ROYAUME DE TONGA PARU DANS CONDÉ NAST TRAVELER. AQUARELLE ET AÉROGRAPHE. (USA)

ART DIRECTOR:
RICHARD ECKERSLEY
DESIGNER:
JUNGSUN WHANG
ILLUSTRATOR:
ED LINDLOF
AGENCY:
UNIVERSITY OF
NEBRASKA PRESS
PUBLISHER:
UNIVERSITY OF
NEBRASKA PRESS
■ 494

ART DIRECTOR:
DAVID WILLARDSON
DESIGNER:
JOHN VAN
HAMERSVELD
ILLUSTRATOR:
PAUL ROGERS
PUBLISHER:
L.A.X. MAGAZINE
■ 495

■ 494 BOOK COVER ILLUSTRATION FOR A NEW BIOGRAPHY OF THE FAMOUS NEW MEXICAN OUTLAW, BILLY THE KID. INDIA INK AND ROTRING ARTIST COLORS. (USA)

■ 495 PORTRAIT OF MUSICIAN AND ACTOR TOM WAITS FOR THE FIRST ISSUE OF L.A.X., A MAGAZINE PRINTED AND PRODUCED IN SOUTHERN CALIFORNIA. THE INITIALS STAND FOR "LANGUAGE", "ART", "EXPRESSION". (USA)

● 494 ILLUSTRATION FÜR DEN UMSCHLAG EINER NEUEN BIOGRAPHIE DES LEGENDÄREN JUGENDLICHEN BANDITEN BILLY THE KID AUS NEUMEXIKO. MISCHTECHNIK. (USA)

● 495 PORTRÄT DES MUSIKERS UND SCHAUSPIELERS TOM WAITS FÜR DIE ERSTE AUSGABE VON L.A.X., EINER ZEITSCHRIFT, DIE IN SÜDKALIFORNIEN HERGESTELLT UND GEDRUCKT WIRD. L.A.X. BEDEUTET «LANGUAGE», «ART», «EXPRESSION». (USA)

▲ 494 ILLUSTRATION POUR LA COUVERTURE D'UNE NOUVELLE BIOGRAPHIE DU JEUNE BANDIT LÉGENDAIRE BILLY THE KID. ENCRE DE CHINE ET ENCRES DE COULEURS. (USA)

▲ 495 PORTRAIT DU MUSICIEN ET ACTEUR TOM WAITS POUR LE PREMIER NUMÉRO DE L.A.X., UN MAGAZINE IMPRIMÉ ET PRODUIT EN CALIFORNIE DU SUD. LES INITIALES L.A.X. SIGNIFIENT «LANGAGE», «ART» ET «EXPRESSION». (USA)

CORPORATE IDENTITY

FIRMENERSCHEINUNGSBILDER

IDENTITÉ CORPORATE

ART DIRECTOR:
KEN CATO
DESIGNER:
KEN CATO
AGENCY:
CATO DESIGN INC.
CLIENT:
MELBOURNE
OLYMPIC
CANDIDATURE
■ 496-502

ART DIRECTOR:
MICHAEL VANDERBYL
DESIGNER:
MICHAEL VANDERBYL
AGENCY:
VANDERBYL DESIGN
CLIENT:
PISCHOFF
▲
▶■ 503

ART DIRECTORS:
CHARLES S.
ANDERSON
DAN OLSON
DESIGNERS:
CHARLES S.
ANDERSON
DAN OLSON
ILLUSTRATORS:
CHARLES S.
ANDERSON
RANDALL DAHLK
DAN OLSON
AGENCY:
CHARLES S.
ANDERSON DESIGN
CLIENT:
PRINT CRAFT, INC.
▶■ 504-506

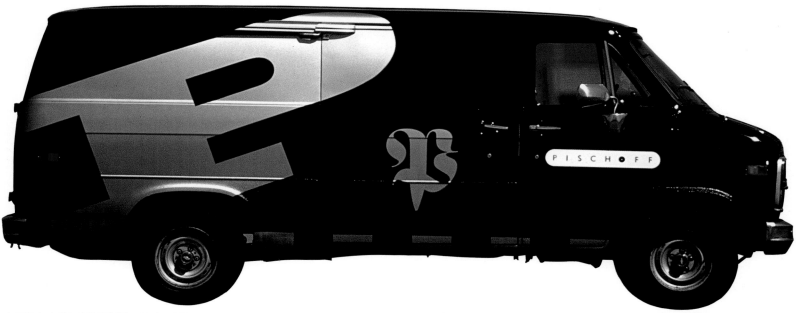

■ 496-502 THESE SPORTING FIGURES WERE DESIGNED TO COMPLEMENT THE SYMBOL AND IDENTITY OF THE MELBOURNE BID FOR THE 1996 OLYMPIC GAMES. THEY ARE CONSTRUCTED FROM 20MM GAUGE STEEL, STAND UP TO FOUR METERS IN HEIGHT AND WEIGH 1 TO 1 1/2 TONS. THE COLOR FINISH WAS APPLIED BY SPRAY-GUN AND BY HAND PAINTING. THE FOLDER CONTAINS THE BID DOCUMENTS. (AUS)

■ 503 PISCHOFF VEHICLE GRAPHICS ARE DEMONSTRATING THEIR DIVERSE LETTERING CAPABILITY ON THEIR OWN VEHICLE. (USA)

■ 504-506 GRAPHICS APPLIED TO DELIVERY VEHICLES FOR AN INDUSTRIAL PRINTER. (USA)

● 496-502 DIESE SPORTFIGUREN WURDEN ALS TEIL DES ERSCHEINUNGSBILDES FÜR MELBOURNES BEWERBUNG ALS AUSTRAGUNGSORT DER OLYMPISCHEN SPIELE 1996 ENTWORFEN. SIE SIND AUS 20MM DICKEM STAHL, BIS ZU 4M HOCH UND WIEGEN ZWISCHEN 1 UND 1 1/2 TONNEN. DIE FARBE WURDE TEILS AUGESPRAYT, TEILS VON HAND AUFGETRAGEN. DIE MAPPE ENTHÄLT DIE BEWERBUNGSUNTERLAGEN. (AUS)

● 503 PISCHOFF, EINE FIRMA FÜR AUTOBESCHRIFTUNGEN, DEMONSTRIERT IHRE VIELSEITIGKEIT AUF DEM EIGENEN FIRMENWAGEN. (USA)

● 504-506 GRAPHISCHE GESTALTUNG DER LIEFERWAGEN EINER DRUCKEREI. (USA)

▲ 496-502 CES SCULPTURES ONT ÉTÉ CONÇUES COMME ÉLÉMENTS D'IDENTITÉ VISUELLE POUR LA CANDIDATURE DE LA VILLE DE MELBOURNE AUX JEUX OLYMPIQUES DE 1996. ELLES SONT RÉALISÉES DANS UN ACIER DE 20 MM D'ÉPAISSEUR, ELLES FONT JUSQU'À 4 M DE HAUT ET PÈSENT ENTRE 1 ET 1,5 T. LA COULEUR A ÉTÉ EN PARTIE SPRAYÉE, EN PARTIE PEINTE À LA MAIN. LE DÉPLIANT RENFERME LE DOSSIER DE CANDIDATURE. (AUS)

▲ 503 DEUX VERSIONS DE L'INITIALE DE PISCHOFF DÉMONTRENT LE SAVOIR-FAIRE DE CE SPÉCIALISTE DES INSCRIPTIONS SUR VÉHICULES. (USA)

▲ 504-506 CONCEPTION GRAPHIQUE DES CAMIONS DE LIVRAISON D'UNE IMPRIMERIE. (USA)

DESIGNERS:
BERNIE LECLERC
(CONSTRUCTION)
TODD WATERBURY
SHARON WERNER
ILLUSTRATOR:
LYNN SCHULTE
TODD WATERBURY
SHARON WERNER
AGENCY:
THE DUFFY DESIGN
GROUP
CLIENT:
THE DUFFY DESIGN
GROUP
■ 507

ART DIRECTOR:
MICHAEL GERBINO
DESIGNER:
MICHAEL GERBINO
AGENCY:
MICHAEL GERBINO
DESIGNS, INC.
CLIENT:
PAUL HELLER
■ 508

ART DIRECTOR:
MATTHEW DRACE
DESIGNERS:
MICHAEL MABRY
JEFF PILOTTE
AGENCY:
MICHAEL MABRY
CLIENT:
SAN FRANCISCO
FOCUS
■ 509

ART DIRECTORS:
LESLIE SAUL
PEGGY KAMEI
ILLUSTRATOR:
PEGGY KAMEI
COPYWRITERS:
NORMAN GERSHENZ
LESLIE SAUL

AGENCY:
KAMEI/GARNAS, INC.
CLIENT:
AMERICAN ASSOC.
OF ZOO KEEPERS/
THE NATURE
CONSERVANCY
■ 510

■ 507 THE NEW DUFFY GROUP SIGN AS PART OF A REVISED CORPORATE IDENTITY THAT WAS TO REFLECT THE GROUP'S NEW SURROUNDINGS AND ATTITUDE AFTER ITS MERGER WITH THE MICHAEL PETERS GROUP. (USA)

■ 508 A SIGNPOST FOR A DENTIST IN MONTAUK, NEW YORK, THAT LEAVES NO DOUBT. (USA)

■ 509 AWARD GIVEN TO THE BEST BAY AREA FASHION DESIGNER, SPONSORED BY THE *SAN FRANCISCO FOCUS* AND ABSOLUT VODKA. (USA)

■ 510 THIS SCENE OF A RAIN FOREST WITH SEVERAL INDIGENOUS JUNGLE BEASTS IS ONE OF THE PICTURES THIS SPECIAL PARKING METER OF THE SAN FRANCISCO ZOO WILL SHOW WHEN FED WITH A QUARTER. THE MONEY THE METERS COLLECT WILL GO TOWARD THE PURCHASE OF ENDANGERED LATIN AMERICAN FOREST LAND. (USA)

● 507 DAS FIRMENZEICHEN DER DUFFY-DESIGN-GRUPPE, DAS DIE NEUE UMGEBUNG UND EIN-STELLUNG DER GRUPPE NACH DEM ZUSAMMEN-SCHLUSS MIT DER MICHAEL PETERS GROUP REFLEKTIEREN SOLL. (USA)

● 508 EIN EINDEUTIGER HINWEIS AUF EINE ZAHN-ARZTPRAXIS IN MONTAUK, NEW YORK. (USA)

● 509 DER PREIS FÜR DEN BESTEN MODEDESIGNER IM UMKREIS VON SAN FRANCISCO, GESTIFTET VON *SAN FRANCISCO FOCUS* UND ABSOLUT-WODKA. (USA)

● 510 DIESES ODER EIN ÄHNLICHES BILD EINES TEILS DES REGENWALDES MIT EINIGEN SEINER BEWOHNER ERSCHEINT, WENN MAN DIESE PARKUHR IM ZOO VON SAN FRANCISCO FÜTTERT. DAS SO GESAMMELTE GELD WIRD FÜR DEN KAUF VON TEILEN DER BEDROHTEN REGENWÄLDER LATEINARMERIKAS EINGESETZT. (USA)

▲ 507 LE PROGRAMME D'IDENTITÉ CORPORATE DU GROUPE DUFFY DESIGN A ÉTÉ TRANSFORMÉ AFIN DE SYMBOLISER LE NOUVEL ENVIRONNEMENT ET LES OBJECTIFS DE LA FIRME APRÈS SA FUSION AVEC LE MICHAEL PETERS GROUP. (USA)

▲ 508 SIGNALISATION TRIDIMENSIONNELLE POUR UN DENTISTE DE MONTAUK, NEW YORK. (USA)

▲ 509 L'OSCAR DU MEILLEUR DESIGNER DE MODE DE LA RÉGION DE SAN FRANCISCO, SPONSORISÉ PAR LE SAN FRANCISCO FOCUS ET ABSOLUT VODKA. (USA)

▲ 510 CETTE IMAGE DE LA FORÊT ÉQUATORIALE ET DES ANIMAUX QUI Y VIVENT EST L'UNE DES SCÈNES QUI APPARAÎT À CHAQUE FOIS QU'UN VISITEUR GLISSE UNE PIÈCE DANS CE PARCMÈTRE DU ZOO DE SAN FRANCISCO. L'ARGENT AINSI COLLECTÉ SERT À L'ACQUISITION DE TERRITOIRES MENACÉS EN AMÉRIQUE DU SUD. (USA)

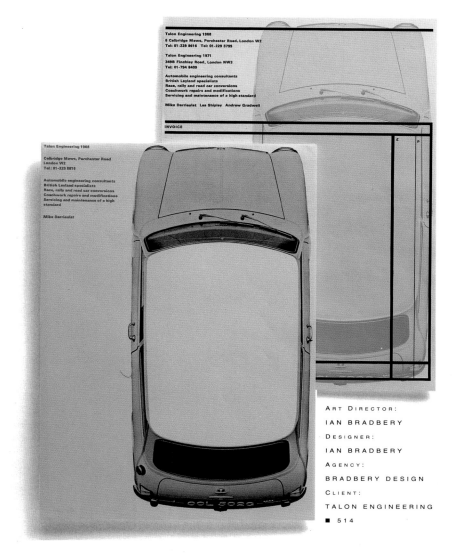

ART DIRECTOR:

JOHN SAYLES

DESIGNER:

JOHN SAYLES

AGENCY:

SAYLES GRAPHIC

DESIGN

CLIENT:

SAYLES GRAPHIC

DESIGN

◀■ 511

ART DIRECTOR:

JOHN BERG

DESIGNER:

JOHN BERG

ILLUSTRATOR:

JOHN BERG

AGENCY:

JOHN BERG

CLIENT:

JOHN BERG

■ 512, 513

ART DIRECTOR:

IAN BRADBERY

DESIGNER:

IAN BRADBERY

AGENCY:

BRADBERY DESIGN

CLIENT:

TALON ENGINEERING

■ 514

■ 511 THE INITIAL OF THE SAYLES GRAPHIC DESIGN FIRM BECAME THE DOMINANT GRAPHIC ELEMENT OF ITS STATIONERY. (USA)

■ 512, 513 LETTERHEAD AND BUSINESS CARD FOR THE JOHN BERG DESIGN FIRM. (USA)

■ 514 LETTERHEAD AND INVOICE FORM PRINTED IN TWO COLORS FOR AN AUTOMOBILE ENGINEERING CONSULTANTS. THIS IS AN EXAMPLE OF HOW A SMALL COMPANY RELIES ON ITS STATIONERY TO MAKE AN IMPACT WITHOUT HAVING TO MAKE BIG INVESTMENTS IN ADVERTISING. (GBR)

● 511 DIE INITIALE DER DESIGN-FIRMA SAYLES WURDE ZUM BESTIMMENDEN ELEMENT FÜR DAS GESCHÄFTSPAPIER. (USA)

● 512, 513 BRIEFBOGEN UND GESCHÄFTSKARTE FÜR DAS DESIGNSTUDIO VON JOHN BERG. (USA)

● 514 BRIEFBOGEN UND RECHNUNGSFORMULAR, IN ZWEI FARBEN GEDRUCKT, FÜR EINE SPEZIELLE AUTOMOBILWERKSTATT. DIES IST EIN BEISPIEL DAFÜR, WIE SICH EINE KLEINE FIRMA DURCH BRIEF-PAPIER EINEN BESONDEREN AUFTRITT VERSCHAFFT, OHNE VIEL FÜR WERBUNG AUSZUGEBEN. (GBR)

▲ 511 L'INITIALE DE LA FIRME DE DESIGN SAYLES A ÉTÉ UTILISÉE COMME ÉLÉMENT GRAPHIQUE DOMI-NANT SUR LE PAPIER À LETTRES. (USA)

▲ 512, 513 PAPIER À LETTRES ET CARTE DE VISITE DU STUDIO DE DESIGN JOHN BERG. (USA)

▲ 514 PAPIER À LETTRES ET FORMULAIRE DE FACTURATION IMPRIMÉS EN DEUX COULEURS, POUR UN SERVICE DE MAINTENANCE DES VOITURES BRITISH LEYLAND. CET EXEMPLE MONTRE COMMENT UN PETIT ATELIER PEUT SOIGNER SON IMAGE DE MARQUE SANS DÉPENSES DE PUBLICITÉ INUTILES. (GBR)

DESIGNER:

HELEN LAWTON

ILLUSTRATOR:

JACK MCCARTHY

AGENCY:

JONES & CO.

DESIGN LTD.

CLIENT:

THE ORCHARD

■ 515

ART DIRECTOR:

BRYAN L. PETERSON

DESIGNER:

SCOTT FEASTER

STUDIO:

PETERSON & CO.

CLIENT:

CONCRETE

PRODUCTIONS, INC.

■ 516

■ 515 THE SCHOOLBOY CHARACTER IS DEPICTED IN THE DIFFERENT ITEMS OF STATIONERY IN VARIOUS NAUGHTY SITUATIONS. IT IS PART OF A CORPORATE IDENTITY FOR A NEW CREATIVE SERVICES GROUP 'THE ORCHARD'. THE IMAGE NEEDED TO EVOKE A FEELING OF A WEALTH OF QUALITY PRODUCTS AVAILABLE FROM ONE SOURCE. (GBR)

■ 516 LETTERHEAD, ENVELOPE AND BUSINESS CARD FOR A FILM PRODUCTION COMPANY. (USA)

■ 517 A ROBIN'S EGG USED AS SYMBOL ON THE STATIONERY OF THE FIRM OF ROBINS ANALYTICS, AS AN ALLUSION TO ITS NAME. (USA)

■ 518 AN ACTUAL TAG BEARING A SALES PRICE HANGING FROM A SHEET OF PAPER FORMS THE LETTERHEAD OF THIS STATIONERY FOR A RETAIL WRITER AND CONSULTANT. IT IS GLUED TO THE ENVELOPE WHILE THE TAG ALONE SERVES AS BUSINESS CARD. (USA)

● 515 DER SCHULJUNGE TAUCHT AUF DEM GE-SCHÄFTSPAPIER IN VERSCHIEDENEN SITUATIONEN AUF. ES IST TEIL DES C.I.-PROGRAMMS DER KREA-TIVEN GRUPPE «THE ORCHARD» (OBSTGARTEN). AUFGABE WAR ES MITZUTEILEN, DASS EINE FÜLLE ERSTKLASSIGER DIENSTLEISTUNGEN VON EINER QUELLE ERHÄLTLICH IST. (GBR)

● 516 GESCHÄFTSPAPIER FÜR EINE FILMPRODUK-TIONSGESELLSCHAFT. (USA)

● 517 EIN ROTKEHLCHENEI ALS SYMBOL FÜR DIE FIRMA ROBINS ANALYTICS, DEREN NAME ROT-KEHLCHEN BEDEUTET. (USA)

● 518 EIN RICHTIGES ETIKETT MIT EINEM SPEZIAL-PREIS DARAUF HÄNGT AN EINEM BLATT PAPIER UND WIRD SO ZUM BRIEFKOPF FÜR EINE TEXTERIN UND WERBEBERATERIN. AUF DEM UMSCHLAG IST DER ANHÄNGER FIXIERT, WÄHREND DER ANHÄNGER ALLEIN ALS GESCHÄFTSKARTE DIENT. (USA)

▲ 515 L'IMAGE D'UN COLLÉGIEN DANS DIVERSES ÉTAPES D'UNE ACTION ILLUSTRE LE PAPIER À LETTRES ET LES CARTES DU GROUPE «THE ORCHARD» (LE VERGER). IL FAIT PARTIE DU PROGRAMME D'IDENTITÉ VISUELLE DE CE SERVICE DE CRÉATION. IL S'AGISSAIT DE MONTRER QU'UNE VARIÉTÉ DE PRODUITS PEUT ÊTRE CONÇUE À PARTIR D'UNE SEULE SOURCE. (GBR)

▲ 516 PAPIER À LETTRES D'UNE SOCIÉTÉ DE PRODUCTION DE FILMS. (USA)

▲ 517 UN ŒUF DE ROUGE-GORGE (EN ANGLAIS, «ROBIN»), SERT D'EMBLÊME À LA FIRME ROBINS ANALYTICS. (USA)

▲ 518 UNE VÉRITABLE ÉTIQUETTE AVEC UN PRIX DE VENTE INSCRIT DESSUS, ACCROCHÉE À UNE FEUILLE DE PAPIER, SERT D'EN-TÊTE DE LETTRE À UNE JEUNE RÉDACTRICE. SUR L'ENVELOPPE, L'ÉTIQUETTE EST COLLÉE. SEULE, ELLE SERT DE CARTE DE VISITE. (USA)

ART DIRECTOR:
JANE TILKA
STUDIO:
TILKA DESIGN
CLIENT:
ROBINS ANALYTICS
■ 517

ART DIRECTOR:
SUE CROLICK
DESIGNER:
SUE CROLICK
AGENCY:
SUE CROLICK
ADVERTISING +
DESIGN
CLIENT:
JOAN OSTRIN
■ 518

ART DIRECTOR:
MARIANNE VOS
DESIGNER:
MARIANNE VOS
ILLUSTRATOR:
TJEERD FREDERIKSE
AGENCY:
SAMENWERKENDE
ONTWERPERS
CLIENT:
DRUKKERIJ
MART.SPRUIJT BV
■ 519

ART DIRECTOR:
GREG SIMPSON
DESIGNER:
GREG SIMPSON
AGENCY:
THE PUSHPIN GROUP
CLIENT:
CRAIG CUTLER
STUDIO, INC.
■ 520

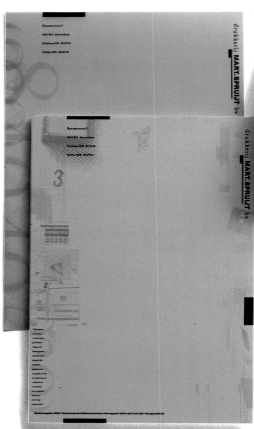

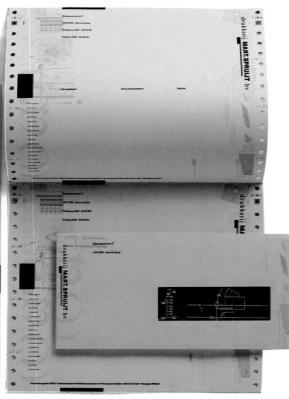

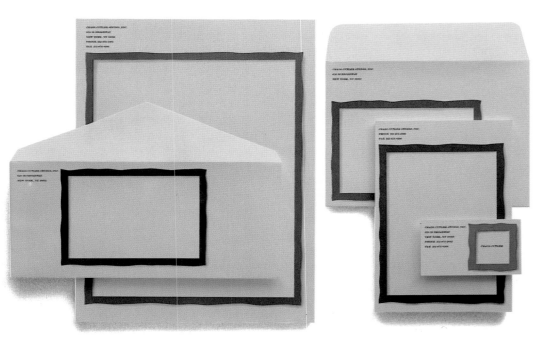

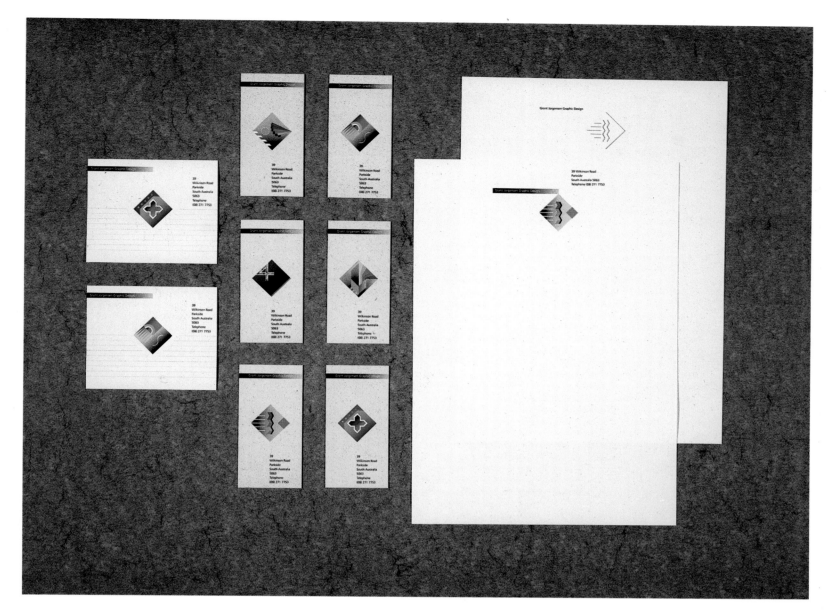

ART DIRECTOR:
GRANT JORGENSEN
DESIGNER:
GRANT JORGENSEN
ILLUSTRATOR:
GRANT JORGENSEN
AGENCY:
GRANT JORGENSEN
GRAPHIC DESIGN
CLIENT:
GRANT JORGENSEN
GRAPHIC DESIGN
■ 521

■ 519 STATIONERY AS PART OF AN IDENTITY WHICH VISUALIZES THE VERSATILITY OF AN AMSTERDAM PRINTERS. THE VARIOUS ITEMS SHOWN SUPPORT THE IMPRESSION OF A PRINTING HOUSE. THE WINDOW OF THE ENVELOPE OFFERS A VIEW ON A MAP SHOWING THE LOCATION OF THE FIRM. (NLD)

■ 520 THE PICTURE FRAME, THE DOMINANT ELEMENT ON THIS STATIONERY, STANDS FOR A PHOTOGRAPHY STUDIO. (USA)

■ 521 RANGE OF STATIONERY FOR A GRAPHIC DESIGNER UTILIZING SMALL STUDIES OF COLOR AND FORM WITH A CONSTRUCTIVIST APPROACH. EACH ITEM PRESENTS A VARIATION OF THE THEME. (AUS)

● 519 BRIEFPAPIER ALS TEIL EINES C.I. PRO-GRAMMS, IN DEM DIE VIELSEITIGKEIT EINER AM-STERDAMER DRUCKEREI ZUM AUSDRUCK KOMMEN SOLL. DIE FORMULARE UNTERSTÜTZEN DAS DRUCKE-REI-THEMA. DURCH DAS FENSTER DES UMSCHLAGS SIEHT MAN EINEN SITUATIONSPLAN. (NLD)

● 520 DAS DOMINIERENDE ELEMENT DIESES BRIEF-PAPIERS, EIN BILDERRAHMEN, SYMBOLISIERT EIN PHOTOSTUDIO. (USA)

● 521 GESCHÄFTSPAPIER FÜR EINEN GRAPHIK-DESIGNER. ER BENUTZTE KLEINE «KONSTRUKTIVI-STISCHE» FARB- UND FORMSTUDIEN, UND ZWAR IN ZAHLREICHEN VARIATIONEN DES THEMAS. (AUS)

▲ 519 CE PAPIER À LETTRES FAIT PARTIE DU PRO-GRAMME D'IDENTITÉ CORPORATE D'UNE IMPRIMERIE D'AMSTERDAM VISUALISANT LES CAPACITÉS MULTI-PLES DE LA FIRME. LES DIVERS FORMULAIRES ÉVO-QUENT L'IMPRIMERIE. AU TRAVERS DE LA FENÊTRE DE L'ENVELOPPE, ON VOIT UN PLAN DE SITUATION. (NLD)

▲ 520 UN CADRE SERT D'ÉLÉMENT D'IDENTIFICATION SUR LES PAPIERS À LETTRES, ENVELOPPES ET CARTES D'UN STUDIO DE PHOTOGRAPHE. (USA)

▲ 521 PAPIER À LETTRES ET CARTES D'UN DESIGNER GRAPHIQUE. IL A UTILISÉ DE PETITES COMPOSITIONS D'ESPRIT CONSTRUCTIVISTE QUI VARIENT SELON LE DESTINATAIRE. (AUS).

■ 522 ART DIRECTOR: LOWELL WILLIAMS DESIGNER: BILL CARSON, LOWELL WILLIAMS AGENCY: LOWELL WILLIAMS DESIGN CLIENT: LOWELL WILLIAMS DESIGN ■ 523 ART DIRECTOR/DESIGNER: MICHAEL STANARD CLIENT: MICHAEL STANARD ■ 524 ART DIRECTOR/DESIGNER/ILLUSTRATOR: DAVID LERCH AGENCY: PENNEBAKER DESIGN CLIENT: CHRISTY ETTER ■ 525 ART DIRECTOR/DESIGNER/ILLUSTRATOR: MICHAEL DORET STUDIO: MICHAEL DORET, INC. CLIENT: EVENTMEDIA INTERNATIONAL INC. ■ 526 ART DIRECTOR/DESIGNER: BRUNO K. WIESE CLIENT: DEUTSCHE FORSCHUNGSANSTALT FÜR LUFT- UND RAUMFAHRT ■ 527 ART DIRECTOR/ILLUSTRATOR: PAUL BLACK AGENCY: JOINER ROELAND, SERIO KOPPEL CLIENT: EDS ■ 528 ART DIRECTOR: LANNY SOMMESE DESIGNER: KRISTIN BRESLIN CLIENT: SOMMESE DESIGN ■ 529 ART DIRECTOR/DESIGNER: BILL THORBURN AGENCY: DAYTON HUDSON/IN HOUSE CLIENT: DAYTON HUDSON DEPT. STORE ■ 530 ART DIRECTOR/DESIGNER: MICHAEL VANDERBYL AGENCY: VANDERBYL DESIGN CLIENT: BEDFORD PROPERTIES ■ 531 ART DIRECTOR/DESIGNER: JOSE SERRANO ILLUSTRATOR: DAN THONER AGENCY: MIRES DESIGN, INC. CLIENT: TEE SHIRT CO. ■ 532 ART DIRECTOR: DOUG RUCKER DESIGNER/ILLUSTRATOR: DICK MITCHELL AGENCY: RICHARDS BROCK MILLER MITCHELL & ASSOCIATES CLIENT: FILMCASTERS ■ 533 ART DIRECTOR/DESIGNER: STEVEN SANDSTROM ILLUSTRATOR: GREE KROLICKI AGENCY: SANDSTROM DESIGN CLIENT: OREGON ART INSTITUTE ■ 534 ART DIRECTOR/DESIGNER: HALEY JOHNSON ILLUSTRATOR: RANALL DAHLK, HALEY JOHNSON STUDIO: CHARLES S. ANDERSON DESIGN AGENCY: WIEDEN & KENNEDY CLIENT: NIKE ■ 535 ART DIRECTOR/ILLUSTRATOR: VADIM GORETSKY AGENCY: STUDIO SILICON CLIENT: T-N-T ENTERPRISES ■ 536 ART DIRECTOR/ILLUSTRATOR: PETER BAKER AGENCY: PETER BAKER CLIENT: MIKE DENIS AVIATION INC. ■ 537 ART DIRECTOR/ILLUSTRATOR: ERIC RICKABAUGH AGENCY: RICKABAUGH GRAPHICS CLIENT: DESIGN WORKS ■ 538 ART DIRECTOR/DESIGNER: DOUGLAS MAY AGENCY: MAY & CO. CLIENT: INTEX SOFTWARE ■ 539 ART DIRECTOR: ANTHONY RUSSELL DESIGNER: SUSAN LIMONCELLI CLIENT: STRATHMORE PAPER COMPANY ■ 540 ART DIRECTOR/DESIGNER: JOHN SAYLES AGENCY: SAYLES GRAPHIC DESIGN CLIENT: BUENA VISTA COLLEGE ■ 541 ART DIRECTOR/DESIGNER: MICHAEL VANDERBYL AGENCY: VANDERBYL DESIGN CLIENT: BERNHARDT FURNITURE COMPANY ■ 542 ART DIRECTOR/DESIGNER: JOHN NORMAN PHOTOGRAPHER: J.W. FRY AGENCY: RICHARDS BROCK MILLER MITCHELL & ASSOCIATES CLIENT: J.W. FRY ■ 543 ART DIRECTOR/DESIGNER: MARGO CHASE AGENCY: MARGO CHASE DESIGN CLIENT: SYDNEY COOPER ■ 544 DESIGNER: STEWART JUNG CLIENT: JANZENS ■ 545 ART DIRECTOR/ILLUSTRATOR: KENNETH J. MEACHAM AGENCY: COOPER COMMUNICATIONS CLIENT: DEPARTMENT OF FISH & GAME STATE OF CALIFORNIA ■ 546 ART DIRECTOR/ILLUSTRATOR: JOHN SWIETER DESIGNER: JOHN SWIETER, JIM VOGEL AGENCY: SWIETER DESIGN CLIENT: SOUTHERN METHODIST UNIVERSITY ■

■ 547 A VISUAL IDENTITY SYSTEM FOR A NEW JAPANESE LUXURY HOTEL COMPRISED OF SIX LOGOTYPE VARIATIONS. THE INTERIOR DESIGN IS BASED ON THIS FLOWER CONCEPT. (JPN) ■ 548 A VARIETY OF BOTTLE LABELS FOR DIFFERENT BEERS OF THE GERMAN CLUSS BREWERY COMPANY. (GER) ■ 549 LOGO FOR THE AVIATION FUEL ENTERPRISES LTD. THE ASSIGNMENT WAS TO DESIGN A LOGO THAT WAS REMINISCENT OF AVIATION EMBLEMS OF THE THIRTIES AND FORTIES. (CAN)

● 547 DIESE SECHS VARIATIONEN EINES LOGOS SIND TEIL EINES FIRMENERSCHEINUNGSBILDES FÜR EIN NEUES JAPANISCHES LUXUSHOTEL. DAS FLOREALE THEMA WURDE AUCH FÜR DIE INNENDEKORATION VERWENDET. (JPN) ● 548 EINE SERIE VON ETIKETTEN FÜR VERSCHIEDENE BIERSORTEN DER BRAUEREI CLUSS.(GER) ● 549 DIESES EMBLEM FÜR DIE AVIATION FUEL ENTERPRISES SOLLTE AN DIE LUFTFAHRTEMBLEME DER DREISSIGER UND VIERZIGER JAHRE ERINNERN. (CAN)

▲ 547 LES SIX VARIATIONS D'UN LOGO FONT PARTIE DE L'IDENTITÉ VISUELLE D'UN NOUVEL HÔTEL DE LUXE JAPONAIS. LE MOTIF FLORAL A ÉTÉ REPRIS DANS LA DÉCORATION INTÉRIEURE. (JPN) ▲ 548 UNE SÉRIE D'ÉTIQUETTES POUR DIFFÉRENTES SORTES DE BIÈRE DE LA BRASSERIE CLUSS. (GER) ▲ 549 CET EMBLÈME CRÉÉ POUR AVIATION FUEL ENTERPRISES DEVAIT RAPPELER LES INSIGNES DE L'AVIATION DES ANNÉES TRENTE ET QUARANTE. (CAN)

■ 547 ART DIRECTOR: COLIN FORBES, MICHAEL GERICKE DESIGNER: JAMES ANDERSON, DONNA CHING, MICHAEL GERICKE ILLUSTRATOR: MCRAY MAGLEBY AGENCY: PENTAGRAM DESIGN CLIENT: OUN CORPORATION ■ 548 ART DIRECTOR/DESIGNER: KNUT HARTMANN CLIENT: BRAUEREI CLUSS AG ■ 549 ART DIRECTOR: FRANK MAYRS DESIGNER: FRANK MAYRS ILLUSTRATOR: BERNIE LOW AGENCY: L.A. DESIGN CLIENT: AVIATION FUEL ENTERPRISES LTD. ■

PACKAGING

PACKUNGEN

PACKAGING

ART DIRECTOR:
TAKU SATOH
DESIGNER:
TAKU SATOH
PHOTOGRAPHERS:
MEGUMU WADA
TOSHIO NAKAJIMA
CLIENT:
TAKU SATOH DESIGN
OFFICE
▲■ 551

ART DIRECTORS:
STANLEY CHURCH
BOB WALLACE
DESIGNER:
STANLEY CHURCH
ILLUSTRATOR:
MARILYN
MONTGOMERY
AGENCY:
WALLACE CHURCH
ASSOCIATES, INC.
CLIENT:
WALLACE CHURCH
ASSOCIATES, INC.
■ 552

ART DIRECTOR:
JAMES KOVAL
DESIGNER:
JAMES KOVAL
ILLUSTRATOR:
MARY FLOCK
AGENCY:
VSA PARTNERS, INC.
CLIENT:
COFFEE
CONSULTANTS INC.
◄■ 550

ART DIRECTOR:
CARLO PAGODA
DESIGNER:
PRIMO ANGELI
ILLUSTRATOR:
ANTAR DAYAL
AGENCY:
PRIMO ANGELI INC.
CLIENT:
THOMAS J. LIPTON,
INC.
■ 553

■ 550 LABEL DESIGN FOR PEABERRY COFFEE. THE COLOR OF GOLD AND BROWN EVOKES THE FEELING OF NATURE AND ROASTED COFFEE BEANS. THE MOTIVE OF THE COFFEE BEANS WITH LEAVES IS REPEATED AS A DELICATE PATTERN ON THE PAPER BAG. (USA)

■ 551 A COFFEE TIN WITH PAPER LABEL SEEN FROM FRONT AND BACK. CITIO COFFEE IS MARKETED IN JAPAN. (JPN)

■ 552 A JAMJAR DESIGNED BY WALLACE CHURCH ASSOCIATES TO SHOWCASE DISTINCTIVE DESIGN INTEGRITY WHILE PROVIDING A MEMORABLE HOLIDAY GREETING. INSIDE WAS A JAZZ CASSETTE WITH "JAM" MUSIC. (USA)

■ 553 A LIMITED EDITION TEA TIN DESIGNED FOR THE 100TH ANNIVERSARY OF LIPTONS. (USA)

● 550 ETIKETTGESTALTUNG FÜR PEABERRY-KAFFEE. DIE FARBEN BRAUN UND GOLD UND DIE ILLUSTRA-TION UNTERSTREICHEN DAS GEFÜHL VON NATUR UND GERÖSTETEM KAFFEE. DAS MOTIV IST GANZ FEIN AUF DER PAPIERTÜTE ALS MUSTER WIEDER-HOLT. (USA)

● 551 EINE KAFFEEDOSE FÜR DEN JAPANISCHEN MARKT, AUS WEISSBLECH MIT PAPIERETIKETT, VON ZWEI SEITEN GESEHEN. (JPN)

● 552 EIN MARMELADENGLAS, DAS VON WALLACE CHURCH ASSOCIATES ALS WEIHNACHTSGRUSS VER-SCHICKT WURDE, UM IHR GESTALTERISCHES KÖN-NEN ZU BEWEISEN. ES ENTHIELT EINE KASSETTE MIT "JAM"-MUSIK (JAM = MARMELADE). (USA)

● 553 TEEDOSE IN LIMITIERTER AUFLAGE ZUM 100JÄHRIGEN BESTEHEN VON LIPTONS. (USA)

▲ 550 ÉTIQUETTE DES EMBALLAGES DE CAFÉ PEABERRY. LES COULEURS, BRUN ET OR, AINSI QUE L'ILLUSTRATION SOULIGNENT LE CÔTÉ NATUREL DU PRODUIT ET ÉVOQUENT LE CAFÉ TORRÉFIÉ. LE MÊME MOTIF A ÉTÉ REPRIS EN GRAND SUR LES SACHETS. (USA)

▲ 551 POUR LE MARCHÉ JAPONAIS, UNE BOÎTE DE CAFÉ EN FER BLANC AVEC ÉTIQUETTE EN PAPIER, VUE DE FACE ET DE DOS. (JPN)

▲ 552 CE VERRE À CONFITURE A ÉTÉ ENVOYÉ PAR WALLACE CHURCH ASSOCIATES AUX CLIENTS COMME CADEAU DE NOËL. IL RENFERMAIT UNE CASSETTE DE MUSIQUE DE JAZZ, DITE «JAM MUSIC» (JAM = CONFITURE). (USA)

▲ 553 UNE BOÎTE À THÉ EN ÉDITION LIMITÉE POUR LE 100E ANNIVERSAIRE DES THÉS LIPTONS. (USA)

ART DIRECTOR/
ILLUSTRATOR:
JOYCE ZAVARRO
CLIENT:
APPLE COMPUTERS
■ 555

ART DIRECTORS:
CHARLES S.
ANDERSON
DAN OLSON
ILLUSTRATORS:
CHARLES S.
ANDERSON
RANDALL DAHLK
DAN OLSON
CLIENT:
LEVI STRAUSS
◀■ 554

ART DIRECTOR/
ILLUSTRATOR:
PERET
AGENCY:
PERET ASOCIADOS
CLIENT:
THE END
■ 556

ART DIRECTOR:
ELLEN SHAPIRO
DESIGNER:
ELLEN SHAPIRO
ILLUSTRATOR:
MICHAEL KELLER
CLIENT:
NATURAL ORGANICS
■ 558

DESIGNERS:
JÖZEF SUMICHRAST
ROBERT VALENTINE
ILLUSTRATOR:
JÖZEF SUMICHRAST
CLIENT:
BLOOMINGDALE'S
◀■ 557

ART DIRECTOR/
PHOTOGRAPHER:
H. ROSS FELTUS
CLIENT:
TON SUR TON
■ 559

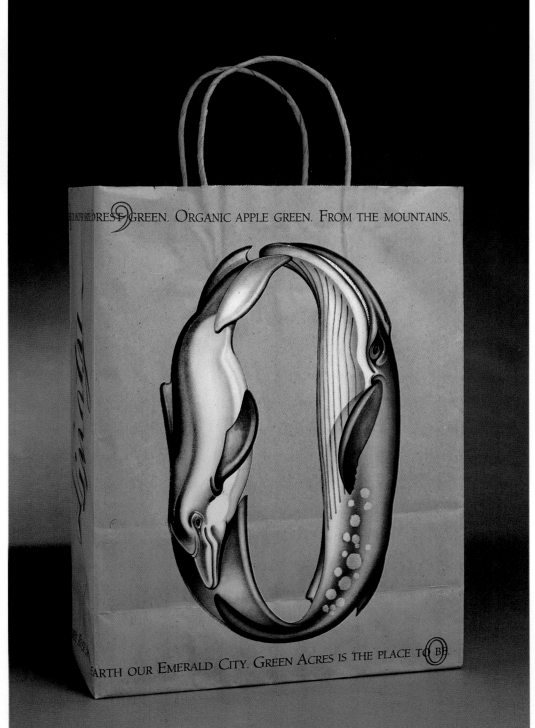

■ 554 A SILVER METAL CASE AS PART OF A NEW IMAGE FOR THE SILVER TAB JEANS LINE. (USA)

● 554 EIN SILBRIGER METALLKOFFER, TEIL EINES NEUEN IMAGES FÜR SILVER TAB-JEANS. (USA)

▲ 554 UNE VALISE DE MÉTAL – UN ÉLÉMENT D'IMAGE DE MARQUE DES JEANS SILVER TAB. (USA)

■ 555 LAMINATED PAPER BAG FOR MACWORLD EXPO 1989, PROMOTING THE APPLE COMMUNICATIONS LIBRARY PUBLISHED BY ADDISON WESLEY. (USA)

● 555 LAMINIERTE TRAGTASCHE FÜR DIE MACWORLD EXPO 1989, ALS WERBUNG FÜR DIE APPLE COMMU-NICATIONS LIBRARY. (USA)

▲ 555 UN SAC EN PAPIER LAMINÉ CRÉÉ POUR LA MACWORLD EXPO 1989 COMME PUBLICITÉ DE APPLE COMMUNICATIONS LIBRARY. (USA)

■ 556 CARRIER BAG FOR "THE END," A FASHION SHOP. (SPA)

● 556 TRAGTASCHE FÜR «THE END», EINE MODE-BOUTIQUE. (SPA)

▲ 556 SAC CRÉÉ POUR «THE END», UNE BOUTIQUE DE MODE. (SPA)

■ 557 1990, THE YEAR OF THE ENVIRONMENT, AS SUBJECT OF A BAG FOR BLOOMINGDALE'S. (USA)

● 557 1990, DAS JAHR DER UMWELT, ALS THEMA EINER TRAGTASCHE FÜR BLOOMINGDALE'S. (USA)

▲ 557 L'ANNÉE DE L'ENVIRONNEMENT, 1990 – SUJET D'UN SAC EN PAPIER POUR BLOOMINGDALE'S. (USA)

■ 558 "BODY, MIND, SOUL", A CARRIER BAG WITH THE LOGO OF THE HOLISTIC CENTER. (USA)

● 558 «KÖRPER, GEIST, SEELE» – TRAGTASCHE MIT DEM ZEICHEN EINES HOLISTIK-ZENTRUMS. (USA)

▲ 558 «CORPS-ESPRIT-ÂME»: SAC ORNÉ DU LOGO DU HOLISTIC CENTER D'HUNTINGTON STATION. (USA)

■ 559 A PAPER CARRIER BAG IN THE COLORS OF MEXICO˝FOR TON SUR TON FASHIONS. (GER)

● 559 EINE PAPIERTRAGTASCHE IN MEXIKANISCHEN FARBEN FÜR TON SUR TON-MODE. (GER)

▲ 559 SAC EN PAPIER POUR LES VÊTEMENTS TON SUR TON. (GER)

ART DIRECTOR:
PAULA SCHER
DESIGNERS:
PAULA SCHER
RON LOUIE
AGENCY:
KOPPEL & SCHER
CLIENT:
ÖOLA CORPORATION
■ 560

ART DIRECTOR:
HARRY ELBERS
DESIGNER:
HARRY ELBERS
PHOTOGRAPHER:
BAREND KÖHLER
AGENCY:
HARRY & ELISABETH
ELBERS B.V.
CLIENT:
OOSTERHOUTSE
ZOETWARENFABRIK
■ 561

ART DIRECTOR:
MICHELE MELANDRI
DESIGNER:
MICHELE MELANDRI
AGENCY:
NIKE DESIGN
CLIENT:
NIKE INC.
■ 562

ART DIRECTOR:
ROGER GOULD
DESIGNER:
TIM POWERS
ILLUSTRATORS:
ROGER GOULD
TIM POWERS
AGENCY:
GOULD DESIGN
CLIENT:
WOLVERINE
WORLDWIDE INC.
■ 563

■ 560 A RANGE OF CANS FOR THE ÖOLA CANDY STORE. THE Ö SERVED AS GRAPHIC ELEMENT. (USA)

■ 561 OPENED AND CLOSED CARTON BOX FOR A DUTCH BRAND OF CHOCOLATES WITH KIRSCH MEANT FOR EXPORT. (NLD)

■ 562 PAPER CARRIER BAG AND BOXES FOR NIKE TOWN WITH PORTRAITS THAT SUPPORT THE SPORTS IMAGE OF THE COMPANY. (USA)

■ 563 BOX DESIGN FOR WOLVERINE BOOTS AND SHOES FOR SPORTS AND WORK. THE SAME MOTIF IS USED ON BOXES AND LABELS. (USA)

● 560 DOSEN FÜR EINEN CANDY STORE. DAS Ö DIENTE ALS GRAPHISCHES ELEMENT. (USA)

● 561 GEÖFFNETE UND GESCHLOSSENE SCHACHTEL FÜR HOLLÄNDISCHE PRALINEN, DIE FÜR DEN EXPORT BESTIMMT SIND. (NLD)

● 562 PAPIERTRAGTASCHE UND SCHACHTELN FÜR NIKE TOWN MIT PORTRÄTS, DIE DAS SPORT-IMAGE DER FIRMA UNTERSTREICHEN. (USA)

● 563 SCHACHTEL FÜR STIEFEL UND SCHUHE DER MARKE WOLVERINE. DAS MOTIV WIRD AUF DEM ETIKETT WIEDERHOLT. (USA)

▲ 560 UNE SÉRIE DE BOÎTES POUR LES CONFISERIES ÖOLA. (USA)

▲ 561 EXEMPLE D'UNE BOÎTE DE GRIOTTES AU CHOCOLAT TIRÉE D'UNE SÉRIE D'EMBALLAGES POUR L'EXPORTATION. (NLD)

▲ 562 EMBALLAGES ET SAC POUR LES PRODUITS DE NIKE TOWN ORNÉS DE PORTRAITS QUI SOULIGNENT LE CARACTÈRE SPORTIF DE CETTE FIRME. (USA)

▲ 563 BOÎTE CRÉÉE POUR LES BOOTS ET CHAUSSURES DE SPORTS ET DE TRAVAIL WOLVERINE. L'ÉTIQUETTE REPREND LE MÊME MOTIF. (USA)

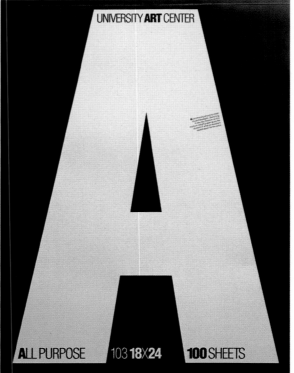

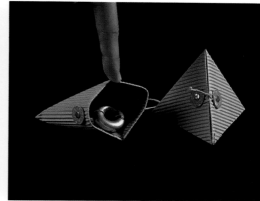

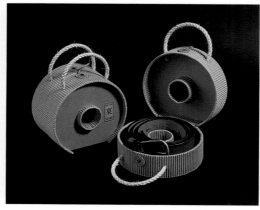
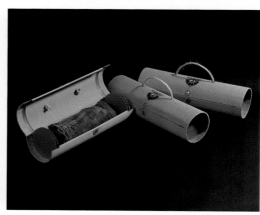

ART DIRECTOR:
MARY LEWIS
DESIGNER:
MARY LEWIS
PHOTOGRAPHER:
ALAN NEWNHAM
AGENCY:
LEWIS MOBERLY
CLIENT:
ASDA
■ 564

ART DIRECTOR:
SAM SMIDT
DESIGNER:
SAM SMIDT
COPYWRITER:
SAM SMIDT
CLIENT:
UNIVERSITY ART
CENTER
▼
◀■ 565-567

DESIGNER:
MARC VOLDENAUER
■ 568-573

■ 564 THE DESIGN APPROACH OF THESE PAINT CANS FOR THE INHOUSE BRAND OF ASDA STORES WAS TO REDUCE EVERYTHING TO THE SIMPLEST LEVEL SO THAT THE COLOR CHIP APPEARS AS THE FOCAL POINT. IT FORMS A BOX OF TISSUES PROVIDING A STRONG VISUAL AND EACH BOX SHOWS THE NAME OF THE PAINT. (GBR)

■ 565-567 THREE ART PADS FOR THE UNIVERSITY ART CENTER OF PASADENA. EACH INITIAL LETTER MARKS THE PAPER QUALITY: M STANDS FOR "MARKERS", A FOR "ALL PURPOSE", AND T FOR "TRACING". (USA)

■ 568-573 A GRADUATE STUDENT'S PACKAGING PROJECT FOR A FICTITIOUS JEANS BRAND. THE STUDENT CONSIDERED CORRUGATED CARDBOARD AS A SPECIAL CHALLENGE. HE TOOK INTO ACCOUNT ITS SPECIAL CHARACTER AND WORKED IT INTO UNUSUAL SHAPES. (GER)

● 564 DAS DESIGN-KONZEPT FÜR DIESE FARBTÖPFE, EINE HAUSMARKE DER ASDA-LÄDEN, WAR REDUZIERUNG AUF DAS NOTWENDIGSTE, SO DASS DAS FARBFELD ZUM MITTELPUNKT WIRD. DURCH DIE UMWANDLUNG IN EINE BOX MIT PAPIERTÜCHERN WIRD DAS FARBFELD MIT DER FARBBEZEICHNUNG ZU EINEM STARKEN VISUELLEN ELEMENT. (GBR)

● 565-567 DREI PAPIERBLÖCKE FÜR DAS UNIVERSITY ART CENTER. DIE ANFANGSBUCHSTABEN BEZEICHNEN DIE PAPIERQUALITÄT: M FÜR «MARKERS» (FILZSTIFTE), A FÜR «ALL PURPOSE» (ALLZWECK) UND T FÜR «TRACING» (DURCHPAUSEN). (USA)

● 568-573 VERPACKUNGEN FÜR EINE FIKTIVE JEANSFIRMA ALS DIPLOMARBEIT EINES STUDENTEN DER FACHHOCHSCHULE FÜR GESTALTUNG, AUGSBURG. ER SETZTE WELLPAPPE BEWUSST ALS GESTALTUNGSELEMENT EIN UND FAND NEUE, UNGEWÖHNLICHE VERPACKUNGSFORMEN. (GER)

▲ 564 DEUX BIDONS DE PEINTURE D'UNE MARQUE EN VENTE DANS LES MAGASINS ASDA. LE CONCEPT SE BASE SUR L'IDENTIFICATION RAPIDE DE LA COULEUR, D'OÙ LA SIMPLIFICATION EXTRÊME DU DESIGN. CHAQUE BIDON PORTE LE NOM DE LA GAMME DE COULEURS ET UN ÉCHANTILLON DE LA NUANCE. (GBR)

▲ 565-567 TROIS BLOCS DE PAPIER POUR LE UNIVERSITY ART CENTER. CHAQUE INITIALE DÉSIGNE LA QUALITÉ DU PAPIER: M POUR «MARKERS» (FEUTRES), A POUR «ALL PURPOSE» (TOUS USAGES) ET T POUR «TRACING» (DÉCALQUE). (USA)

▲ 568-573 PROJET D'EMBALLAGES POUR JEANS, CHEMISES ET ACCESSOIRES D'UNE FIRME FICTIVE. POUR CE TRAVAIL DE DIPLÔME À LA FACHHOCHSCHULE FÜR GESTALTUNG D'AUGSBOURG, LE DESIGNER A TIRÉ PARTI AU MAXIMUM DES PROPRIÉTÉS DU CARTON ONDULÉ. (GER)

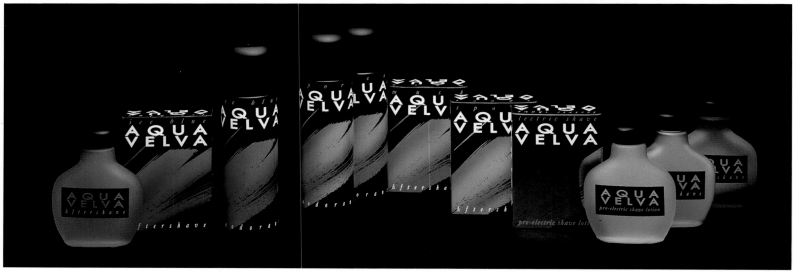

■ 574 BOXES, BAGS AND LABELS FOR ERNO LASZLO SKIN CARE PRODUCTS USING A STYLIZED CLOCK WHICH SHOWS DIFFERENT TIMES AS VISUAL ELEMENT. (USA)

■ 575 A RANGE OF PACKAGING FOR MEN'S AFTER SHAVE AND DEODORANT OF THE AQUA VELVA BRAND. (SAF)

■ 576-578 PRODUCT DESIGN FOR DECORATIVE COSMETICS: EYE SHADOW AND LIPSTICK (SHOWN CLOSED) FOR MAX FACTOR AND A LIPSTICK FOR KANEBO. (JPN)

● 574 SCHACHTELN, TRAGTASCHEN UND ETIKETT FÜR ERNO LASZLO KOSMETIK. DAS EINHEITLICHE GRAPHISCHE ELEMENT IST EINE STILISIERTE UHR, DIE VERSCHIEDENE ZEITEN ANZEIGT. (USA)

● 575 VERPACKUNGSREIHE FÜR DIE AQUA VELVA AFTER SHAVE- UND DEODORANT-LINIE IN VERSCHIE-DENEN DUFTNOTEN FÜR MÄNNER. (SAF)

● 576-578 PRODUKT-DESIGN FÜR DEKORATIVE KOSMETIK: AUGENSCHATTEN UND LIPPENSTIFT (GE-SCHLOSSEN) FÜR MAX FACTOR UND EIN LIPPEN-STIFT FÜR KANEBO. (JPN)

▲ 574 EMBALLAGES, SACS ET ÉTIQUETTES POUR LES COSMÉTIQUES ERNO LASZLO RÉPÉTANT COMME ÉLÉMENT VISUEL UN CADRAN DE MONTRE STYLISÉ INDIQUANT DES HEURES DIFFÉRENTES. (USA)

▲ 575 LA GAMME DE CONDITIONNEMENTS DES LOTIONS APRÈS-RASAGE ET DÉODORANTS DE LA MARQUE AQUA VELVA. (SAF)

▲ 576-578 PROJET D'UNE GAMME DE CONDITION-NEMENTS POUR DES PRODUITS DE MAQUILLAGE: FARD À YEUX ET ROUGE À LÈVRES MAX FACTOR; EN BAS, TUBE DE ROUGE À LÈVRES KANEBO. (JPN)

ART DIRECTORS:
THOMAS G. FOWLER
LOIS SLACHOWITZ
LISA DELGRANDE
DESIGNER:
THOMAS G. FOWLER
AGENCY:
TOM FOWLER, INC.
CLIENT:
CHESEBROUGH-
POND'S CREATIVE
PACKAGING
DESIGN DEPT.
◀■ 574

ART DIRECTOR:
TAKU SATOH
DESIGNER:
TAKU SATOH
PHOTOGRAPHERS:
MEGUMU WADA
TOSHIO NAKAJIMA
CLIENT:
TAKU SATOH DESIGN
OFFICE
■ 576-578

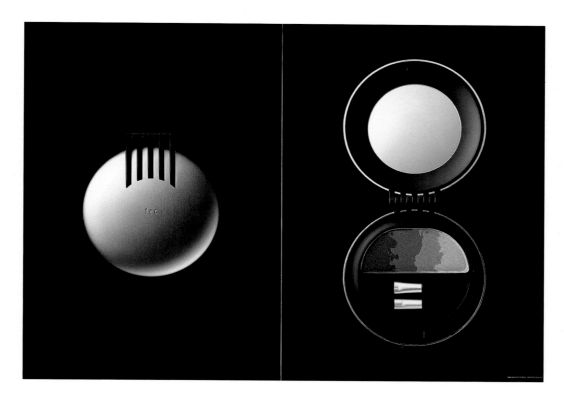

ART DIRECTOR:
KEES SCHILPEROORT
DESIGNER:
ROBYN BAJKAI
AGENCY:
PENTAGRAPH (PTY)
LTD.
CLIENT:
BEECHAMS
◀■ 575

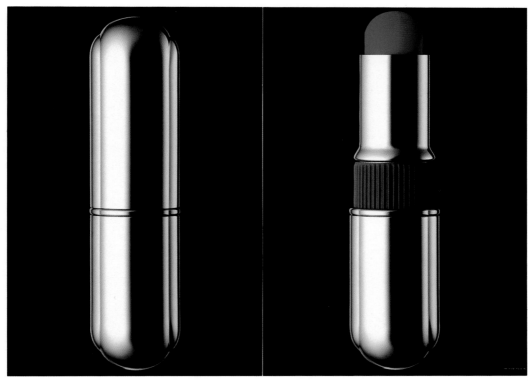

ART DIRECTOR:
ALAIN WANNAZ
DESIGNER:
ALAIN WANNAZ
CLIENT:
MARC-ETIENNE
DUBOIS
■ 580, 582

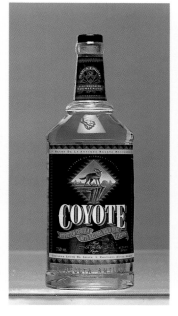

ART DIRECTORS:
HEATHER
ARMSTRONG
JONATHAN FORD
JOHN MOTHERSOLE
ILLUSTRATORS:
TOM CARNASE
WENDELL MINOR
AGENCY:
MICHAEL PETERS
DESIGN
CLIENT:
HOUSE OF SEAGRAM
■ 581

ART DIRECTOR:
TODD WATERBURY
DESIGNER:
TODD WATERBURY
ILLUSTRATOR:
TODD WATERBURY
LETTERERS:
TODD WATERBURY
LYNN SCHULTE
COPYWRITER:
CHUCK CARLSON
AGENCY:
THE DUFFY DESIGN
GROUP
CLIENT:
JIM BEAM BRANDS
◄■ 579

ART DIRECTOR:
KATJA SCHUMACHER
DESIGNER:
KATJA SCHUMACHER
■ 583

■ 579 CARDBOARD BOX WITH CUT-OUTS AND BOTTLE
LIVERY FOR A NEW TYPE OF AQUAVIT MADE IN
DENMARK, FORMULATED AND POSITIONED TO COM-
PETE WITH PREMIUM VODKAS AND GINS ON THE U.S.
MARKET. (USA)

■ 580, 582 LABEL DESIGNS FOR CÔTES DE PRO-
VENCE WINE BOTTLES. (FRA)

■ 581 PRODUCT CONCEPT FOR COYOTE, AN
IMPORTED TEQUILA WITH NATURAL WILD HERB
FLAVORS. (USA)

■ 583 BOTTLE LIVERY FOR DIFFERENT WINES FROM
ONE VINEYARD. STUDENT'S PROJECT. (GER)

● 579 KARTONSCHACHTEL MIT AUSSTANZUNGEN UND
FLASCHE FÜR EINEN NEUEN AQUAVIT AUS DÄNE-
MARK, DER DANK QUALITÄT UND AUFTRITT MIT
ERSTKLASSIGEN WODKA- UND GIN-MARKEN KON-
KURRIEREN SOLL. (USA)

● 580, 582 ETIKETTGESTALTUNG FÜR CÔTES DE
PROVENCE-WEINFLASCHEN. (FRA)

● 581 FLASCHENAUSSTATTUNG FÜR COYOTE, EINEN
IMPORTIERTEN TEQUILA MIT GESCHMACKSZUSÄTZEN
WILDER KRÄUTER. (USA)

● 583 FLASCHENAUSSTATTUNG FÜR VERSCHIEDENE
WEINE EINES WEINGUTS. STUDIENPROJEKT. (GER)

▲ 579 ÉTIQUETTE ET EMBALLAGE AVEC JEU DE
DÉCOUPES POUR UNE NOUVELLE MARQUE D'EAU DE
VIE FABRIQUÉE AU DANEMARK, QUI DEVRAIT CON-
CURRENCER LES GRANDES MARQUES DE VODKAS ET
DE GINS. (USA)

▲ 580, 582 DEUX PROJETS D'ÉTIQUETTES POUR DES
BOUTEILLES DE CÔTES DE PROVENCE. (FRA)

▲ 581 ÉTIQUETTE CONÇUE POUR UNE BOUTEILLE DE
TEQUILA IMPORTÉE, COYOTE, PARFUMÉE AUX
HERBES SAUVAGES. (USA)

▲ 583 PROJETS D'ÉTIQUETTES D'EMBALLAGES POUR
UNE GAMME DE BOUTEILLES DE VINS. (GER)

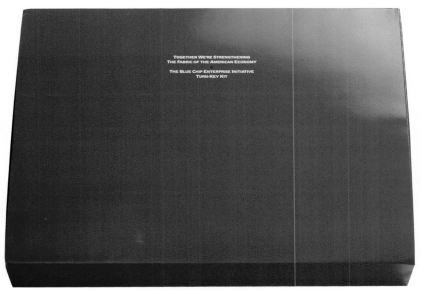

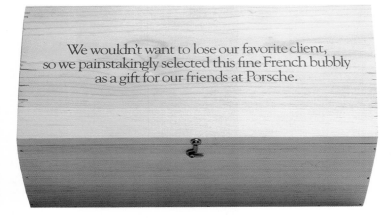

ART DIRECTOR:

ANDREÉ CORDELLA

PHOTOGRAPHER:

AARON JONES

COPYWRITER:

EVAN STONE

CLIENT:

CONNECTICUT

MUTUAL

■ 584, 585

ART DIRECTOR:

MARK JOHNSON

COPYWRITER:

JOHN STINGLEY

AGENCY:

FALLON MCELLIGOTT

CLIENT:

PORSCHE CARS

NORTH AMERICA

■ 586, 587

■ 584, 585 THIS BOX SHOWN WITH AND WITHOUT ITS WRAPPER WAS MAILED TO LOCAL AND STATE CHAMBERS OF COMMERCE BY THE MUTUAL INSURANCE CO. IT CONTAINS INFORMATION MATERIAL ON AN AWARD PROGRAM FOR SMALL FIRMS WITH THE AIM TO ENCOURAGE INNOVATIVE THINKING: "TOGETHER WE'RE STRENGTHENING THE FABRIC OF THE AMERICAN ECONOMY." (USA)

■ 586, 587 "DRIVE CAREFULLY THIS HOLIDAY SEASON." FALLON MCELLIGOTT SENT THIS WOODEN BOX WITH A BOTTLE OF PERRIER MINERAL WATER TO THEIR CLIENT PORSCHE CARS NORTH AMERICA AS A CHRISTMAS REMINDER SHOWCASING AGENCY CREATIVITY. (USA)

● 584, 585 DIESE SCHACHTEL, MIT UND OHNE WICKLER GEZEIGT, WURDE VON EINER VERSICHERUNGSGESELLSCHAFT AN LOKALE UND NATIONALE HANDELSKAMMERN VERSCHICKT. SIE ENTHÄLT INFORMATIONSMATERIAL ÜBER EINEN WETTBEWERB, DER DIE EIGENINITIAVE KLEINER UNTERNEHMEN FÖRDERN SOLL: «GEMEINSAMEN STÄRKEN WIR DAS GEWEBE DER AMERIKANISCHEN WIRTSCHAFT.» (USA)

● 586, 587 «GUTE FAHRT» WÜNSCHT DIE AGENTUR FALLON MCELLIGOTT MIT DIESER HOLZSCHACHTEL, DIE EINE FLASCHE PERRIER ENTHÄLT, IHREM KUNDEN PORSCHE CARS NORTH AMERICA. MIT DIESEM WERBEGESCHENK WILL DIE AGENTUR IHRE KREATIVITÄT UNTER BEWEIS STELLEN. (USA)

▲ 584, 585 CETTE BOÎTE, MONTRÉE AVEC ET SANS BANDE-ENVELOPPE, RENFERME DU MATÉRIEL PUBLICITAIRE ENVOYÉ PAR LA POSTE AUX CHAMBRES DE COMMERCE PAR UNE MUTUELLE D'ASSURANCES POUR LES INFORMER D'UN CONCOURS RÉCOMPENSANT L'ESPRIT D'INITIATIVE DES PETITES ENTREPRISES. «ENSEMBLE, NOUS CONSOLIDERONS LE TISSU DE L'ÉCONOMIE AMÉRICAINE.» (USA)

▲ 586, 587 CETTE PETITE BOÎTE RENFERMANT UNE BOUTEILLE DE PERRIER A ÉTÉ ENVOYÉE COMME CADEAU DE NOËL À LA DIRECTION DE PORSCHE: L'AGENCE FALLON MCELLIGOTT SE PRÉSENTE DE MANIÈRE ORIGINALE EN CONSEILLANT LA PRUDENCE ET LA SOBRIÉTÉ AU VOLANT. (USA)

BOOKS, RECORD COVERS, CALENDARS

BÜCHER, SCHALLPLATTEN, KALENDER

LIVRES, DISQUES, CALENDRIERS

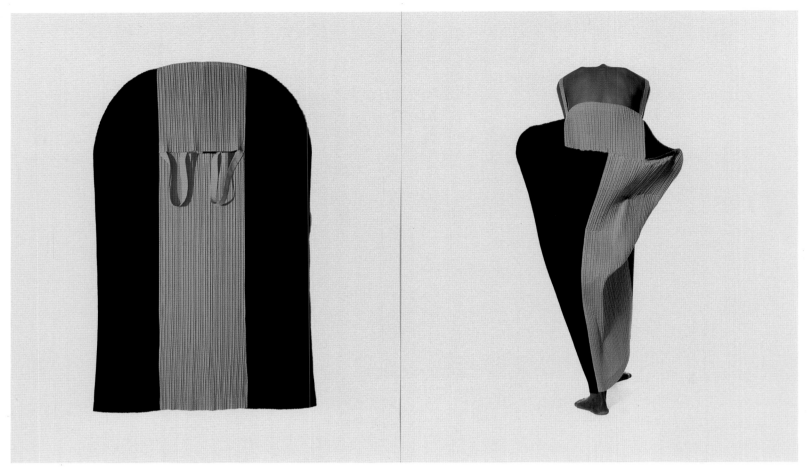

ART DIRECTOR:
IKKO TANAKA
DESIGNER:
IKKO TANAKA
PHOTOGRAPHER:
IRVING PENN
CLIENT:
MIYAKE DESIGN
STUDIO
■ 588-592

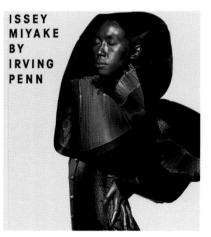

■ 588-592 SPREADS AND COVER (ABOVE) OF A BOOK DEDICATED TO THE FASHION OF ISSEY MIYAKE, INTERPRETED BY FAMOUS PHOTOGRAPHER IRVING PENN. THE BOLD SHAPES OF MIYAKE'S CREATIONS ARE SUPPORTED BY THE PHOTOGRAPHY AND THE WAY IT IS PRESENTED. ALL MODELS SHOWN ARE MADE OF PLEATED FABRICS, A FAVORITE MATERIAL OF THE DESIGNER. (JPN)

● 588-592 DOPPELSEITEN UND UMSCHLAG (OBEN) EINES BUCHES, DAS DER MODE VON ISSEY MIYAKE GEWIDMET IST. DER BERÜHMTE PHOTOGRAPH IRVING PENN INTERPRETIERTE DIE KÜHNEN FORMEN VON MIYAKES KREATIONEN, DIE ALLE FREIGESTELLT GEZEIGT WERDEN. DIE HIER ABGEBILDETEN MODELLE SIND AUS PLISSIERTEM STOFF, EIN MATERIAL, DAS MIYAKE BESONDERS GERN VERARBEITET. (JPN)

▲ 588-592 COUVERTURE ET DOUBLES PAGES D'UN LIVRE CONSACRÉ AUX CRÉATIONS D'ISSEY MIYAKE, INTERPRÉTÉES PAR LE CÉLÈBRE PHOTOGRAPHE IRVING PENN. L'AUDACE DES FORMES EST SOULIGNÉE PAR UNE PHOTOGRAPHIE D'UNE GRANDE RIGUEUR. TOUS LES VÊTEMENTS PRÉSENTÉS SUR CES DOUBLES PAGES SONT SUR LE THÈME DU PLISSÉ. (JPN)

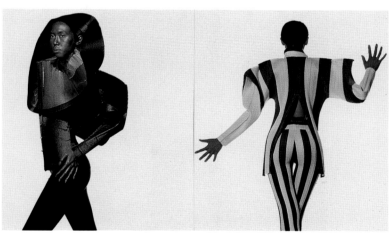

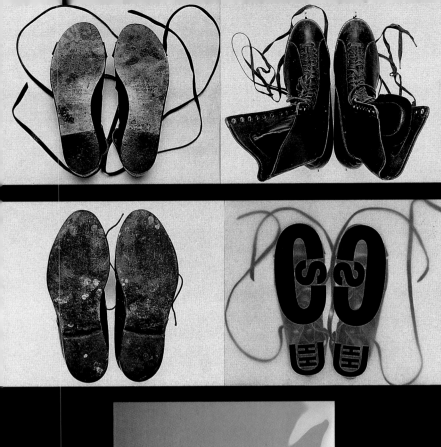

SCHUH
WERK

SCHON IMMER WAR DER
SCHUH
GERADE IN SEINEN
EXZESSEN
EIN VERLÄSSLICHER
SPIEGEL
ZEIT.

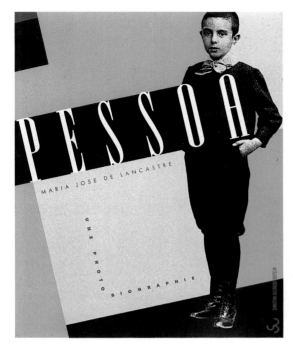

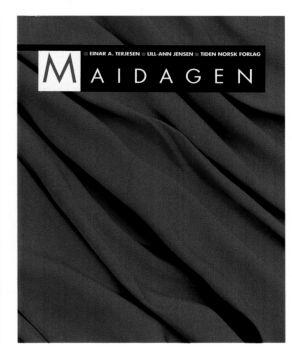

ART DIRECTOR:
FRANK KOSCHEMBAR
DESIGNER:
FRANK KOSCHEMBAR
PHOTOGRAPHER:
FRANK KOSCHEMBAR
COPYWRITER:
FRANK KOSCHEMBAR
PUBLISHER:
JENS NAGELS, VER-
LAG IM WASSERWEG
◀■ 593-597

ART DIRECTOR:
ERNESTO APARICIO
DESIGNERS:
ERNESTO APARICIO
DENIS HOCH
AGENCY:
ERNESTO APARICIO
DESIGN
PUBLISHERS:
CHRISTIAN BOUR-
GEOIS EDITEUR/
FANVAL
■ 598, 599

DESIGNER:
JUNN PAASCHE-
AASEN
PUBLISHER:
TIDEN NORSK FORLAG
■ 600

■ 593-597 SPREADS AND COVER OF A BOOK ENTITLED "SCHUHWERK" (SHOES). EACH PAIR WAS PHOTOGRAPHED IN BLACK AND WHITE FROM ABOVE AND BELOW. THE LEFT PAGE ALWAYS SHOWS THE SOLES OF THE PAIR FROM THE PRECEDING RIGHT PAGE. A SHOELACE SERVES AS BOOKMARK. ALL PHOTOGRAPHS ARE ACCOMPANIED BY CITATIONS THAT EXPRESS THE SHOE AS SYMBOL OF INDIVIDUAL LIFE AND EXPERIENCE, THUS BECOMING A SOCIAL DOCUMENT. (GER)

■ 598 COVER OF A PHOTOGRAPHIC BIOGRAPHY DOCUMENTING THE MYSTERIOUS LIFE OF THE GREAT PORTUGUESE POET FERNANDO PESSOA. (FRA)

■ 599 COVER OF A BOOK ON THE ACTRESS ARLETTY WHO IS KNOWN FOR HER REPARTEE. (FRA)

■ 600 JACKET FOR A BOOK ABOUT THE 100 YEARS' CELEBRATION OF LABOR DAY, THE 1ST OF MAY, IN NORWAY. (NOR)

● 593-597 DOPPELSEITEN UND UMSCHLAG EINES BUCHES MIT DEM TITEL «SCHUHWERK». JEDES PAAR WURDE IN SCHWARZWEISS VON OBEN UND UNTEN AUFGENOMMEN. AUF DEN DOPPELSEITEN LINKS SIND DIE SOHLEN DES AUF DER VORANGEHENDEN DOPPELSEITE VON OBEN GEZEIGTEN PAARS ZU SEHEN. ALS LESEZEICHEN DIENT EIN SCHNÜRSENKEL. ALLE AUFNAHMEN SIND VON ZITATEN ZUM THEMA DES SCHUHS BEGLEITET, DER ZUM SYMBOL INDIVIDUELLEN ERLEBENS, ZUM DOKUMENT WIRD. (GER)

● 598 UMSCHLAG EINES BILDBANDES, DER DAS GEHEIMNISVOLLE LEBEN DES PORTUGIESISCHEN DICHTERS FERNANDO PESSOA DOKUMENTIERT. (FRA)

● 599 UMSCHLAG EINES BUCHES ÜBER DIE SCHLAGFERTIGE SCHAUSPIELERIN ARLETTY. (FRA)

● 600 SCHUTZUMSCHLAG FÜR EIN BUCH ÜBER DIE HUNDERTJAHRFEIER DES TAGS DER ARBEIT (1. MAI) IN NORWEGEN. (NOR)

▲ 593-597 DOUBLES PAGES ET COUVERTURE D'UN LIVRE INTITULÉ «SCHUHWERK» (CHAUSSURES). CHAQUE PAIRE A ÉTÉ PHOTOGRAPHIÉE EN NOIR ET BLANC RECTO-VERSO: LA SEMELLE DE GAUCHE CORRESPOND TOUJOURS AU MODÈLE DE LA PAGE DE DROITE PRÉCÉDENTE. UN LACET SERT DE SIGNET. LES PHOTOS SONT ACCOMPAGNÉES DE CITATIONS SUR LE THÈME DE LA CHAUSSURE, TÉMOIGNAGE SOCIO-HISTORIQUE DE LA VIE INDIVIDUELLE, EN UNE SORTE DE DIALOGUE ASSOCIATIF. (GER)

▲ 598 COUVERTURE D'UN LIVRE DE PHOTOGRAPHIES DOCUMENTANT LA VIE MYSTÉRIEUSE DU GRAND POÈTE PORTUGAIS, FERNANDO PESSOA. (FRA)

▲ 599 COUVERTURE D'UN LIVRE SUR L'ACTRICE ARLETTY, CÉLÈBRE POUR SES RÉPARTIES. (FRA)

▲ 600 COUVERTURE D'UN LIVRE SUR L'HISTOIRE DE LA FÊTE DU TRAVAIL DU 1ER MAI, INTRODUITE VOICI 100 ANS EN NORVÈGE. (NOR)

ART DIRECTOR:
RENÉE KHATAMI
DESIGNER:
ADRIANE STARK
PUBLISHER:
ABBEVILLE PRESS
■ 601

DESIGNERS:
PAUL EUBEL
IKUKO MATSUMOTO
ARTIST:
GEORG KARL
PFAHLER
PUBLISHER:
GOETHE-INSTITUT
OSAKA
■ 602

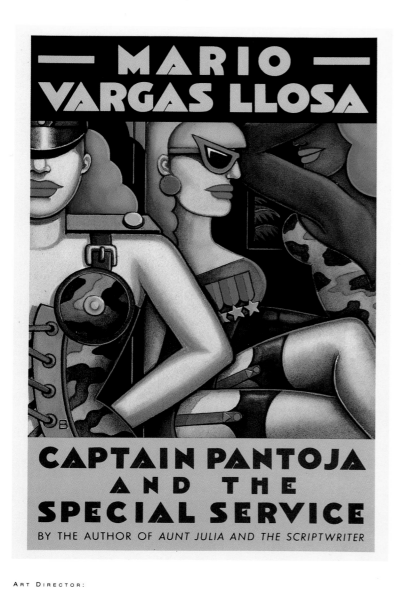

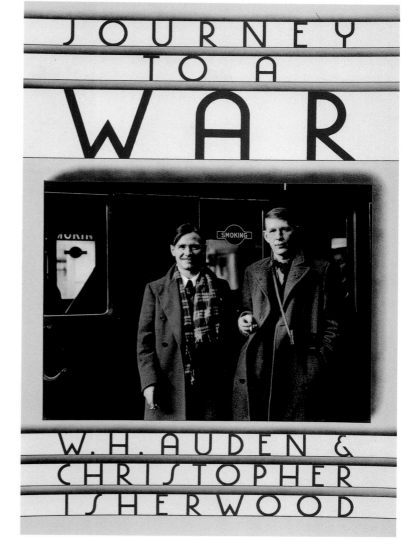

ART DIRECTOR:
DORIS JANOWITZ
DESIGNER:
BASCOVE
ILLUSTRATOR:
BASCOVE
PUBLISHER:
FARRAR STRAUS &
GIROUX
■ 603

ART DIRECTOR:
SUSAN NEWMAN
DESIGNER:
SUSAN NEWMAN
HAND-TINTING:
CHRISTINE RODIN
PUBLISHER:
PARAGON HOUSE
■ 604

■ 601 COVER OF A BOOK ON THE DESIGN OF THE EIGHTIES PUBLISHED BY ABBEVILLE PRESS. (USA)

■ 602 COVER OF A BOOK/CATALOG ON A TRAVELLING EXHIBITION OF KITES WHICH WERE DESIGNED BY ARTISTS FROM ALL OVER THE WORLD UPON THE INITIATIVE OF THE GOETHE INSTITUTE IN OSAKA, JAPAN. SHOWN IS PART OF THE BACK OF A HAMAMATSU KITE DESIGNED BY GERMAN ARTIST GEORG KARL PFAHLER. (GER)

■ 603 COVER FOR A PAPERBACK TO BE SOLD IN THE UNITED STATES. (USA)

■ 604 BOOK COVER WITH HAND-TINTED PHOTOGRAPH REFERRING TO A WAR STORY. (USA)

● 601 UMSCHLAG EINES BUCHES ÜBER DAS DESIGN DER ACHTZIGER JAHRE. (USA)

● 602 UMSCHLAG EINES BUCHES/KATALOGS ÜBER EINE VOM GOETHE INSTITUT IN OSAKA INITIIERTE WANDERAUSSTELLUNG VON DRACHEN, DIE VON KÜNSTLERN AUS ALLER WELT ENTWORFEN WURDEN. GEZEIGT IST EIN TEIL DER RÜCKSEITE DES HAMAMATSU-DRACHENS DES DEUTSCHEN KÜNSTLERS GEORG KARL PFAHLER. (GER).

● 603 UMSCHLAG EINES TASCHENBUCHES FÜR DEN AMERIKANISCHEN MARKT. (USA)

● 604 «REISE IN EINEN KRIEG» – BUCHUMSCHLAG MIT HANDKOLORIERTER PHOTOGRAPHIE. (USA)

▲ 601 PAGE DE COUVERTURE D'UN LIVRE SUR LE DESIGN DES ANNÉES 80. (USA)

▲ 602 COUVERTURE DE LA JAQUETTE D'UN CATALOGUE POUR UNE EXPOSITION DE CERFS-VOLANTS CRÉÉS PAR DES ARTISTES PROVENANT DE TOUS PAYS, ORGANISÉE PAR LE GOETHE INSTITUT D'OSAKA. ON VOIT ICI UN FRAGMENT DE CERF-VOLANT HAMAMATSU RÉALISÉ PAR GEORG KARL PFAHLER. (GER)

▲ 603 COUVERTURE D'UN LIVRE DE POCHE POUR LE MARCHÉ AMÉRICAIN. (USA)

▲ 604 COUVERTURE D'UN LIVRE INTITULÉ: «VOYAGE VERS LA GUERRE». PHOTO COLORÉE MAIN. (USA)

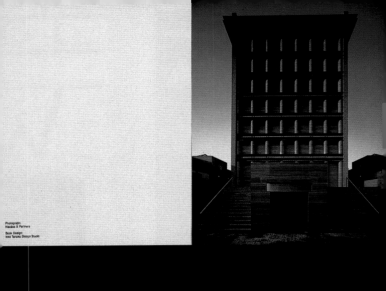

Photograph:
Nacása & Partners

Book Design:
Ikko Tanaka Design Studio

都市を触発する建築

Hotel IL PALAZZO

A City Stimulated

by Architecture

ART DIRECTOR:
IKKO TANAKA
PUBLISHER:
RIKUYO-SHA
PUBLISHING, INC.
◀■ 605-607

ART DIRECTOR:
OSWALDO MIRANDA
DESIGNER:
OSWALDO MIRANDA
ILLUSTRATOR:
ROBERT CHEVEUX
(1928)
AGENCY:
CASA DE IDEIAS
CLIENT:
LIVRARIA DO ESTADO
■ 608

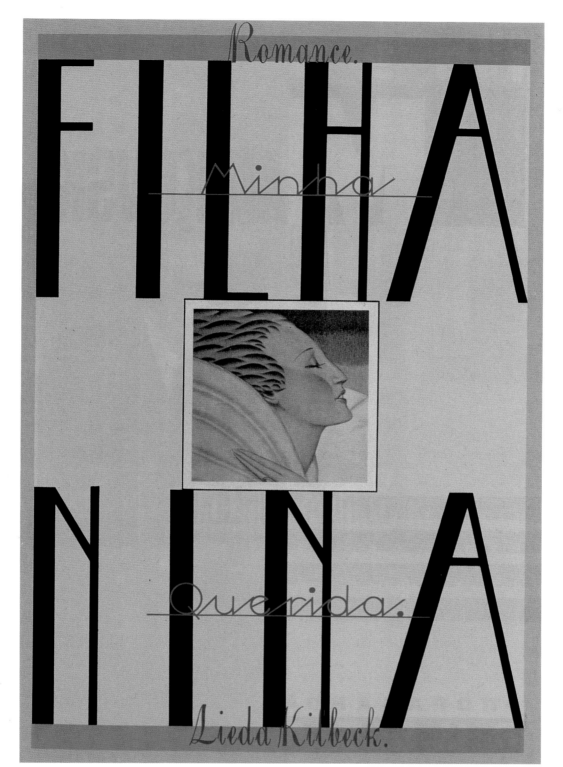

Romance.

FILHA

Minha

NINA

Querida.

Lieda Kilbeck.

■ 605-607 SPREADS AND COVER OF A BOOK ON THE HOTEL IL PALAZZO DESIGNED BY ALDO ROSSI IN THE JAPANESE TOWN OF FUKUOKA. *605:* THE RED STONE OF THE FACADE CHANGES ITS COLOR WITH DIFFERENT LIGHT. GREEN LINTELS GIVE POWER AND ORDER TO THE COMPOSITION. *607:* EXAMPLES OF THE FURNITURE USED IN THE ROOMS. THE CONSTRUCTION OF THE HOTEL RESULTED IN THE CREATION OF A WHOLE NEW CITY DISTRICT WITH BARS AND RESTAURANTS. (JPN)

● 605-607 DOPPELSEITEN UND UMSCHLAG EINES BUCHES ÜBER DAS VON ALDO ROSSI ENTWORFENE HOTEL IL PALAZZO IN DER JAPANISCHEN STADT FUKUOKA. 605: DIE FARBE DER ROTEN STEINFASSADE VERÄNDERT SICH JE NACH LICHT. DIE GRÜN BEMALTEN STÜRZE UNTERSTÜTZEN UND ORDNEN DIE ARCHITEKTONISCHE KOMPOSITION. 607: BEISPIELE DER MÖBLIERUNG DER RÄUME. DURCH DEN HOTELBAU ENTSTAND EIN GANZ NEUES STADTVIERTEL MIT RESTAURANTS UND BARS. (JPN)

▲ 605-607 COUVERTURE DE LA JAQUETTE ET DOUBLES PAGES D'UN LIVRE SUR L'HÔTEL IL PALAZZO DE FUKUOKA, «UNE VILLE STIMULÉE PAR L'ARCHITECTURE». 605: LA FAÇADE DE TRAVERTIN ROUGE ET DE POUTRES MÉTALLIQUES REPREND LE MOTIF DU PORTIQUE, CHER À ALDO ROSSI. 607: EXEMPLES DU MOBILIER DES CHAMBRES. LA CONSTRUCTION DE CET HÔTEL SUSCITA LA CRÉATION DE TOUT UN QUARTIER DE BARS ET RESTAURANTS. (JPN)

■ 608 COVER FOR A NOVEL ENTITLED "MY SWEET DAUGHTER NINA", A STORY THAT TAKES PLACE IN PARIS OF THE 20'S AND 30'S. (BRA)

● 608 «MEINE GELIEBTE TOCHTER NINA», EINE GESCHICHTE, DIE IM PARIS DER 20ER UND 30ER JAHRE SPIELT. TASCHENBUCHUMSCHLAG. (BRA)

▲ 608 JAQUETTE D'UN ROMAN INTITULÉ: «MA CHÈRE FILLE, NINA». L'ILLUSTRATION DE ROBERT CHEVEUX A ÉTÉ RÉALISÉE VERS 1927. (BRA)

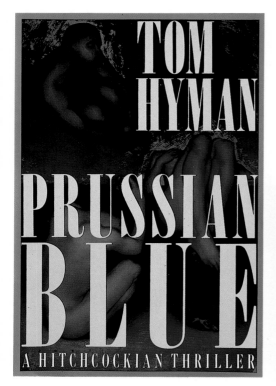

ART DIRECTOR:
NEIL STUART
DESIGNER:
NEIL STUART
ILLUSTRATOR:
JOEL PETER
JOHNSON
PUBLISHER:
VIKING BOOK
PENGUIN USA
■ 609

ART DIRECTORS:
SAVAS GEKIG
SAHIN AYMERGEN
ILLUSTRATOR:
SAVAS GEKIG
AGENCY:
VALOR
PUBLISHER:
PATIKA
■ 610

ART DIRECTOR:
JOSEPH MONTEBELLO
DESIGNER:
SUZANNE NOLI
ILLUSTRATOR:
CATHLEEN TOELKE
PUBLISHER:
HARPER COLLINS
■ 611

■ 609 BOOK JACKET FOR A THRILLER PUBLISHED BY PENGUIN BOOKS. (USA)

■ 610 COVER DESIGN FOR A PAPERBACK BY A TURKISH AUTHOR. (TUR)

■ 611 FROM A SERIES OF COVERS FOR BOOKS BY GABRIEL GARCIA MARQUEZ WHICH ARE REPUBLISHED BY HARPER COLLINS. SHOWN IS A SOUTH AMERICAN COUPLE WAITING FOR THEIR FATE AND AT THE SAME TIME LOOKING FOR THEIR CHANCES, A DUALITY THAT COEXISTS IN MARQUEZ' WORK. (USA)

■ 612 JACKET OF A CLOTH-BOUND BOOK FOR A THRILLER. (USA)

■ 613 COVER FOR A VOLUME FROM A POETIC SERIES. IT IS FOLDED AND GLUED IN A SPECIAL WAY TO OBTAIN THE THREEDIMENSIONAL EFFECT. (POR)

■ 614 ILLUSTRATION WITH CANVAS CHARACTER FOR A NOVEL. (USA)

● 609 UMSCHLAG FÜR EINEN KRIMINALROMAN MIT DEM TITEL «PREUSSISCH BLAU». (USA)

● 610 UMSCHLAG FÜR EIN TASCHENBUCH EINES TÜRKISCHEN AUTORS. (TUR)

● 611 AUS EINER REIHE VON UMSCHLÄGEN FÜR BÜCHER VON GABRIEL GARCIA MARQUEZ, DIE NEU AUFGELEGT WURDEN. HIER EIN SÜDAMERIKANISCHES PAAR, DAS SEIN SCHICKSAL ERWARTET, ABER AUCH NACH AUSWEGEN SUCHT. DIESE DUALITÄT EXISTIERT IN MARQUEZ' WERK. (BRA)

● 612 UMSCHLAG FÜR EIN LEINENGEBUNDENES BUCH MIT EINER KRIMINALGESCHICHTE. (USA)

● 613 UMSCHLAG FÜR EINE POESIE-BUCHREIHE. ER IST SPEZIELL GEFALTET UND VERKLEBT, UM DEN DREIDIMENSIONALEN EFFEKT ZU ERREICHEN. (POR)

● 614 ILLUSTRATION MIT LEINWANDCHARAKTER FÜR EINEN ROMAN. (USA)

▲ 609 JAQUETTE D'UN ROMAN POLICIER INTITULÉ: «BLEU DE PRUSSE». (USA)

▲ 610 COUVERTURE D'UN LIVRE DE POCHE PUBLIÉ EN TURQUIE. (TUR)

▲ 611 PREMIÈRE D'UNE SÉRIE DE CINQ JAQUETTES DE LIVRES DE GABRIEL GARCIA MARQUEZ, ICI UN RECUEIL DE NOUVELLES. L'ILLUSTRATION REPRÉSENTE UN COUPLE SUD-AMÉRICAIN DANS L'ATTENTE DE SON PROPRE DESTIN, MAIS AUSSI DE SA CHANCE – THÈME DE PRÉDILECTION DE L'ÉCRIVAIN. (USA)

▲ 612 JAQUETTE D'UN ROMAN À SUSPENSE POUR UN LIVRE RELIÉ EN TOILE. (USA)

▲ 613 EXEMPLE DE COUVERTURE D'UNE COLLECTION DE LIVRES DE TEXTES POÉTIQUES: LE JEU DE PLIAGE CRÉE UN EFFET DE RELIEF. (POR)

▲ 614 JAQUETTE D'UN ROMAN AVEC ILLUSTRATION SUR TOILE. (USA)

ART DIRECTOR:
STEVEN BROWER
DESIGNER:
STEVEN BROWER
ILLUSTRATOR:
MARC BURCKHARDT
PUBLISHER:
CAROL PUBLISHING
GROUP
■ 612

ART DIRECTOR:
GIL MAIA
DESIGNER:
GIL MAIA
ILLUSTRATOR:
GIL MAIA
PUBLISHER:
EDIÇOES
AFRONTAMENTO
■ 613

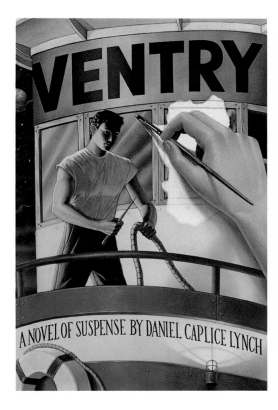

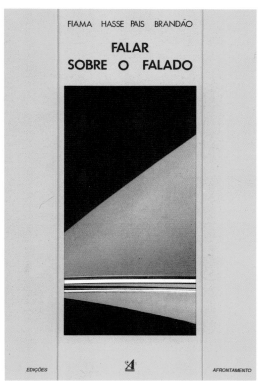

ART DIRECTOR:
NEIL STUART
DESIGNER:
BASCOVE
ILLUSTRATOR:
BASCOVE
PUBLISHER:
VIKING BOOK
PENGUIN USA
■ 614

ART DIRECTOR:
CHRISTOPER
AUSTOPCHUK
DESIGNER:
MARK BURDETT
PHOTOGRAPHER:
CHIP SIMONS
AGENCY:
SONY MUSIC
CLIENT:
COLUMBIA RECORDS
◄■ 615, 616

ART DIRECTOR:
ALLEN WEINBERG
DESIGNER:
ALLEN WEINBERG
PHOTOGRAPHER:
CHIP SIMONS
AGENCY:
SONY MUSIC
CLIENT:
COLUMBIA RECORDS
■ 617

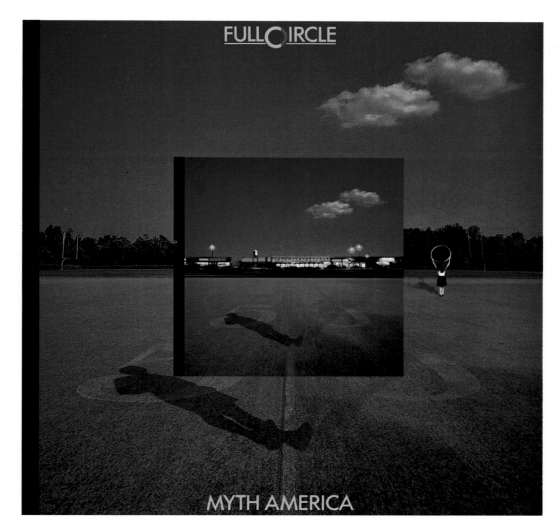

■ 615, 616 THIS CBS COMPACT DISC OF THE DISCO/TEENY BOP GROUP "NEW KIDS ON THE BLOCK" COMES IN A CARTON PACKAGE. AT LEFT THE COVER PRESENTED LIKE A DOOR WITH A LOCK, AT RIGHT THE CONTENTS. (USA)

■ 617 COVER FOR AN ALBUM BY THE GROUP "FULL CIRCLE." THE PICTURE IN THE PICTURE EVOKES CERTAIN SURREALISTIC PAINTINGS BY RENÉ E. (USA)

● 615, 616 DIESE CBS-COMPACT DISC DER DISCO/TEENY BOB-GRUPPE «NEW KIDS ON THE BLOCK» WIRD IN EINER KARTONVERPACKUNG PRÄSENTIERT. LINKS DER UMSCHLAG ALS TÜR MIT SCHLOSS, RECHTS DER INHALT. (USA)

● 617 HÜLLE FÜR EINE LANGSPIELPLATTE DER GRUPPE «FULL CIRCLE». DAS BILD IM BILD ERINNERT AN BESTIMMTE WERKE DES SURREALISTISCHEN MALERS RENÉ MAGRITTE. (USA)

▲ 615, 616 CE DISQUE COMPACT CBS DU GROUPE DE MUSIQUE DISCO/TEENY-BOP «NEW KIDS ON THE BLOCK» EST PRÉSENTÉ DANS UN EMBALLAGE CARTONNÉ. À G.: EN COUVERTURE, UNE PORTE FERMÉE PAR UN CADENAS; À DR., LE CONTENU. (USA)

▲ 617 POCHETTE DE L'ALBUM DU GROUPE «FULL CIRCLE». L'IMAGE DANS L'IMAGE N'EST PAS SANS RAPPELER CERTAINS TABLEAUX DU PEINTRE SURRÉALISTE RENÉ MAGRITTE. (USA)

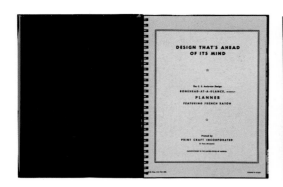

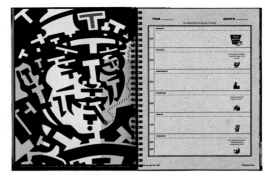

ART DIRECTOR:

DOUGLAS OLIVER

DESIGNERS:

DEANNA KUHLMANN

JANE KOBAYASHI

RITCH

AGENCY:

MORAVA OLIVER

BERTÉ

CLIENT:

ART CENTER

COLLEGE OF DESIGN

◄■ 618-621

ART DIRECTORS:

CHARLES S.

ANDERSON

DAN OLSON

ILLUSTRATORS:

CHARLES S.

ANDERSON

DAN OLSON

RANDALL DAHLK

AGENCY:

CHARLES S.

ANDERSON DESIGN

PUBLISHER:

CHARLES S.

ANDERSON DESIGN

■ 622-628

■ 618-621 A DIARY/CATALOG PUBLISHED BY THE ART CENTER COLLEGE OF DESIGN IN PASADENA. 618: THIS SPIRAL-BOUND DIARY COMES IN A JACKET MADE OF STRONG LEATHER. 619: COVER OF THE DIARY WITH OPENED JACKET; 620, 621: INSIDE SPREADS. THE CATALOG PART PRESENTS WORKS OF ALUMNI, HERE THE "MACHINE GUN" POSTER FOR THE FILM "DICK TRACY" BY ILLUSTRATOR JONNY C. KWAN AND THE BOOKLET DESIGNED BY JAMES MIHO TO ACCOMPANY THE "DESIGN USA" EXHIBIT IN MOSCOW IN SEPTEMBER 1989. (USA)

■ 622-628 SPREADS AND COVER WITH ITS BOX FOR A THREE-YEAR WEEKLY PLANNER PUBLISHED BY ANDERSON OLSON DESIGN AND FEATURING HISTORICAL GRAPHIC DESIGN OF THE COMPANY. IT IS PRINTED ON "FRENCH RAYON PAPER" MADE BY THE FRENCH PAPER CO. AT THE BOTTOM THE COVER OF THE DIARY IS SHOWN WITH ITS CARTON. A MINIATURE CALENDAR IS GLUED TO THE COVER. (USA)

● 618-621 AGENDA/KATALOG DES ART CENTER COLLEGE OF DESIGN IN PASADENA. 618: DIESE SPIRALGEBUNDENE AGENDA HAT EINE HÜLLE AUS SEHR FESTEM LEDER. 619: UMSCHLAGSEITE DER AGENDA BEI GEÖFFNETER LEDERHÜLLE; 620, 621: DOPPELSEITEN AUS DEM INHALT. DER KATALOG ZEIGT ARBEITEN EHEMALIGER STUDENTEN, HIER DAS «MACHINE GUN»-PLAKAT VON JONNY C. KWAN FÜR DEN FILM «DICK TRACY» UND DIE BROSCHÜRE VON JAMES MIHO FÜR DIE AUSSTELLUNG «DESIGN USA» IM SEPTEMBER 1989 IN MOSKAU. (USA)

● 622-628 DOPPELSEITEN UND UMSCHLAG EINER SPIRALGEBUNDENEN AGENDA FÜR DREI JAHRE, DIE VON ANDERSON OLSON DESIGN HERAUSGEGEBEN WURDE. SIE IST AUF «FRENCH RAYON»-PAPIER DER FRENCH PAPER CO. GEDRUCKT UND MIT WICHTIGEN ARBEITEN DES STUDIOS ILLUSTRIERT. UNTEN SIEHT MAN DIE AGENDA MIT DER KASSETTE. EIN MINIATUR-KALENDER IST AUF DEN UMSCHLAG GEKLEBT. (USA)

▲ 618-621 AGENDA PUBLIÉ PAR LE ART CENTER COLLEGE OF DESIGN. CE CALENDRIER-CATALOGUE À RELIURE SPIRALE EST PROTÉGÉ PAR UNE JAQUETTE DE CUIR RIGIDE. 631: COUVERTURE DE L'AGENDA, AVEC JAQUETTE DE PROTECTION OUVERTE; 632, 633: DEUX PAGES INTÉRIEURES. LE CATALOGUE PRÉSENTE DES ŒUVRES D'ANCIENS ÉLÈVES, ICI L'ILLUSTRATEUR JONNY C. KWAN, AUTEUR DE L'AFFICHE DU FILM «DICK TRACY» ET LE DESIGNER JAMES MIHO, QUI A RÉALISÉ LA BROCHURE DE L'EXPOSITION «DESIGN USA» À MOSCOU EN 1989. (USA)

▲ 622-628 DOUBLES PAGES ET COUVERTURE D'UN AGENDA SEMAINIER À RELIURE SPIRALE PUBLIÉ PAR ANDERSON OLSON DESIGN. IL EST IMPRIMÉ SUR UN PAPIER «FRENCH RAYON» DE LA FRENCH PAPER CO. ET ILLUSTRÉ DE DÉTAILS D'IMAGES CRÉÉES PAR CE STUDIO DE DESIGN. EN BAS, L'AGENDA ET SON BOÎTIER DE CARTON. UN CALENDRIER MINIATURE EST COLLÉ SUR LA COUVERTURE. (USA)

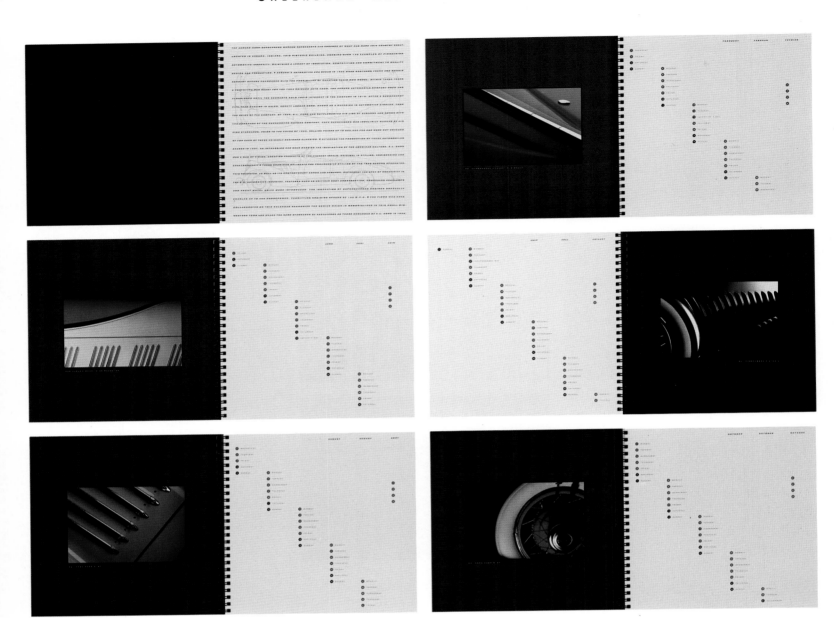

DESIGNERS:
MICHAEL
GUNSELMAN
KERRY POLITE
PHOTOGRAPHER:
MICHAEL FURMAN
AGENCY:
GUNSELMAN + POLITE
CLIENT:
GUNSELMAN + POLITE
■ 629-634

ART DIRECTOR:
TAKENOBU IGARASHI
DESIGNER:
TAKENOBU IGARASHI
CLIENT:
ALPHABET GALLERY
▶■ 635

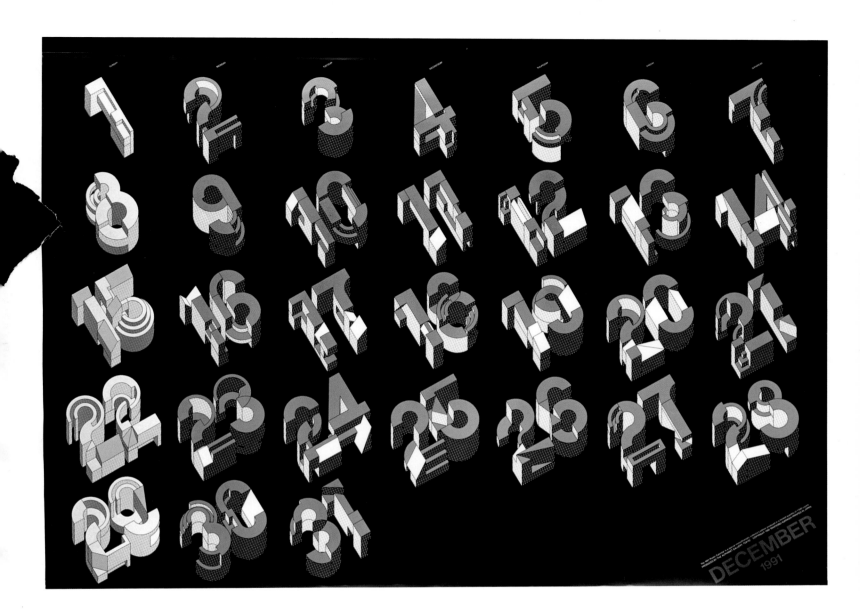

DECEMBER
1991

■ 629-634 SPREADS FROM A SPIRAL-BOUND DIARY PUBLISHED BY THE AUBURN-CORD-DUESENBERG MUSEUM WHICH HOUSES A COLLECTION OF OVER 130 VINTAGE CARS. THE PHOTOS ILLUSTRATING THE DIARY SHOW DETAILS OF THE CARS WHICH ARE PRESENTED LIKE WORKS OF ART. THE DIARY IS PROTECTED BY A CARDBOARD JACKET. (USA)

■ 635 THIS POSTER CALENDAR, ORIGINALLY A PROJECT BY THE MUSEUM OF MODERN ART OF NEW YORK IT IS NOW PUBLISHED IN A LIMITED EDITION BY THE ALPHABET GALLERY IN TOKYO. EVERY MONTH OF THIS SERIES HAS A DIFFERENT DESIGN. NOW IN ITS SEVENTH YEAR, 3776 NUMERALS HAVE BEEN DESIGNED SO FAR, IN THE TENTH YEAR IT WILL BE 6226. (JPN).

● 629-634 DOPPELSEITEN AUS EINER SPIRALGE-BUNDENEN AGENDA DES AUBURN-CORD-DUESEN-BERG MUSEUMS, DAS EINE SAMMLUNG VON ÜBER 130 OLDTIMERN BESITZT. ALS ILLUSTRATIONEN DIENEN DETAILAUFNAHMEN DER AUTOS, DIE WIE GEMÄLDE PRÄSENTIERT WERDEN. EINE KARTON-HÜLLE SCHÜTZT DIE AGENDA. (USA)

● 635 EIN POSTER-KALENDAR, DER IN LIMITIERTER AUFLAGE VON DER ALPHABET GALLERY, TOKIO, HER-AUSGEGEBEN WIRD. URSPRÜNGLICH WAR ES EIN PROJEKT DES NEW YORKER MUSEUMS OF MODERN ART, JEDER MONAT WIRD UNTERSCHIEDLICH GE-STALTET. NACH JETZT SIEBEN JAHREN SIND BISHER 3776 ZAHLEN ENTSTANDEN, NACH ZEHN JAHREN WERDEN ES 6226 SEIN. (JPN)

▲ 629-634 PAGES INTÉRIEURES DE L'AGENDA À RELIURE SPIRALE DU AUBURN-CORD-DUESENBERG MUSEUM QUI PRÉSENTE UNE COLLECTION DE 130 VIEILLES VOITURES. LES PHOTOS MONTRENT DES DÉTAILS DE CAROSSERIES, PRÉSENTÉS COMME DES TABLEAUX ABSTRAITS. IL SE GLISSE DANS UNE JAQUETTE DE PROTECTION CARTONNÉE. (USA)

▲ 635 CE CALENDRIER-AFFICHE PUBLIÉ EN ÉDITION LIMITÉE PAR LE MUSEUM OF MODERN ART DE NEW YORK A ÉTÉ CONÇU DANS LE CADRE D'UN PROJET DE L'ALPHABET GALLERY DE TOKYO. LANCÉ DEPUIS 7 ANS ET PRÉVU POUR DIX ANS, CE PROJET SE BASE SUR LES VARIATIONS DU DESIGN DES CHIFFRES, QUI DIFFÈRE CHAQUE MOIS. EN 10 ANS, 6226 NOMBRES AURONT AINSI ÉTÉ CRÉÉS. (JPN)

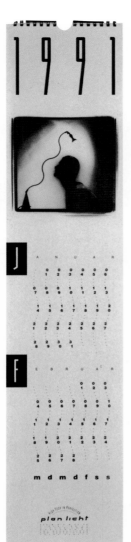

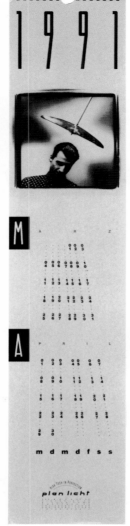

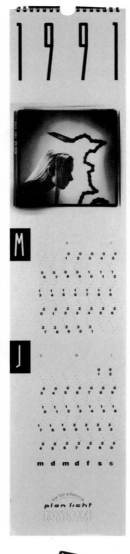

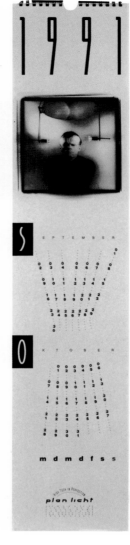

ART DIRECTOR:
MICHAEL
KALTENHAUSER
DESIGNER:
MICHAEL
KALTENHAUSER
PHOTOGRAPHER:
ANDREAS SMETANA
CLIENT:
PLAN LICHT
■ 636-641

ART DIRECTOR:
SHIN MATSUNAGA
DESIGNER:
SHIN MATSUNAGA
AGENCY:
I&S CORPORATION
CLIENT:
SHIN MATSUNAGA
DESIGN INC.
■ 642

■ 636-641 CALENDAR IN AN UNUSUALLY NARROW SIZE FOR PLAN LICHT, A COMPANY SPECIALIZING IN THE DESIGN OF LAMPS. THE PHOTOGRAPHS SHOW SOME OF THE LAMPS DESIGNED BY THE COMPANY. THE VARIOUS SHAPES OF THE LAMPS ARE TAKEN UP BY THE WAY THE NUMBERS ARE PRESENTED. (AUT)

■ 642 DOUBLE SPREAD FROM A DIARY FOR CREATORS WHICH COMES IN TWO VOLUMES STORED IN A CASE. A SMALL ANNUAL CALENDAR SERVES AS BOOKMARK. (JPN)

● 636-641 KALENDER IN UNGEWÖHNLICH SCHMALEM HOCHFORMAT FÜR PLAN LICHT, EINEN LAMPEN-HERSTELLER. DIE PHOTOS ZEIGEN VERSCHIEDENE MODELLE DER LAMPEN, WÄHREND DAS DESIGN DES KALENDARIUMS JEWEILS DIE FORM DER LAMPE AUFNIMMT. (AUT)

● 642 DOPPELSEITE AUS EINEM TAGEBUCH/KALENDER FÜR KREATIVE, DER AUS ZWEI BÄNDEN BESTEHT. ALS LESEZEICHEN DIENT EIN KLEINER JAHRESKALENDER. (JPN)

▲ 636-641 CALENDRIER DE PLAN LICHT, UNE FIRME SPÉCIALISÉE DANS LE DESIGN DE LAMPES. DE FORMAT INHABITUELLEMENT ALLONGÉ, CE CALENDRIER SE CARACTÉRISE PAR LA DISPOSITION ORIGINALE DES CHIFFRES, QUI REPRENNENT LA FORME DES LAMPES. (AUS)

▲ 642 DOUBLE PAGE D'UN JOURNAL-AGENDA AVEC SIGNET-CALENDRIER. CE «JOURNAL POUR CRÉATEURS», PUBLIÉ EN 1990, EST PRÉSENTÉ EN DEUX VOLUMES DANS UN BOÎTIER DE CARTON. (JPN)

INDEX

VERZEICHNIS

INDEX

ABERNETHY, MILES — SCOTTSDALE, USA 422
ACOCELLA, MARISA — NEW YORK, USA 112
ADAMEK, TINA — MINNEAPOLIS, USA 471
AICHER, OTL — LÜDENSCHEID, GER 126
ALBRECHT, RON — NEW YORK, USA 380-382
ANDERSON, CHARLES S. — MINNEAPOLIS, USA 217, 245-252, 504-506, 554, 622-628
ANDERSON, GAIL — NEW YORK, USA 354
ANELLO, FRANK — CHICAGO, USA 255
APARICIO, ERNESTO — PARIS, FRA 598, 599
APPLETON, ROBERT — HARTFORD, USA 310
ARMSTRONG, HEATHER — NEW YORK, USA 581
ARNOLD, JEANNE — NEW YORK, USA 380
ASHWORTH, LISA — MIAMI, USA 308, 309
AUSTOPCHUK, CHRISTOPHER — USA 615, 616
AYMERGEN, SAHIN — ISTANBUL, TUR 610

BACCARI, ALBERTO — NEW YORK, USA 24, 25
BADRUTT-GIRON, OLIVIA — USA 364-370
BAKER, PETER — TORONTO, USA 536
BALKIND, AUDREY — NEW YORK, USA 454-457
BARNES, JEFF — CHICAGO, USA 78, 79
BARNETT, DAVID — NEW YORK, USA 435
BARON, FABIEN — USA 19-21
BARRIE, BOB — MINNEAPOLIS, USA 57-61
BAUR, RUEDI — PARIS, FRA 403-406
BEDESCHI, GIOVANNI — MILANO, ITA 111
BENTKOWSKI, TOM — NEW YORK, USA 402
BERG, JOHN — NEW YORK, USA 512, 513
BERGMANS, HÉLÉNE — DEN HAAG, NLD 253
BERTÉ, JIM — SANTA MONICA, USA 445-453
BESSER, RIK — SANTA MONICA, USA 462-465
BEST, ROBERT — NEW YORK, USA 421
BIERI, DANY — ZURICH, SWI 110
BJÖRKMAN, KLAS — STOCKHOLM, SWE 134-136
BLACK, PAUL — DALLAS, USA 527
BLOCH, BRUCE — NEW YORK, USA 6
BONAVITA, DONNA M. — MONTCLAIR, USA 423
BRADBERY, IAN — GLEBE, AUS 514
BRADLEY, MARK — INDIANAPOLIS, USA 340
BROCK, MICHAEL — LOS ANGELES, USA 394, 395
BROWER, STEVEN — NEW YORK, USA 612
BURNS, BOB — NEW YORK, USA 276
BURRONI, ROBERTO — NEW YORK, USA 379
BUTCHER, SEAN — BURLEY, GBR 339

CAHAN, BILL — USA 270-274
CAMPISI, RON — BOSTON, USA 489
CARSON, DAVID — DEL MAR, USA 429, 430
CARTER, DAVID — DALLAS, USA 342-344
CATO, KEN — RICHMOND, AUS 496-502

CHASE, MARGO — LOS ANGELES, USA 543
CHERMAYEFF, IVAN — USA 486
CHRISTENSEN, JEFF — NEW YORK, USA 418, 420
CHURCH, STANLEY — NEW YORK, USA 552
CHWAST, SEYMOUR — NEW YORK, USA 317-320
CIMA, DANIELE — MILANO, ITA 22, 23
CLARK CHERMAYEFF, JANE — USA 486
COATES, JACQUI — MELBOURNE, AUS 41-43
COLE, BOB — NEW YORK, USA 66
COLMET DAAGE, ERIC — PARIS, FRA 378
COLOMBO, ROLANDO — ITA 56
CONCATO, AUGUSTO — ITA 56
COPPIN, MARIA PIA — MILANO, ITA 392, 393
CORDELLA, ANDREÉ — BOSTON, USA 584, 585
COVERDALE, JAC — USA 73, 105, 106
COZZI, MARTINA — MILANO, ITA 392, 393
CRAIG-TEERLINK, JEAN — USA 152, 153
CROLICK, SUE — MINNEAPOLIS, USA 518
CRONAN, MICHAEL PATRICK — USA 256-262
CRONENWETT, DREW — MIAMISBURG, USA 254

D'ADDA, MAURIZIO — MILANO, ITA 111
DALTHORP, JAMES — NEW YORK, USA 48-51
DELGRANDE, LISA — STAMFORD, USA 574
DENNY, MICHAEL — LONDON, GBR 148-151
DOBSON, TERRY — NEW YORK, USA 346
DORET, MICHAEL — NEW YORK, USA 525
DOYLE, JOHN — BOSTON, USA 158-161
DRACE, MATTHEW — USA 398, 509
DUFFY DESIGN GROUP — USA 311-316

ECKERSLEY, RICHARD — LINCOLN, USA 494
EDELMANN, HEINZ — NLD 473, 475
EIBER, RICK — SEATTLE, USA 326
ELBERS, HARRY — OUDENBOSCH, NLD 561
ERKMEN, BÜLENT — ISTANBUL, TUR 425
EWAN, ANDY — LONDON, GBR 303-307

FELTUS, ROSS H. — DÜSSELDORF, GER 559
FORBES, COLIN — NEW YORK, USA 547
FORD, JONATHAN — NEW YORK, USA 581
FOWLER, THOMAS G. — STAMFORD, USA 574
FREEMAN, DAVID — LONDON, GBR 458-460
FULLER, JOEL — MIAMI, USA 308, 309

GATTI, JUAN — MILANO, ITA 356-360
GEKIG, SAVAS — ISTANBUL, TUR 610
GERBINO, MICHAEL — NEW YORK, USA 508
GERICKE, MICHAEL — NEW YORK, USA 547
GLASER, MILTON — NEW YORK, USA 263, 264
GORETSKY, VADIM — PALO ALTO, USA 535

GORI, FRANCA — FIRENZE, ITA 197-209
GOULD, ROGER — GRAND RAPIDS, USA 563
GRIFFITH, JEFF — NEW YORK, USA 101
GROSS, MAGGIE — SAN FRANCISCO, USA 7-9

HARTMANN, KNUT — FRANKFURT/M., GER 548
HASLINGER, WOLFGANG — VIENNA, AUT 210, 211
HAUMERSEN, MARK — MINNEAPOLIS, USA 114
HAYASHI, HIROYUKI — TOKYO, JPN 137
HERRINGTON, WALTER — USA 162-165
HESS, RICHARD — USA 226-236, 426
HILL, CHRIS — HOUSTON, USA 266-269
HINRICHS, KIT — USA 218-225, 424, 433, 434
HIROMURA, MASAAKI — TOKYO, JPN 13-18
HOCHWARTER, FRANZ — VIENNA, AUT 265
HOGLUND, RUDY — NEW YORK, USA 477
HOLDEMAN, BRUCE — DENVER, USA 479
HONDA, YUKAKO — TOKYO, JPN 492
HOWE, AUSTIN — PORTLAND, USA 92
HUNTER, KENT — NEW YORK, USA 454-457

IGARASHI, TAKENOBU — TOKYO, JPN 635

JANOWITZ, DORIS — NEW YORK, USA 603
JAY, JOHN — USA 167, 168, 192-196
JENSON, KRIS — MILWAUKEE, USA 115
JOHNSON, HALEY — MINNEAPOLIS, USA 534
JOHNSON, MARK — USA 52-54, 325, 586, 587
JOINER, ERICH — USA 113
JORGENSEN, GRANT — PARKSIDE, AUS 521
JOSEPH, DOUGLAS — USA 462-465
JULIANO, ANGELO — NEW YORK, USA 100

KALTENHAUSER, MICHAEL — VOMP, AUT 636-641
KAMEI, PEGGY — USA 510
KATONA, DIDI — TORONTO, CAN 283, 285
KAYALAR, MESUT — ISTANBUL, TUR 132, 133
KHATAMI, RENÉE — NEW YORK, USA 601
KIRNER, PAUL — NEW YORK, USA 65
KLEIN, DEBBIE — BOSTON, USA 432
KOEPKE, GARY — MAGNOLIA, USA 383
KOPPEL, TERRY R. — USA 414-417, 436, 490
KOSCHEMBAR, FRANK — GER 593-597
KOVAL, JAMES — CHICAGO, USA 550
KOWALL, WOLFGANG — GER 409
KRAFCHEK, KENNETH — WASHINGTON, USA 467
KRATOCHVIL, LAURIE — USA 348-353, 355

LAGUARDIA, DIANA — NEW YORK, USA 493
LARAMORE, JEFF — INDIANAPOLIS, USA 340
LEE, EDDIE — USA 152, 153

LEE GRANT, KAREN　NEW YORK, USA 371-375
LEES, ANDREW　MELBOURNE, AUS 41-43
LEHMANN-HAUPT, CARL　NEW YORK, USA 419
LEPLY, ANN　CHICAGO, USA 255
LERCH, DAVID　HOUSTON, USA 524
LÉVY, STAN　PARIS, FRA 4, 5
LEWIS, MARY　LONDON, GBR 564
LEWIS, TOM　DEL MAR, USA 284
LICHTENHELD, TOM　MINNEAPOLIS, USA 45, 91
LITTLE, MONICA　MINNEAPOLIS, USA 155

MACMANUS, TOM　NEW YORK, USA 63, 64
MADSEN, BETH　MINNEAPOLIS, USA 155
MAIA, GIL　PORTO, POR 613
MANLEY, BOB　USA 277-282, 439-443
MARTIN, JEFF　KALAMAZOO, USA 62
MATSUNAGA, SHIN　TOKYO, JPN 642
MAY, DOUGLAS　DALLAS, USA 538
MAYRS, FRANK　AYLMER, CAN 549
MCCARTHY, KEVIN　LOS ANGELES, USA 76
MCCARTY, HELEN　LOS ALAMOS, USA 438
MEACHAM, KENNETH J.　OAKS, USA 545
MELANDRI, MICHELE　BEAVERTON, USA 562
MENSINGA, SIBYLLE　GER 409
MESCHER, SABINE　GER 120-123, 125
MIRANDA, OSWALDO　BRA 427, 428, 608
MITCHELL, BONO　BOSTON, USA 489
MITCHELL, PATRICK　GLOUCESTER, USA 401
MONTEBELLO, JOSEPH　NEW YORK, USA 611
MORALDI, SUSANNA　NEW YORK, USA 166
MORRIS, DON　NEW YORK, USA 390, 391
MORTAROLI, MAURO　TORINO, ITA 1
MOTAMEDI, GHOLAM-REZA　IRN 474
MOTHERSOLE, JOHN　NEW YORK, USA 581
MUI, KAI　ROCHESTER, USA 102-104

NEUSSL, MANFRED　MUNICH, GER 361-363
NEWMAN, SUSAN　NEW YORK, USA 604
NHER, RAY　GER 408
NORMAN, JOHN　DALLAS, USA 542

OLIVER, DOUGLAS　USA 618-621
OLSON, DAN　MINNEAPOLIS, USA 217, 245-252, 504-506, 554, 622-628
O'STILLY, SEYMON　NEW YORK, USA 90

PAGNIEZ, RÉGIS　USA 364-370, 379
PAGODA, CARLO　USA 553
PARAMSKI, SCOTT　DALLAS, USA 327
PARSLEY, JOSEPH　BEAVERTON, USA 157
PATRICK, SEAN　USA 266-269

PERET　BARCELONA, SPA 556
PETERS, MICHAEL　LONDON, GBR 311-316
PETERSON, BRYAN L.　DALLAS, USA 516
PFIFFNER, JERRY　IRVINE, USA 55
PHILLIPS, JENNIFER　USA 481
PIRDAVARI, HOUMAN　MINNEAPOLIS, USA 26-35
PIRTLE, WOODY　NEW YORK, USA 299-302
PONCHIELLI, AMILCARE　MILANO, ITA 431
POSPISCHIL, HANS-GEORG　GER 386-389, 461
POSTAER, JEREMY　SAN FRANCISCO, USA 36
PRIEVE, MICHAEL　PORTLAND, USA 75
PULFER, ADRIAN　SALT LAKE CITY, USA 329-335
PYLYPCZAK, JOHN　TORONTO, CAN 283, 285

RABANUS, CHRISTOF　GER 408
RAZZINI, ANNELISE　MILANO, ITA 400
RICKABAUGH, ERIC　GAHANNA, USA 537
ROTH, HERMANN　COLOGNE, GER 468
RUBESS, BALVIS　TORONTO, CAN 482-485
RUCKER, DOUG　DALLAS, USA 532
RUNYAN, ROBERT MILES　USA 341
RUSSELL, ANTHONY　NEW YORK, USA 138, 539

SANDSTROM, STEVEN　PORTLAND, USA 156, 533
SANNA, GAVINO　MILANO, ITA 80-83
SATOH, TAKU　JPN 286-297, 551, 576-578
SAUL, LESLIE　SAN FRANCISCO, USA 510
SAYLES, JOHN　USA 212-216, 511, 540
SCHER, PAULA　NEW YORK, USA 560
SCHILPEROORT, KEES　SUNNINGHILL, SAF 575
SCHNEIDER, ERIC　LE LANDERON, SWI 275
SCHNELL, CINDY　MIAMISBURG, USA 437
SCHUMACHER, KATJA　HAAN, GER 583
SEMAN, RICHARD M.　PITTSBURGH, USA 345
SERRANO, JOSE　SAN DIEGO, USA 531
SHAHID, SAM　NEW YORK, USA 2, 3
SHAPIRO, ELLEN　NEW YORK, USA 558
SIEGER, DIETER　SASSENBERG, GER 321-324
SILVERSTEIN, RICH　USA 37, 70-72
SIMPSON, GREG　NEW YORK, USA 520
SINNI, GIANNI　FIRENZE, ITA 197-209
SLACHOWITZ, LOIS　STAMFORD, USA 574
SMIDT, SAM　PALO ALTO, USA 565-567
SMITH, AARON　PORTLAND, USA 92
SMITH, TYLER　PROVIDENCE, USA 440
SMOKLER, JEROLD　NEW YORK, USA 377
SOMMESE, LANNY　STATE COLLEGE, USA 528
STANARD, MICHAEL　EVANSTON, USA 523
STONE, STEVE　SAN FRANCISCO, USA 36
STOUT, D.J.　AUSTIN, USA 399

STUART, NEIL　NEW YORK, USA 472, 609, 614
SWIETER, JOHN　DALLAS, USA 328, 546

TAKE STUDIO　HAMBURG, GER 407
TAN, ARTY　USA 10-12, 46, 67-69, 107
TANAKA, IKKO　TOKYO, JPN 588-592, 605-607
TERRELONGE, DEL　TORONTO, CAN 175-181
THOMPSON, TIM　BALTIMORE, USA 145-147
THORBURN, BILL　MINNEAPOLIS, USA 529
TILKA, JANE　MINNEAPOLIS, USA 517

UIBERREITHER, SIGRID　SALZBURG, AUT 347
UNGLESS, DEREK　NEW YORK, USA 410-413

VALENTINE, ROBERT　USA 167, 168, 557
VALICENTI, RICK　CHICAGO, USA 237-244
VAN BLOOMESTEIN, HANS　NLD 396, 397
VAN BOKHOVEN, MARC　DEN HAAG, NLD 253
VAN BRAGT, TON　DEN HAAG, NLD 253
VAN VELSEN, PIETER　AMSTERDAM, NLD 94-96
VANDERBYL, MICHAEL　SAN FRANCISCO, USA 77, 84-86, 127-131, 298, 503, 530, 541
VANSEGHBROECK, PHILIPPE　BOULOGNE, FRA 93
VIGORELLI, GIANPIETRO　MILANO, ITA 111
VINSON, LESLEY　NEW YORK, USA 376
VOS, MARIANNE　AMSTERDAM, NLD 519

WALLACE, BOB　NEW YORK, USA 552
WANNAZ, ALAIN　BELMONT, SWI 580, 582
WATERBURY, TODD　MINNEAPOLIS, USA 579
WEBSTER, STEPHEN　NEW YORK, USA 380
WEINBERG, ALLEN　NEW YORK, USA 617
WELLER, DON　PARK CITY, USA 480
WELLS VERLANDER, KAREN　USA 380-382
WERNER, SHARON　MINNEAPOLIS, USA 336, 337
WIESE, BRUNO K.　HAMBURG, GER 526
WILLARDSON, DAVID　USA 495
WILLIAMS, LOWELL　HOUSTON, USA 154, 522
WILLIAMS, LOWELL, DESIGN　USA 139-144
WISE, GARY　BLOOMFIELD HILLS, USA 44, 47
WOLF, GERD　HAMBURG, GER 87, 88
WONG, TRACY　USA 38, 40, 108, 109
WOODWARD, FRED　NEW YORK, USA 348-355
WÖRTMANN, RAINER　HAMBURG, GER 384, 385

YOUNG, DAVID　INDIANAPOLIS, USA 340

ZABOWSKI, BILL　MINNEAPOLIS, USA 97-99
ZANON, CIRIANO　ITA 74, 169-174
ZAVARRO, JOYCE　SAN FRANCISCO, USA 555
ZIMMERMANN, BETSY　SAN FRANCISCO, USA 39

ABERNETHY, MILES	483 3700, SCOTTSDALE, USA	422
ALEXANDER, DOUG	523 7363, HOUSTON, USA	266-269
ANDERSON, CHARLES S.	339 5181, MINNEAPOLIS, USA	217,
	245-252, 504-506, 554, 622-628	
ANDERSON, GAIL	758 3800, NEW YORK, USA	349, 354
ANDERSON, JAMES	683 7000, NEW YORK, USA	547
ANGELI, PRIMO	974 6100, SAN FRANCISCO,	USA 553
APARICIO, ERNESTO	43 25 44 06, PARIS, FRA	598, 599
APPLETON, ROBERT	296 4111, HARTFORD, USA	310
ASHWORTH, LISA	854 1000, MIAMI, USA	308, 309
AYMERGEN, SAHIN	145 5009, ISTANBUL, TUR	610
BAJKAI, ROBYN	803 5815, SUNNINGHILL, SAF	575
BAKER, PETER	927 7094, TORONTO, CAN	536
BARLOW, PAUL	LONDON, GBR	458-460
BARNES, JEFF	527 0157, CHICAGO, USA	78, 79
BARNETT, DAVID	431 7130, NEW YORK, USA	435
BARRIE, BOB	332 2445, MINNEAPOLIS, USA	57-61
BASCOVE	888 0038, NEW YORK, USA	603, 614
BATESON, JOHN	731 6946, LONDON, GBR	148-151
BAUR, RUEDI	48 70 20 18, PARIS, FRA	403-406
BECKER, SYNDI	880 0700, NEW YORK, USA	421
BENTKOWSKI, TOM	522 5962, NEW YORK, USA	402
BERG, JOHN	684 3267, NEW YORK, USA	512, 513
BERNARDIN, JOHN	261 0330, IRVINE, USA	55
BERTÉ, JIM	453 3523, SANTA MONICA, USA	445-453
BEST, ROBERT	880 0700, NEW YORK, USA	421
BISHOP, DEBRA	758 3800, NEW YORK, USA	353
BJÖRKMAN, KLAS	155 557, STOCKHOLM, SWE	134-136
BLACK, PAUL	871 2305, DALLAS, USA	527
BLANK, PETER	687 1784, NEW YORK, USA	338
BOCHERT, MARLIES	HAMBURG, GER	384, 385
BONAVITA, DONNA M.	MONTCLAIR, USA	423
BRADBERY, IAN	660 0268, GLEBE, AUS	514
BRADLEY, CHRIS	731 6946, LONDON, GBR	148-151
BRESLIN, KRISTIN	238 7484, STATE COLLEGE, USA	528
BROCK, MICHAEL	932 0283, LOS ANGELES, USA	394, 395
BROWER, STEVEN	418 4067, NEW YORK, USA	612
BURDETT, MARK	NEW YORK, USA	615, 616
BURNS, BOB	255 5542, NEW YORK, USA	276
BUSTAD, JOE	243 2922, DES MOINES, USA	212-216
BUTCHER, SEAN	04253 2209, BURLEY, GBR	339
CARDIN, FRANCO	495 836, CASTELFRANCO, ITA	169-174
CARSON, BILL	529 7651, HOUSTON, USA	139-144, 154, 522
CARSON, DAVID	481 0609, DEL MAR, USA	429, 430
CARTER, DAVID	826 4631, DALLAS, USA	342-344
CATO, KEN	429 6577, RICHMOND, AUS	496-502
CHASE, MARGO	688 1055, LOS ANGELES, USA	543
CHING, DONNA	683 7000, NEW YORK, USA	547
CHRISTIE, SCOTT	366 9908, TORONTO, CAN	283, 285
CHURCH, STANLEY	755 2903, NEW YORK, USA	552
CHWAST, SEYMOUR	674 8080, NEW YORK, USA	486
CIMA, DANIELE	581 931, MILANO, ITA	22, 23
CORDELLA, ANDREÉ	954 1840, BOSTON, USA	584, 585
CRAIG-TEERLINK, JEAN	366 0900, REDWOOD CITY, USA	152, 153
CROLICK, SUE	375 9359, MINNEAPOLIS, USA	518
CRONAN, MICHAEL PATRICK	543 6745, SAN FRANCISCO, USA	256-262
CRONENWETT, DREW	866 4013, MIAMISBURG, USA	254
CROXTON, BRENT	USA	277-282
DANZINGER, SYLVIA	588 460, VIENNA, AUT	265
DEARWATER, ANDY	529 7651, HOUSTON, USA	139-144
DIAS, MICHAEL	345 8086, MONTREAL, CAN	469, 470
DINNIS, RACHAEL	731 6946, LONDON, GBR	148-151
DOBSON, TERRY	924 9148, NEW YORK, USA	346
DORET, MICHAEL	929 1688, NEW YORK, USA	525
DRACE, MATTHEW	553 2800, SAN FRANCISCO, USA	398
DRISCOLL, TERRI	981 6612, USA	424, 433, 434
DUFFY, JOE	339 3247, MINNEAPOLIS, USA	311-316
EDMONDSON, DALE	424 1844, BOSTON, USA	158-161
EISNER, ELLIE	542 5529, NORFOLK, USA	426
ELBERS, HARRY	01652 16319, OUDENBOSCH, NLD	561
ERKMEN, BÜLENT	141 3560, ISTANBUL, TUR	425
EUBEL, PAUL	GER	602
EWAN, ANDY	928 7801, LONDON, GBR	303-307
FEASTER, SCOTT	954 0522, DALLAS, USA	516
FELS, THEO	431 7130, NEW YORK, USA	435
FELTUS, ROSS H.	306 011, DÜSSELDORF, GER	559
FERRETTI, RICHARD	USA	391
FOSTER, SUSAN	USA	391
FOWLER, THOMAS G.	329 1105, STAMFORD, USA	574
GEKIG, SAVAS	145 5009, ISTANBUL, TUR	610
GERBINO, MICHAEL	941 0445, NEW YORK, USA	508
GERICKE, MICHAEL	683 7000, NEW YORK, USA	547
GIAMMANCO, MICHAEL	951 5251, CHICAGO, USA	237-244
GILMORE-BARNES, CATHERINE	758 3800, NEW YORK, USA	355
GLASER, MILTON	889 3161, NEW YORK, USA	263, 264
GOLON, MARTI	522 5962, NEW YORK, USA	402
GORETSKY, VADIM	856 9356, PALO ALTO, USA	535
GOTTSCHALL, RALF	9250 3360, MUNICH, GER	361-363

GUNSELMAN, MICHAEL	655 7077, WILMINGTON, USA	116-119, 124, 629-634
GUREGHIAN, TALIN	621 0915, SAN FRANCISCO, USA	270-274
HAMM, GARRICK	339 3247, MINNEAPOLIS, USA	311-316
HARTMANN, KNUT	756 1920, FRANKFURT/M., GER	548
HERRINGTON, WALTER	LOS ANGELES, USA	162-165
HILL, CHRIS	523 7363, HOUSTON, USA	266-269
HINRICHS, KIT	981 6612, SAN FRANCISCO, USA	218-225, 424, 433, 434
HIROMURA, MASAAKI	TOKYO, JPN	13-18
HOCH, DENIS	43 25 44 06, PARIS, FRA	598, 599
HOEFLER, JONATHAN	NEW YORK, USA	354
HOHL-PHILLIPS, KATHLEEN	542 5529, NORFOLK, USA	226-236, 426
HOPES, KIM	364 5349, WASHINGTON, USA	444
HOW, BELLE	981 6612, SAN FRANCISCO, USA	218-225
HOWARD, JOAN	366 0900, REDWOOD CITY, USA	152, 153
HUNTER, KENT	421 5888, NEW YORK, USA	454-457
IGARASHI, TAKENOBU	498 3621, TOKYO, JPN	635
JANERKA, ANDRZEJ	NEW YORK, USA	372-375
JAY, JOHN	705 3472, NEW YORK, USA	192-196
JOHNSON, HALEY	339 3247, MINNEAPOLIS, USA	245-252, 311-316, 534
JOHNSON, MARK	332 2445, MINNEAPOLIS, USA	52-54, 325, 586, 587
JOINER, ERICH	392 0669, SAN FRANCISCO, USA	113
JORGENSEN, GRANT	271 7753, PARKSIDE, AUS	521
JOSEPH, DOUGLAS	458 1899, SANTA MONICA, USA	462-465
JULIANO, ANGELO	768 5054, NEW YORK, USA	100
JUNG, STEWART	920 0708, TORONTO, CAN	544
KALMAN, TIBOR	NEW YORK, USA	441
KALTENHAUSER, MICHAEL	VOMP, AUT	636-641
KAMEI, PEGGY	566 0868, SAN FRANCISCO, USA	510
KAN, CHI-MING	889 3161, NEW YORK, USA	263, 264
KAYALAR, MESUT	167 6750, ISTANBUL, TUR	132, 133
KLEIN, DEBBIE	BOSTON, USA	432
KOBAYASHI RITCH, JANE	453 3523, SANTA MONICA, USA	618-621
KOEPKE, GARY	525 2229, MAGNOLIA, USA	277-282, 383, 439-443
KOPPEL, TERRY R.	NEW YORK, USA	414-417, 436, 490
KOSCHEMBAR, FRANK	693 917, DÜSSELDORF, GER	593-597
KOVAL, JAMES	427 6413, CHICAGO, USA	550
KUHLMANN, DEANNA	453 3523, SANTA MONICA, USA	618-621
KUSAGAYA, TAKAFUMI	TOKYO, JPN	13-18
LAARAKKER, TINY	573 4811, AMSTERDAM, NLD	397
LAWTON, HELEN	482 4324, LONDON, GBR	515
LECLERC, BERNIE	USA	507
LEE GRANT, KAREN	NEW YORK, USA	371
LERCH, DAVID	963 8607, HOUSTON, USA	524
LÉVY, STAN	45 02 18 92, PARIS, FRA	4, 5
LEWIS, MARY	580 9252, LONDON, GBR	564
LICHTENHELD, TOM	332 2445, MINNEAPOLIS, USA	45, 91
LIMONCELLI, SUSAN	431 8770, NEW YORK, USA	539
LOESCH, UWE	589 961, DÜSSELDORF, GER	253
LONG, LARRY	823 0975, MARINA DEL REY, USA	341
LOUIE, RON	627 9330, NEW YORK, USA	560
LUSSMANN, ANITA	463 9910, ZURICH, SWI	110
LYON, JENNIFER	248 9466, PORTLAND, USA	156
MABRY, MICHAEL	982 7336, SAN FRANCISCO, USA	509
MAIA, GIL	560 818, PORTO, POR	613
MATSUMOTO, IKUKO	JPN	602
MATSUNAGA, SHIN	499 0291, TOKYO, JPN	642
MAY, DOUGLAS	528 4770, DALLAS, USA	538
MAYRS, FRANK	827 0201, AYLMER, CAN	549
MCCARTY, HELEN	455 2642, LOS ALAMOS, USA	438
MCCARTHY, KEVIN	471 4333, LOS ANGELES, USA	76
MEACHAM, KENNETH J.	497 3226, OAKS, USA	545
MELANDRI, MICHELE	526 6800, BEAVERTON, USA	562
MENEGAZ, LAURA	523 7363, HOUSTON, USA	266-269
MESCHER, SABINE	855 685, STUTTGART, GER	120-123, 125
MIRANDA, OSWALDO	232 4240, CURITIBA, BRA	427, 428, 608
MITCHELL, BONO, GRAPHICS	WASHINGTON, USA	467
MITCHELL, DICK	987 4800, DALLAS, USA	532
MITCHELL, PATRICK	281 3110, GLOUCESTER, USA	401
MORALDI, SUSANNA	988 0335, NEW YORK, USA	166
MORRIS, DON	551 7153, NEW YORK, USA	390, 391
MORTAROLI, MAURO	88 011, TORINO, ITA	1
MUNSTERMAN, PAUL	720 6020, DALLAS, USA	328
MURAKAMI, PIPER	981 6612, SAN FRANCISCO, USA	433, 434
NEWMAN, SUSAN	620 2820, NEW YORK, USA	604
NIEMINEN, BARBARA	431 8770, NEW YORK, USA	138
NOLI, SUZANNE	NEW YORK, USA	611
NOMA, TAKAYOSHI	TOKYO, JPN	492
NORMAN, JOHN	987 4800, DALLAS, USA	542
OLSON, DAN	339 5181, MINNEAPOLIS, USA	217, 245-252, 504-506, 554, 622-628
O'STILLY, SEYMON	408 2100, NEW YORK, USA	90

PAASCHE-AASEN, JUNN	290 357, OSLO, NOR	600
PARAMSKI, SCOTT	954 0522, DALLAS, USA	327
PARISI, JOE	837 0070, BALTIMORE, USA	145-147
PARSLEY, JOSEPH	641 6453, BEAVERTON, USA	157
PENNY, NICOLA	928 7801, LONDON, GBR	303-307
PERET	242 2006, BARCELONA, SPA	556
PHILLIPS, JENNIFER	USA	481
PILOTTE, JEFF	SAN FRANCISCO, USA	509
PIRDAVARI, HOUMAN	332 2445, MINNEAPOLIS, USA	26-35
PIRTLE, WOODY	683 7000, NEW YORK, USA	299-302
POLITE, KERRY	655 7077, WILMINGTON, USA	116-199, 124, 629-634
POSTAER, JEREMY	392 0669, SAN FRANCISCO, USA	36
POWERS, TIM	774 0510, GRAND RAPIDS, USA	563
PRIEVE, MICHAEL	228 4381, PORTLAND, USA	75
PULFER, ADRIAN	378 3890, SALT LAKE CITY, USA	329-335
PÜTZ, ROBERT	2236 39070, COLOGNE, GER	473, 475
PYLYPCZAK, JOHN	366 9908, TORONTO, CAN	283, 285
RAZGAITIS, AUDREY	NEW YORK, USA	493
RAZZINI, ANNELISE	MILANO, ITA	400
RICKABAUGH, ERIC	337 2229, GAHANNA, USA	537
RÖHRIG, CARL W.	257 248, HAMBURG, GER	491
ROMNEY, ROZ	SAN FRANCISCO, USA	7, 9
ROTACH, YVES	513 819, LE LANDERON, SWI	275
SAKHEIM, RUTH	SAN FRANCISCO, USA	8
SANDSTROM, STEVEN	248 9466, PORTLAND, USA	156, 533
SASSON, MAURICE	768 2888, NEW YORK, USA	19-21
SATOH, TAKU	546 7901, TOKYO, JPN	286-297, 551, 576-578
SAYLES, JOHN	243 2922, DES MOINES, USA	212-216, 511, 540
SCHER, PAULA	627 9330, NEW YORK, USA	560
SCHNELL, CINDY	866 4013, MIAMISBURG, USA	437
SCHULTE, LYNN	339 3247, MINNEAPOLIS, USA	579
SCHUMACHER, KATJA	02129 7148, HAAN, GER	583
SEMAN, MICHAEL M.	261 3511, PITTSBURGH, USA	345
SERRANO, JOSE	234 6631, SAN DIEGO, USA	531
SETHIADI, RIKI	421 5888, NEW YORK, USA	454-457
SHAPIRO, ELLEN	460 8544, NEW YORK, USA	558
SHINOHARA, KEN	442 1091, TOKYO, JPN	137
SILVERSTEIN, RICH	392 0669, SAN FRANCISCO, USA	37, 70-72
SIMPSON, GREG	674 8080, NEW YORK, USA	317-320, 520
SISMAN, LUCY	598 3733, NEW YORK, USA	410-413
SMIDT, SAM	327 0707, PALO ALTO, USA	565-567
SMITH, TYLER	PROVIDENCE, USA	440
STANARD, MICHAEL	869 9820, EVANSTON, USA	523
STARK, ADRIANE	888 1969, NEW YORK, USA	601
STONE, STEVE	392 0669, SAN FRANCISCO, USA	36
STOUT, D.J.	476 7085, AUSTIN, USA	399
STRATOTI, ELENA	495 836, CASTELFRANCO, ITA	74
STREEPER JEFF	378 3890, SALT LAKE CITY, USA	329-335
STUART, NEIL	366 2170, NEW YORK, USA	472, 609
SUMICHRAST, JÖZEF	295 0255, LAKE FOREST, USA	557
SWIETER, JOHN	720 6020, DALLAS, USA	328, 546
TAN, ARTY	332 2445, MINNEAPOLIS, USA	10-12, 46, 67-69, 107
TANAKA, IKKO	470 2611, TOKYO, JPN	588-592
TERRAGNI, GUIDO	MILANO, ITA	431
TERRELONGE, DEL	462 1960, TORONTO, CAN	175-181
THORBURN, BILL	375 3286, MINNEAPOLIS, USA	529
TIXADOR, JULIETTE	48 70 20 18, PARIS, FRA	403-406
TUTSSEL, GLENN	339 3247, MINNEAPOLIS, USA	311-316
UIBERREITHER, SIGRID	840 8840, SALZBURG, AUT	347
UNGLESS, DEREK	598 3733, NEW YORK, USA	410-413
VALENTINE, ROBERT	705 3472, NEW YORK, USA	167, 168, 557
VALICENTI, RICK	951 5251, CHICAGO, USA	237-244
VAN HAMERSVELD, JOHN	MALIBU, USA	495
VANDERBYL, MICHAEL	543 8447, SAN FRANCISCO, USA	77, 84-86, 127-131, 298, 503, 530, 541
VINSON, LESLEY	598 3733, NEW YORK, USA	376
VOGEL, JIM	720 6020, DALLAS, USA	328, 546
VOLDENAUER, MARC	08261 6380, MINDELHEIM, GER	568-573
VOOGT, LOUIS	573 4811, AMSTERDAM, NLD	396
VOS, MARIANNE	240 547, AMSTERDAM, NLD	519
WANNAZ, ALAIN	617 7445, BELMONT, SWI	580, 582
WATERBURY, TODD	339 3247, MINNEAPOLIS, USA	507, 579
WEINBERG, ALLEN	454 4954, NEW YORK, USA	617
WELLER, DON	649 9859, PARK CITY, USA	480
WERNER, SHARON	339 3247, MINNEAPOLIS, USA	311-316, 336, 337, 507
WESTON, LINDA	LONDON, GBR	458-460
WHANG, JUNGSUN	USA	494
WIESE, BRUNO K.	603 8982, HAMBURG, GER	526
WILLIAMS, LOWELL	529 7651, HOUSTON, USA	139-144, 522
WONG, TRACY	392 0669, SAN FRANCISCO, USA	38, 40, 108, 109
WOODWARD, FRED	758 3800, NEW YORK, USA	348, 350-353, 355
ZAVARRO, JOYCE	255 9575, SAN FRANCISCO, USA	555
ZIMMERMANN, BETSY	392 0669, SAN FRANCISCO, USA	39
ZUMPANO, SUZANNE	889 3161, NEW YORK, USA	263, 264

ARTISTS/ILLUSTRATORS/PHOTOGRAPHERS

ACA STUDIO	02372 3722, HEMER, GER	321-324
ALLEN JULIAN	NEW YORK, USA	410
ANDERSON, CHARLES S.	339 5181, MINNEAPOLIS, USA	245-252, 504-506, 554, 622-628
ARISMAN, MARSHALL	662 2289, NEW YORK, USA	477
ARNDT, JIM	MINNEAPOLIS, USA	26, 67-69, 73, 105, 106
BACCEGA, GIANNI	ITA	74, 169-174
BAKER, PETER	927 7094, TORONTO, CAN	536
BARABAN, JOE	526 0317, HOUSTON, USA	154
BARGSTÄDT, YVONNE	GER	408
BARNAUD, BRIAN	USA	399
BASCOVE	888 0038, NEW YORK, USA	603, 614
BATISTA, FERNANDO	USA	37
BEGUÉ, SIGREDO MARTIN	SPA	167
BELLIA, GIORGIO	ITA	56
BELLINCAMPI, CARLO	ITA	400
BENE ARCHIV (PAUSCH)	VIENNA, AUT	265
BENSIMON, GILLES	42 89 04 22, PARIS, FRA	364, 366, 368-370, 379
BENSON, HANK	SAN FRANCISCO, USA	39
BERG, JOHN	684 3267, NEW YORK, USA	512, 513
BICE, PAUL	USA	450-453
BILLOUT, GUY	431 6350, NEW YORK, USA	492, 493
BIRNBAUM, LILIAN	GER	388
BLACK, PAUL	871 2305, DALLAS, USA	527
BLAUSTEIN, JOHN	BERKELEY, USA	71
BORTHWICK, MARC	GBR	397
BRAASCH, GARY	PORTLAND, USA	222, 224
BRINKSCHMIDT, H.C.	GER	408
BRONSTEIN, STEVE	USA	63, 64
BRYANT, RICHARD	USA	419
BURCKHARDT, MARC	NEW YORK, USA	612
BURKE, KEVIN	USA	437
BYBEE, GERRY	SAN FRANCISCO, USA	108, 109
CAMERON, BETSY	324 9688, EAST HAMPTON, USA	338
CAPELA, JAY	USA	152, 153
CARCAMO, RUBEM	BRA	428
CARNASE, TOM	NEW YORK, USA	581
CHAMBER OF COAL TRADERS	LONDON, GBR	115
CHEVEUX, ROBERT		608
CHWAST, SEYMOUR	674 8080, NEW YORK, USA	461, 486
COATES, JACQUI	612 3444, MELBOURNE, AUS	41-43
COLLINS, CHRIS	633 1670, NEW YORK, USA	65
COMSTOCK, INC.	USA	424
CONNERS, TOM	USA	91
CORBIJN, ANTON	USA	429
CORNELLI, FRANCESCO	ITA	80-83
CORWIN, JEFF	USA	139-144
CRANCE, CHRIS	USA	416
CRANE, TOM	BRYN MAWR, USA	116-119, 124
CRONAN, MICHAEL	USA	256-262
CRUMPTON, MICHAEL	USA	276
DAHLK, RANDALL	339 5181, MINNEAPOLIS, USA	217, 245-252, 504-506, 534, 554, 622-628
DAKOTA, MICHAEL	USA	308, 309
DALLA CHIESA, CARLO	USA	162-165
DALVAND, AHMAD-REZA	IRN	474
DARIGO	FRA	93
DAVID-TU, ALAN	722 3913, LONDON, GBR	396
DAVIDSON, ANDREW	884 650, STROUD, GBR	315
DAYAL, ANTAR	USA	553
DE LA FUENTE, JUAN	SPA	182-191
DEARWATER, ANDY	529 7651, HOUSTON, USA	139-144
DELBECK, THOMAS	GER	363
DIOR	GER	253
DOBRUNZ, KLAUS	362 926 DÜSSELDORF, GER	89
DOLE, JODY	691 9888, NEW YORK, USA	66
DORET, MICHAEL	929 1688, NEW YORK, USA	525
DRESSLER, OTTO	GER	384
DUBLIN, RICK	USA	57-61
DUDZINSKI, ANDRZEJ	772 3098, NEW YORK, USA	489
ECCLES, ANDREW	USA	381
EDELMANN, HEINZ	AMSTERDAM, NLD	385
EDWARDES, GORDON	USA	72
FALLAI, ALDO	FIRENZE	4, 5, 197-209
FEINBERG, MITCHELL	USA	104
FELLA, EDWARD	USA	443
FELTUS, H. ROSS	306 011, DÜSSELDORF, GER	559
FERRATO, DONNA	USA	402
FLOCK, MARY	USA	550
FORD, TROY	USA	139-144
FREDERIKSE, TJEERD	NLD	519
FRY, J.W.	724 6895, ROCHESTER, USA	542
FURMAN, MICHAEL	925 4233, PHILADELPHIA, USA	629-634
GAGE, ROB	494 7265, LAGUNA BEACH, USA	44, 47
GALL, CHRIS	USA	435
GAMMA LIAISON	USA	412
GATNARCZYK, THOMAS	419 776, COLOGNE, GER	476
GEKIG, SAVAS	145 5009, ISTANBUL, TUR	610
GEMELLI, PIERO	ITA	6
GEORGE, JOHN P.	USA	334
GERSTEN, PAUL	USA	76
GERVASE, MARK	USA	76
GILLASPY, DENNIS	298 3500, SAN DIEGO, USA	284
GIUSTI, ROBERT	354 6539, NEW MILFORD, USA	467
GLASER, MILTON	889 3161, NEW YORK, USA	263, 264
GLASS, GREG	USA	254
GOLDMAN, BART	USA	480
GORETSKY, VADIM	856 9356, PALO ALTO, USA	535
GOULD, ROGER	774 0510, GRAND RAPIDS, USA	563
GREENFIELD-SANDERS, T.	USA	372
GREENLEIGH, JOHN	USA	152, 153
GUZMAN	NEW YORK, USA	7, 371

255

HAAK, KEN	NEW YORK, USA	409
HANSEN, HANS	824 040, HAMBURG, GER	87, 88, 126
HANSON, PAMELA	535 7473, NEW YORK, USA	410
HARDING, C.B.	281 9907, PORTLAND, USA	156
HEFFERNAN, TERRY	626 1999, SAN FRANCISCO, USA	49, 70, 221, 225
HELLER, STEVEN A.	PASADENA, USA	433, 434
HENDLER, SANDRA	735 7380, PHILADELPHIA, USA	354
HENNEKA, DIETMAR	605 040, STUTTGART, GER	121-123
HESS, RICHARD	NEW YORK, USA	473, 475
HIRO	580 8000, NEW YORK, USA	27-35
HODGES, ROSS	SAN FRANCISCO, USA	127-131
HOFFMAN, NEIL	USA	256-262
HOLCOMBE, KIMBERLY	USA	432
HOLDEMAN, BRUCE	825 7913, DENVER, USA	479
HOLLAND, BRAD	226 3675, NEW YORK, USA	481
HOLZ, GEORGE	USA	395
HULL, RICHARD	USA	333
JANSSON, ROLF	HORTEN, NOR	487
JASMIN, PAUL	USA	394
JEFFS, PETER	AUS	41-43
JINKS, JOHN	675 2901, NEW YORK, USA	472
JOHNSON, HALEY	339 5181, MINNEAPOLIS, USA	534
JOHNSON, STEVE	USA	462-465
JOHNSON, JOEL PETER	982 6533, NEW YORK, USA	609
JONES, AARON	988 5730, SANTA FE, USA	584, 585
JORGENSEN, GRANT	271 7753, PARKSIDE, AUS	521
JURKOVIC, GERHARD	GER	415
KAMEI, PEGGY	566 0868, SAN FRANCISCO, USA	510
KANDER, NADAV	359 5207, LONDON, GBR	113
KASSER, TOM	USA	412
KASTERINE, DMITRI	226 0401, NEW YORK, USA	226-236
KAZUMOTO, YOSHI	JPN	22, 23
KELLER, MICHAEL	USA	558
KELLEY, GARY	277 2330, CEDAR FALLS, USA	471
KERN, GEOF	USA	436, 454-457
KLEIN AND WILSON	747 1714, DALLAS, USA	342-344
KLOVSTAD, RICK	GBR	316
KÖHLER, BAREND	NLD	561
KOISHIZAWA, HARUO	JPN	137
KOSCHEMBAR, FRANK	633 917, DÜSSELDORF, GER	593-597
KRÄMER, PETER	210 8087, DÜSSELDORF, GER	468
KROESKAMP, HANS	AMSTERDAM, NLD	94-96
KROLICKI, GREE	224 9299, PORTLAND, USA	533
LAFAVOR, MARK	USA	45, 46
LAMB, DAN	MANHATTAN BEACH, USA	157
LATEGAN, BARRY	NEW YORK, USA	102
LAXTON, WILLIAM	47 04 28 41, PARIS, FRA	375
LEIBOVITZ, ANNIE	NEW YORK, USA	8, 350
LERCH, DAVID	963 8607, HOUSTON, USA	524
LESCH, DAVID	USA	332
LEVY, KAREN	TORONTO, CAN	283, 285
LIGHTSTRUCK STUDIO	727 2220, BALTIMORE, USA	145-147
LINDLOF, ED	472 0195, AUSTIN, USA	494
LLEWELLYN, MICHAEL	535 1948, SAN FRANCISCO, USA	401
LLOYD, HARVEY	NEW YORK, USA	37, 39
LOMBARD, RALPH	ITA	431
LOOK PHOTO	ITA	400
LORANT, TERRY	USA	256-262
LOW, BERNIE	728 7646, OTTAWA, CAN	549
LUBARSKY, DAVID	NEW YORK, USA	127-131
MACPHERSON, ANDREW	LONDON, GBR	348, 351, 413
MAGLEBY, MCRAY	378 4711, PROVO, USA	332, 547
MAIA, GIL	560 818, PORTO, POR	613
MAILL, WARREN	USA	313
MAISEL, JAY	431 5013, NEW YORK, USA	36, 38, 39
MANARCHY, DENIS	829 9272, CHICAGO, USA	90, 98, 99
MARKUS, KURT	COLORADO SPRINGS, USA	168, 353
MARSCH, JAMES	USA	314
MARSEL, STEVE	547 4445, CAMBRIDGE, USA	277-282, 383, 439
MARVY!	935 0307, MINNEAPOLIS, USA	114
MASCARDI, NINO	ITA	1
MASER, WAYNE	USA	19-21, 392, 413
MATRIX	USA	421
MAUSKOPF, NORMAN	USA	331
MAUSS, PETER	USA	391
MAYER, BILL	USA	427
MAYOR, RANDY	933 2818, BIRMINGHAM, USA	62
MCCARTHY, JACK	GBR	515
MCGRAW, K.D.	USA	267, 269
MEACHAM, KENNETH J.	497 3226, OAKS, USA	545
MEISEL, STEVEN	206 0737, NEW YORK, USA	192-196, 356, 358, 359
MELNICK, STEVE	874 9552, NEW YORK, USA	376
MEYERSON, ARTHUR	660 0405, HOUSTON, USA	423
MICHIENZI, SHAWN	USA	10-12
MICHL, JOE	MINNEAPOLIS, USA	73
MILES, KENT	USA	331
MILLER, RANDY	MIAMI, USA	38
MILLMAN, ROBERT	USA	268, 269
MINOR, WENDELL	NEW YORK, USA	581
MITCHELL, DICK	987 4800, DALLAS, USA	532
MONDINO, JEAN-BAPTISTE	40 68 08 11, PARIS, FRA	377
MONTGOMERY, MARILYN	829 2135, SEBASTOPOL, USA	552
MORELLA, DENNIS	USA	108, 109
MORGAN, SCOTT	VENICE, USA	454-457
NACASA & PARTNERS	GER	362
NAKAJIMA, TOSHIO	JPN	551, 576-578
NEIDHART, WOLF	SWI	110
NELLANS, BILL	DES MOINES, USA	212-216

NELSON, WILL	USA	222
NEWNHAM, ALAN	LONDON, GBR	564
NGAN, HENRY	USA	92
OCKENFELS, FRANK W.	USA	349
OLSON, DAN	339 5181, MINNEAPOLIS, USA	245-252,
		504-506, 554, 622-628
OMEGA STUDIOS	USA	84
OUELLET, ODILE	MONTREAL, CAN	469, 470
OVERACRE, GARY	USA	219
PAPETTI, F. & M.	ITA	111
PENN, IRVING	880 8426, NEW YORK, USA	588-592
PERET	240 2006, BARCELONA, SPA	556
PETA	USA	412
PETERSON, DAVID	USA	270-274, 398
PETERSON, KERRY	MINNETONKA, USA	57-61, 107
PETRAKES, GEORGE	695 0556, BOSTON, USA	158-161, 440
PFAHLER, GEORG KARL	GER	602
PFISTER, CORINNE	USA	237-244
PICAYO, JOSE	USA	374
PIERCE, RICHARD	NEW YORK, USA	382
PLOTEMA, MARIE	632 420, BRNO, CSR	466
POWERS, TIM	774 0510, GRAND RAPIDS, USA	563
PSIHOYOS, LOUIS	USA	421
PULIATTI, JOEL	USA	256-262
RANDALL, BOB	USA	92
RASCONA, RODNEY	437 0866, PHOENIX, USA	422
RAUSCH, MIKE	USA	55
RESSMEYER, ROGER	USA	72
RICKABAUGH, ERIC	337 2229, GAHANNA, USA	537
RITTS, HERB	826 6366, LOS ANGELES, USA	9
ROBINSON, BARRY	USA	108, 109, 219, 223
RODIN, CHRISTINE	NEW YORK, USA	604
RODRIGUEZ, ROBERT	USA	24, 25
ROGERS, PAUL	564 8128, PASADENA, USA	495
RÖHRIG, CARL W.	257 248, HAMBURG, GER	491
ROLSTON, MATTHEW	HOLLYWOOD, USA	414, 417
ROOLAART, HARRY	USA	376
RUBESS, BALVIS	927 7071, TORONTO, CAN	482-485
RUSSO, ANTHONY	USA	490
RUTH, ERNST HERMANN	NICE, FRA	48, 50, 51
RYAN, TOM	651 7085, DALLAS, USA	327
SAKANO, YUTAKA	JPN	13-18
SANDERS, CHRIS	645 6111, NEW YORK, USA	454-457
SAYLES, JOHN	243 2922, DES MOINES, USA	212-216
SCHER, PAULA	627 9330, NEW YORK, USA	441
SCHMITZ, HEINER	DÜSSELDORF, GER	253
SCHULTE, LYNN	339 3247, MINNEAPOLIS, USA	507
SCHWARTZ, DANIEL	533 0237, NEW YORK, USA	478
SCOTT, STEVEN	USA	76
SENG, WALT	PITTSBURGH, USA	345
SIM, DUNCAN	LONDON, GBR	36, 40
SIMONS, CHIP	USA	615-617
SIROTA, PEGGY	344 2020, TARZANA, USA	75
SMETANA, ANDREAS	AUT	639-641
SMETEK, WIESLAW	GDANSK, POL	488
SMITH, RON BAXTER	365 1429, TORONTO, CAN	175-181
SNYDER, ISABEL	USA	410
SPINELLI, FRANK	NEW YORK, USA	100
SPIRO, ED	USA	317-320
STAUBITZ, KRISTIN	MINNEAPOLIS, USA	155
STEELE, BILL	USA	411
STEELE-PERKINS, CHRIS	USA	387, 389
STODDART, JOHN	USA	355
STONE & STECCATI	USA	85, 86
STRONG, TOM	USA	442
SUMICHRAST, JÖZEF	295 0255, LAKE FOREST, USA	557
SWIETER, JOHN	720 6020, DALLAS, USA	546
TAKE STUDIO	HAMBURG, GER	407
TEDESKINO, MARKUS	GER	363
TELFORD, JOHN	USA	334
THONER, DAN	234 6631, SAN DIEGO, USA	531
TILL, TOM	USA	330
TOELKE, CATHLEEN	876 8776, RHINEBECK, USA	611
TOLOT, ALBERTO	ITA	393
TOSCANI, OLIVIERO	ITA	111
TOSCANI	USA	365
TYEN	FRA	103, 367
UHLMANN, GINA	871 1025, CHICAGO, USA	78, 79
VALERIUS, GEORG	529 226, COLOGNE, GER	361-363
VAN PIETERSON LEX	399 5893, RIJSWIJK, NLD	253
VON UNWERTH, ELLEN	GER	378
WADA, MEGUMU	JPN	286-297, 551, 576-578
WATERBURY, TODD	339 3247, MINNEAPOLIS, USA	507, 579
WATERMAN, GREG	USA	380
WATSON, ALBERT	627 0077, NEW YORK, USA	357, 360, 410
WEBER, BRUCE	226 0814, NEW YORK, USA	2, 3, 352
WEGMAN, WILLIAM	NEW YORK, USA	112
WERNER, SHARON	339 3247, MINNEAPOLIS, USA	507
WESENER, WOLFGANG	GER	386
WHITMAN, ED	727 2220, BALTIMORE, USA	145-147
WIEMANN, ROY	USA	138
WILCOX, GWENNE	NEW YORK, USA	38
WOLFE, ART	SEATTLE, USA	101
WONG, PETER	340 0798, MINNEAPOLIS, USA	97
WRIGHT, JONATHAN	USA	76
ZAVARRO, JOYCE	255 9575, SAN FRANCISCO, USA	555
ZWART, JEFF	USA	52-54

A.K.A. ADVERTISING & SASS	224 4930, PORTLAND, USA	92
ALFSTAD BLANK GROUP	687 1784, NEW YORK, USA	338
ALTMAN & MANLEY	362 2470, SAN FRANCISCO, USA	
		277-282, 439-443
AMMIRATI & PURIS	337 9455, NEW YORK, USA	48-51
ANDERSON, CHARLES S., DESIGN	339 5181, MINNEAPOLIS, USA	217,
	245-252, 504-506, 534, 554, 622-628	
ANGELI, PRIMO, INC.	974 6100, SAN FRANCISCO, USA	553
APARICIO, ERNESTO, DESIGN	43 25 44 06, PARIS, FRA	598, 599
APPLETON DESIGN	296 4111, HARTFORD, USA	310
ARNELL/BICKFORD	219 8400, NEW YORK, USA	166
BACKER SPIELVOGEL BATES	261 0330, IRVINE, USA	55
BAKER, PETER	927 7094, TORONTO, CAN	536
BARNES DESIGN OFFICE	527 0157, CHICAGO, USA	78, 79
BARTON GILLET	USA	481
BBDO	NEW YORK, USA	65
BERG, JOHN	684 3267, NEW YORK, USA	512, 513
BESSER JOSEPH PARTNERS	458 1899, SANTA MONICA, USA	462-465
BLOOMINGDALE'S	705 3472, NEW YORK, USA	167, 168,
		192-196
BRADBERY DESIGN	660 0268, GLEBE, AUS	514
BROCK, MICHAEL, DESIGN	932 0283, LOS ANGELES, USA	394, 395
BURNS, CONNACHER & WALDRON	255 5542, NEW YORK, USA	276
BUTCHER, SEAN	04253 2209, BURLEY, GBR	339
CAHAN & ASSOC.	621 0915, SAN FRANCISCO, USA	270-274
CARSON DESIGN	481 0609, DEL MAR, USA	429, 430
CARTER, DAVID, GRAPHIC DESIGN ASSOCIATES		
	826 4631, DALLAS, USA	342-344
CASA DE IDÉIAS	232 4240, CURITIBA, BRA	427, 428, 608
CATO DESIGN INC.	429 6577, RICHMOND, AUS	496-502
CATO JOHNSON	46 84 34 44, BOULOGNE, FRA	93
CHASE, MARGO, DESIGN	668 1055, LOS ANGELES, USA	543
CHIAT/DAY/MOJO	612 3444, MELBOURNE, AUS	41-43
CLARITY COVERDALE RUEFF	339 3902, MINNEAPOLIS, USA	73, 105, 106
CONCRETE DESIGN	366 9908, TORONTO, CAN	283-285
COOPER COMMUNICATIONS	SAN FERNANDO, USA	545
CORDELLA DESIGN	954 1840, BOSTON, USA	584, 585
CRK ADVERTISING	719 2600, NEW YORK, USA	2, 3
CROLICK, SUE, ADVERTISING	375 9359, MINNEAPOLIS, USA	518
CRONAN DESIGN	543 6745, SAN FRANCISCO, USA	256-262
DAI NIPPON PRINTING	213 7524, NEW YORK, USA	492
DAYTON HUDSON/IN HOUSE	375 3286, MINNEAPOLIS, USA	529
DEMNER & MERLICEK	588 460, VIENNA, AUT	265
DESIGN MATTERS	USA	162-165
DORET, MICHAEL, INC.	929 1688, NEW YORK, USA	525
DOYLE ADVERTISING/DESIGN	424 1844, BOSTON, USA	158-161
DUFFY DESIGN GROUP	339 3247, MINNEAPOLIS, USA	311-316,
	336, 337, 507, 579	
DUMBAR, STUDIO	354 6304, DEN HAAG, NLD	253
ELBERS, HARRY & ELISABETH B.V.	01652 16319, OUDENBOSCH, NLD	561
EMA ADVERTISING	167 6750, ISTANBUL, TUR	132, 133
ERVACO/BJÖRKMAN & MITCHELL	155 557, STOCKHOLM, SWE	134-136
FALLON MCELLIGOTT	332 2445, MINNEAPOLIS, USA	10-12,
	26-35, 45, 46, 52-54, 57-61,	
	67-69, 91, 107, 325, 586, 587	
FORMA, STUDIO	ITA	56
FOWLER, TOM, INC.	329 1105, STAMFORD, USA	574
FRANKENBERRY, LAUGHLIN + CONSTABLE		
	272 2400, MILWAUKEE, USA	115
FRANKFURT GIPS BALKIND	421 5888, NEW YORK, USA	454-457
GAP/IN-HOUSE	291 2151, SAN FRANCISCO, USA	7-9
GATTI, STUDIO	275 6292, MADRID, SPA	182-191
GERBINO, MICHAEL, DESIGNS	941 0445, NEW YORK, USA	508
GLASER, MILTON, INC.	889 3161, NEW YORK, USA	263, 264
GOODBY, BERLIN & SILVERSTEIN	392 0669, SAN FRANCISCO, USA	36-40,
	70-72, 108, 109, 113	
GOULD DESIGN	774 0510, GRAND RAPIDS, USA	563
GRAFFITO	837 0070, BALTIMORE, USA	145-147
GRAPHICA, INC.	866 4013, MIAMISBURG, USA	254, 437
GUNSELMAN + POLITE	655 7077, WILMINGTON, USA	116-119,
	124, 629-634	
HESS & HESS	542 5529, NORFOLK, USA	226-236, 426
I&S CORPORATION	5391 6480, TOKYO, JPN	642
IKKS, INC.	TOKYO, JPN	13-18
IMPACT GROUP AGENCY	923 1526, SNOWMASS VILLAGE, USA	
		266-269
INTEGRAL CONCEPT	48 70 20 18, PARIS, FRA	403-406
JOINER ROELAND SERIO KOPPEL	871 2305, DALLAS, USA	527
JONES & CO. DESIGN LTD.	482 4324, LONDON, GBR	515
JORGENSEN, GRANT	271 7753, PARKSIDE, AUS	521
KAMEI/GARNAS, INC.	566 0868, SAN FRANCISCO, USA	510
KANSAI SUPER STUDIO	TOKYO, JPN	137
KOEPKE DESIGN	525 2229, MAGNOLIA, USA	383, 439-443
KOPPEL & SCHER	627 9330, NEW YORK, USA	560
L.A. DESIGN	235 0424, OTTAWA, CAN	549
LAWLER BALLARD	KALAMAZOO, USA	62
LCD GRAPHICS	280 560, FIRENZE, ITA	197-209

LEWIS MOBERLY	580 9252, LONDON, GBR	564
LEWIS, TOM, INC.	481 7600, DEL MAR, USA	284
LINTAS:HAMBURG	339 7501, HAMBURG, GER	87, 88
LIPMAN HEARNE	946 1900, CHICAGO, USA	255
LITTLE & COMPANY	375 0077, MINNEAPOLIS, USA	155
LORD, DENTSU & PARTNERS	408 2100, NEW YORK, USA	90
MABRY, MICHAEL, DESIGN	982 7336, SAN FRANCISCO, USA	509
MARTIN/WILLIAMS ADVERTISING	340 0800, MINNEAPOLIS, USA	97-99, 114
MAY & CO.	528 4770, DALLAS, USA	538
MCCANN ERICKSON	984 3386, NEW YORK, USA	66
MCCARTY, HELEN, DESIGN	SANTA FE, USA	438
MIRES DESIGN, INC.	234 6631, SAN DIEGO, USA	531
MORAVA OLIVER BERTÉ	453 3523, SANTA MONICA, USA	618-621
NEXT COMPUTER	366 0900, REDWOOD CITY, USA	152, 153
NIKE DESIGN	526 6800, BEAVERTON, USA	157, 562
PENNA, POWERS, CUTTING & HAYNES	USA	329-335
PENNEBAKER DESIGN	963 8607, HOUSTON, USA	524
PENTAGRAM DESIGN	683 7000, NEW YORK, USA	299-302, 547
PENTAGRAM DESIGN	981 6612, SAN FRANCISCO, USA	218-225, 424, 433, 434
PENTAGRAPH LTD.	803 5815, SUNNINGHILL, SAF	575
PERET ASOCIADOS	240 2006, BARCELONA, SPA	556
PETERS, MICHAEL, DESIGN	371 1919, NEW YORK, USA	581
PETERSON & COMPANY	954 0522, DALLAS, USA	327, 516
PINKHAUS	854 1000, MIAMI, USA	308, 309
PPGH/J. WALTER THOMPSON	646 0166, AMSTERDAM, NLD	94-96
PUSHPIN GROUP	674 8080, NEW YORK, USA	317-320, 486, 520
PÜTZ, ROBERT, GMBH	39 070, COLOGNE, GER	473, 475
REDGATE COMMUNICATIONS	USA	383
REKLAMEVY Y&R	TUR	425
RICHARDS BROCK MILLER MITCHELL & ASSOCIATES	987 4800, DALLAS, USA	532, 542
RICKABAUGH GRAPHICS	221 2229, COLUMBUS, USA	537
RINEY, HAL & PARTNERS	973 2127, NEW YORK, USA	101, 112
ROSS ROY ADVERTISING	433 6270, BLOOMFIELD HILLS, USA	44-47
ROUNDEL DESIGN GROUP	731 6946, LONDON, GBR	148-151
RUMRILL-HOYT	272 6100, ROCHESTER, USA	102-104
RUNYAN, ROBERT MILES & ASSOC.	USA	445-453
RUNYAN HINSCHE ASSOCIATES	823 0975, MARINA DEL REY, USA	341
RUSSEL, ANTHONY & ASSOCIATES	431 8770, NEW YORK, USA	138
SAATCHI & SAATCHI ADVERTISING	75 711, MILANO, ITA	111
SAMENWERKENDE ONTWERPERS	240 547, AMSTERDAM, NLD	519
SAMPSON TYRELL	379 7124, LONDON, GBR	458-460
SANDSTROM DESIGN, INC.	248 9466, PORTLAND, USA	156, 533
SAYLES GRAPHIC DESIGN	243 2922, DES MOINES, USA	212-216, 511, 540
SCALI, MCCABE, SLOVES	735 8000, NEW YORK, USA	100
SCHNEIDER, AGENCE	513 819, LE LANDERON, SWI	275
SEMAN DESIGN GROUP	261 3511, PITTSBURGH, USA	345
SHAPIRO DESIGN ASSOCIATES	460 8544, NEW YORK, USA	558
SHR DESIGN COMMUNICATIONS	483 3700, SCOTTSDALE, USA	422
SIEGER DESIGN	05426 2796, SASSENBERG, GER	321-324
SILICON, STUDIO	856 9356, PALO ALTO, USA	535
601 DESIGN	825 7913, DENVER, USA	479
SOMMESE DESIGN	238 7484, STATE COLLEGE, USA	528
SONY MUSIC	445 5790, NEW YORK, USA	615-617
STANARD, MICHAEL, INC.	869 9820, EVANSTON, USA	523
STEIN ROBAIRE HELM	471 4333, LOS ANGELES, USA	76
SUCCESS SLAD	45 02 18 92, PARIS, FRA	4, 5
SWIETER DESIGN	720 6020, DALLAS, USA	328, 546
TBWA ADVERTISING	725 1150, NEW YORK, USA	63, 64
TERRELONGE DESIGN INC.	462 1960, TORONTO, CAN	175-181
TESTA, ARMANDO, S.P.A.	88 011, TORINO, ITA	1
TESTA, ARMANDO, ADVERTISING	683 3030, NEW YORK, USA	24, 25
THIRST	951 5251, CHICAGO, USA	237-244
TILKA DESIGN	822 6422, MINNEAPOLIS, USA	517
UI-IDEEN	840 8840, SALZBURG, AUT	347
UNIVERSITY OF NEBRASKA PRESS	472 3581, LINCOLN, USA	494
VALOR	145 5009, ISTANBUL, TUR	610
VANDERBYL DESIGN	543 8447, SAN FRANCISCO, USA	77, 84-86, 127-131, 298, 503, 530, 541
VERBA	581 931, MILANO, ITA	22, 23
VSA PARTNERS, INC.	427 6413, CHICAGO, USA	550
WALLACE CHURCH ASSOCIATES	755 2903, NEW YORK, USA	552
WELLER INSTITUTE FOR THE CURE OF DESIGN INC.	649 9859, PARK CITY, USA	480
WELLS, RICH, GREENE	303 5000, NEW YORK, USA	6
WERKSTUDIO	567 671, VIENNA, AUT	210, 211
WIEDEN & KENNEDY	228 4381, PORTLAND, USA	75, 534
WILLIAMS, LOWELL, DESIGN	529 7651, HOUSTON, USA	139-144, 154, 522
WIRZ WERBEBERATUNG AG	463 9910, ZURICH, SWI	110
YOUNG & LARAMORE	264 8000, INDIANAPOLIS, USA	340
YOUNG & RUBICAM	MILANO, ITA	80-83
ZAN ON DESIGN	495 836, CASTELFRANCO, ITA	74, 169-174

ALDRICH, LANCE   USA 44, 47
ASHWORTH, LISA   MIAMI, USA 308, 309
ATWOOD, JUDITH   NEW YORK, USA 100

BAGOT, ROB   SAN FRANCISCO, USA 38
BARRETT, JAMIE   MINNEAPOLIS, USA 46, 57-61
BECKER, BEVERLY   SANTA FE, USA 438
BELEFANT, BRIAN   LOS ANGELES, USA 76
BILDSTEN, BRUCE   MINNEAPOLIS, USA 26-35
BONOMINI, ENRICO   MILANO, ITA 22, 23
BRUCE, BILL   NEW YORK, USA 65

CARLSON, CHUCK   USA 311-316, 579
CHALMERS, IRENE, INC.   USA 263, 264
COBURN, MARSHA   DALLAS, USA 342-344
COHRS, TIM   SAN FRANCISCO, USA 7-9
COURRIER, GEOFF   BOSTON, USA 158-161
CRAYTON, ED   SAN FRANCISCO, USA 36, 39
CUNNINGHAM, FRANK   MIAMI, USA 308, 309

DAKOTA, IRENE   MIAMI, USA 308, 309
DE VAUBLANC, HERVÉ   BOULOGNE, FRA 93
DELBAR, RENÉ   NEW YORK, USA 276
DOBRUNZ, KLAUS   DUSSELDORF, GER 89
DURDEN-SMITH, JO   NORFOLK, USA 226-236

FLESHER, BOB   BALTIMORE, USA 145-147
FLORENDO, NORBERT   NEW YORK, USA 276
FORST, DONNA   CHICAGO, USA 78, 79
FOWLER, DAVID   USA 37, 40, 108, 109
FRIEDEL, RAV   NEW YORK, USA 51
FROLICK, STUART   PASADENA, USA 433, 434
FURY, JERRY   MINNEAPOLIS, USA 105, 106

GANON COLLEEN   USA 432
GERSHENZ, NORMAN SAN FRANCISCO, USA 510
GIBBS, MIKE   USA 10-12, 67-69, 107
GIUA, GASPARE   MILANO, ITA 80-83
GLASER, MILTON   NEW YORK, USA 263, 264
GOODMAN, TONNE   NEW YORK, USA 2, 3
GRANDESSO, PIERA   MILANO, ITA 346
GREENWOOD, GALEN   NEW YORK, USA 50
GREGORY, DAN   NEW YORK, USA 112

HANFT, PHIL   MINNEAPOLIS, USA 45
HARRINGTON SHEA, KATE   USA 394
HAYASHI, HIROYUKI   TOKYO, JPN 137
HAYDEN, ANN   ROCHESTER, USA 102-104
HELLER, STEVE   NEW YORK, USA 317-320
HESS, RICHARD   NORFOLK, USA 226-236
HILLS, LIZANN   CHICAGO, USA 255
HIRASUNA, DELPHINE   USA 218-225
HOOTNICK, SARA   BOSTON, USA 432
HOPES, KIM   WASHINGTON, USA 444
HOWE, AUSTIN   PORTLAND, USA 92

JARVIS, JOHN   MINNEAPOLIS, USA 97-99

KATZ, HOWARD   WILMINGTON, USA 116-119, 124
KORDIC, LÉNA   USA 365
KOSCHEMBAR, FRANK DÜSSELDORF, GER 593-597
KUYPER, AAD   AMSTERDAM, NLD 94-96

LANEY, LOREN   NEW YORK, USA 369, 370
LEES, ANDREW   MELBOURNE, AUS 41-43
LIEF, TODD   CHICAGO, USA 237-244
LOESCH, UWE   DÜSSELDORF, GER 253
LONG, LARRY   MARINA DEL REY, USA 341

MACINTOSH, BRUCE   USA 439-443
MACKAY, JOHN   TORONTO, CAN 175-181
MARTINE, SUZANNE   USA 364
MILLER, BILL   MINNEAPOLIS, USA 325
MITCHELL, CHERYL   SANTA FE, USA 438

NINNEMANN, KAREN   MILWAUKEE, USA 115
NOCERINO, FRANCESCA   MILANO, ITA 392, 393

O'HARE, DAVID   SAN FRANCISCO, USA 70-72
OBJECT WORKS, THE   PITTSBURGH, USA 345

PAGNIEZ, FANNY NEW YORK, USA 366, 368, 370
PARONE, EDWARD   USA 162-165
PATRICK, SEAN SNOWMASS VILLAGE, USA 266-269
PEARSON, CANDACE   USA 480
PEMRICK, LISA   MINNEAPOLIS, USA 245-252

RAUSCHER, MAX   MUNICH, GER 120-123, 125

RAVENNA, DANIELE   MILANO, ITA 22, 23
REGEBRO, MARGARETA STOCKHOLM, SWE 134-136
RISWOLD, JIM   PORTLAND, USA 75
ROBINSON, ANN   NEW YORK, USA 276
ROCKMORE, PATTY   NEW YORK, USA 6
RUBIN, PAM   CHICAGO, USA 78, 79
RYAN, KEVIN   USA 329-335

SALA, MAURIZIO   TORINO, ITA 1
SAUL, LESLIE   SAN FRANCISCO, USA 510
SCHARFF, JENS   HAMBURG, GER 87, 88
SCHMIDT, LEE   MINNEAPOLIS, USA 73
SCHULMAN, ROBERT   NEW YORK, USA 24, 25
SEGALL, KEN   NEW YORK, USA 48, 49
SENN, PATRICK   ZURICH, SWI 110
SHIFFRAR, BOB   NEW YORK, USA 101
SHINOHARA, KEN   TOKYO, JPN 137
SLOAN, LEE   KALAMAZOO, USA 62
SMIDT, SAM   PALO ALTO, USA 565-567
SMITH, HEATHER   LEYBURN, GBR 148-151
SMITH, PETE   MINNEAPOLIS, USA 114
SOLIS, DENISE TERESE   USA 395
SOMMERLOT, JULIE   DES MOINES, USA 212-216
STEIN, STEVE   IRVINE, USA 55
STILES, LYNN   NEW YORK, USA 90
STINGLEY, JOHN   USA 52-54, 91, 586, 587
STONE, EVAN   BOSTON, USA 584, 585
STONE, JOANNE   HOUSTON, USA 139-144

TEAM   USA 432
TOKUNARI, OSAMU   TOKYO, JPN 137
TOSI, MICHELE   MILANO, ITA 111
TROTT, SUE   NEW YORK, USA 66

UI, JÖRG   SALZBURG, AUT 347

VANDERBYL DESIGN   USA 127-131

WARREN, DAVID   NEW YORK, USA 63, 64
WILLIAMS, CLAY   SAN FRANCISCO, USA 113

YOUNG, DAVID   INDIANAPOLIS, USA 340

ZANON, CIRIANO   CASTELFRANCO, ITA 74
ZIMMERMANN, PETRA   COLOGNE, GER 253

ABBEVILLE PRESS — NEW YORK, USA 601
ADDISON-WESLEY — USA 555
AFRONTAMENTO, EDIÇOES — PORTO, POR 613
AGFA CORPORATION — USA 276-282, 310, 439-443
AIGA SAN DIEGO — SAN DIEGO, USA 284
ALFA ROMEO DISTRIBUTORS OF AMERICA — ORLANDO, USA 44, 47
ALPHA GRAPHIX — USA 480
ALPHABET GALLERY — TOKYO, JPN 635
AMBIENTE — MUNICH, GER 361-363
AMERICAN ASSOC. OF ZOO KEEPERS — USA 510
AMERICAN ADVERTISING FEDERATION — USA 328
AMOCO OIL CO. — USA 45, 46
ANDERSON, CHARLES S., DESIGN — USA 622-628
APOGEE DESIGNS — BALTIMORE, USA 145-147
APPLE COMPUTERS, INC. — CUPERTINO, USA 555
AREA — TORONTO, CAN 283, 285
ARREDAMENTO DEKORASYON — TUR 425
ART DIRECTORS CLUB, INC. — NEW YORK, USA 436
ART CENTER COLLEGE OF DESIGN — PASADENA USA 433, 434, 618-621
ASDA — LEEDS, GBR 564
ASMP — DALLAS, USA 327
AT&T — PARSIPPANY, USA 426
ATELIER 2000 FOTOGMBH — SALZBURG, AUT 347
AUDI OF AMERICA — TROY, USA 422
AVENUE MAGAZINE — AMSTERDAM, NLD 396, 397
AVIA GROUP INT'L — PORTLAND, USA 156
AVIATION FUEL ENTERPRISES LTD — CAN 549

BEACH CULTURE — DANA POINT, USA 429, 430
BEAUX-ART MAGAZINE — FRA 403-406
BEDFORD PROPERTIES — LAFAYETTE, USA 530
BEECHAMS — SAF 575
BELLEROPHON PUBLICATIONS — USA 418-420
BENE BÜROMÖBEL — VIENNA, AUT 265
BERG, JOHN — NEW YORK, USA 512, 513
BERNHARDT FURNITURE CO. — LENOIR, USA 77, 127-131, 541
BILLBOARD — NEW YORK, USA 401
BIRNBAUM, ROBERT — BOSTON, USA 432
BLOOMINGDALE'S — USA 167, 168, 192-196, 557
BMW OF NORTH AMERICA INC. — USA 48-51
BOSTON GLOBE MAGAZINE — BOSTON, USA 489
BOURGEOIS, CHRISTIAN, EDITEUR — FRA 598, 599
BOYUT PUBLISHING GROUP — TUR 425
BROWN & ROOT USA — HOUSTON, USA 139-144
BUENA VISTA COLLEGE — STORM LAKE, USA 540
BULL HN WORLDWIDE — BURLINGTON, USA 383
BURDA VERLAG — MUNICH, GER 361-363

CALIFORNIA COLLEGE OF ARTS AND CRAFTS — OAKLAND, USA 256-262
CALVIN KLEIN COSMETICS — NEW YORK, USA 2, 3

CARILLON IMPORTERS, LTD. — USA 63, 64
CAROL PUBLISHING GROUP — NEW YORK, USA 612
CARTER, DAVID, GRAPHIC DESIGN ASSOCIATES — DALLAS, USA 342-344
CASIO — ITA 22, 23
CASTELLARANO FIANDRE CERAMICHE — ITA 80-83
CHAMBRE NEUCHATELOISE DU COMMERCE ET DE L'INDUSTRIE — SWI 275
CHAMPION INT'L — STAMFORD, USA 226-236
CHESEBROUGH-POND'S CREATIVE PACKAGING DESIGN DEPT. — GREENWICH, USA 574
CILAG GMBH — VIENNA, AUT 210, 211
CLUB MÉDITERRANÉE — SYDNEY, AUS 41-43
CLUSS AG, BRAUEREI — HEILBRONN, GER 548
COFFEE CONSULTANTS INC. — USA 550
COLGATE-PALMOLIVE — COURBEVOIE, FRA 93
COLUMBIA RECORDS — NEW YORK, USA 615-617
CONCRETE PRODUCTIONS — DALLAS, USA 516
CONDE NAST TRAVELER — NEW YORK, USA 493
CONNECTICUT MUTUAL — HARTFORD, USA 584, 585
CONTINENTAL BANK — USA 57-61
COOPER, SIDNEY — LOS ANGELES, USA 543
CORRIERE DELLA SERA — MILANO, ITA 431
CUTLER, CRAIG, STUDIO — NEW YORK, USA 520

D'AMICO & PARTNERS — USA 336, 337
DAYTON CONTEMPORARY DANCE COMPANY — DAYTON, USA 254
DAYTON HUDSON DEPT. STORE — USA 529
DE LAAT, WILLEM — NLD 488
DE VOLKSKRANT — NLD 94-96
DENIS, MIKE, AVIATION — MESSINES, CAN 536
DEPARTMENT OF FISH & GAME STATE OF CALIFORNIA — SACRAMENTO, USA 545
DESIGN WORKS — COLUMBUS, USA 537
DETAILS MAGAZINE — USA 376, 410-413
DEUTSCHE FORSCHUNGSANSTALT FÜR LUFT- UND RAUMFAHRT — COLOGNE, GER 526
DEUTSCHE LUFTHANSA AG — COLOGNE, GER 468
DKNY COVERINGS — NEW YORK, USA 166
DUBOIS, MARC-ETIENNE — FRA 580, 582
DUFFY DESIGN GROUP — USA 311-316, 507

EASTMAN KODAK CO. — ROCHESTER, USA 102-104
EDIZIONE CONDÉ NAST — MILANO, ITA 356-360
EDS — USA 527
EIBER, RICK, DESIGN — SEATTLE, USA 326
ELLE — NEW YORK, USA 364-370, 379
EMPORIO ARMANI — MILANO, ITA 197-209
END, THE — IBIZA, SPA 556
ERCO LEUCHTEN — LÜDENSCHEID, GER 126
ESQUIRE MAGAZINE — USA 414-417, 436, 490
ETTER, CHRISTY — HOUSTON, USA 524
EVENTMEDIA INT'L INC. — NEW YORK, USA 525

FALLON MCELLIGOTT — MINNEAPOLIS, USA 107, 325
FANVAL — PARIS, FRA 599
FARRAR STRAUS & GIROUX — NEW YORK, USA 603
FIL DESIGN CENTRE — ISTANBUL, TUR 132, 133
FILMCASTERS — USA 532
FIRST OF AMERICA BANK — KALAMAZOO, USA 62
FRANKFURTER ALLGEMEINE MAGAZIN — FRANKFURT/M., GER 386-389, 461
FRENCH PAPER COMPANY — NILES, USA 217
FRY, J.W. — ROCHESTER, USA 542
FUJI PHOTO FILM USA — USA 101, 112

GAP, THE — SAN FRANCISCO, USA 7-9
GILBERT PAPER — MENASHA, USA 212-216, 237-244
GIORGIO ARMANI PARFUMS — MILANO, ITA 4, 5
GIRO SPORT DESIGN — SOQUEL, USA 76
GOETHE-INSTITUT OSAKA — OSAKA, JPN 602
GOLDEN VALLEY HEALTH CENTER — USA 105, 106
GRAFICA — CURITIBA, BRA 427, 428
GRAPHIC ARTS CENTER — PORTLAND, USA 218-225
GUNSELMAN + POLITE — WILMINGTON, USA 629-634

HACHETTE MAGAZINES, INC. — USA 364-370, 379
HARPER COLLINS — NEW YORK, USA 611
HARPER'S BAZAAR — NEW YORK, USA 377
HEARST CORP. — NEW YORK, USA 377, 414-417
HELLER, PAUL — MONTAUK, USA 508
HEUBLEIN, INC. — HARTFORD, USA 66
HICKORY BUSINESS FURNITURE — USA 84-86
HM GRAPHICS — USA 115
HOUSE OF SEAGRAM — NEW YORK, USA 581
HYUNDAI MOTOR AMERICA — USA 55

ICEBOX — USA 67-69
ILLUSTRATORS CLUB OF WASHINGTON — ARLINGTON, USA 467
IM WASSERWEG, VERLAG — KASSEL, GER 593-597
INFORMATIONSZENTRUM WEISSBLECH — DUSSELDORF, GER 87, 88
INT'L DAIRY QUEEN — MINNEAPOLIS, USA 155
INT'L DESIGN CONFERENCE OF ASPEN — USA 486
INTEX SOFTWARE, INC. — USA 538
IVY HILL CORP. — NEW YORK, USA 317-320

JANZENS — TORONTO, CAN 544
JIM BEAM BRANDS CO. — DEERFIELD, USA 579
JOHNSON INDUSTRIES — ELGIN, USA 78, 79
JORGENSEN, GRANT, GRAPHIC DESIGN — PARKSIDE AUS 521

K.ONE MODASOLARIS — ITA 74, 169-174
KIDDER, PEABODY — NEW YORK, USA 138

KING	MILANO, ITA	392, 393
KPMG PEAT MARWICK	MONTVALE, USA	423
L.A. STYLE	LOS ANGELES, USA	384, 395
L.A.X. MAGAZINE	GLENDALE, USA	495
LEAR'S MAGAZINE	NEW YORK, USA	380-382
LEE COMPANY	USA	10-12
LEITNER GMBH	WAIBLINGEN, GER	120-123, 125
LEVI STRAUSS	SAN FRANCISCO, USA	554
LIBREX COMPUTERS	USA	113
LIFE MAGAZINE	NEW YORK, USA	402
LINCOLN BANCORP	ENCINO, USA	462-465
LIPTON, THOMAS J., INC.	USA	553
LIVRARIA DO ESTADO	BRA	608
LOGICON, INC.	TORRANCE, USA	450-453
LOWELL SHOE INC.	HUDSON, USA	158-161
MARC LAURENT	TORONTO, CAN	175-181
MART.SPRUJIT, DRUKKERIJ	AMSTERDAM, NLD	519
MATSUNAGA, SHIN, DESIGN	TOKYO, JPN	642
MELBOURNE OLYMPIC CANDIDATURE	AUS	496-502
MERCURY MARINE	FOND DU LAC, USA	114
MEREDITH CORP.	DES MOINES, USA	390, 391
METROPOLIS MAGAZINE	NEW YORK, USA	418-420
METROPOLITAN HOME	NEW YORK, USA	390, 391
MIAMI UNIVERSITY	OXFORD, USA	255
MIRABELLA	NEW YORK, USA	371-375
MITSUI DESIGNTEC	JPN	137
MIYAKE DESIGN STUDIO	TOKYO, JPN	13-18, 588-592
MODA	MILANO, ITA	400
MURDOCH MAGAZINES	NEW YORK, USA	421
MUSEUM OF NEW MEXICO	SANTA FE, USA	438
MUSICA AG	SWI	110
NAGELS, JENS	KASSEL, GER	593-597
NATIONAL CONFERENCE OF STATE LEGISLATURES	DENVER, USA	479
NATURAL ORGANICS	FARMINGDALE, USA	558
NATURE COMPANY	BERKELEY, USA	108, 109
NATURE CONSERVANCY	WASHINGTON, USA	510
NCR CORPORATION	DAYTON, USA	437
NEW SCHOOL FOR SOCIAL RESEARCH	NEW YORK, USA	481
NEW YORK MAGAZINE	NEW YORK, USA	421
NEW YORKER, THE	NEW YORK, USA	90
NEW YORK CITY TRANSIT AUTHORITY	NEW YORK, USA	127-131
NEXT COMPUTER	REDWOOD CITY, USA	152, 153
NIKE INC.	BEAVERTON, USA	75, 157, 534, 562
NIKON	USA	100
NIXDORF COMPUTER	WALTHAM, USA	473, 475
NUOVA ERI-EDIZIONI RAI	ITA	392, 393, 400
OAKLAND MUSEUM	OAKLAND, USA	298
ÖOLA CORPORATION	STAMFORD, USA	560
OOSTERHOUTSE ZOETWARENFABRIK	NLD	561
ORCHARD, THE	LONDON, GBR	515
OREGON ART INSTITUTE	PORTLAND, USA	533
OSTRIN, JOAN	ST. PAUL, USA	518
OUN CORPORATION	TOKYO, JPN	547
PANTONE, INC.	MOONACHIE, USA	245-252
PARAGON HOUSE	NEW YORK, USA	604
PATIKA	ISTANBUL, TUR	610
PENGUIN USA	NEW YORK, USA	472, 609, 614
PEPSI CO, INC.	USA	65
PETERS, MICHAEL, GROUP	LONDON, GBR	311-316
PHILIPS	ITA	111
PHOTO	PARIS, FRA	378
PHYSICIAN AND SPORTSMEDICINE, THE	USA	471
PININFARINA	TORINO, ITA	56
PISCHOFF	OAKLAND, USA	503
PLAN LICHT	VOMP, AUT	636-641
PORSCHE CARS NORTH AMERICA	USA	52-54, 586, 587
PRINT CRAFT, INC.	ST. PAUL, USA	504-506
PRO TERRA	MUNICH, GER	491
RAINYDAY FLOWERS	USA	92
RCS EDITORIALE QUOTIDIANI SPA	ITA	431
REX THREE	SUNRISE, USA	308, 309
RICHARDSON-VICKS, INC.	USA	6
RIKUYO-SHA PUBLISHING	TOKYO, JPN	605-607
ROBERN, INC.	BENSALEM, USA	116-119, 124
ROBIN WOOD	BREMEN, GER	89
ROBINS ANALYTICS	ST. PAUL, USA	517
ROCKEFELLER CENTER CLUB	NEW YORK, USA	263, 264
ROLLING STONE	NEW YORK, USA	348-355
ROYAL VIKING LINE	CORAL GABLES, USA	36-40, 424
RUNYAN HINSCHE ASSOC.	MARINA DEL REY, USA	341
SALT LAKE CITY WINTER OLYMPIC BID COMMITTE	USA	329-335
SAN FRANCISCO FOCUS	USA	398, 509
SAN'AT-E HAML-O NAGHL	TEHRAN, IRN	474
SASSON, MAURICE	NEW YORK, USA	19-21
SATOH, TAKU, DESIGN OFFICE.	TOKYO, JPN	286-297, 551, 576-578
SAYLES GRAPHIC DESIGN	DES MOINES, USA	511
SCHIAPPARELLI BENESSERE PIKENZ S.P.A.	ITA	1
SCHULZ FOERSTEN, PETER	GER	407-409
SHEARSON LEHMAN BROTHERS	USA	435
SHOJI, MATSUZAKI	JPN	492
SKALD	CORAL GABLES, USA	424
SMITHSONIAN INSTITUTION	USA	489
SOFTSEL COMPUTER PRODUCTS	EL SEGUNDO USA	445-449
SOMMESE DESIGN	STATE COLLEGE, USA	528
SOUTHERN METHODIST UNIVERSITY	USA	546
SPECIALIZED BICYCLES	USA	70-72
SPIRIT ACTIVWEAR	SANTA FE, USA	162-165
STANARD, MICHAEL	EVANSTON, USA	523
STRAIGHT ARROW PUBLISHERS	NEW YORK, USA	348-355
STRATHMORE PAPER CO.	WESTFIELD, USA	539
STUFF MAGAZINE	BOSTON, USA	432
SURFER PUBLICATIONS	USA	429, 430
SVENSK MÖBEL CENTER	SWE	134-136
SYBILLA	MADRID, SPA	182-191
TALON ENGINEERING	LONDON, GBR	514
TEE SHIRT CO.	SAN DIEGO, USA	531
TEXAS MONTHLY	AUSTIN, USA	399
TIDEN NORSK FORLAG	OSLO, NOR	600
TIME EXCHANGE	USA	24, 25
TIME, INC.	NEW YORK, USA	402
TIME MAGAZINE	NEW YORK, USA	477
TIME WARNER INC.	NEW YORK, USA	454-457
TIMEX CORP.	USA	26-35
TISHMAN SPEYER PROPERTIES	USA	270-274
T-N-T ENTERPRISES	WALNUT CREEK, USA	535
TON SUR TON	GER	559
2029 MAGAZIN	HAMBURG, GER	407-409
TRANSATLANTIK	HAMBURG, GER	384, 385
TRANSPORT DESIGN CONSORTIUM	GBR	148-151
TUNDRA BOOKS INC.	MONTREAL, CAN	469, 470
UNIVERSITY ART CENTER	PALO ALTO, USA	565-567
UNIVERSITY OF NEBRASKA PRESS	USA	494
USPCI	HOUSTON, USA	154
VOGUE ITALIA	MILANO, ITA	356-360
WALLACE CHURCH ASSOC., INC.	USA	552
WILDCAT LAND CO.	ASPEN, USA	266-269
WILHELM CONSTRUCTION	USA	340
WILLIAMS, LOWELL, DESIGN	HOUSTON, USA	522
WOLVERINE WORLDWIDE INC.	USA	563
WORLD MONITOR	USA	91
WORLD	MONTVALE, USA	423
WPP GROUP PLC.	LONDON, GBR	458-460
YELLOW PENCIL COMPANY	LONDON, GBR	303-307
YELLOW PAGES PUBLISHERS ASSOC.	USA	97-99
YMCA OF MINNEAPOLIS	MINNEAPOLIS, USA	73
ZANDERS FEINPAPIERE AG	GER	253

CALL FOR ENTRIES

EINLADUNGEN

APPEL D'ENVOIS

CALL FOR ENTRIES

....

GRAPHIS DESIGN 93

ENTRY DEADLINE: NOVEMBER 30, 1991

ADVERTISING: Newspaper and magazine. **DESIGN**: Promotion brochures, catalogs, invitations, record covers, announcements, logos and/or corporate campaigns, calendars, books, book covers, packaging (single or series, labels and/or complete packages). **EDITORIAL**: Company magazines, newspapers, consumer magazines, house organs, annual reports. **ILLUSTRATION**: All categories, black and white or color. **ELIGIBILITY**: All work produced between December 1, 1990 through November 30, 1991, as well as unpublished work from this period by professionals and students.

ANNUAL REPORTS 4

ENTRY DEADLINE: APRIL 30, 1992

All annual reports, capability brochures, public interest reports, and other corporate public relations material produced in a brochure format. **ELIGIBILITY**: All work published between April 30, 1991 and April 30, 1992.

GRAPHIS POSTER 93

ENTRY DEADLINE: APRIL 30, 1992

Cultural Posters: exhibitions, film, music theater, etc. Advertising Posters: consumer goods, self-promotion, etc. Social posters: education, conferences, and meetings, political, etc. **ELIGIBILITY**: All work produced between May 1, 1991 and April 30, 1992.

GRAPHIS PHOTO 93

ENTRY DEADLINE: JUNE 30, 1992

Advertising Photography: Ads, promotional brochure, catalogs, invitations, announcements, record covers, and calendars on all subjects. Editorial Photography: for press media (journalism and feature stories), books, corporate publications, etc. on all subjects. Fine Art Photography: Personal studies on all subjects. Unpublished Photography: Experimental and student work on all subjects. **ELIGIBILITY**: All work produced between July 1, 1991 and June 30, 1992.

RULES

By submitting work to **GRAPHIS**, the sender grants permission for his or her publication in any **GRAPHIS** book, as well as any article in **GRAPHIS** magazine, or any advertisement, brochure, or other printed matter produced specifically for the purpose of promoting the sale of these publications.

ELIGIBILITY

....

All work produced in the 12-month period previous to the submission deadlines, as well as rejected or unpublished work from this period, by professionals and students.

WHAT TO SEND

....

Please send the printed piece (unmounted but well protected). Do not send original art. For large, bulky or valuable pieces, please submit color photos or (duplicate) slides. **Entries cannot be returned.** Only in exceptional cases and by contacting us in advance will material be sent back.

HOW AND WHERE TO SEND

....

Please tape (do not glue) the entry form provided (or copy)—with full information—on the back of each piece. Entries can be sent by air mail, air parcel post or surface mail. Please do not send anything by air freight. Declare, "No Commercial Value" on packages, and label "Art for Contest." The number of transparencies and photos should be indicated on the parcel. (If sent by air courier, please mark "documents, Commercial Value 00.00.")

ENTRIES

....

SINGLE ENTRY: North America: US $10.00 Germany: DM 10.00 All other countries: SFr. 10.00

FOR EACH CAMPAIGN ENTRY OF 3 OR MORE PIECES: North America: US $25.00 Germany: DM 25.00 All other countries: SFr 25.00

Please make checks payable to **GRAPHIS PRESS CORP. ZURICH** and include in parcel. These fees do not apply to students, if copy of student identification is included. (For entries from countries with exchange controls, please contact us.) A confirmation of receipt will be sent to each entrant, and all entrants will be notified whether or not their work has been accepted for publication. By submitting work you qualify for a 25% discount on the purchase of the respective book. Thank you for you entry.

GRAPHIS PRESS CORP. 107 DUFOURSTRASSE CH-8008 ZURICH, SWITZERLAND

EINLADUNG

GRAPHIS DESIGN 93

EINSENDESCHLUSS: 30. NOVEMBER 1991

WERBUNG: In Zeitungen und Zeitschriften. **DESIGN:** Werbeprospekte, Kataloge, Einladungen, Schallplattenhüllen, Anzeigen, Signete und/oder Image-Kampagnen, Kalender, Bücher, Buchumschläge, Packungen. **REDAKTIONELLES DESIGN:** Firmenpublikationen, Zeitungen, Zeitschriften, Jahresberichte. **ILLUSTRATION:** Alle Kategorien, schwarzweiss oder farbig. **IN FRAGE KOMMEN:** Alle Arbeiten von Fachleuten und Studenten - auch nicht publizierte. Arbeiten -, die zwischen Dezember 1990 und November 1991 entstanden sind.

ANNUAL REPORTS 4

EINSENDESCHLUSS: 30. APRIL 1992

Alle Jahresberichte einer Firma oder Organisation (Tabellen und Diagramme, Illustrationen und Photos). **IN FRAGE KOMMEN:** Alle Jahresberichte und ähnliche Firmenpublikationen für Öffentlichkeitsarbeit in Form von Broschüren von 1991 bis 1992.

GRAPHIS POSTER 93

EINSENDESCHLUSS: 30. APRIL 1992

KULTUR: Plakate für Ausstellungen, Film-, Theater- und Balletaufführungen usw. **WERBUNG:** Plakate für Konsumgüter, Eigenwerbung usw. **GESELLSCHAFT:** Plakate für Ausbildung, die Ankündigung von Tagungen usw. **IN FRAGE KOMMEN:** Alle Arbeiten, die zwischen Mai 1991 und April 1992 entstanden sind.

GRAPHIS PHOTO 93

EINSENDESCHLUSS: 30. JUNI 1992

Werbephotographie: Anzeigen, Prospekte, Kataloge, Einladungen, Bekanntmachungen, Schallplattenhüllen, Kalender. Redaktionelle Photographie: Pressephotos, Firmenpublikationen usw. In den Bereichen Mode, Architektur, Kunst, Natur, Wissenschaft und Technik, Alltag, Sport, Porträts, Stilleben usw. Künstlerische Photographie: Persönliche Studien. Unveröffentlichte Aufnahmen: Experimentelle Photographie und Arbeiten von Studenten und Schülern. **IN FRAGE KOMMEN:** Alle Arbeiten, die zwischen Juli 1991 und Juni 1992 entstanden sind.

TEILNAHMEBEDINGUNGEN

GRAPHIS erhält die Erlaubnis zur Veröffentlichung der eingesandten Arbeiten sowohl im entsprechenden Jahrbuch als auch in der Zeitschrift **GRAPHIS** oder für die Wiedergabe im Zusammenhang mit Besprechungen und Werbematerial für **GRAPHIS**-Publikationen.

IN FRAGE KOMMEN

Alle Arbeiten von Fachleuten und Studenten - auch nicht publizierte Arbeiten -, welche in den zwölf Monaten vor Einsendeschluss entstanden sind.

WAS EINSENDEN

Bitte senden Sie uns das gedruckte Beispiel (gut geschützt). Senden Sie keine Originale. Bei unhandlichen, umfangreichen und wertvollen Sendungen bitten wir um Farbphotos oder Duplikat-Dias. **Bitte beachten Sie, dass Einsendungen nicht zurückgeschickt werden können** (Ausnahmen möglich).

WIE SCHICKEN

Bitte befestigen Sie das vorgesehene Etikett (oder Kopie) - vollständig ausgefüllt - mit Klebstreifen (nicht mit Klebstoff) auf der Rückseite jeder Arbeit. Bitte per Luftpost oder auf normalem Postweg einsenden. **Keine Luftfrachtsendungen.** Deklarieren Sie «ohn jeden Handelswert» und «Arbeitsproben für Wettbewerb». Die Anzahl der Dias und Photos sollte auf dem Paket angegeben werden (bei Luftkurier-Sendungen vermerken Sie «Dokumente, ohne jeden Handelswert»).

GEBÜHREN

SFR. 10.--/DM 10.-- FÜR EINZELNE ARBEITEN
SFR. 25.--/DM 25.-- FÜR KAMPAGNEN ODER SERIEN (MEHR ALS 3 STÜCK)
Bitte senden Sie uns einen Scheck (SFr.-Schecks bitte auf eine Schweizer Bank ziehen) oder überweisen Sie den Betrag auf PC Zürich 80-23071-9 oder PSchK Frankfurt 3000 57-602. Diese Gebühren gelten nicht für Studenten. Senden Sie bitte eine Kopie des Studentenausweises. (Für Einsendungen aus Ländern mit Devisenbeschränkungen bitten wir Sie, uns zu kontaktieren.) Jeder Einsender erhält eine Empfangsbestätigung und wird über Erscheinen oder Nichterscheinen seiner Arbeit informiert. Durch Ihre Einsendung erhalten Sie 25% Rabatt auf das betreffende Buch. Herzlichen Dank für Ihre Mitarbeit.

GRAPHIS VERLAG AG, DUFOURSTRASSE 107 CH-8008 ZURICH, SCHWEIZ

GRAPHIS DESIGN 93

DATE LIMITE D'ENVOI: 30 NOVEMBRE 1992

PUBLICITÉ: journaux, magazines. **DESIGN:** brochures de promotion, catalogues, invitations, pochettes de disques, annonces, emblèmes, en-têtes, campagnes de prestige, calendriers, livres, jaquettes, emballages (spécimen ou série, étiquettes ou emballages complets). **DESIGN ÉDITORIAL:** magazines de sociétés, journaux, revues, rapports annuels. **ILLUSTRATION:** toutes catégories en noir et blanc ou en couleurs. **ADMISSION:** Tous les travaux réalisés entre décembre 1990 et novembre 1991 par des professionnels ou étudiants, ainsi que les travaux refusés ou non publiés durant cette période.

ANNUAL REPORTS 4

DATE LIMITE D'ENVOI: 30 AVRIL 1992

Tous travaux publiés en relation avec le rapport annuel d'une entreprise ou d'une organisation. **ADMISSION:** Tous les rapports annuels et autre rapports destinés au grand public publiés sous forme de brochure en 1991 ou en 1992.

GRAPHIS POSTER 93

DATE LIMITE D'ENVOI: 30 AVRIL 1992

AFFICHES CULTURELLES: expositions, film, théâtre, ballet, concerts etc. **AFFICHES PUBLICITAIRES:** produits de consommation, autopromotion, etc. **AFFICHES SOCIALES:** formation, conférences et annonces de manifestations ou de réunions politiques, etc. **ADMISSION:** Tous les travaux réalisés entre mai 1991 et avril 1992.

GRAPHIS PHOTO 93

DATE LIMITE D'ENVOI: 30 JUIN 1992

PHOTO PUBLICITAIRE: annonces, brochures de promotion, catalogues, pochettes de disques, calendriers. **PHOTO RÉDACTIONNELLE:** reportages, livres, publications d'entreprises, etc. dans les domaines suivants: mode, arts, architecture, nature, sciences, techniques, vie quotidienne, sports, portraits, nature morte, etc. **PHOTO D'ART:** études personnelles. **PHOTOS NON-PUBLIÉES:** travaux expérimentaux et projets d'étudiants. **ADMISSION:** Les travaux réalisés entre juillet 91 et juin 92.

MODALITES D'ENVOI

Par votre envoi, vous donnez expressément à **GRAPHIS** l'autorisation de reproduire les travaux reçus aussi bien dans le livre en question que dans le magazine **GRAPHIS**, ou dans tout imprimé concernant des comptes rendus ou du matériel publicitaire sur les publications **GRAPHIS**.

ADMISSION
. . . .

Sont acceptés tous les travaux de professionnels et d'étudiants - même inédits - réalisés pendant les douze mois précédant le délai limite d'envoi.

QUE NOUS ENVOYER
. . . .

Veuillez nous envoyer un exemplaire imprimé. N'envoyez pas d'originaux. Pour les travaux de grand format, volumineux ou de valeur, veuillez nous envoyer des photos ou des duplicata. **Veuillez noter que les travaux ne peuvent pas être retournés,** sauf dans des cas exceptionnels et si vous nous en avisez à l'avance.

COMMENT ET OU ENVOYER
. . . .

Veuillez scotcher (ne pas coller) au dos de chaque spécimen les étiquettes ci-jointes (ou photocopies) dûment remplies. Envoyez les travaux de préférence par avion, ou par voie de surface. **Ne nous envoyez rien en fret aérien.** Indiquez «Sans aucune valeur commerciale» et «Echantillons de spécimens pour concours». Le nombre de diapositives et de photos doit être indiqué sur le paquet. (Pour les envois par courrier, inscrire «Documents, sans aucune valeur commerciale».)

DROITS D'ADMISSION
. . . .

SFR. 10.00 pour les envois concernant un seul travail
SFR. 25.00 pour chaque série de 3 travaux ou davantage
Veuillez joindre à votre envoi un chèque tiré sur une banque suisse ou verserez ce montant au compte chèque postal Zurich 80.23071.9. Les étudiants sont exemptés de cette taxe. Prière de joindre une photocopie de la carte d'étudiant. (Si vous résidez dans un pays qui connaît le contrôle des changes, veuillez nous contacter préalablement.) Nous vous ferons parvenir un accusé de réception. Vous serez informé par la suite de la parution ou non-parution de vos travaux. Votre envoi vous vaudra une réduction de 25% sur l'annuel en question. Veuillez faire parvenir vos travaux à l'adresse suivante:

ÉDITIONS GRAPHIS, DUFOURSTRASSE 107 CH-8008 ZURICH, SWITZERLAND

ENTRY LABEL

PLEASE TAPE (DO NOT GLUE) THIS LABEL OR A PHOTOCOPY TO THE BACK OF EACH ENTRY.

SENDER:
FIRM, ADDRESS, TELEPHONE

ART DIRECTOR:
NAME, CITY, STATE

DESIGNER:
NAME, CITY, STATE

ILLUSTRATOR, PHOTOGRAPHER:
NAME, CITY, STATE

STYLIST:
NAME, CITY, STATE

COPYWRITER:
NAME, CITY, STATE

AGENCY, STUDIO:
NAME, CITY, STATE

CLIENT, PUBLISHER:
COMPLETE ADDRESS

DESCRIPTION OF ASSIGNMENT/OTHER INFORMATION:

I HEREBY GRANT **GRAPHIS PRESS** NON-EXCLUSIVE PERMISSION FOR USE OF THE SUBMITTED MATERIAL, FOR WHICH I HAVE FULL REPRODUCTION RIGHTS (COPY, PHOTOGRAPHY, ILLUSTRATION, AND DESIGN).

SIGNATURE:

ADDRESS LABEL

GRAPHIS PRESS CORP.
107 DUFOURSTRASSE CH-8008
ZURICH, SWITZERLAND

ETIKETT / FICHE

BITTE AUF DER RÜCKSEITE JEDER AFBEIT BEFESTIGEN
VEUILLEZ SCOTCHER AU DOS DE CHAQUE SPÉCIMEN.

ABSENDER/ENVOYÉ PAR:
FIRMA(E), ADRESSE, TELEPHON(E)

ART DIRECTOR/DIRECTEUR ARTISTIQUE:
NAME, ORT,/NOM, LIEU

GESTALTER/DESIGNER:
NAME, ORT,/NOM, LIEU

KÜNSTLER/ARTISTE, PHOTOGRAPH(E):
NAME, ORT,/NOM, LIEU

STYLIST/STYLISTE:
NAME, ORT,/NOM, LIEU

TEXTER/RÉDACTEUR:
NAME, ORT,/NOM, LIEU

AGENTUR/AGENCE:
NAME, ORT,/NOM, LIEU

KUNDE/CLIENT:
ADRESSE

ZWECK/UTILISATION:
INFORMATION

ICH ERTEILE HIERMIT DEM **GRAPHIS VERLAG** DIE NICHT-EXKLUSIVE ERLAUBNIS ZUR VERÖFFENTLICHUNG DER EINGEREICHTEN ARBEITEN, FÜR DIE ICH DIE REPRODUKTIONSRECHTE BESITZE (TEXT, PHOTOGRAPHIE, ILLUSTRATION UND DESIGN).

J'ACCORDE PAR LA PRÉSENTE AUX **EDITIONS GRAPHIS** L'AUTORISATION NON EXCLUSIVE D'UTILISER LE MATÉRIEL SOUMIS À LEUR APPRÉCIATION, POUR LEQUEL JE DÉTIENS LES DROITS DE REPRODUCTION (TEXTE, PHOTOGRAPHIE, ILLUSTRATION ET DESIGN).

UNTERSCHRIFT/SIGNATURE:

ADDRESS LABEL

GRAPHIS PRESS CORP.
107 DUFOURSTRASSE CH-8008
ZURICH, SWITZERLAND

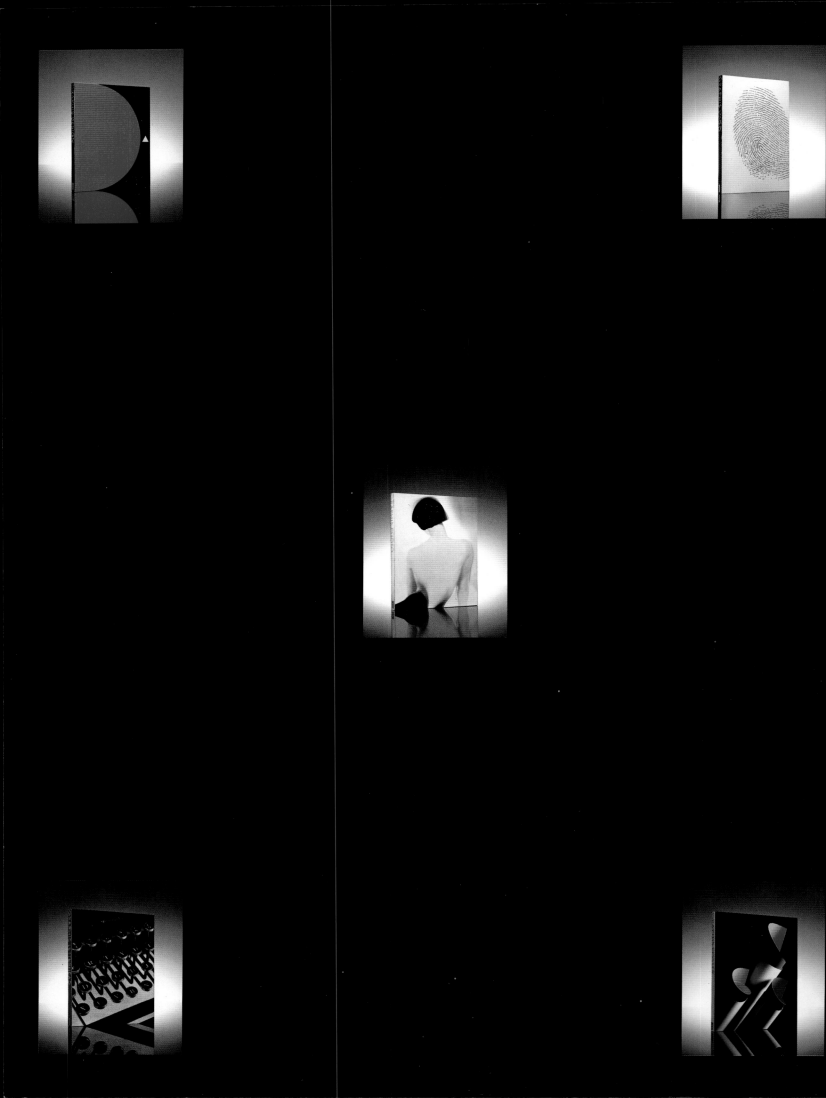